BARRON'S

THE TRUSTED NAME IN TEST PREP

7 ACT® Practice Tests

SIXTH EDITION

Patsy J. Prince, M.Ed.,
and James D. Giovannini

About the Author

Jim Giovannini, an educator for more than thirty years, is the owner and founder of Academic Tutoring, LLC. Nationally recognized as a leading expert in both ACT and SAT test preparation, Mr. Giovannini's company partners with hundreds of school districts across the country and serves tens of thousands of students each year. Mr. Giovannini's passion is to help students achieve their Personal A+ on both the ACT and SAT exams by raising both skills and scores.

Published by Kaplan North America, LLC d/b/a Barron's Educational Series
1515 West Cypress Creek Road
Fort Lauderdale, Florida 33309
www.barronseduc.com

ISBN: 978-1-5062-9152-9

10 9 8 7 6 5 4 3 2 1

Kaplan North America, LLC, d/b/a Barron's Educational Series print books are available at special quantity discounts to use for sales promotions, employee premiums, or educational purposes. For more information or to purchase books, please call the Simon & Schuster special sales department at 866-506-1949.

Contents

Introductory Words

This must be a stressful time in your life: balancing schoolwork, family, friends, extracurriculars, jobs, AND college admissions! Whew . . . that's a lot! Not to worry, this ACT prep program has been created with your busy life in mind.

The ACT is a five-section test: English, math, reading, science, and an optional essay (writing). Our prep program covers all of these areas. We made a point of reviewing and teaching only material that is presented on this high-stakes test.

The ACT is unlike any test you have ever taken. It requires a new way of thinking. Look at it this way: in your math class or English courses, 70% is typically the lowest percentage to earn a grade of C. However, on the ACT, 70% correct would equate to a score of about a 25, and while a 25 might or might not be a good score for you, it is far above the national average (typically about a 21). This means that you can actually get a lot of questions wrong on the ACT and still earn a good score! The key is to learn the correct strategies for each section and to never give up while taking the test.

The rules and strategies that follow have been used successfully by thousands of students. They are the perfect tool to help you reach your maximum score.

COMPUTER BASED TESTING (CBT), SECTION RETESTING, AND SUPERSCORING

Students who have previously taken a full-length, paper and pencil ACT will be allowed to register for additional ACT section tests that are administered via computer.

As the push for Computer Based Testing (CBT) grows, we fully expect the ACT to eventually offer students the option of taking the entire exam via computer. For now, students should prepare using a combination of pencil and paper along with at least a familiarity with CBT and how it works. Either way, the strategies and skills required to earn your top score are the same.

ACT will superscore your multiple test administrations. In other words, if you take the ACT more than once, they will automatically submit your best section scores from each administration to the colleges and universities where you apply, thus giving you the highest possible composite score.

STUDENTS WITH ACCOMMODATIONS

If you have been pre-approved by ACT for extended time testing or for any other accommodation, please utilize those same accommodations while practicing. For the majority of students with learning differences, the most common accommodation is called extended time, but there are many others. Again, no matter your official, pre-approved accommodation, please practice accordingly.

About the ACT

FORMAT

The ACT test consists of four multiple-choice sections plus an optional writing exercise. Here's the breakdown:

Section	Time	No. of Questions
English	45 minutes	75
Math	60 minutes	60
Reading	35 minutes	40
Science	35 minutes	40
Writing (optional)	40 minutes	1 essay

SCORING

The four multiple-choice sections (English, Mathematics, Reading, and Science) are scored on a scale from 1 to 36; the more questions you answer correctly, the higher your score will be. You will receive an individual score for each subject test, as well as a *composite* score. Your composite score is found by averaging your four subject test scores—that is, adding them all together and dividing the sum by 4—rounding up at .5 or above.

For example, let's say you took a practice test and received the following scores:

English: 26

Mathematics: 21

Reading: 24

Science: 24

Your composite score would be 24. (Added together, these scores total 95. Divide that value by 4, and you get 23.75. Because 23.75 has a decimal value greater than or equal to .5, you round up to 24.)

When colleges speak of ACT scores or list the median ACT score of their student bodies, they are referring to composite scores.

The only aspect of the ACT not scored from 1 to 36 is the Writing section. Every essay is read by two essay graders, who each give the writing sample a score ranging from 1 to 6. These scores are added together, resulting in a Writing score ranging from 2 to 12. Students will also receive a combined English/Writing score (on a scale of 1–36), drawing one-third from your Writing score and two-thirds from your English score.

PRACTICE TESTS

The best way to prepare for the ACT is to take several full-length practice tests. Once you have reviewed all of the skills presented in this book and learned our proven strategies, you can truly begin to measure your progress as a test taker. Do not expect to reach your score goals on the first practice test. **It takes time to familiarize yourself with the ACT**. As you move through the various practice tests, always keep one goal in mind—**steady progress**.

Although scale scores (explained earlier) are certainly important, the most helpful tool to measure your progress is actually your raw score on each subject test. In other words, on each successive practice test, your goal should always be to answer more questions correctly than you did on the previous test. Always think of how many questions you answer correctly, because in most cases, for every one question you get right on the Reading and Science sections, your scale scores go up by a full point; on the English and Mathematics sections, you get 1 scale point for every two questions you answer correctly. Keep track of your scores on the sheets provided after each practice test, and push yourself to answer at least one more question correctly per section as you move through the tests. If you can reach this very modest goal, **by the time you finish working through this book, you will have raised your composite score by 3 points!**

You might think that one little question doesn't matter, but nothing could be further from the truth. Getting one or two more questions right might just help you get into the college of your dreams! Since there is no penalty for incorrect answers, be sure you answer every question. Do not leave blanks.

MONITORING TIME

We will discuss pacing for each section in the strategies for that particular section. To succeed on this test, both during practice and on the actual test, you need to be responsible for keeping track of time. Practice pacing yourself so that you are not surprised during the actual ACT.

Suggestion for timekeeping: Use a digital watch on both the practice tests and on the actual test. Be sure it has a stopwatch feature and does not beep. If you must use a watch with a sweeping second hand, set it to noon before you begin each test. It is far easier to gauge your time from this setting.

Regardless of which type of watch you choose, **the most important thing is that you use the same watch for the practice tests and for the actual ACT**.

BUILDING ENDURANCE

The ACT is nearly 4 hours long. Your ultimate goal should be to complete at least one full practice test in one sitting before the actual test. Begin to build endurance by doing at least two sections together (e.g., English, then Mathematics or Reading, then Science). Additionally, the ACT is always given in the morning, so it is a good idea to do at least some of your practicing in the morning (especially if you are not a "morning person!").

English Rules

The ACT English test is possibly the easiest section for you to make vast skill and score improvements.

HIGHLIGHTS

- 5 passages, each with 15 questions
- 75 questions total
- 45 minutes
- Answer *every* question

DO'S AND DON'TS

- **DO** know the difference between a sentence and a fragment. A sentence has a subject and a verb and expresses a complete thought.

  Fragment: *She, acting like an infant, crying and whining.*

  Sentence: *I swim.*
- **DO** pick the clearest, most concise way of stating something. SHORTEST IS BEST, as long as you have a complete sentence.
- **DO** read to the very end of a sentence before answering a question. This way you will be sure that you pick an answer that creates a complete sentence.
- **DO** test the "DELETE the underlined portion" choice first: it is the correct answer about 50 percent of the time. Remember, though, that means it is a wrong answer 50 percent of the time as well, so choose DELETE when the underlined portion is repetitive or does not fit the main idea of the passage.
- **DO** be cautious when considering any answer with the word *being* in it, as it is seldom correct.
- **DO** look for wrong answers. Wrong answers are often much easier to find than right ones. Unless the right answer comes to you immediately, **ELIMINATE WRONG ANSWERS!**
- **DON'T** jump from question to question.
- **DON'T** be afraid to pick NO CHANGE. It is typically correct as often as any other answer.

PACING AND PRACTICING

- You have 45 minutes to complete the five English passages—that's 9 minutes per passage.
- Here's a tip for practicing your pacing: Draw a box at the end of each section. Under each box write in multiples of 9 (9, 18, 27, 36, and 45). Don't forget, you only have 45 minutes. As you take the exam, time yourself and write in the actual time it took you to finish each passage. This will help you know whether you need to speed up or slow down.
- The sections do not get more difficult as you go, so it is better to finish even if you have to make a few guesses along the way.

- It takes practice to get used to the English section. If you apply the rules and strategies while taking the practice tests, you will be fully prepared for the actual test.

PUNCTUATION

COMMAS

There are six comma rules to learn for the ACT.

1. Commas are used to mark the end of an introductory clause and are followed by a complete sentence. Introductory clauses often begin with words such as *although, when, while, since, if,* and *because.* (Yes. The word *because* can start a sentence!)

   EXAMPLE: *When it stops raining, Mark is going to wash his car.*

   EXAMPLE: *Although I'd love to go to the movie with you, I need to study for the ACT.*

   Please notice that each clause is followed by a comma and then a complete sentence. Also, the subject of the sentence must be mentioned immediately after the comma in order for it to make sense.

   EXAMPLE: *Feeling very sad, she felt a tear run down her cheek.*

   This is correct because it is clear that "she" was feeling very sad. If the sentence were written, "Feeling very sad, a tear ran down her cheek" it would be incorrect. A tear cannot feel sad!

2. Commas are used to set off nonrestrictive clauses/appositives (phrases that interrupt the flow of the sentence).

   EXAMPLE: *Jim, a champion swimmer, hoped to make the Olympic team.*

   To check for interruptions, remove the words between the commas. If the remaining portion is a complete sentence and the meaning is not changed, then the commas are correct. If not, then test another answer. <u>Be sure to read the whole sentence!</u> Words such as *however, for example, for instance,* and *although* are usually surrounded by commas.

3. Commas are used to separate two or more coordinate adjectives preceding a noun.

   EXAMPLE: *The ACT is not a stressful, difficult test.*

   However, do not use a comma if the adjectives are cumulative.

4. Commas separate more than two words in a series.

   EXAMPLE: *I bought eggs, cheese, milk, and butter at the store.*

   (The last comma after "milk" is optional, although the ACT tends to leave it in.)

5. A comma <u>before a conjunction</u> can be used to separate two complete sentences. (Conjunction words are *and, but, or, so.*)

   EXAMPLE: *The palm trees blew softly in the wind, and the hot sun beat down from the sky.*

   Do not use a comma without the conjunction to separate two complete sentences!

   EXAMPLE: *The palm trees blew softly in the wind, the hot sun beat down from the sky.*

6. A comma can be used at the end of a sentence followed by an afterthought.

   EXAMPLE: *The football game was a massacre, 49 to 0.*

OTHER COMMA TIPS

- When in doubt, leave the comma out!
- Just because you pause when reading a sentence does not mean the sentence requires a comma.
- If all four answer choices are identically worded and three of the four answer choices contain commas in various places, the correct answer is likely to be the one that omits the commas.

DASH

There are two dash rules used on the ACT.

1. The dash, like the comma, is used to mark an interruption.

   EXAMPLE: *The Chicago Marathon—a race of endurance, strength, and skill—is difficult to complete.*

   Two dashes or two commas can be used interchangeably; however, never use one of each.

2. The dash can also be used just like a colon.

   EXAMPLE: *Roxann's hair is unlike anyone else's in the family—thick and dark.*

COLON

There are three colon rules for the ACT.

1. The colon is used **after a complete sentence** followed by a summary list.

   EXAMPLE: *I have many hobbies: golfing, rock climbing, sailing, and windsurfing.*

   Complete sentence + COLON + list

2. The colon is also used at the end of a complete sentence followed by an afterthought.

   EXAMPLE: *Japan has a high literacy rate: 99 percent.*

   Complete sentence + COLON + afterthought

3. The colon is also used to separate two complete sentences when the second sentence explains or restates an idea in the first.

   EXAMPLE: *These seat covers are the most durable kind: they are reinforced with double stitching and covered with a heavy plastic coating.*

   Complete sentence + COLON + explanation

SEMICOLON

There are two semicolon rules to know for the ACT.

1. The semicolon is used to separate complete sentences.

   EXAMPLE: *Harris practiced diligently for the ACT; he wanted to maximize his score.*

2. The semicolon is also used before a coordinating adverb (*however, therefore, since*) to separate two sentences.

   EXAMPLE: *I enjoy living in a small community; however, the neighbors are often too nosy.*

APOSTROPHE

An apostrophe is used to show ownership.

1. If there is one owner, use *'s.*

   EXAMPLE: *Patsy's car is brand new.*

2. If there is more than one owner, use *s'.*

   EXAMPLE: *Ten boys' bikes were stolen.*

3. Words that are plural without adding the *s* form the possessive by adding *'s.*

   EXAMPLE: *Women's, men's, people's, children's*

GRAMMAR

POSSESSIVES

One owner = *'s*
More than one owner = *s'*
Words that are plural without adding *s* like *women, men,* or *people*: use *'s.*

EXAMPLE: *I went into the men's locker room to change into my bathing suit.*

It's = it is
Its = one owner
Its' = **THIS IS NOT A WORD**, but ACT gives it as an answer choice—**NEVER** choose it!

Their = more than one owner
They're = they are
There = location

SUBJECT-VERB AGREEMENT

Always check for agreement. Within a sentence, a singular subject must be followed by a singular verb and a plural subject must be followed by a plural verb.

EXAMPLE: *The stack of books is on the floor.*

The subject here is "stack," which is singular, so the verb *is* is correct.

BE CAREFUL!

Verbs are not made plural just by putting an *s* on the end. If you want a singular verb, put the word *he* or *she* in front of it and make sure it works. If you want a plural verb, put the word *they* in front of it and make sure it works.

EXAMPLE: *He sits*

They sit.

One of the ACT's most common questions begins with a singular subject and is followed by several prepositional phrases with plural nouns and then a verb. This verb MUST be singular so as to agree with the sentence's singular subject.

EXAMPLE: *The color of the glass in the panes of glass in the windows of the nearby house is actually a reflection of the sun's rays.*

Although there are multiple nouns in the prepositional phrase above, the subject in this sentence is in fact *color*. You must, therefore, use the singular verb *is*.

SUBJECT-PRONOUN AGREEMENT

Within a sentence a singular subject must be followed by a singular pronoun, and a plural subject must be followed by a plural pronoun.

EXAMPLE: *Each of the boys took his seat on the bus.*

Since the subject is "each of the boys" it is singular. *His* is a singular pronoun.

PARALLEL PHRASING

Express ideas in a consistent, grammatical way. Phrases or words in a series must be in the same form.

DO THIS: *I like to run, bike, and swim.*

NOT THIS: I like to run, biking, and swimming.

TRANSITIONS

If all answers except one have a transition, read the sentence before to see whether you really need a transition.

A. Consequently, the dog
B. Therefore, the dog
C. *The dog*
D. For example, the dog

If all answers contain transitions ...

1. Look for two transitions that have similar meanings.
2. Eliminate the two with similar meanings.
3. Look at the sentence before and after the transition to determine how the sentences should be linked. One of the two remaining answers should clearly be the better choice.

Math Rules

The ACT Math test covers most areas of high school mathematics. Regardless of your math level or proficiency, you will achieve your maximum potential score by completing the practice tests in this book.

HIGHLIGHTS

- 60 multiple-choice questions
- 60 minutes
- No penalty for guessing; answer *every* question
- Questions increase in difficulty throughout the test
- The TI-83 and TI-84 calculators are allowed on the test. The TI-89 is **not** allowed.

The Math test is the only section of the ACT arranged in order of difficulty; generally speaking, you will find significantly easier questions toward the beginning of the test and more difficult questions toward the end. (This is not to say, of course, that you will never find a "tough" question on the first half or an "easy" question at the end.) Knowing that the test is laid out in this way can help you tremendously as you work through the section on test day. For instance, if one of the first questions seems extremely complicated, you are probably overthinking it; if the answer to one of the last 10 questions appears extremely obvious and straightforward, it likely is not the correct answer.

While there is no precise point where the Math section jumps from easy to difficult questions, a good rule of thumb is that typically the first 30 questions cover the more basic skill sets, and the last 30 questions test more advanced topics. You might find that you are entirely unfamiliar with some of the advanced topics, and that's okay! If you have never taken an advanced algebra or a trigonometry class, you are not expected to know the answers to these questions. **Remember: You can still receive an excellent score on the ACT Math section without any knowledge of these advanced skills!**

DO'S AND DON'TS

- **DO** use your test booklet! Often a quick sketch will help you solve the problem. If a diagram is already provided, begin by marking all known information.
- **DO** work backwards. This is especially true when there are variables in the question and numbers in the answer choices. For these questions, use the "**Plug and Chug**" strategy: Plug answer choices back into the problem to find the correct solution to the problem.
- **DO** use the "**Plug in C Strategy**" when working backwards: all ACT math answers are listed in numerical order, either smallest to largest or vice versa. Therefore, when possible, plug in choice C (or H). If it is not the right answer, it will be immediately clear whether a larger or smaller answer choice would have led you to the correct answer. If you need a larger number, you can immediately eliminate choices A and B; if you need a smaller one, you can eliminate D and E. By using this method, you can eliminate three choices by checking only one!
- **DO** read the question first on long word problems. Previewing the actual question helps you eliminate unnecessary words and information.

- **DO** assign the variable(s) a number and evaluate the problem accordingly if a question has variables in the answer choices. Plug in an easy number to work with, like 2 or 3. (Beware of using zero or 1—they are more trouble than they are worth!)
- **DO** be sure to **answer the question being asked!** One of the most commonly made mistakes on the ACT is also one of the most avoidable. A good way to avoid this scenario is to underline the part of the question that directly poses the question (e.g., "What is the value of x?"). That way, after you finish solving the problem, you can quickly glance back at the part of the question that you have underlined and double check that you are answering the right question (i.e., circling the answer that corresponds to the value of x, rather than the value of y).
- **DO** assume that diagrams are drawn to scale if you don't know where to start on a problem or cannot find the answer mathematically and estimate lengths and angle measures from the diagram.
- **DO** look for wrong answers in addition to correct ones, and use **process of elimination**. Even if you do not find the answer, guessing after eliminating three answer choices will increase your probability of guessing correctly from 20 percent to 50 percent!
- **DO** start the test with your calculator in degree mode. To put a TI-83 or TI-84 in degree mode, first press the "MODE" button, located directly to the right of the yellow "2nd" button. Once in the "MODE" screen, look to the third line down. It will say "Radian" and "Degree." Make sure "Degree" is highlighted. If it is not, place the cursor on "Degree" and press the "ENTER" button. "Degree" should now be highlighted, and your calculator will be in degree mode.
- **DO** be alert for charts/graphs that apply to more than one question.
- **DON'T** spend too much time on any one question.

PACING AND PRACTICING

Sixty minutes to answer 60 questions corresponds to 1 minute per question. However, you should limit yourself to 25 minutes for the first 30 questions, and save the extra time to work through the more difficult questions on the second half of the test.

Remember, DO NOT leave any answers blank! However, on the practice tests, it is helpful to mark which questions you guessed on, so you can see which math concepts you might need to review again.

Reading Rules

To be successful on the Reading test, you must be an **active reader**. This means being able to determine main ideas, evaluate supporting details, and arrive at appropriate conclusions. Don't let your mind wander; stay focused on what the passage is saying.

Completing the practice tests in this book will enable you to improve your reading proficiency. The reading tests/passages in this book reflect the word count of actual ACT test passages.

HIGHLIGHTS

- 35 minutes
- 4 reading passages, each with 10 questions

PASSAGE 1: PROSE FICTION/LITERARY NARRATIVE

- This passage is a story.
- The first paragraph will indicate who (the character or characters) and what about that person.
- Use the **CAPS** strategy by identifying: **C**haracters, **A**ttitudes, **P**roblems (or issues), and **S**olutions (or ending). Know each character's personality traits and to whom they are related in the passage.

PASSAGE 2: SOCIAL SCIENCE

- This passage is informative.
- Read the first paragraph carefully for the author's purpose. To determine the author's purpose, ask yourself, "Why did the author write this?" or "What is the one main thing the author wants me to know after reading this passage?"
- Pay close attention to the first sentence or two of each paragraph and to the last paragraph, particularly the last sentence, because it often restates the main idea.
- If often helps to write down a key word for each paragraph.

PASSAGE 3: HUMANITIES

- This passage is often a narrative but sometimes resembles a social science passage.
- While reading, focus on the author/narrator's attitudes toward the subject of the passage.
- If it's a narrative, use the **CAPS** strategy.
- If it's informative, use the **T**hesis and **D**etails (**TD**) strategy.

PASSAGE 4: NATURAL SCIENCE

- This passage is also informative, so use the **TD** strategy.
- Read the passage for the big picture, focusing on the first and last paragraphs for the thesis.
- Don't spend too much time learning details; read for location of information.

TEST-TAKING STRATEGIES

1. Questions about a passage usually follow one main idea. The author wrote the passage for a reason; once you figure out the point that the author is trying to make, you will be well on your way to answering questions correctly.

Placing a star (*) next to the main points helps you to focus and locate important information as you read. Main points are key ideas in the passage.

2. On the prose fiction and (sometimes) the humanities passages, use the **CAPS** strategy: look for **C**haracters, **A**ttitudes, **P**roblems, and **S**olutions. There is always an issue (the problem) in the passage, so identify it! Every prose fiction passage will also have a conclusion or resolution, even if it's not a final one.
3. On the nonfiction passages—social science, natural science, and (sometimes) humanities—focus on the **TD:** **T**hesis and **D**etails. Be sure to read the first two paragraphs carefully, as they generally contain the author's purpose, thesis, or main idea. The rest of the passage contains details that support the author's main idea. You do not need to memorize them all on your initial read. If you can simply pick out the author's important supporting details (each paragraph generally corresponds to one major detail), you will be in great shape as you move on to the questions.
4. Each student will approach the ACT Reading test slightly differently. No two brains are identical; therefore, no two strategies are identical. However, for most students there is a definitive reading strategy that produces the highest possible ACT reading score, and it's very simple.

   Step 1: Read the entire passage quickly but actively, seeking out the most important information. Place a star in the margin next to significant information. When you finish reading the passage, you should be able to mentally answer the **CAPS** or **TD** questions! If you cannot do this easily, you were not actively reading! (Reading the passage should take between 4 and 5 minutes.)

   Step 2: Answer the questions. Be sure to read ALL FOUR answer choices, using the process of elimination, BEFORE looking back to the passage. (Answering questions should take about 4–5 minutes.) Do not keep looking back. Keep moving.

No matter what, you must complete each passage in LESS THAN 9 MINUTES! In order to reach your maximum reading score, it is imperative that you get to all four passages. Remember, it is possible to get some answers wrong on the ACT and still achieve a great score.

An alternative strategy that works for some students is to actively read only the first and last paragraphs while skimming the body of the passage and then answering the questions as described above.

You waste precious time by reading the questions first. On a rare occasion, this strategy will work, but for 99 percent of students it does not help with comprehension or with earning a high reading score.

5. Although the content of the passages changes from test to test, the types of questions do not. If you know how to answer each type of question, you will be in good shape.

   - **Main Idea or Author's Purpose**
     Look for a general, vague, or broad answer.
   - **Inferences**
     Make an assumption based on what you read; don't bother looking back.
   - **Tone**
     Usually positive; look for a "nice" answer.
   - **Detail**
     If the question includes "the passage states" or "the passage indicates," the answer is in the passage. When referring to line numbers, read before and after the lines given.

However, be sure to still read all the answer choices before looking back in order to save valuable time.

- **Vocabulary Words**
  You must look back for context: read the lines before and after for clues as to meaning and then plug in words.
- **"Except" or "Not" Questions**
  Answer as if they are true/false questions.

DO'S AND DON'TS

- **DO** read all choices and try to eliminate some before looking back. It is acceptable to look back as long as you first use the process of elimination. If you do look back, you must do so very quickly!
- **DO** be consistent with theme; questions often repeat themselves.
- **DO** be careful on questions with specific line references. When looking back in the passage, make sure to read a few lines before and after the given line reference for context.
- **DO** look at the title of the passage for social science, humanities, and natural science. It can often give you a clear hint as to what the passage is primarily about.
- **DO** match ideas from the passage to the questions.
- **DO** choose moderate words such as *sometimes, tend to be,* and *likely.*
- **DON'T** look back for the answer without reading all choices and eliminating wrong answers first.
- **DON'T** just match words, match ideas. Be sure your selection answers the question.
- **DON'T** choose answers containing definitive words such as *always, never, only,* and *alone.*

PACING AND PRACTICING

- You have approximately 9 minutes per passage. Always spend more time answering questions (e.g., 5 minutes) than reading the passage (e.g., 4 minutes).
- You can speed up your reading by using an index card or pencil to help you focus. Be sure to place a star next to key ideas.
- It is better to make educated guesses throughout the test than to guess on an entire passage. Remember, each passage contains easy, medium, and difficult questions. If you spend too much time on the truly difficult questions early on, you might run out of time and end up missing some easy questions because you never got to them. You want to get to all questions if possible.
- Try the following to practice your pacing: Draw a box at the end of each reading passage. Under the first box, write in 8–9. Under the second, write in 17–18. Under the third, write in 26–27, and under the fourth, write in 35. With 35 minutes to complete four passages, you actually get 8 minutes and 45 seconds per passage, so try your best to complete each passage in less than 9 minutes! You MUST be finished in 35 minutes. As you take the practice exams, time yourself and write in the actual time you take to finish. This will give you a strong idea of where you need to speed up or slow down.

REMEMBER

To get a good score on the Reading test, you must finish it—even if you have to guess along the way!

Science Rules

For most students, the ACT Science Reasoning test appears to be the most difficult of the four, but with a little practice, it becomes fairly straightforward. This is the point in the test where many students lose focus. *Do not let this happen!*

HIGHLIGHTS

- The Science section is not arranged in order of difficulty. Each passage contains a difficult question or two, so it is important not to spend too much time on challenging questions. If necessary, make an educated guess and move on.
- The Science section is really a reasoning or logic test. You may need to have prior knowledge of the subject matter, although usually it is a basic concept.
- Think of the Science section as a puzzle or riddle that you have to figure out.
- The focus is on interpreting data and information and making logical conclusions.
- It is important to be FLEXIBLE and to be able to SHIFT GEARS in the Science section. In other words, if one method doesn't work, try another. If looking at one piece of information doesn't help you, look in a different place.
- With all of the information put in front of you and only 35 minutes to answer all of the questions, the Science section can seem overwhelming. The most important thing you can do to conserve time is orient yourself. Use the headings on charts and graphs the same way you would at the grocery store, and the ACT Science Reasoning test can be as straightforward as buying a loaf of bread.
- The Science section contains three distinct types of passages.

  1. **Data representation**
  2. **Research summaries**
  3. **Conflicting viewpoints**

The conflicting viewpoints passage is unique and is not usually accompanied by charts and graphs. Instead, it involves interpreting data. It can fall anywhere in the test, but you will easily recognize it because it will consist of a brief introduction to the topic followed by two to four sections (e.g., Scientist 1, Scientist 2 ... or The Dust Theory, The Dirt Theory, The Rock Theory) written in paragraph form. It may look like you need to read everything but you do not!

In many ways, the conflicting viewpoints passage is similar to the passages in the Reading section: It is essential that you determine the MAIN IDEA of each view.

REMEMBER

"Conflicting viewpoints" is called that for a reason. Although they will discuss the same general topic, the views must oppose each other in some fundamental way. Once you have figured out each view's main idea and where the views disagree, you will be in great shape on the questions.

Follow these steps on the conflicting viewpoints passage:

1. Skim the introductory paragraph.
2. Then read enough of each viewpoint to determine the main idea of each one. (The main idea can usually be found in the first two sentences of each viewpoint.)

3. Then go straight to the questions. Look back when you need to, using as much logic as possible.
4. There are two basic types of questions. The first is a simple word match—just look for the words in the passages. The second asks you to define the viewpoint. These may seem more difficult, but they should revolve around the first two sentences of each viewpoint that you read.
5. Questions often ask about one of the viewpoints but list answer choices that correspond to the other(s). Look to eliminate these extraneous answer choices first.

In general, there are three types of questions on the Science section:

1. **PATTERNS AND TRENDS**: For this type of question, you need to find the answer based on the data. Focus on investigating the information *directionally* (e.g., Does the pressure increase or decrease when velocity increases? When exposed to more sunlight, do the plants flower more frequently, less frequently, or is there no relationship?).
2. **HYPOTHESIS**: This question involves yes/no or true/false answers. These questions can be best tackled by a **"Plug and Chug"** method. Try out each answer as you go through them.
3. **LOGIC**: These questions are designed to challenge your thinking. You should focus on connecting the information. If the question talks about the *design* of the experiment, you may need to read a little bit.

ACT science questions can also be thought of as either navigation or manipulation questions.

Navigation. Within each passage there are typically three questions that you can answer simply by locating (navigating) the necessary information in a chart or graph.

Manipulation. There are approximately two per passage. These questions involve three steps: first you must locate the appropriate information, then you must use the data in some way to find the correct answer, and finally you must decide if you need additional information from the reading.

TEST-TAKING STRATEGIES

1. For most of the passages, your first step should be to skim the introduction. Look at the data, reading the labels and headings quickly. Your goal is to just get a general idea of where everything is. DO NOT WORRY IF YOU DON'T UNDERSTAND WHAT'S GOING ON. It may be confusing, but there isn't enough time to try to completely comprehend each experiment.
2. Your focus then becomes the questions. Read through the first question and underline key words. DO NOT go straight to the data yet.
3. Next, match the information in the question to the appropriate chart/graph(s). BE SURE THAT YOU ARE LOOKING AT THE CORRECT GRAPH OR CHART! **Then, work backward from the answers.** Use the process of elimination to help you determine the true answer. Almost every question refers to a data table even though the question might not specifically mention that table. *Use the answers as a guide to locate the correct table.*
4. Think simply and linearly! Try not to overthink—the answers are usually simpler than you realize.
5. If you are not able to find the answer using just the charts and graphs, then you may have to go to the text. Sometimes italicized words can be helpful. If the question states "based on the information," you should look at the text. The introductory passage may have some information to help you.

DO'S AND DON'TS

- **DO** focus on the charts and graphs. You may have to use data from two sources to answer the question.
- **DO** pretend that you are shopping at an unfamiliar grocery store. Use the headings on the tables, charts, and graphs to help you!
- **DO** look for patterns, trends, and directions. If there is an obvious pattern, such as a column of numbers increasing or decreasing, it might be helpful to draw an arrow showing that trend.
- **DO** write in the test booklet. Circling and underlining both help prevent careless errors.
- **DO** work backward from each answer—using the process of elimination. (Check each answer to see if it is true. There should only be one true answer.)
- **DON'T** let the wording of the questions confuse you. Break them down; underline key words. There is often more information in the questions than you actually need to answer.

PACING AND PRACTICING

- Over the last several years, ACT Science has presented students with 6 passages. However, ACT still states that the Science section could have either 6 or 7 passages. With 6 or 7 passages and 35 minutes, you have essentially 5 or 6 minutes per passage; however, some will take a minute less while others may take a minute more. Try to use pacing boxes during practice.
- Don't rush; just be conscious of your time from the beginning.
- If you can't figure out a question, **make your best guess and move on.** You will not have enough time to dwell on questions, and it is better to guess on one or two than to not even make it to an entire passage.
- If you find yourself struggling with finishing, complete the conflicting views passage last. (Be careful on your answer sheet!)
- Don't panic as you begin to practice. It may take you longer at first! You *will* get the hang of it!

Writing Rules

The ACT Writing will be administered about five minutes after the end of the ACT Science test. During the Writing test, you will have 40 minutes to plan and write an analytical essay in response to a prompt. Although there is no length requirement, the higher-scoring essays tend to be at least 1.5 pages long (more like 2 pages if you have very big handwriting), and although you should *definitely* spend more time writing than you should spend on planning, making outlines or whatever your personal pre-writing process is important.

You will be provided with three hypothetical people's opinions—i.e., "some quotes"—at least one of which you are required to address in your response. Overall, your essay response represents the "fourth perspective." Think of your essay as "joining a conversation" in which you are the fourth person, rather than as "judging" any or all of the other perspectives in turn as "right" or "wrong"—although you may of course say so, if that is your real opinion. You will *always* write a better essay by saying what you *really* think than you will if you worry about guessing what the graders "want to hear."

After the specific issue that your essay must concern is explained, and the three hypothetical perspectives are given, the instructions at the bottom will state:

- clearly state your own perspective on the issue and analyze the relationship between your perspective and at least one other perspective
- develop and support your ideas with reasoning and examples
- organize your ideas clearly and logically
- communicate your ideas effectively in standard written English

Regarding these instructions, here are some things to notice and keep in mind:

- Although you are only *required* to discuss *one* of the three provided perspectives, you can discuss more than one of them.
- Although no one way of structuring your essay is "the right way," be advised that it is NOT the best idea to use a "first half/second half" structure, where "first" you discuss the perspectives and "then" you give your own opinion. You'll note that the directions specifically tell you to "analyze the *relationship between*" your own opinion and the provided perspective(s) that you choose to discuss—not just to talk about both things separately. Yes, by the "home stretch" of your essay you should have dispensed with the provided perspectives and just be discussing your own views, but you certainly shouldn't "wait" until you are "done" discussing the other perspectives to introduce it. Instead, let the other perspectives "help" you introduce your own views bit-by-bit, adding a "this makes me think of ..." or an "I think that's interesting because ..." to your assessments of the perspectives you pick. Think of the provided perspectives as being like the "boosters" that help a space shuttle take off: their assistance is needed in order for the shuttle (i.e., your own opinion) to get off the ground, and they do most of the work at first, but then, as the shuttle gains altitude and momentum, they fall away one by one as their fuel is spent, until finally the shuttle is soaring under its own power!
- You are asked to "develop and support your ideas with reasoning and examples." Be careful not to be repetitive. You may use examples from your own experiences, but remember, your examples are your evidence. Make sure to have a clear thesis (it need not be complex), strong topic sentences, and transitions between paragraphs.

OVERALL APPROACH: THE "BOW" STRATEGY

BRAINSTORM

Think about the issue in general as described in the prompt, and also about the three provided perspectives. What popped into your head when you were thinking about *just* the issue? And did any or all of the three perspectives make you want to *modify* those initial ideas? If so, then you've already gotten some ideas on how to "pay respect to" the three perspectives (e.g., "I was inclined to think this way until Perspective Two reminded me of how ...").

ORGANIZE

While it *is* important that you *use paragraphs* (when a reader sees that an essay is just one long paragraph, she or he will expect it to be bad—because, frankly, most essays written as one long paragraph really *are* bad), it is by no means required that you use the traditional five-paragraph "Introduction, Three Points, Conclusion" essay. Nor do you have to open with a rhetorical question, or make the second sentence the "topic sentence," or any other rule you may have learned in school. If you like some or all of those rules, and feel more comfortable using them, then go right ahead—but using them is not mandatory, or even necessarily the best idea. All that the first paragraph has to do is get the reader interested and make you seem like you understand the issue and have interesting things that you're eager to start saying about it (be advised that quoting word-for-word from the opening paragraph of the prompt is NOT the way to make this impression—that's what students do when they can't think of anything to say!); all that the last paragraph has to do is provide a satisfying "sense of an ending" (i.e., it seems like you meant for that to be the end, rather than seeming like you ran out of time); and all that the paragraphs in the middle have to do is demonstrate understanding of one or more perspectives, provide original ideas that are somehow connected to them, and back up these original ideas with effective persuasion... in *whatever order you're comfortable with!* After all, the *most* important thing is NOT to worry so much about organization that you end up not writing enough! As long as everything you need is in there *somewhere*, the graders aren't going to lose their minds over whether everything is in the "right" place!

WRITE

As the saying goes, "you never get a second chance to make a first impression," and your first paragraph is the first impression you make on the graders. This doesn't mean you should be terrified that it's going to "make or break" your essay—but it does mean that you should try to make it interesting! If you think of a great quotation or an interesting fact that is relevant to the issue, for example, don't "save it for later"—put it right at the beginning and open with a bang! The graders, of course, *have to* read your essay (just like you *have to* write it), but you should be thinking about what might make people *want to* read it: If somebody just came across your essay somewhere and read the beginning, would he or she be "hooked" and want to keep going?

While the opening paragraph should be "motivating," the keyword for the rest of the essay is "memorable." Are your ideas and examples you use to support them going to "stick with" a reader? Are they insightful? Moving? Amusing? Whatever sort of rhetoric you use to get the reader interested, the idea is that you want *your* essay to be the one that the readers remember at the end of the day! So, ask yourself: What sort of ideas make *you* remember a piece of writing?

As far as conclusions go, keep in mind that the oft-repeated advice of "tell them what you told them" is NOT the best strategy for the ACT Writing. While you do want to provide a sense of "summing up" your big ideas (i.e., the end should *feel like the end*), it makes for dull writing to simply repeat them, "ticking them off" one-by-one as though the conclusion were a checklist. You want to end "with a bang," just like you started with one in the introduction! (And whatever you do, DON'T begin the last paragraph with the words "In conclusion ..."—after all, "real" essays in magazines never do that, but you can still tell when it's the end!)

It is better to have a longer essay that may involve some "twists and turns" than to have a meticulously organized essay that is too short. The best strategy is to do a "good enough" amount of pre-planning and then just "jump in," as opposed to wasting precious writing time making sure that you will have exactly five paragraphs of precisely equal length.

SCORING

Two readers will read your essay, and each will assign it a score from 1 to 6. If, by chance, these two scorers disagree by more than one point, then the scoring supervisor will step in to resolve the discrepancy. The Writing Score is based on Ideas and Analysis, Development and Support, and Organization—Language Use and Conventions. Performance on the Writing test will not affect the English, Math, Reading, Science, or composite scores. You will receive two additional scores on your score sheet—a combined English/Writing score (1–36) and a Writing test sub-score (2–12). Neither of these scores will affect your composite score.

EXERCISES TO IMPROVE YOUR ESSAY-WRITING SKILLS, AND TIPS TO IMPROVE YOUR ACT WRITING SCORE

- Just as you use every muscle during a game but build up your strength by working out one muscle group at a time in the gym, you can build up your writing skills by practicing one part of an essay at a time: Using the prompts and skill-builders in this book, try practicing writing only topic sentences, or only introductions or conclusions, or only listing quotes, examples, and interesting facts, rather than feeling as though you need to only practice writing an entire essay at a time (although you should *certainly* practice writing entire essays, too).
- A stirring (or insightful, or amusing) quotation can enhance an essay, especially if it appears in the introduction. The "Big Four" people to Google when it comes to great quotations are Abraham Lincoln, Mark Twain, Albert Einstein, and Oscar Wilde!
- You don't always need to say "In my opinion ..." before stating an opinion. After all, it's your essay, so the reader already knows it's your opinion! However, doing this *once or twice* can be a good idea, especially when the opinion you're about to state might be controversial, because it makes you seem humble.
- It's important to vary your sentence structure. So, try to write as few sentences as possible that begin with the word "The." And you *definitely* want to avoid beginning sentences with the word "Also," especially consecutive sentences!
- Vocabulary is important but using words correctly is even more important. (If you are not used to using a particular word, then there's a good chance you'll end up using it *incorrectly*, which will make your score go *down*.)
- Although the prompt provides you with "three perspectives" representing other people's opinions, these people are not named or identified in any way, so you do not know whether they are male or female (the quotes aren't real, so there is no right answer). Feel free to use what ever pronouns make you most comfortable.

How to Practice Effectively for the ACT

A SUGGESTED LESSON PLAN

Preparing for the ACT is one of the most important steps a high school student can take. Your ACT score helps determine where you will go to college and whether or not schools will offer you scholarship money.

When taking the practice exams in this book, please simulate actual test conditions:

- Find a quiet location that is free from distractions.
- Leave your phone in a separate room!
- Be sure to wear the same wrist watch during practice that you will wear during the actual exam.
- Be sure to use the same calculator, as well.
- Try to do an entire test in one sitting, whenever possible.
- Do not "read out loud" as this is not allowed during the ACT.

After completing a practice test, it is imperative that you carefully review your errors. Each test is accompanied by a set of explanations. When you miss a question, carefully review the explanation for the correct answer. It is virtually impossible to improve your ACT score without this corrective input.

All students should carefully read, review, and learn the strategies listed at the beginning of this book, found in the "About the ACT" section. These "Rules" will help you score to your maximum potential.

We suggest the following lesson plans:

Full Prep: (12 week plan)

Ideally, students will begin their prep twelve weeks (about 3 months) prior to their test date. There are seven full exams in this book. Be sure to review the "Rules" found in the "About the ACT" section at the beginning of the book. We then suggest taking and reviewing one practice exam every two weeks or so.

Fast Prep: (4–8 week plan)

When time is a bit short, students should attempt to complete and review at least 3–4 of the practice exams found in this book. Be sure to first review the "Rules" found in the "About the ACT" section at the beginning of the book.

Lightning Prep: (1–4 week plan)

We understand that sometimes time is limited and that some prep is better than no prep. In this case, be sure to review the "Rules" found in the "About the ACT" section at the beginning of the book. Then, try to take and review at least 2 of the practice exams found in the book.

Practice Tests

ANSWER SHEET
Practice Test 1

Directions: Mark one answer only for each question. Make the mark dark. Erase completely any mark made in error. (Additional or stray marks will be counted as mistakes.)

English

1. Ⓐ Ⓑ Ⓒ Ⓓ	**16.** Ⓕ Ⓖ Ⓗ Ⓙ	**31.** Ⓐ Ⓑ Ⓒ Ⓓ	**46.** Ⓕ Ⓖ Ⓗ Ⓙ	**61.** Ⓐ Ⓑ Ⓒ Ⓓ
2. Ⓕ Ⓖ Ⓗ Ⓙ	**17.** Ⓐ Ⓑ Ⓒ Ⓓ	**32.** Ⓕ Ⓖ Ⓗ Ⓙ	**47.** Ⓐ Ⓑ Ⓒ Ⓓ	**62.** Ⓕ Ⓖ Ⓗ Ⓙ
3. Ⓐ Ⓑ Ⓒ Ⓓ	**18.** Ⓕ Ⓖ Ⓗ Ⓙ	**33.** Ⓐ Ⓑ Ⓒ Ⓓ	**48.** Ⓕ Ⓖ Ⓗ Ⓙ	**63.** Ⓐ Ⓑ Ⓒ Ⓓ
4. Ⓕ Ⓖ Ⓗ Ⓙ	**19.** Ⓐ Ⓑ Ⓒ Ⓓ	**34.** Ⓕ Ⓖ Ⓗ Ⓙ	**49.** Ⓐ Ⓑ Ⓒ Ⓓ	**64.** Ⓕ Ⓖ Ⓗ Ⓙ
5. Ⓐ Ⓑ Ⓒ Ⓓ	**20.** Ⓕ Ⓖ Ⓗ Ⓙ	**35.** Ⓐ Ⓑ Ⓒ Ⓓ	**50.** Ⓕ Ⓖ Ⓗ Ⓙ	**65.** Ⓐ Ⓑ Ⓒ Ⓓ
6. Ⓕ Ⓖ Ⓗ Ⓙ	**21.** Ⓐ Ⓑ Ⓒ Ⓓ	**36.** Ⓕ Ⓖ Ⓗ Ⓙ	**51.** Ⓐ Ⓑ Ⓒ Ⓓ	**66.** Ⓕ Ⓖ Ⓗ Ⓙ
7. Ⓐ Ⓑ Ⓒ Ⓓ	**22.** Ⓕ Ⓖ Ⓗ Ⓙ	**37.** Ⓐ Ⓑ Ⓒ Ⓓ	**52.** Ⓕ Ⓖ Ⓗ Ⓙ	**67.** Ⓐ Ⓑ Ⓒ Ⓓ
8. Ⓕ Ⓖ Ⓗ Ⓙ	**23.** Ⓐ Ⓑ Ⓒ Ⓓ	**38.** Ⓕ Ⓖ Ⓗ Ⓙ	**53.** Ⓐ Ⓑ Ⓒ Ⓓ	**68.** Ⓕ Ⓖ Ⓗ Ⓙ
9. Ⓐ Ⓑ Ⓒ Ⓓ	**24.** Ⓕ Ⓖ Ⓗ Ⓙ	**39.** Ⓐ Ⓑ Ⓒ Ⓓ	**54.** Ⓕ Ⓖ Ⓗ Ⓙ	**69.** Ⓐ Ⓑ Ⓒ Ⓓ
10. Ⓕ Ⓖ Ⓗ Ⓙ	**25.** Ⓐ Ⓑ Ⓒ Ⓓ	**40.** Ⓕ Ⓖ Ⓗ Ⓙ	**55.** Ⓐ Ⓑ Ⓒ Ⓓ	**70.** Ⓕ Ⓖ Ⓗ Ⓙ
11. Ⓐ Ⓑ Ⓒ Ⓓ	**26.** Ⓕ Ⓖ Ⓗ Ⓙ	**41.** Ⓐ Ⓑ Ⓒ Ⓓ	**56.** Ⓕ Ⓖ Ⓗ Ⓙ	**71.** Ⓐ Ⓑ Ⓒ Ⓓ
12. Ⓕ Ⓖ Ⓗ Ⓙ	**27.** Ⓐ Ⓑ Ⓒ Ⓓ	**42.** Ⓕ Ⓖ Ⓗ Ⓙ	**57.** Ⓐ Ⓑ Ⓒ Ⓓ	**72.** Ⓕ Ⓖ Ⓗ Ⓙ
13. Ⓐ Ⓑ Ⓒ Ⓓ	**28.** Ⓕ Ⓖ Ⓗ Ⓙ	**43.** Ⓐ Ⓑ Ⓒ Ⓓ	**58.** Ⓕ Ⓖ Ⓗ Ⓙ	**73.** Ⓐ Ⓑ Ⓒ Ⓓ
14. Ⓕ Ⓖ Ⓗ Ⓙ	**29.** Ⓐ Ⓑ Ⓒ Ⓓ	**44.** Ⓕ Ⓖ Ⓗ Ⓙ	**59.** Ⓐ Ⓑ Ⓒ Ⓓ	**74.** Ⓕ Ⓖ Ⓗ Ⓙ
15. Ⓐ Ⓑ Ⓒ Ⓓ	**30.** Ⓕ Ⓖ Ⓗ Ⓙ	**45.** Ⓐ Ⓑ Ⓒ Ⓓ	**60.** Ⓕ Ⓖ Ⓗ Ⓙ	**75.** Ⓐ Ⓑ Ⓒ Ⓓ

Mathematics

1. Ⓐ Ⓑ Ⓒ Ⓓ Ⓔ	**16.** Ⓕ Ⓖ Ⓗ Ⓙ Ⓚ	**31.** Ⓐ Ⓑ Ⓒ Ⓓ Ⓔ	**46.** Ⓕ Ⓖ Ⓗ Ⓙ Ⓚ
2. Ⓕ Ⓖ Ⓗ Ⓙ Ⓚ	**17.** Ⓐ Ⓑ Ⓒ Ⓓ Ⓔ	**32.** Ⓕ Ⓖ Ⓗ Ⓙ Ⓚ	**47.** Ⓐ Ⓑ Ⓒ Ⓓ Ⓔ
3. Ⓐ Ⓑ Ⓒ Ⓓ Ⓔ	**18.** Ⓕ Ⓖ Ⓗ Ⓙ Ⓚ	**33.** Ⓐ Ⓑ Ⓒ Ⓓ Ⓔ	**48.** Ⓕ Ⓖ Ⓗ Ⓙ Ⓚ
4. Ⓕ Ⓖ Ⓗ Ⓙ Ⓚ	**19.** Ⓐ Ⓑ Ⓒ Ⓓ Ⓔ	**34.** Ⓕ Ⓖ Ⓗ Ⓙ Ⓚ	**49.** Ⓐ Ⓑ Ⓒ Ⓓ Ⓔ
5. Ⓐ Ⓑ Ⓒ Ⓓ Ⓔ	**20.** Ⓕ Ⓖ Ⓗ Ⓙ Ⓚ	**35.** Ⓐ Ⓑ Ⓒ Ⓓ Ⓔ	**50.** Ⓕ Ⓖ Ⓗ Ⓙ Ⓚ
6. Ⓕ Ⓖ Ⓗ Ⓙ Ⓚ	**21.** Ⓐ Ⓑ Ⓒ Ⓓ Ⓔ	**36.** Ⓕ Ⓖ Ⓗ Ⓙ Ⓚ	**51.** Ⓐ Ⓑ Ⓒ Ⓓ Ⓔ
7. Ⓐ Ⓑ Ⓒ Ⓓ Ⓔ	**22.** Ⓕ Ⓖ Ⓗ Ⓙ Ⓚ	**37.** Ⓐ Ⓑ Ⓒ Ⓓ Ⓔ	**52.** Ⓕ Ⓖ Ⓗ Ⓙ Ⓚ
8. Ⓕ Ⓖ Ⓗ Ⓙ Ⓚ	**23.** Ⓐ Ⓑ Ⓒ Ⓓ Ⓔ	**38.** Ⓕ Ⓖ Ⓗ Ⓙ Ⓚ	**53.** Ⓐ Ⓑ Ⓒ Ⓓ Ⓔ
9. Ⓐ Ⓑ Ⓒ Ⓓ Ⓔ	**24.** Ⓕ Ⓖ Ⓗ Ⓙ Ⓚ	**39.** Ⓐ Ⓑ Ⓒ Ⓓ Ⓔ	**54.** Ⓕ Ⓖ Ⓗ Ⓙ Ⓚ
10. Ⓕ Ⓖ Ⓗ Ⓙ Ⓚ	**25.** Ⓐ Ⓑ Ⓒ Ⓓ Ⓔ	**40.** Ⓕ Ⓖ Ⓗ Ⓙ Ⓚ	**55.** Ⓐ Ⓑ Ⓒ Ⓓ Ⓔ
11. Ⓐ Ⓑ Ⓒ Ⓓ Ⓔ	**26.** Ⓕ Ⓖ Ⓗ Ⓙ Ⓚ	**41.** Ⓐ Ⓑ Ⓒ Ⓓ Ⓔ	**56.** Ⓕ Ⓖ Ⓗ Ⓙ Ⓚ
12. Ⓕ Ⓖ Ⓗ Ⓙ Ⓚ	**27.** Ⓐ Ⓑ Ⓒ Ⓓ Ⓔ	**42.** Ⓕ Ⓖ Ⓗ Ⓙ Ⓚ	**57.** Ⓐ Ⓑ Ⓒ Ⓓ Ⓔ
13. Ⓐ Ⓑ Ⓒ Ⓓ Ⓔ	**28.** Ⓕ Ⓖ Ⓗ Ⓙ Ⓚ	**43.** Ⓐ Ⓑ Ⓒ Ⓓ Ⓔ	**58.** Ⓕ Ⓖ Ⓗ Ⓙ Ⓚ
14. Ⓕ Ⓖ Ⓗ Ⓙ Ⓚ	**29.** Ⓐ Ⓑ Ⓒ Ⓓ Ⓔ	**44.** Ⓕ Ⓖ Ⓗ Ⓙ Ⓚ	**59.** Ⓐ Ⓑ Ⓒ Ⓓ Ⓔ
15. Ⓐ Ⓑ Ⓒ Ⓓ Ⓔ	**30.** Ⓕ Ⓖ Ⓗ Ⓙ Ⓚ	**45.** Ⓐ Ⓑ Ⓒ Ⓓ Ⓔ	**60.** Ⓕ Ⓖ Ⓗ Ⓙ Ⓚ

ANSWER SHEET
Practice Test 1

Reading

1. Ⓐ Ⓑ Ⓒ Ⓓ	9. Ⓐ Ⓑ Ⓒ Ⓓ	17. Ⓐ Ⓑ Ⓒ Ⓓ	25. Ⓐ Ⓑ Ⓒ Ⓓ	33. Ⓐ Ⓑ Ⓒ Ⓓ
2. Ⓕ Ⓖ Ⓗ Ⓙ	10. Ⓕ Ⓖ Ⓗ Ⓙ	18. Ⓕ Ⓖ Ⓗ Ⓙ	26. Ⓕ Ⓖ Ⓗ Ⓙ	34. Ⓕ Ⓖ Ⓗ Ⓙ
3. Ⓐ Ⓑ Ⓒ Ⓓ	11. Ⓐ Ⓑ Ⓒ Ⓓ	19. Ⓐ Ⓑ Ⓒ Ⓓ	27. Ⓐ Ⓑ Ⓒ Ⓓ	35. Ⓐ Ⓑ Ⓒ Ⓓ
4. Ⓕ Ⓖ Ⓗ Ⓙ	12. Ⓕ Ⓖ Ⓗ Ⓙ	20. Ⓕ Ⓖ Ⓗ Ⓙ	28. Ⓕ Ⓖ Ⓗ Ⓙ	36. Ⓕ Ⓖ Ⓗ Ⓙ
5. Ⓐ Ⓑ Ⓒ Ⓓ	13. Ⓐ Ⓑ Ⓒ Ⓓ	21. Ⓐ Ⓑ Ⓒ Ⓓ	29. Ⓐ Ⓑ Ⓒ Ⓓ	37. Ⓐ Ⓑ Ⓒ Ⓓ
6. Ⓕ Ⓖ Ⓗ Ⓙ	14. Ⓕ Ⓖ Ⓗ Ⓙ	22. Ⓕ Ⓖ Ⓗ Ⓙ	30. Ⓕ Ⓖ Ⓗ Ⓙ	38. Ⓕ Ⓖ Ⓗ Ⓙ
7. Ⓐ Ⓑ Ⓒ Ⓓ	15. Ⓐ Ⓑ Ⓒ Ⓓ	23. Ⓐ Ⓑ Ⓒ Ⓓ	31. Ⓐ Ⓑ Ⓒ Ⓓ	39. Ⓐ Ⓑ Ⓒ Ⓓ
8. Ⓕ Ⓖ Ⓗ Ⓙ	16. Ⓕ Ⓖ Ⓗ Ⓙ	24. Ⓕ Ⓖ Ⓗ Ⓙ	32. Ⓕ Ⓖ Ⓗ Ⓙ	40. Ⓕ Ⓖ Ⓗ Ⓙ

Science

1. Ⓐ Ⓑ Ⓒ Ⓓ	9. Ⓐ Ⓑ Ⓒ Ⓓ	17. Ⓐ Ⓑ Ⓒ Ⓓ	25. Ⓐ Ⓑ Ⓒ Ⓓ	33. Ⓐ Ⓑ Ⓒ Ⓓ
2. Ⓕ Ⓖ Ⓗ Ⓙ	10. Ⓕ Ⓖ Ⓗ Ⓙ	18. Ⓕ Ⓖ Ⓗ Ⓙ	26. Ⓕ Ⓖ Ⓗ Ⓙ	34. Ⓕ Ⓖ Ⓗ Ⓙ
3. Ⓐ Ⓑ Ⓒ Ⓓ	11. Ⓐ Ⓑ Ⓒ Ⓓ	19. Ⓐ Ⓑ Ⓒ Ⓓ	27. Ⓐ Ⓑ Ⓒ Ⓓ	35. Ⓐ Ⓑ Ⓒ Ⓓ
4. Ⓕ Ⓖ Ⓗ Ⓙ	12. Ⓕ Ⓖ Ⓗ Ⓙ	20. Ⓕ Ⓖ Ⓗ Ⓙ	28. Ⓕ Ⓖ Ⓗ Ⓙ	36. Ⓕ Ⓖ Ⓗ Ⓙ
5. Ⓐ Ⓑ Ⓒ Ⓓ	13. Ⓐ Ⓑ Ⓒ Ⓓ	21. Ⓐ Ⓑ Ⓒ Ⓓ	29. Ⓐ Ⓑ Ⓒ Ⓓ	37. Ⓐ Ⓑ Ⓒ Ⓓ
6. Ⓕ Ⓖ Ⓗ Ⓙ	14. Ⓕ Ⓖ Ⓗ Ⓙ	22. Ⓕ Ⓖ Ⓗ Ⓙ	30. Ⓕ Ⓖ Ⓗ Ⓙ	38. Ⓕ Ⓖ Ⓗ Ⓙ
7. Ⓐ Ⓑ Ⓒ Ⓓ	15. Ⓐ Ⓑ Ⓒ Ⓓ	23. Ⓐ Ⓑ Ⓒ Ⓓ	31. Ⓐ Ⓑ Ⓒ Ⓓ	39. Ⓐ Ⓑ Ⓒ Ⓓ
8. Ⓕ Ⓖ Ⓗ Ⓙ	16. Ⓕ Ⓖ Ⓗ Ⓙ	24. Ⓕ Ⓖ Ⓗ Ⓙ	32. Ⓕ Ⓖ Ⓗ Ⓙ	40. Ⓕ Ⓖ Ⓗ Ⓙ

ENGLISH TEST

Time: 45 Minutes—75 Questions

Directions: In the five passages that follow, certain words and phrases are underlined and numbered. In the right-hand column, you will find alternatives for the underlined part. In most cases, you are to choose the one that best expresses the idea, makes the statement appropriate for standard written English, or is worded most consistently with the style and tone of the passage as a whole. If you think the original version is best, choose "NO CHANGE." In some cases, you will find in the right-hand column a question about the underlined part. You are to choose the best answer to the question.

You will also find questions about a section of the passage, or about the passage as a whole. These questions do not refer to an underlined portion of the passage, but rather are identified by a number or numbers in a box.

For each question, choose the alternative you consider best and fill in the corresponding oval on your answer sheet. Read each passage through once before you begin to answer the questions that accompany it. For many of the questions, you must read several sentences beyond the question to determine the answer. Be sure that you have read far enough ahead each time you choose an alternative.

PASSAGE I

No Place I'd Rather Be

[1]

I started taking group skating lessons when I was four. I progressed through various levels rapidly and gave my first ice performance at age seven, soon I started (1) winning local and regional competitions. I began seriously training when I was nine years old. Mom and I would wake up at four o'clock in the morning, six days a week. I'd skate for five hours. Then I'd go to school.

1. A. NO CHANGE
   B. seven. Soon I started
   C. seven, soon I was
   D. seven. Soon I had

[2]

Saying good-bye to my family, and friends made me homesick before I even left, but I knew deep down that I had to leave and train full-time in Canada to give my dreams a chance at reality. I went to compete in the Olympic Games in 1992. No one, not my coach or even my family, ever talked to me about giving up. In fact, I wouldn't even allow myself to think about it. I thought my thoughts would jinx me. Yet, I went with the attitude that I wanted to enjoy the Olympic spirit. [6]

2. F. NO CHANGE
   G. family, and, friends
   H. family and friends,
   J. family and friends

3. Which of the following alternatives to the underlined portion would NOT be acceptable?
   A. even left yet I knew
   B. even left. I knew
   C. even left; I knew
   D. even left; however, I knew

4. Given that all of the choices are true, which one provides information that is most relevant at this point in the essay?
   F. NO CHANGE
   G. all the hard work required
   H. the joy of competing in the Olympics
   J. winning a gold medal

5. A. NO CHANGE
   B. Nevertheless, I
   C. However, I
   D. I

6. Which of the following statements, if added at the beginning of Paragraph 2, would most effectively introduce readers to the information presented in the paragraph?
   F. I had always wanted to move away from home, so when the opportunity presented itself, I jumped.
   G. Knowing that it was time to leave my childhood behind, I followed my coach's advice and randomly moved to Canada.
   H. Twenty-four hours after graduating from high school, I moved to Canada to train with other Olympic candidates.
   J. There was only one road to success, and hanging around my hometown waiting to be discovered wasn't it.

[3]

My practice sessions felt great leading up to the competition. Finally, the day arrived. I remember stepping onto the ice and thinking, *I can't do this.* How am I going to keep myself from freaking out? I took a deep breath and begun[7] a solid performance that placed me first going into the finals.

7. A. NO CHANGE
   B. begin
   C. began
   D. had begun

[4]

When medals were awarded, I found myself on the top step, the gold hanging[8] around my neck and Americas national anthem[9] playing. Words can't describe the overwhelming mixture of emotions I felt.

8. F. NO CHANGE
   G. top step the gold, hanging
   H. top, step the gold hanging
   J. top step the gold hanging

9. A. NO CHANGE
   B. Americas national anthem's
   C. Americas' national anthem
   D. America's national anthem

[5]

[1] Two days later, I was the first of the final six skaters on the cold, but shimmering ice.[10] [2] My long performance started well, but I slipped while completing one of my easiest triple jumps, and my hand touched the ice. [3] I didn't want to make two mistakes in a row, so next I did a jump with just two spins to play it safe. [4] Usually jumps have three

10. F. NO CHANGE
    G. cold yet shimmering, ice
    H. cold, shimmering, ice
    J. cold, shimmering ice

spins. [5] As I neared the end, I had one more jump, the triple Lutz. [6] Okay, this is it. [7] You have to do this, I told myself. [8] I landed perfectly. [11]

11. Which of the following sentences in this paragraph is LEAST relevant to the purpose of describing the narrator's actions, and therefore, could be deleted?
   A. Sentence 3
   B. Sentence 4
   C. Sentence 5
   D. Sentence 7

[6]

<u>Why is ice so popular?</u> [12] Frozen water can be so painfully hard and oh so cold—just as life can be. Ice doesn't care who skates across its surface. It doesn't care who loses balance and falls on <u>its</u> [13] slippery back. Still, when the lights go on and the crowd roars its welcome, there's no place I'd rather be.

12. Which of the following choices best introduces this paragraph?
   F. NO CHANGE
   G. There are so many reasons to love ice.
   H. How can anyone love ice?
   J. Ice has been around forever.

13. **A.** NO CHANGE
   B. it's
   C. their
   D. there

Questions 14 and 15 ask about the preceding passage as a whole.

14. For the sake of the logic and coherence of this essay, Paragraph 5 should be placed:
   F. where it is now.
   G. after Paragraph 3.
   H. before Paragraph 1.
   J. after Paragraph 6.

15. Suppose the writer's goal had been to write a brief essay about a significant event in her life. Would this essay successfully accomplish that goal?
   A. Yes, because it focuses on a specific time in the narrator's life and goes into detail about winning an Olympic gold medal.
   B. Yes, because it details every event that indirectly led to an important achievement in the narrator's life.
   C. No, because it is more of a persuasive essay motivating the readers to pursue their dreams, even if it means personal sacrifice.
   D. No, because the narrator mentions several events and doesn't go into much detail about any one event.

PASSAGE II

A Journey on Cane River

Growing up, I knew for an absolute fact that no one on the planet was stronger than my mother. So when she told me stories of people she admired growing up, I paid attention. She was clearly in awe of her grandmother, Emily. She described [16] her grandmother as iron-willed and devilish, physically beautiful and demanding of beauty from others, determined to make her farmhouse in central Louisiana a fun place to be on Sundays when family gathered, and fanatical and unforgiving about the

16. **F.** NO CHANGE
   G. She describes
   H. Describing
   J. Because she described

responsibilities generated from family ties. On one hand, Emily was refined, graceful, elegant, [17] soft-spoken, and classy. On the other, she was a woman from the backwoods of Louisiana, possibly born a slave, unapologetic about dipping snuff, who buzzed on her homemade muscadine wine each and every day.

Emily intrigued me, and the puzzle [18] of this woman simmered on the back burner of my conscious mind for decades, undoubtedly activating [19] questions about who I was as well. Hooked, I traced my mother's line to a place in Louisiana called Cane River, a unique area that before the Civil War housed one of the largest and wealthiest collections of free people of color in the United States. [20]

17. **A.** NO CHANGE
B. Emily was, refined, graceful, elegant,
C. Emily was refined, and graceful and elegant
D. Emily was; refined, graceful, elegant,

18. **F.** NO CHANGE
G. intrigued me, and, the puzzle
H. intrigued me and, the puzzle
J. intrigued me and the puzzle,

19. Which of the following alternatives to the underlined portion would be LEAST acceptable?
A. prompting
B. halting
C. stirring
D. triggering

20. If the writer were to delete the underlined portion from the sentence, the paragraph would primarily lose:
F. details that emphasize the historical importance of the geographical location.
G. a comparison of this location with the rest of the state of Louisiana.
H. information that explains the narrator's reasons for wanting to explore the Cane River.
J. nothing at all, since these geographical details are irrelevant to the paragraph.

I decided to hire a specialist on Cane River <u>culture; a genealogist to</u> [21] find my great-grandmother Emily's grandmother.

In a collection of ten thousand unindexed local records written in <u>poor preserved</u> [22] Creole French, she found the bill of sale for my great-great-great-great-grandmother Elisabeth, <u>whom was</u> [23] sold in 1850 in Cane River, Louisiana, for eight hundred dollars.

<u>One day,</u> [24] I had no choice. I had to write their story and document their lives—my history. <u>They were,</u> [25] after all, real flesh-and-blood people. I pieced their

21. A. NO CHANGE
    B. culture a genealogist, to
    C. culture—a genealogist—to
    D. culture a genealogist

22. F. NO CHANGE
    G. poorly preserved
    H. preserved poorly
    J. preserved poor

23. A. NO CHANGE
    B. whom
    C. who have
    D. who was

24. Given that all choices are true, which one provides the best transition between paragraphs?
    F. NO CHANGE
    G. Sooner or later,
    H. At this point,
    J. However,

25. A. NO CHANGE
    B. They are,
    C. I am,
    D. We could be,

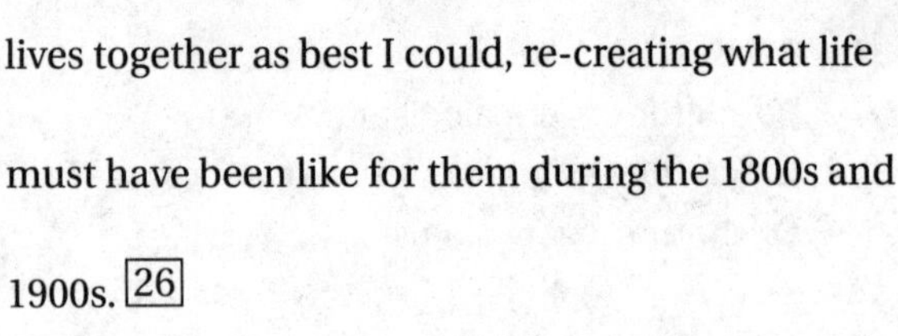

lives together as best I could, re-creating what life must have been like for them during the 1800s and 1900s. [26]

26. The writer is considering adding the following phrase to the preceding sentence, after the word *could*:

from over a thousand documents uncovered in my years of research.

Should the writer make this addition?

F. Yes, because it emphasizes how much work the writer had to do in order to complete the book.
G. Yes, because it provides details that prove that *Cane River* is a fictional novel.
H. No, because the information is unnecessary and detracts from the main idea of the sentence.
J. No, because the phrase fails to specify the precise number of documents examined.

Resulting with (27) *Cane River*, a novelized account covering one hundred years in America's history and following four generations of Creole slave women in Cane River, Louisiana. As they (28) struggled to keep their families intact through the dark days of slavery, the Civil War, Reconstruction, and the pre-civil rights era of Jim Crow South. The book ended up on Oprah's book list and made the *New York Times* Bestseller list. (29)

27. **A.** NO CHANGE
B. The result was
C. Having the result of
D. Results were

28. **F.** NO CHANGE
G. Louisiana when they
H. Louisiana, they
J. Louisiana, who

29. Given that all of the choices are true, which one best concludes this essay by tying this paragraph to the essay's introduction?

A. NO CHANGE
B. I had always wanted to write a book, and was proud of my accomplishment.
C. Finally I, along with the rest of the world, had an idea of who Emily really was.
D. This was the first book published about Creole slave women.

Question 30 asks about the preceding passage as a whole.

30. Suppose the writer's goal had been to describe the personal benefits of writing a book. Does this essay successfully accomplish that goal?

F. Yes, the author explains how writing *Cane River* made her a better person.
G. Yes, the author discusses why she wanted to write a book and then details the many steps involved.
H. No, because it focuses instead on biographical information about the author's family.
J. No, the essay fails to provide enough information about what the author gained from the experience of writing the book.

PASSAGE III

Illinois Prairies

There are different kinds of prairies in Illinois depending on the moisture gradient and soil type. The different kinds of prairie <u>wildflowers, are often</u> [31] associated with these different moisture gradients and soil types. As an ecological habitat, grasses and herbaceous wildflowers, rather than trees and shrubs, or areas with more or less permanent water, <u>dominated</u> [32] prairies.

31. **A.** NO CHANGE
B. wildflowers are often
C. wildflowers often
D. wildflowers: often

32. **F.** NO CHANGE
G. dominates
H. dominating
J. dominate

[33] High-quality prairies are interesting and colorful places to visit during the growing season <u>because they demonstrate high biodiversity.</u> 34

Black soil prairie was the dominant type of prairie in central and northern <u>Illinois, until</u> 35 it was almost totally destroyed by agricultural development during the 19th century. The landscape of such prairies is rather flat. A high-quality black soil prairie has lots of wildflowers in bloom from late spring until

33. At this point in the opening paragraph, the writer is considering adding the following true statement:

In Iowa, six different types of coneflowers sway in summer breezes.

Should the writer make this addition here?

A. Yes, because it helps establish that the essay is set in the Midwest.
B. Yes, because it helps reinforce the main idea of the paragraph.
C. No, because it does not make clear whether coneflowers grow in every state.
D. No, because it distracts from the main focus of the paragraph.

34. The writer is considering deleting the underlined portion from the sentence. Should the phrase be kept or deleted?

F. Kept, because it provides supporting details that reinforce the main idea of the sentence.
G. Kept, because it establishes that prairies contain more biodiversity than any other habitat.
H. Deleted, because it has already been established earlier in the paragraph that prairies have low biodiversity.
J. Deleted, because it draws attention away from the different types of prairies.

35. **A.** NO CHANGE
B. Illinois,
C. Illinois: until
D. Illinois. Until

the middle of fall. Today, small remnants of original black soil prairie can be found in pioneer <u>cemeteries or at construction sites.</u> 36

[1] Gravel and dolomite prairies were never very common in Illinois, and can be found primarily in northern Illinois. [2] Gravel and dolomite prairies can be rather flat, or slightly hilly. [3] <u>Yet,</u> 37 the original gravel and dolomite prairies have been largely destroyed by modern development. [4] They tend to be rather dry and well drained. [5] More recently, such prairies have been found along the gravelly ballast of railroads, where they probably did not formerly exist. [38]

36. Given that all choices are grammatically correct, which one best establishes that black soil prairies are difficult to find today?
- **F.** NO CHANGE
- **G.** cemeteries or along old railroads.
- **H.** cemeteries, state parks, and surrounding farmland.
- **J.** cemeteries and in many neighborhoods.

37.
- **A.** NO CHANGE
- **B.** However,
- **C.** Unfortunately,
- **D.** Accordingly,

38. The writer is considering deleting the phrase "where they probably did not formerly exist" from the preceding sentence (and placing a period after the word *railroads*). Should the phrase be kept or deleted?
- **F.** Kept, because the information helps to establish the rampant proliferation of gravel and dolomite prairies in Illinois.
- **G.** Kept, because it strengthens the paragraph's focus on the unchanging landscape of prairies.
- **H.** Deleted, because it is not relevant to the description of gravel and dolomite prairies found in Illinois.
- **J.** Deleted, because the speculation is inconsistent with the claim made earlier in the paragraph that the prairies have been largely destroyed.

[6] In this case, they are degraded and often contain flora from Western states. [40]
39

Hill prairies occur primarily along the Illinois and Mississippi Rivers, hill prairies are very dry and exposed to prevailing winds from the south or west. The wildflowers of hill prairies are similar to those who are found in the drier areas of gravel and dolomite prairies.
41
42

Some species that are found in hill prairies is typical of western areas.
43

Sand prairies can be moist mesic or dry and their landscape is either flat or slightly hilly. They usually
44

39. **A.** NO CHANGE
B. and many bird species migrate to them
C. consisting of a mix of native grasses and flowers and flora
D. and are of particular interest to tourists

40. For the sake of the logic and coherence of this paragraph, Sentence 4 should be placed:
F. where it is now.
G. before Sentence 1.
H. before Sentence 3.
J. before Sentence 6.

41. **A.** NO CHANGE
B. rivers. Hill
C. rivers hill
D. rivers; hill,

42. **F.** NO CHANGE
G. which are finding
H. if found
J. that can be found

43. **A.** NO CHANGE
B. are more typical
C. typify
D. are more usual

44. **F.** NO CHANGE
G. moist mesic, or dry; and
H. moist: mesic or dry, and
J. moist, mesic, or dry, and

occur near current or former bodies of water. Their vegetation is sparser than that of black soil prairies. 45

45. Given that all of the choices are true, which best concludes the paragraph with a colorful image that relates to the description of a sand prairie?
   A. NO CHANGE
   B. Vegetation includes woody shrubs, wildflowers, and native prairie grasses.
   C. The spectacular vegetation includes the vibrant hues of purple spiderwort, orange butterfly weed, and yellow goldenrod.
   D. More than sixty colorful species of wildflowers have been identified as being native to sand prairies.

PASSAGE IV

Money Monkeys

The mountainous regions of northern Japan renowned 46 not only for their beauty but also for their hot springs, known as *onsen.* Created naturally by the same volcanic activity that formed the Japanese islands initially, 47 the springs are not only relaxing but believed to be therapeutic, due to the high mineral content of their waters.

[1] At many onsen, native populations of Japanese Macaques, a gray, pink-faced monkey species famed for the 48 intelligence, make a habit of dipping in them as well. [2] For the most part, the monkeys are well mannered and cause no problems for humans. [3] Tourists are always especially entertained by them, and so the monkeys

46. F. NO CHANGE
   G. renown
   H. are renowned
   J. have been renown

47. Which of the following alternatives to the underlined portion would NOT be acceptable?
   A. later,
   B. themselves,
   C. on which they sit,
   D. DELETE the underlined portion (but preserve the comma).

48. F. NO CHANGE
   G. it's
   H. its
   J. they're

are gladly tolerated by the operators of the various springs. [4] Humans are not the only creatures who enjoy bathing in the springs. [49]

At one onsen however, the clever apes are causing an amusing problem. Visitors to this particular location encourage strongly to keep their cars locked and their wallets and purses hidden, because the monkeys are focused on getting their money! After years of observing humans in line at the gift and snack shops, the macaques at this onsen have deduced that certain special objects namely paper money and coins can be exchanged for food. In short order, the hungry simians were sneaking into unlocked cars, grabbing money, and trotting over to the shops to purchase themselves a snack.

49. For the sake of the logic and coherence of this paragraph, Sentence 4 should be placed:
- **A.** where it is now.
- **B.** before Sentence 1.
- **C.** before Sentence 2.
- **D.** before Sentence 3.

50.
- **F.** NO CHANGE
- **G.** onsen, however the
- **H.** onsen, however, the
- **J.** onsen—however, the

51.
- **A.** NO CHANGE
- **B.** are strong with encouragement
- **C.** being strongly encouraged
- **D.** are strongly encouraged

52. Which of the following alternatives to the underlined portion would be LEAST acceptable?
- **F.** fixated on getting
- **G.** intent on getting
- **H.** centered on getting
- **J.** seeking on getting

53.
- **A.** NO CHANGE
- **B.** objects—namely, paper money and coins—can be exchanged
- **C.** objects, namely, paper money—and coins—can be exchanged
- **D.** objects, namely paper money and coins—can be exchanged

At first, the flabbergasted employees didn't know what to do. [54] After all, the monkeys were waiting politely in line and paying for their purchases, just like the human customers, so there was no real reason not to accept their business.

Meanwhile, [55] however, someone pointed out that there was no possible way a monkey could get money other than [56] stealing it from a human. So now, when a cash-carrying macaque steps into line, special monkey-specific security guards are on hand to chase him out in the hopes that [57] this will eliminate the monkey's motive for theft.

I suppose that makes sense, but I'm disappointedly personable. [58] I'm not much of a traveler, but if there was one thing that could have motivated me to fly [59]

54. If the writer were to delete the underlined portion, the paragraph would primarily lose:
F. an explanation of the fact that the employees at this onsen were particularly inexperienced.
G. further detail about the cleverness of this species of monkey.
H. emphasis on the extremely bizarre nature of the situation.
J. foreshadowing of the fact that things are not going to turn out well for the monkeys.

55. A. NO CHANGE
B. Additionally,
C. Eventually,
D. Although

56. Which of the following alternatives to the underlined portion would be LEAST acceptable?
F. would be
G. except for
H. besides
J. outside of

57. A. NO CHANGE
B. out, in the hopes that
C. out in the hopes, that
D. out, in the hopes, that

58. F. NO CHANGE
G. I disappoint people.
H. personally I'm disappointed.
J. I'm personally disappointed.

59. A. NO CHANGE
B. motivate me flying
C. be motivating me flying
D. be motivating me to fly

halfway around the world, it's the possibility of seeing a monkey with a wad of bills in his paw waiting in line to buy a bag of chips. [60]

60. At this point, the writer is considering adding the following true statement:

Although I'm not even sure monkeys like chips, so I suppose I shouldn't buy my ticket just yet.

Should the writer make this addition here?

F. Yes, because it provides the necessary information that the author is a cautious person.
G. Yes, because this is a question about monkeys that is important for the reader to consider.
H. No, because the previous sentence already effectively and humorously ended the passage.
J. No, because the tone of the sentence is inconsistent with that of the rest of the passage.

PASSAGE V

The Birth of Surrealism

Joan Miró was a Catalan painter, sculptor, and ceramicist born in Barcelona, Spain, in 1893. His work has been interpreted with international acclaim, earning a reputation (61) as Surrealism, a sandbox for the subconscious mind, a re-creation of the childlike, and a manifestation of Catalan pride. In numerous interviews dating from the 1930s onwards, Miró expressing (62) contempt for conventional painting methods as a way of

61. A. NO CHANGE
B. He has earned international acclaim, his work
C. Interpreted as having earned international acclaim, his work is seen
D. Earning international acclaim, his work has been interpreted

62. F. NO CHANGE
G. expressed
H. had express
J. were to express

supporting bourgeois society, and famously declared an "assassination of painting" in favor of <u>utilizing common traditional methods of blending colors.</u> 63

63. Which choice best illustrates Miró's contempt for conventional painting and helps explain the "assassination of painting" mentioned earlier in the sentence?
A. NO CHANGE
B. applying works of art by famous Renaissance painters.
C. boycotting painting as an art form and turning to sculpting instead.
D. rejecting the visual elements of established painting.

<u>Born to the family of a goldsmith and watchmaker, the young Miró was drawn toward the arts community</u> 64 that was gathering in Montparnasse and in 1920 moved to Paris. There, under the influence of the poets and <u>writers, developing</u> 65 his unique style: organic forms and flattened picture planes drawn with a sharp line. Generally thought of as a Surrealist because of his interest in automatism and the use of sexual symbols, Miró was influenced in <u>varying</u> 66 degrees by Surrealism and Dada, yet he rejected membership in any artistic movement in the interwar European years.

64. F. NO CHANGE
G. Miró was drawn to the arts community, born to the family of a goldsmith and watchmaker
H. The arts community, born to the family of a goldsmith and watchmaker, the young Miró was drawn to
J. The young Miró was drawn to the family of a goldsmith and watchmaker, born to the arts community

65. A. NO CHANGE
B. writers. He developed
C. writers, he developed
D. writers develops

66. F. NO CHANGE
G. variety
H. different and varying
J. various, multiple

Andre Breton, the founder of Surrealism described (67) him as "the most Surrealist of us all."

67. A. NO CHANGE
B. Breton the founder of Surrealism, described
C. Breton: the founder of Surrealism, describe
D. Breton, the founder of Surrealism, described

Miró often received inspiration for his paintings in visions, (68) and thus, with Andre Masson, represented the beginning of Surrealism as an art movement.

68. At this point in the essay, the writer wants to highlight the influence that Miró had on painting as an art form. Given that all of the choices are true, which one would best accomplish that purpose?
F. NO CHANGE
G. Miró greatly disliked all bourgeois art, especially Cubism,
H. Miró was the first artist to develop automatic drawing as a way to undo previous established techniques in painting,
J. Miró worked heavily in ceramics in the last phase of his career,

However, (69) Miró chose not to become an official member of the Surrealists in order to be free to experiment with other artistic styles without compromising his position within the group.

69. A. NO CHANGE
B. Consequently,
C. Furthermore,
D. Thus,

He pursued his own interests in the art world, ranges (70) from automatic drawing and Surrealism to Expressionism and Color Field painting.

70. F. NO CHANGE
G. world, ranging
H. world which ranges
J. world and range

In his final decades, Miró were to accelerate (71) his work in different media and produced hundreds of ceramics, including the *Wall of the Moon* and

71. A. NO CHANGE
B. is accelerating
C. accelerates
D. accelerated

Wall of the Sun. He also made temporary window paintings (on glass) for an exhibit. In the last years of his life Miró wrote his most radical and least known ideas: explored the possibilities of gas sculpture and four-dimensional painting.
72

He died bedridden, at his home in Palma, Mallorca, on December 25, 1983. He suffered from heart disease, and visits a clinic for respiratory problems two weeks before his death. Many of his pieces are exhibited today in the Fundació Joan Miró in Barcelona and the U.S. National Gallery in Washington, D.C. he is buried in Barcelona at the Montjuïc cemetery. Today, his paintings sell for between $250,000 and $17 million, that was the auction price for the *La Caresse des Etoiles* on May 6, 2008, and is the highest amount paid for one of Miró's works to date.
73
74
75

72. **F.** NO CHANGE
G. known ideas exploring—
H. known ideas. He explored
J. known ideas, he explored

73. **A.** NO CHANGE
B. had visited
C. visiting
D. were to visit

74. **F.** NO CHANGE
G. Washington D.C. he is buried in Barcelona,
H. Washington, D.C., he is buried, in Barcelona
J. Washington, D.C.; he is buried in Barcelona

75. **A.** NO CHANGE
B. million and that
C. million, which
D. million which

STOP

If there is still time remaining, you may review your answers.

MATHEMATICS TEST

Time: 60 Minutes—60 Questions

Directions: Solve each problem, choose the correct answer, and then fill in the corresponding oval on your answer sheet.

Do not linger over problems that take too much time. Solve as many as you can; then return to the others in the time you have left for this test.

You are permitted to use a calculator on this test. You may use your calculator for any problems you choose, but some of the problems may best be done without using a calculator.

Note: Unless otherwise stated, all of the following should be assumed.

1. Illustrative figures are NOT necessarily drawn to scale.
2. Geometric figures lie in a plane.
3. The word *line* indicates a straight line.
4. The word *average* indicates arithmetic mean.

DO YOUR FIGURING HERE

1. If $x = 3$, then $x^2 + 2x - 12 = ?$

A. –3
B. 0
C. 3
D. 6
E. 21

2. If $3(2x - 1) = 11x + 27$, then $x = ?$

F. –6
G. –2
H. 2
J. 6
K. 7

3. To make space for new merchandise, a clothing store offered a 15% discount on all current stock. What is the sale price of a jacket that regularly sells for $42?

A. $6.30
B. $8.40
C. $35.70
D. $37.80
E. $41.85

4. In the figure below, line m is parallel to line n. One angle formed with transversal line t measures 60°, as shown. What is the measure of $\angle a$?

DO YOUR FIGURING HERE

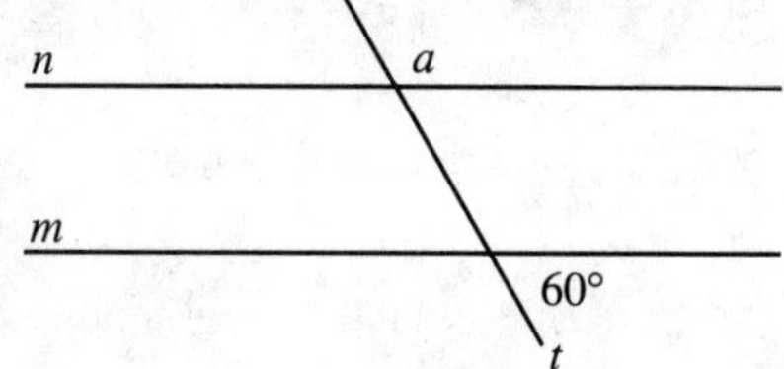

F. 30°
G. 60°
H. 90°
J. 120°
K. Cannot be determined

5. If $x = 3$, $y = 5$, and $w = 4$, what is the value of $xw^3 + \frac{3w}{2} - x^2y$?

A. 9.0
B. 12.0
C. 79.5
D. 153.0
E. 1,689.0

6. For all x, $(3x - 5)(4x + 3) = ?$

F. $12x^2 - 15$
G. $12x^2 + 11x - 15$
H. $12x^2 - 11x - 15$
J. $12x^2 + 29x - 15$
K. $12x^2 - 29x - 15$

7. $|5 - 8| - |9 - 3| = ?$

A. -9
B. -3
C. 1
D. 3
E. 9

8. $(5\sqrt{3})^2 = ?$

F. 15
G. $10\sqrt{6}$
H. 45
J. $34 + 10\sqrt{3}$
K. 75

DO YOUR FIGURING HERE

9. An urn contains 7 blue balls, 5 white balls, and 3 red balls. What is the probability that the first ball drawn at random from the urn will NOT be red?

A. $\frac{7}{45}$

B. $\frac{1}{5}$

C. $\frac{1}{3}$

D. $\frac{7}{15}$

E. $\frac{4}{5}$

10. A certain watch costs $100 and a certain pearl necklace costs $300. If the cost of the watch increases by 5% and the cost of the pearl necklace decreases by 10%, what will be the sum of their new costs?

F. $375

G. $385

H. $395

J. $405

K. $415

11. In the figure below, $\overline{CA}$ is tangent to circle O at point T. If $\overline{AT} = 6$ units, $\overline{CT} = 8$ units, and $\overline{CO} = 10$ units, how many units long is the radius of the circle?

A. 2

B. 5

C. 6

D. 8

E. 10

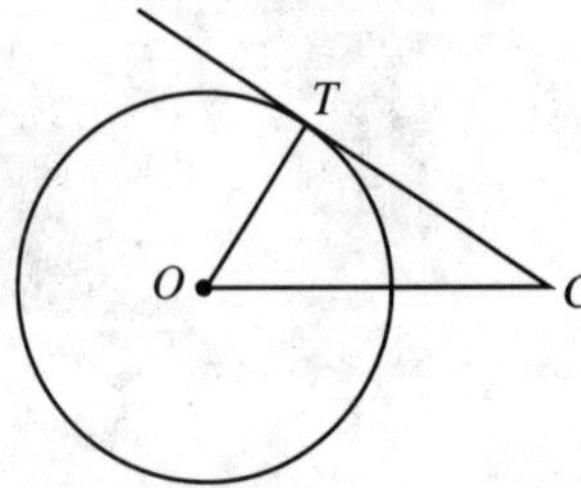

12. If $A = BC$, $B = x$, and $C = yz$, then $AB = ?$

F. $xyzx$

G. $yzxy$

H. $zxyz$

J. $xyyz$

K. xyz

DO YOUR FIGURING HERE

13. Which of the following inequalities specifies precisely the real values of x that are solutions to the inequality $-5 < -3x - 7$?

A. $x < 4$

B. $x < -\frac{2}{3}$

C. $x > -\frac{2}{3}$

D. $x < \frac{2}{3}$

E. $x > 4$

14. Which of the following expresses the equation $4x - 2y = 12$ in slope-intercept form?

F. $x = \frac{1}{2}y + 3$

G. $x = -\frac{1}{2}y + 3$

H. $y = 2x - 6$

J. $y = -2x + 6$

K. $y = -2x - 6$

15. Which of the following values for a in the equation $3x + 3a - 5 = 5x - a$ causes the solution for x to be 6?

A. −8.5

B. −4.25

C. 4.25

D. 8.5

E. 13.25

16. The centers of 3 identically sized circles lie on the diameter of a larger circle, as shown in the figure below. Each of the 4 circles is tangent to 2 other circles, as shown. If the circumference of each small circle is 8π inches, what is the circumference of the largest circle, in inches?

F. 16π

G. 24π

H. 48π

J. 64π

K. 144π

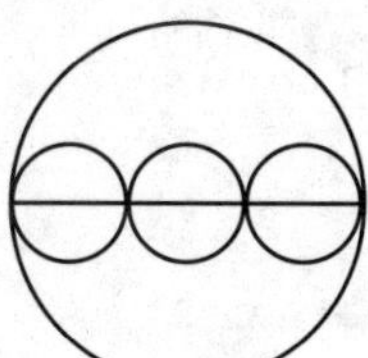

DO YOUR FIGURING HERE

17. A recipe calls for cooking a turkey 1 hour for every 3 pounds it weighs. How long should a 19-pound turkey cook?

A. 6 hours and 15 minutes
B. 6 hours and 20 minutes
C. 6 hours and 30 minutes
D. 6 hours and $33\frac{1}{3}$ minutes
E. 6 hours and 40 minutes

18. Dee and 4 of her friends went to a Chicago Cubs game. Their 5 seats were consecutive in the same row. The 5 people were seated randomly in those 5 seats. What is the probability that Dee would be in the middle seat?

F. $\frac{1}{625}$
G. $\frac{5}{625}$
H. $\frac{1}{120}$
J. $\frac{1}{5}$
K. $\frac{4}{5}$

19. A photocopy machine enlarges a small triangle to produce a larger, similar triangle, as shown below. If the lengths of the sides, in inches, are as marked on the figure, and the triangles are similarly oriented, what is the value of x in inches?

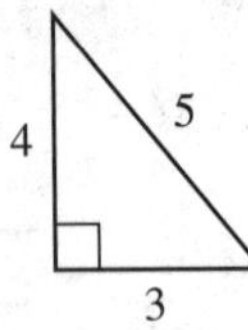

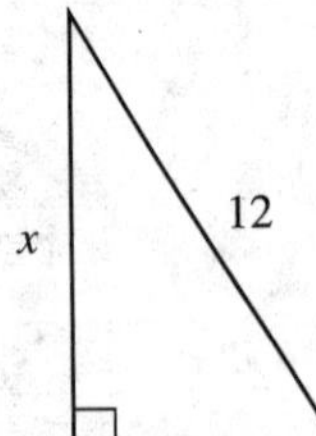

A. $7\frac{1}{5}$
B. 9
C. $9\frac{1}{2}$
D. $9\frac{3}{5}$
E. 11

DO YOUR FIGURING HERE

20. If the lengths of adjacent sides of a rectangular playground have measures of $4x - 3$ and $2x^2 + 7$ units, respectively, then which of the following expressions represents the area, in square units, of the playground?

F. $2x^2 + 4x + 4$
G. $4x^2 + 8x + 8$
H. $8x^3 - 21$
J. $8x^3 - 6x^2 + 28x - 21$
K. $8x^3 + 6x^2 + 28x + 21$

21. Which of the following is a prime factorization of 2,100?

A. $2 \cdot 3 \cdot 5 \cdot 7$
B. $2^2 \cdot 3 \cdot 5^2 \cdot 7$
C. $2^2 \cdot 3 \cdot 5 \cdot 35$
D. $2^2 \cdot 5^2 \cdot 21$
E. $2^2 \cdot 550$

22. After Jean spent 90% of her vacation money, \$100 remained. How much vacation money did she originally have?

F. \$111
G. \$191
H. \$900
J. \$1,000
K. \$1,111

23. Which of the following is a simplified version of $\frac{2x+1}{x} - \frac{x-3}{5x}$ whenever $x \neq 0$?

A. $9x + 2$
B. $9x^2 + 2x$
C. $\frac{-(x-4)}{4x}$
D. $\frac{9x+8}{5x}$
E. $\frac{9x^2+8x}{5x^2}$

DO YOUR FIGURING HERE

24. If $2x^2 - x - 15 = 0$, what are the 2 possible values for x?

F. -5 and $\frac{3}{2}$

G. -3 and $\frac{2}{5}$

H. -3 and $\frac{5}{2}$

J. 3 and $-\frac{5}{2}$

K. 5 and $-\frac{3}{2}$

25. All angles in the figure shown below are right angles. If each side has a length of 4 centimeters, what is the area of the figure in square centimeters?

A. 32
B. 40
C. 44
D. 48
E. 80

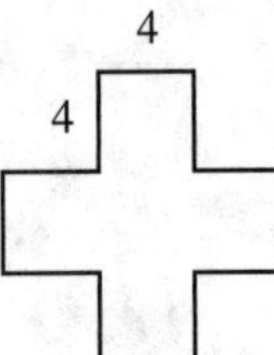

26. In the figure below, lengths in units and angle measures in degrees are as marked. How many units long is $\overline{BC}$?

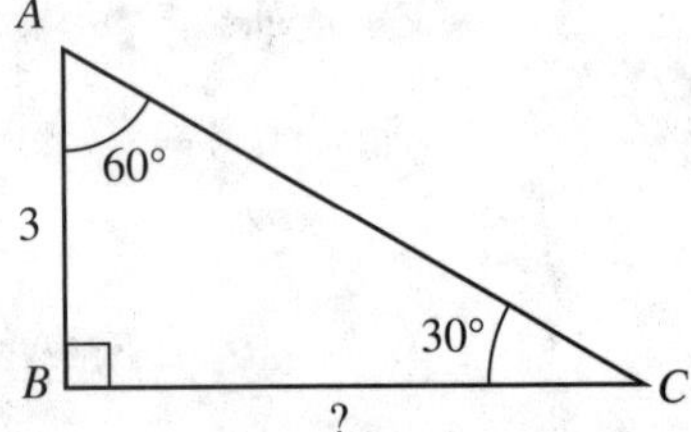

F. 3
G. $3\sqrt{2}$
H. $3\sqrt{3}$
J. 6
K. $3\sqrt{5}$

DO YOUR FIGURING HERE

27. To increase the mean of 5 numbers by 3, by how much would the sum of the 5 numbers need to increase?

A. 3
B. 6
C. 9
D. 15
E. 18

28. Josh pounded a stake into the ground. When he attached a leash to both the stake and his dog's collar, the dog could walk 12 feet from the stake in any direction. Using 3.14 for π, what is the approximate area of the lawn, in square feet, that the dog could roam while tied to the stake?

F. 38
G. 75
H. 151
J. 377
K. 452

29. Television screen sizes are determined by the diagonal length of the rectangular screen. Chad recently changed from watching a television with a 19-inch screen to a television with a similarly shaped 32-inch screen. If a car on the 19-inch screen appeared 12 inches long, how long, to the nearest inch, would the same car appear on the 32-inch screen?

A. 16
B. 18
C. 20
D. 22
E. 24

DO YOUR FIGURING HERE

Use the following information to answer questions 30–32.

The figure below shows the top view of the Wright family's house and yard. The Wrights' rectangular house is 48 feet wide and 36 feet long, and their rectangular yard is 90 feet wide and 120 feet long. The Wrights have a rectangular garden in the back corner of their yard that is 36 feet wide and 30 feet long. The garden currently contains 60 flower bulbs: 14 hyacinth bulbs, 20 daffodil bulbs, and 26 tulip bulbs.

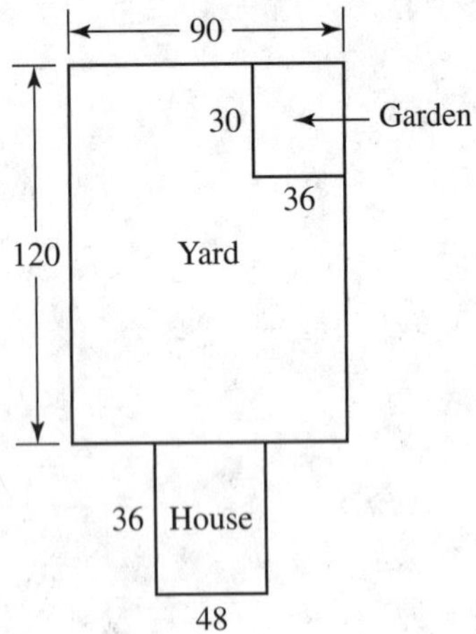

30. The yard will be enclosed by a fence and the back side of the house. The fence will begin at one back corner of the house and will end at the other. What is the minimum number of feet of fencing needed to enclose the yard?

F. 330
G. 360
H. 372
J. 378
K. 420

31. The area of the garden is what percent of the area of the yard (rounded to the nearest percent)?

A. 10%
B. 16%
C. 30%
D. 33%
E. 63%

DO YOUR FIGURING HERE

32. Beginning next year, Mr. Wright will increase the number of bulbs in the garden each year so that the numbers form a geometric sequence. In 3 years, there will be 480 bulbs in the garden. By what factor will the number of bulbs be multiplied by each year?

F. 1.5

G. 2

H. 8

J. 140

K. Cannot be determined from the given information

---

33. In the figure below, *ABCD* is a square. Points are connected on each pair of adjacent sides of *ABCD* to form 4 congruent right triangles, as shown below. Each of these triangles has one leg that is twice as long as the other leg. If the area of the shaded region is 25 square feet, what is the area of square *ABCD* in square feet?

A. 225

B. 112.5

C. 56.25

D. 45

E. 27

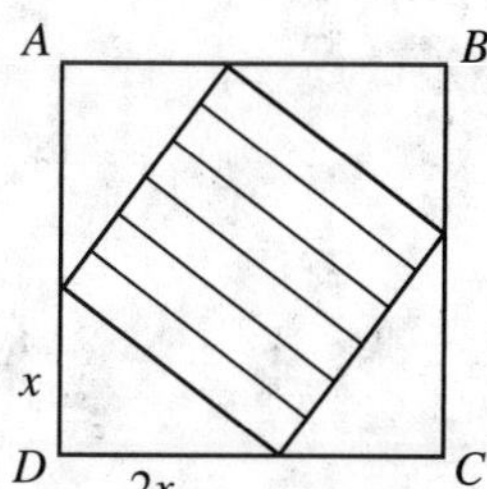

34. Which of the following is the graph of the equation $y = \dfrac{4x - 2x^2}{x}$ in the standard (x, y) coordinate plane?

DO YOUR FIGURING HERE

F.

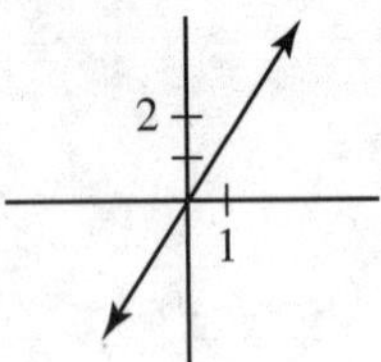

G.

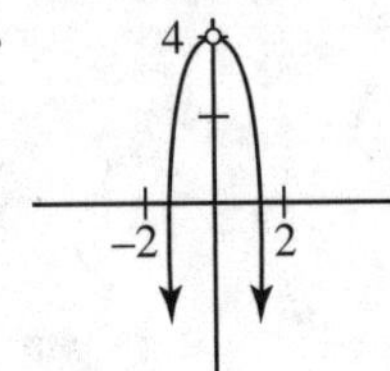

H.

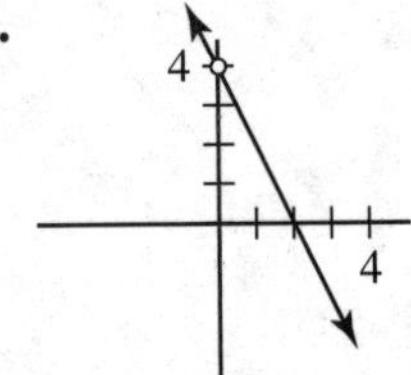

J.

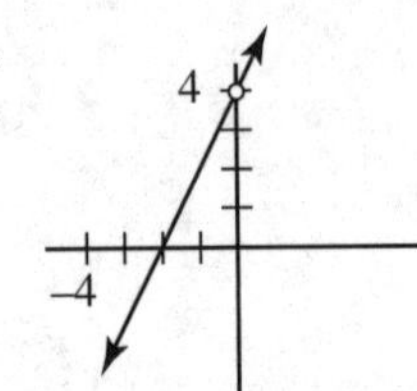

K.

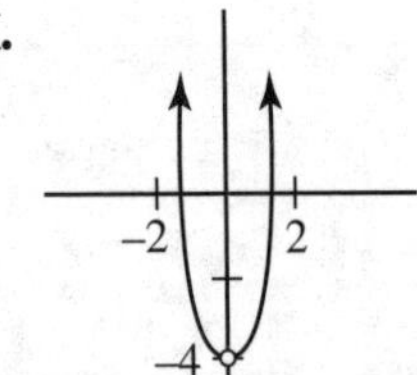

35. A line in a plane separates the plane into how many regions of points that do not contain the line?

A. 0
B. 1
C. 2
D. 3
E. Cannot be determined

DO YOUR FIGURING HERE

36. What is the maximum number of distinct diagonals that can be drawn in the hexagon shown below?

F. 12
G. 9
H. 6
J. 5
K. 4

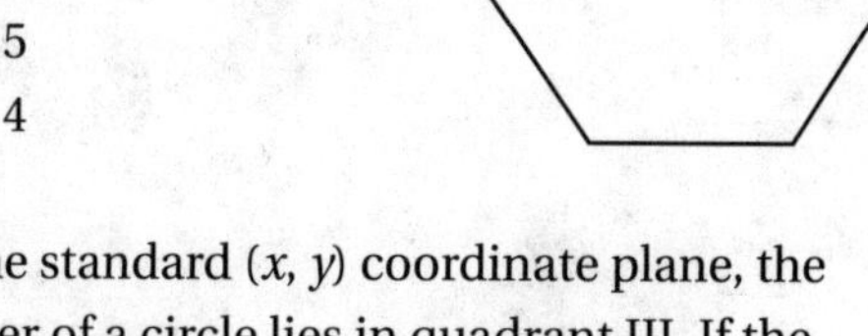

37. In the standard (x, y) coordinate plane, the center of a circle lies in quadrant III. If the circle is tangent to the x-axis and the y-axis and its radius is 4, which of the following is an equation for the circle?

A. $(x+4)^2 + (y+4)^2 = 4$
B. $(x-4)^2 + (y-4)^2 = 4$
C. $x^2 + (y-4)^2 = 16$
D. $(x+4)^2 + (y+4)^2 = 16$
E. $(x+4)^2 + (y-4)^2 = 16$

38. How must $-\frac{3}{5}$, $-\frac{4}{7}$, $-\frac{5}{6}$, and $-\frac{8}{9}$ be arranged so that they are listed in increasing order?

F. $-\frac{8}{9} < -\frac{5}{6} < -\frac{3}{5} < -\frac{4}{7}$
G. $-\frac{8}{9} < -\frac{5}{6} < -\frac{4}{7} < -\frac{3}{5}$
H. $-\frac{4}{7} < -\frac{3}{5} < -\frac{5}{6} < -\frac{8}{9}$
J. $-\frac{3}{5} < -\frac{4}{7} < -\frac{5}{6} < -\frac{8}{9}$
K. $-\frac{5}{6} < -\frac{8}{9} < -\frac{3}{5} < -\frac{4}{7}$

Use the following information to answer questions 39–42.

In the standard (x, y) coordinate plane below, P is located at (0, 2), Q is located at (4, 2), and R is located at (0, 5) to form right triangle $\triangle PQR$. The given lengths are in coordinate units.

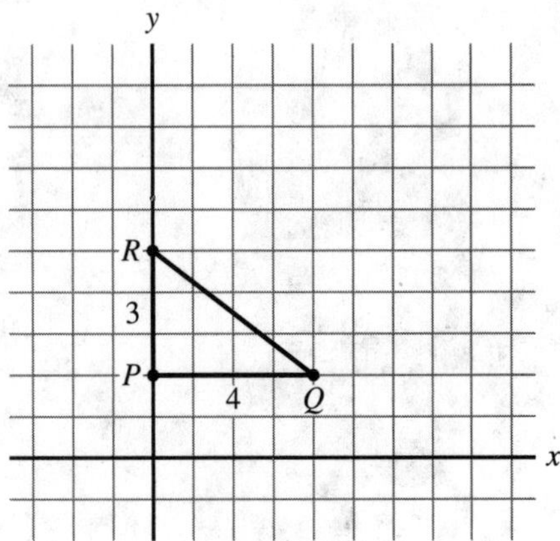

39. What is the slope of $\overline{QR}$?

A. $-\frac{4}{3}$

B. $-\frac{3}{4}$

C. 0

D. $\frac{3}{4}$

E. $\frac{4}{3}$

40. What is the midpoint of $\overline{QR}$?

F. $\left(2, \frac{3}{2}\right)$

G. $\left(2, \frac{7}{2}\right)$

H. $\left(\frac{7}{2}, 2\right)$

J. 4, 2

K. $\left(4, \frac{3}{2}\right)$

DO YOUR FIGURING HERE

DO YOUR FIGURING HERE

41. Which of the following expressions gives the measure of $\angle PRQ$?

A. $\cos^{-1}\left(\frac{4}{3}\right)$

B. $\cos^{-1}\left(\frac{3}{4}\right)$

C. $\sin^{-1}\left(\frac{4}{3}\right)$

D. $\tan^{-1}\left(\frac{4}{3}\right)$

E. $\tan^{-1}\left(\frac{3}{4}\right)$

42. Right triangle $\triangle PQR$ will be rotated about the y-axis to form a right circular cone. How long, in coordinate units, is the diameter of the cone's base?

F. 3

G. 4

H. 6

J. 8

K. 16

---

43. The perimeter of an elliptical billiard table is to be covered with red velvet. The perimeter of an ellipse is given by the formula $p = \frac{\pi}{2}\sqrt{2(l^2 + w^2)}$, where l is the length and w is the width, as shown in the diagram below. If the length is 4 feet and the width is 3 feet, what is the outside perimeter of the ellipse in feet?

A. 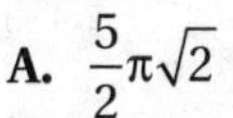 $\frac{5}{2}\pi\sqrt{2}$

B. 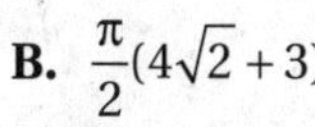 $\frac{\pi}{2}(4\sqrt{2} + 3)$

C. 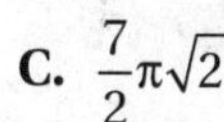 $\frac{7}{2}\pi\sqrt{2}$

D. $(4\pi + 3)\sqrt{2}$

E. $5\pi\sqrt{2}$

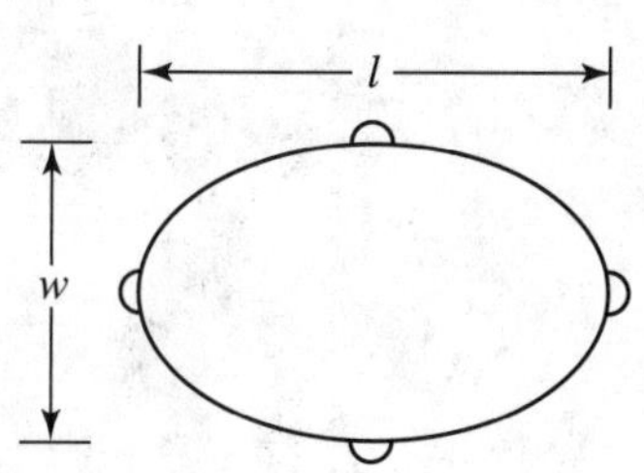

DO YOUR FIGURING HERE

44. If $\frac{A}{28}+\frac{B}{126}=\frac{9A+2B}{x}$, and A, B, and x are integers greater than 1, what must x equal?

F. 11
G. 154
H. 252
J. 1,134
K. 3,528

45. Which one of the following expresses the number of meters that a contestant must travel in a 5-lap race around a circular track with a radius of R meters?

A. $5R$
B. $5\pi R$
C. $5\pi R^2$
D. $6R$
E. $10\pi R$

46 In $\triangle ABC$, shown below, the measure of $\angle B$ is 40°, the measure of $\angle C$ is 35°, and $\overline{AB}$ is 27 units long. Which one of the following is an expression of the length, in units, of $\overline{BC}$?

(Note: The law of sines states that for any triangle, the ratio between the sine of an angle and the length of the side opposite that angle is the same for all of the interior angles in the triangle.)

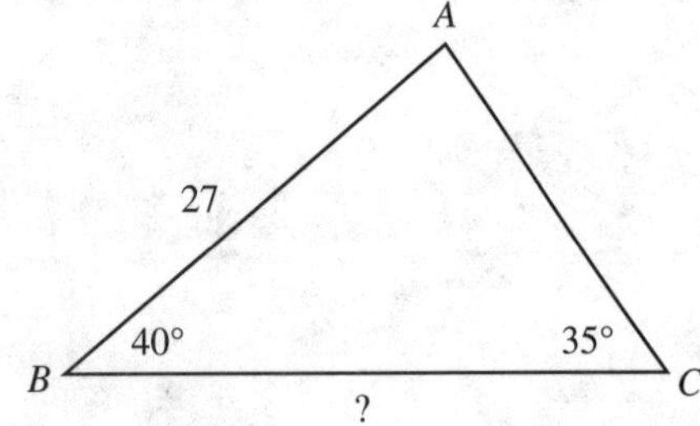

F. $\frac{27(\sin 105°)}{\sin 40°}$

G. $\frac{27(\sin 105°)}{\sin 35°}$

H. $\frac{27(\sin 75°)}{\sin 40°}$

J. $\frac{27(\sin 40°)}{\sin 105°}$

K. $\frac{27(\sin 35°)}{\sin 75°}$

47. For $i^2 = -1$, $(5 - i)^2 = ?$

A. 24
B. 26
C. $24 - 5i$
D. $24 - 10i$
E. $26 + 10i$

DO YOUR FIGURING HERE

48. If x and y are integers such that $y > 12$ and $2x + y = 19$, which of the following is the solution set for x?

F. $x \geq 4$
G. $x \geq 3$
H. $x \leq 4$
J. $x \leq 3$
K. $x \leq 0$

49. If $pq^3t^4 > 0$, which of the following products must be positive?

A. pq
B. pt
C. qt
D. pqt
E. pq^2

50. If $\log_3 81 = x + 1$, then $x = ?$

F. 3
G. 4
H. 5
J. 6
K. 243

51. A flight instructor charges \$75 per lesson, plus an additional fee for the use of his plane. The charge for the use of his plane varies directly with the cube root of the time the plane is used. If a lesson plus 27 minutes of plane usage costs \$120, what is the total amount charged for a lesson involving 64 minutes of plane usage?

A. \$195
B. \$180
C. \$157
D. \$135
E. \$60

52. In $\triangle ABD$ shown below, C is on $\overline{BD}$, $\overline{AC} \perp \overline{BD}$, the length of $\overline{AD}$ is 6 inches, the length of $\overline{BD}$ is 10 inches, and $\sin d = 0.8$. What is the area of $\triangle ABD$ in square inches?

F. 6
G. 12
H. 24
J. 30
K. 60

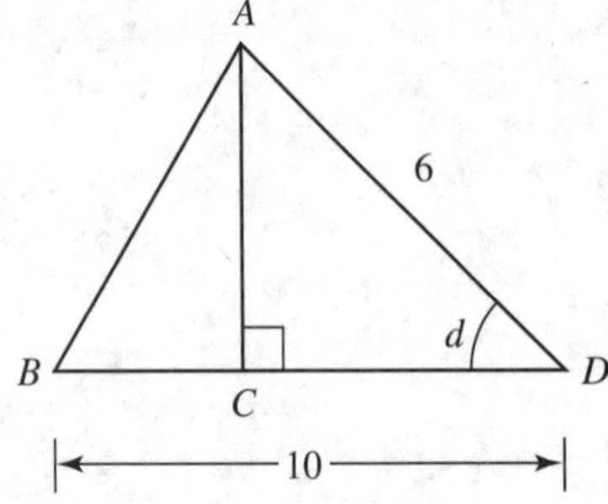

DO YOUR FIGURING HERE

53. For real numbers x and y, when is the equation $|2x + 3y| = |2x - 3y|$ true?

A. Never
B. Always
C. Only when $2x = 3y$
D. Only when $x = 0$ and $y = 0$
E. Only when $x = 0$ or $y = 0$

54. Bronwyn has $4.23 in quarters ($0.25), dimes ($0.10), nickels ($0.05), and pennies ($0.01). She arranges these coins in rows and notices that there are 6 more dimes than quarters, 3 more nickels than quarters, and 20 more pennies than quarters. How many pennies does Bronwyn have?

F. 8
G. 13
H. 20
J. 27
K. 28

55. For some real number A, the graph of $y = (A + 3)x + 5$ in the standard (x, y) coordinate plane passes through the point $(3, 11)$. What is the slope of this line?

A. −5
B. −2
C. −1
D. 2
E. $5\frac{1}{3}$

DO YOUR FIGURING HERE

56. In the figure below, $\overline{BF}$ is a line segment with point C between B and F; all distances are given in inches. What is the ratio of the area of quadrilateral *RBCS* to the area of quadrilateral *SCFT*?

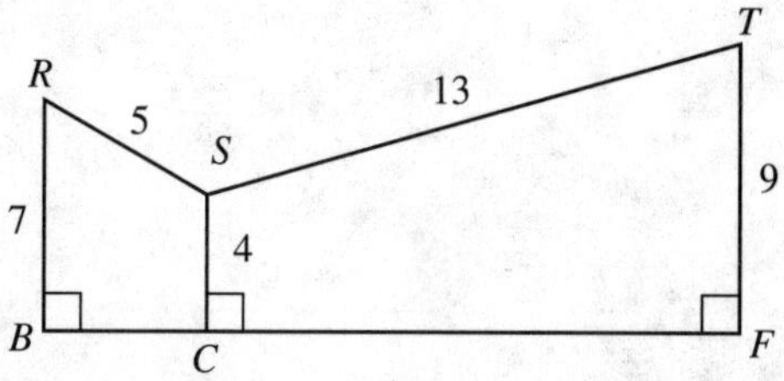

F. 9:7
G. 7:9
H. 11:13
J. 11:39
K. 11:50

57. When graphed in the standard (x, y) coordinate plane, the graphs of $y = x^2 - 5$ and $y = x + 1$ intersect at which of the following points?
A. (–3, 2) and (2, 3)
B. (–3, 4) and (2, –1)
C. (3, –4) and (–2, 1)
D. (3, 4) and (–2, –1)
E. The graphs do not intersect.

58. In septagon *ABCDEFG* shown below, $\angle A = 115°$ and $\angle G = 70°$. What is the sum of the measures of the other 5 interior angles?

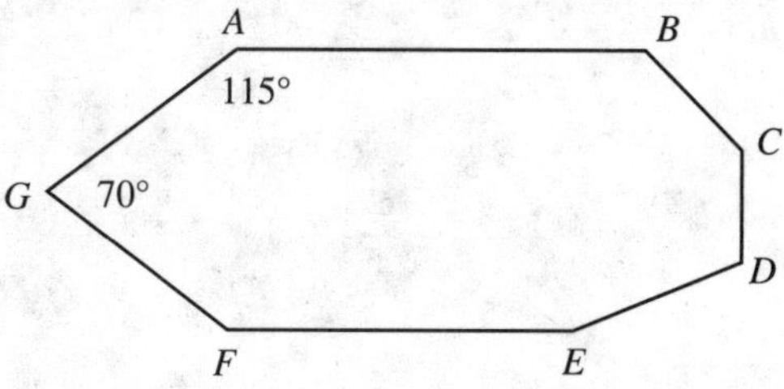

F. 585°
G. 595°
H. 655°
J. 690°
K. 715°

DO YOUR FIGURING HERE

59. For all real numbers x and y such that the product of y and 4 is x, which of the following expressions represents the sum of y and 4 in terms of x?

A. $x+4$

B. $4x+4$

C. $4(x+4)$

D. $\frac{x+4}{4}$

E. $\frac{x+16}{4}$

60. What is $\cos\frac{7\pi}{12}$ given that $\frac{7\pi}{12}=\frac{\pi}{3}+\frac{\pi}{4}$ and that $\cos(A+B)=\cos A(\cos B)-\sin A(\sin B)$?

(Note: You may use the following table of values.)

θ	sin θ	cos θ
$\frac{\pi}{6}$	$\frac{1}{2}$	$\frac{\sqrt{3}}{2}$
$\frac{\pi}{4}$	$\frac{\sqrt{2}}{2}$	$\frac{\sqrt{2}}{2}$
$\frac{\pi}{3}$	$\frac{\sqrt{3}}{2}$	$\frac{1}{2}$

F. $\frac{\sqrt{2}-\sqrt{6}}{4}$

G. $-\frac{1}{4}$

H. $\frac{\sqrt{2}-\sqrt{3}}{4}$

J. 0.999

K. $\frac{1+\sqrt{2}}{2}$

If there is still time remaining, you may review your answers.

READING TEST

Time: 35 Minutes—40 Questions

Directions: There are four passages in this test. Each passage is followed by several questions. After reading a passage, choose the best answer to each question and fill in the corresponding oval on your answer sheet. You may refer to the passages as often as necessary.

PASSAGE I—LITERARY NARRATIVE

This passage is adapted from the short story *The First Sense* by Nadine Gordimer (© 2006).

She has never felt any resentment that he became a musician and she didn't. Could hardly call her amateur flute playing a vocation. She sits at a computer in a city-government office earning a salary that has at least provided regularly for their basic needs.

She found when she was still an adolescent that her father, with his sports shop and the beguiling heartiness that is a qualification for that business, and her mother, with her groupies exchanging talk of female maladies, did not have in their comprehension what it was that she wanted to do.

A school outing at sixteen had taken her to a concert where she heard, coming out of a slim tube held to human lips, the call of the flute. The teacher who had arranged the cultural event was understanding enough to put the girl in touch with a musical youth group in the city. She babysat on weekends to pay for the hire of a flute, and began to attempt to learn how to produce with her own breath and fingers something of what she had heard.

He was among the Youth Players. His instrument was the very antithesis of the flute. The sounds he drew from the overgrown violin between his knees: the complaining moo of a sick cow, the rasp of a blunt saw. "Excuse me!" he would say, with a clownish lift of the eyebrows and a down-twisted mouth. Within a year, his exceptional talent had been recognized by the professional musicians who coached these young people.

They played together when alone, to amuse themselves and secretly imagine that they were already in concert performance, the low, powerful cadence coming from the golden-brown body of the cello making her flute voice sound, by contrast, more like that of a squeaking mouse. In time, she reached a certain level of minor accomplishment. He couldn't deceive her and let her suffer the disillusions of persisting with a career that was not open to her level of performance. "You'll still have the pleasure of playing the instrument you love best." She would always remember what she said: "The cello is the instrument I love best."

Sometimes she fell asleep to the low tender tones of what had become his voice, the voice of that big curved instrument, sharing the intimacy that was hers. At concerts, when his solo part came, she did not realize that she was smiling in recognition, that his was a voice she would have recognized anywhere. She was aware that, without a particular ability of her own, she was privileged enough to have an interesting life, and a remarkably talented man whose milieu was also hers.

He began to absent himself from her at unexplained times or for obligations that he must have known she knew didn't exist. She had suggestions for relaxation: a film or a dinner. He was not enthusiastic. "Next week, next week." He took the revered cello out of its solitude in the case and played, to himself, to her—well, she was in the room those evenings. It was his voice, that glorious voice of his cello, saying something different, speaking not to her but to some other. The voice of the cello doesn't lie.

She waited for him to speak. About what had happened. To trust the long confidence between them. He never did. And she did not ask, because she was also afraid that what had happened, once admitted, would be irrevocably real.

One night, he got up in the dark, took the cello out of its bed, and played. She woke to the voice, saying something passionately angry in its deepest bass. She knew that the affair was over. She felt a pull of sadness—for him. For herself, nothing. By never confronting him she had stunned herself.

1. If the fourth paragraph (lines 24–32) were omitted from the passage, the reader would not know:
   A. that he played the violin.
   B. how the couple met.
   C. that he became a famous musician.
   D. that he was an angry person.

2. Which of the following best describes what the first paragraph reveals about her character?
   F. She has a rewarding and high-paying career.
   G. She earns money playing a flute.
   H. She is generous and pragmatic.
   J. She regrets not becoming a musician.

3. Which of the following can most reasonably be inferred from the passage about her parents' feelings about music?
   A. They are accomplished musicians.
   B. They do not have a capacity for music themselves, but support her interest.
   C. They are opposed to her becoming a musician.
   D. They didn't understand why she would want to pursue a career in music.

4. In lines 45–46 the statement "The cello is the instrument I love best" most nearly communicates what?
   F. She would rather play the cello than play the flute.
   G. She will stop playing the flute so that she can play the cello.
   H. She never really loved playing the flute.
   J. She loves him more than she loves playing the flute.

5. The main conflict in this passage can best be described as:
   A. both he and she want to become famous musicians, but only one of them is able.
   B. challenges she faces as the girlfriend of a famous musician.
   C. tension created when he starts distancing himself from her.
   D. her need to choose between the flute and the cello.

6. It can reasonably be inferred from the passage that she views him as:
   F. a competent competitor.
   G. a teacher and a mentor.
   H. someone whose responsibility it is to entertain her.
   J. a talented musician whose opinion she respects.

7. In line 68 the statement "The voice of the cello doesn't lie" mostly means:
   A. that she can tell something is wrong because of the music he plays.
   B. the cello is telling her what is bothering him.
   C. he is using music to communicate his love for her.
   D. he is playing the cello in order to demonstrate its power to deliver a message to her.

8. Which of the following statements describing how she feels about his musical ability is most clearly supported by the passage?
   F. She respects him, but gets annoyed at how often he is out of town playing concerts.
   G. She is jealous that he is so much better than she is.
   H. She loves listening to him play, and enjoys the life of a musician's partner.
   J. She is proud of his success and takes advantage of the opportunities that brings for her to play the flute.

9. The main purpose of the sixth paragraph (lines 47–57) is to:
   A. illustrate his success.
   B. show how intimate their relationship is.
   C. explain why she gets upset when he leaves her.
   D. tell the reader more about his voice.

10. Why didn't he encourage her to pursue a career as a musician?
   F. He didn't want the competition.
   G. He was jealous of her abilities.
   H. He wanted her to earn steady money for them.
   J. He didn't think she was talented enough.

PASSAGE II—SOCIAL SCIENCE

This passage is adapted from "The Disappearing Computer" by Bill Gates, which appeared in *The World in 2003* (*The Economist*) (© 2002 by The Economist).

A few years from now, the average home entertainment system might not look much different than it does today. But it will probably have an Internet connection that enables it to download and play digital music and video, display album artwork and song titles on the television, and even interrupt your listening if an important message arrives. It will have a central processor, disk storage, graphics hardware and some kind of intuitive user interface. Add a wireless mouse and keyboard, and this home entertainment system will start looking a lot like a personal computer. Will people buy and use these systems in large numbers? Absolutely. Will they think of them as computers? Probably not.

According to Gartner Dataquest, an American research firm, the world computer industry shipped its one billionth PC in 2002, and another billion more are expected to be built in the next six years. Add to this the exploding number of embedded computers—the kind found in mobile phones, gas pumps and retail point-of-sale systems—which are fast approaching the power and complexity of desktop PCs. On one estimate, people in the United States already interact with about 150 embedded systems every day, whether they know it or not. These systems, which use up to 90 percent of the microprocessors produced today, will inevitably take on more PC-like characteristics, and will be able to communicate seamlessly with their traditional PC counterparts. They will also become amazingly ubiquitous. In 2001, according to the Semiconductor Industry Association, the world microchip industry produced around 60 million transistors for every man, woman and child on earth. That number will rise to one billion by 2010.

At the same time, the general-purpose PC as we know it today will continue to play an important, and increasingly central, role in most people's lives, but it will be at the center of a wide range of intelligent devices that most people wouldn't think of as "computers" today. This scenario is in sharp contrast to the computers of just a few years ago—back in the pre-Internet age—which were still mostly passive appliances that sat in the corner of the den or living room. Back then, people used their PCs for little more than writing letters and documents, playing games or managing their family finances.

But today we are truly in a digital decade, in which the intelligence of the PC is finding its way into all kinds of devices, transforming them from passive appliances into far more significant and indispensable tools for everyday life. Many of the core technologies of computing-processing power, storage capacity, graphics capabilities and network connectivity are all continuing to advance at a pace that matches or even exceeds Moore's Law (which famously, and correctly, predicted that the number of transistors on a computer chip would double every two years).

As people find more ways to incorporate these inexpensive, flexible and infinitely customizable devices into their lives, the computers themselves will gradually "disappear" into the fabric of our lives. We are still a long way from a world full of disembodied intelligent machines, but the computing experience of the coming decade will be so seamless and intuitive that, increasingly, we will barely notice it. At the same time, computing will become widespread enough that we will take it for granted—just as most people in the developed world today trust the telephone service.

The pervasiveness and near-invisibility of computing will be helped along by new technologies such as cheap, flexible displays, fingernail-sized chips capable of storing terabytes of data, or inductively powered computers that rely on heat and motion from their environment to run without batteries.

The economics of computing will also bring change. Decreasing costs will make it easy for electronics manufacturers to include PC-like intelligence and connectivity in even the most mundane devices.

All this will lead to a fundamental change in the way we perceive computers. Using one will become like using electricity when you turn on a light. Computers, like electricity, will play a role in almost everything you do, but computing itself will no longer be a discrete experience. We will be focused on what we can do with computers, not on the devices themselves. They will be all around us, essential to almost every part of our lives, but they will effectively have "disappeared."

11. This passage is best described as being:
A. an analysis of how computers are vanishing from everyday use in society.
B. an argument in support of introducing more computer-friendly products.
C. an examination of the changing roles computers have in people's lives.
D. a thorough evaluation of the benefits and drawbacks of using computers.

12. The author uses all of the following sources of evidence to support his claims EXCEPT:
F. research data gathered by professionals.
G. the opinion of a scientist.
H. statistics provided by industry experts.
J. reference to a famous mathematical prediction.

13. The word *ubiquitous*, as used in line 33, most likely means:
A. small.
B. difficult to find.
C. inexpensive.
D. ever-present.

14. According to the passage, new technologies and decreasing costs of electronics will lead directly to an increase in all of the following EXCEPT:
F. interconnectivity among objects.
G. the presence of computer intelligence in everyday objects.
H. the amount of power and batteries that will be required to run computers.
J. computers being involved in most aspects of life.

15. Which of the following best describes how the author predicts people will perceive computers in the future?
    A. Computers will be so much a part of everyday life that people will hardly notice them.
    B. Computers will have disappeared from people's lives.
    C. People will be afraid of how invasive computers have become and will use them less.
    D. Computers will be everywhere and people will be very aware of using them constantly and will become dependent on them.

16. The word *disappeared* used in line 98 most likely refers to the idea that:
    F. people will no longer use computers.
    G. computers will be so embedded in people's everyday lives that they won't even notice them anymore.
    H. computers will become invisible.
    J. computers will become so small and will be inside so many other objects that people will not be able to see them anymore.

17. All of the following are identified in the passage as parts of a future entertainment system EXCEPT:
    A. a satellite.
    B. graphics hardware.
    C. a wireless keyboard.
    D. an Internet connection.

18. The author refers to computers of the past as "passive appliances" (line 55) because:
    F. they were indispensable tools for everyday life.
    G. they were incapable of complex tasks.
    H. they remained in one location.
    J. people only used them occasionally for specific tasks.

19. The main point of the second paragraph (lines 16–38) can best be summarized as:
    A. there are more microchips than people.
    B. microprocessors are being produced more quickly than we can use them.
    C. both the number of and uses for microprocessors is rapidly increasing.
    D. there is more need for microprocessors than for personal computers.

20. In the first paragraph, the author suggests that all of the following are core technologies EXCEPT:
    F. storage capacity.
    G. power profiles.
    H. graphics capabilities.
    J. network connectivity.

PASSAGE III—HUMANITIES

Passage A is adapted from "A Defence of Poetry" by Percy Bysshe Shelley (1821). Passage B is adapted from "The Poetics of Disobedience" by Alice Notley (1998).

Passage A by Percy Bysshe Shelley

A poem is the very image of life expressed in its eternal truth. There is this difference between a story and a poem, that a story is a catalogue of detached facts, which have no other connection than time, place, circumstance, cause and effect; the other is the creation of actions according to the unchangeable forms of human nature, which is itself the image of all other minds. Time, which destroys the beauty and the use of the story of particular facts, stripped of the poetry which should invest them, augments that of poetry, and forever develops new and wonderful applications of the eternal truth which it contains.

The functions of the poetical faculty are two-fold: by one it creates new materials of knowledge, and power, and pleasure; by the other it engenders in the mind a desire to reproduce and arrange them according to a certain rhythm and order which may be called the beautiful and the good. The cultivation of poetry is never more to be desired than at periods when, from an excess of the selfish and calculating principle, the accumulation of the materials of external life exceed the quantity of the power of assimilating them to the internal laws of human nature. Poetry is the record of the best and happiest moments of the happiest and best minds.

The most unfailing herald, companion, and follower of the awakening of a great people to work a beneficial change in opinion or institution, is poetry. At such periods there is an accumulation of the power of communicating and receiving intense and impassioned conceptions respecting man and nature. The person in whom this power resides, may often, as far as regards many portions of their nature, have little apparent correspondence with that spirit of good of which they are the ministers. But even whilst they deny, they are yet compelled to serve that power which is seated on the throne of their own soul.

It is impossible to read the compositions of the most celebrated writers without being startled with the electric life which burns within their words. They measure the circumference and sound the depths of human nature with a comprehensive and all-penetrating spirit, and they are themselves perhaps the most sincerely astonished at its manifestations; for it is less their spirit than the spirit of the age. Poets are the hierophants of an unapprehended inspiration; the mirrors of the gigantic shadows which futurity casts upon the present; the words which express what they understand not; the trumpets which sing to battle, and feel not what they inspire; the influence which is moved not, but moves. Poets are the unacknowledged legislators of the world.

Passage B by Alice Notley

For a long time I've seen my job as bound up with the necessity of noncompliance with pressures, dictates, atmospheres of society at large, my own past practices as well. For a long time—well in fact since the beginning, since I learned how to be a poet inside the more rebellious wing of poetry. Learning itself meant a kind of disobedience, so like most words the Dis word, the Dis form, cannot be worshipped either—that would be an obedience anyway. I've spoken in other places of the problems, too, of subjects that hadn't been broached much in poetry and of how it seemed one had to disobey the past and the practices of literary males in order to talk about what was going on most literarily around one.

It seems as if one must disobey everyone else in order to see at all. This is a persistent feeling in a poet, but staying alert to all the ways one is coerced into denying experience, sense, and reason is a huge task. I recently completed a very long poem called *Disobedience* but I didn't realize that disobeying was what I was doing, what perhaps I'd always been doing until the beginning of the end of it, though the tone throughout was one of rejection of everything I was supposed to be or to affirm.

It's possible that my biggest act of disobedience has consistently, since I was an adolescent, been against the idea that all truth comes from books, really other people's books. I hate the fact that whatever I say or write, someone reading or listening will try to find something out of their reading I "sound like." 'You sound just like ...,' 'you remind me of ...,' 'have you read ...?' I've been trying to train myself for thirty or forty years not to believe anything anyone tells me. It's necessary to maintain a state of disobedience against ... everything.

Questions 21–24 ask about Passage A.

21. The passage characterizes poetry as being all of the following EXCEPT:

A. produced by special and advanced people.
B. an accurate source of scientific information.
C. true for all time.
D. a valuable corrective to society.

22. As it is used in line 14, the word *faculty* most nearly means:
    F. easiness.
    G. staff.
    H. goal.
    J. ability.

23. The passage cites "the selfish and calculating principle" (line 22) as an example of:
    A. something that keeps the work of inferior poets from being truly great and immortal.
    B. a character flaw that even the greatest poets seek to cover up in themselves.
    C. a socially influenced human tendency that makes poetry immediately necessary.
    D. a reason why certain politically powerful individuals pretend to dislike poetry.

24. The passage closes by suggesting that poets:
    F. have a much greater influence on the course of human civilization than most people realize.
    G. are on rare occasions even imbued with the ability to predict the future.
    H. are generally less emotionally affected by their own work than other people are.
    J. may have had a hand in starting wars from time to time in history.

Questions 25–27 ask about Passage B.

25. The author characterizes disobedience as being all of the following EXCEPT:
    A. a healthy way of taking people's opinions.
    B. an attitude that she even applies to poetry.
    C. the title of her own most famous work.
    D. something that must itself be disobeyed.

26. In the context of the passage, the phrases that appear in quotation marks in the final paragraph function as examples of:
    F. "pressures, dictates, atmospheres of society" (line 60).
    G. "subjects that hadn't been broached much in poetry" (lines 69–70).
    H. "all the ways one is coerced into denying experience" (lines 76–77).
    J. "my biggest act of disobedience" (lines 85–86).

27. Based on the passage, the author seems to regard her duty as a poet as involving:
    A. protest against traditional concept of ethics and justice.
    B. preventing her mode of expression from becoming contaminated.
    C. questioning whether writing poetry is a morally acceptable way of making a living.
    D. preventing male poets of the past from being taught so frequently in schools.

Questions 28–30 ask about both passages.

28. One of the most obvious differences between the two passages is that:
    F. Passage B regards society with skepticism, whereas Passage A is in agreement with most of society's opinions.
    G. Only Passage A makes reference to any of the author's own poetical works.
    H. Only Passage B attempts to explain the essential difference between poetry and fiction.
    J. Passage A sees poetry as serving something objective, whereas Passage B sees it as a totally subjective matter.

29. Which of the following does *neither* of the two passages contain?
   A. An opinion about whether poetry should be read in books or heard aloud
   B. A characterization of what poets themselves are like as people
   C. An assertion that poets speak for someone or something other than themselves
   D. A reference to the types of poetical subjects the author favors in his or her work

30. Despite their many differences, which of the following is something about which the two passages *agree*?
   F. The idea that only a certain rare type of person is able to write poetry well
   G. The fact that poetry ideally performs a necessary moral duty for society
   H. The suggestion that writing poetry the right way will make one a happier person
   J. The assertion that the poetry of the past is less valuable than the poetry of the present

PASSAGE IV—NATURAL SCIENCE

This passage is adapted from "The Truth Behind Lightsaber Technology" by Matt Gluesenkamp (© 2010 General Electric).

There are a lot of myths and legends about lasers that Hollywood has generated or perpetuated over the years, but perhaps the most well-known instance of "lasers" in cinema are the lightsabers from the *Star Wars* saga. I put quotes around "lasers" because the way lightsabers behave in these movies is quite a bit different from the way lasers behave in real life.

In the *Star Wars* universe, lightsabers are typically custom-built by Jedi and Sith warriors, and all have several common elements. Each has a power source, a lightsaber crystal, one or more focusing crystals, and a stabilizing emitter system. The power source is typically a diatium power cell, often with a capacity of several megawatt-hours. The lightsaber crystal converts the power cell's energy into a plasma that is then passed through and directed by the focusing crystals. Finally, the emitter system stabilizes the plasma into a blade shape using a mix of power modulation and magnetic field containment.

Did that make sense to anyone? No? Good, then I'm not alone. Science fiction is typically a blend of materials or physical laws that exist and some that don't. Although real-life battery technology is coming along great, we are a long way off from creating handheld batteries with capacities like the ones found in the lightsaber's diatium power cell. Perhaps the key lies in discovering this fictional "diatium" material? And although crystals do have many useful optical and piezoelectric properties, I don't know of one that could magically create plasma from electricity. (However, I read that the crystals must be "attuned to the Force" by a Jedi or Sith in a meditation ritual that can take days, so maybe we should start there.)

Where the explanations of lightsaber technology get really convoluted is when they start talking about how the blade is shaped and contained. Magnetic fields are currently used to contain plasmas, but they are generated by machinery that must also surround it—generating such a magnetic envelope from a single, unidirectional source would likely require some new laws of physics. There are no crystals that can "direct" a plasma.

In fact, a plasma being "directed" by a crystal lens doesn't even make any physical sense. A plasma is really just an ionized gas—a gas in which the electrons have been stripped from their atomic nuclei. We see plasmas all the time. They make up and are emitted from every star, like our solar wind and solar flares. The interaction of the solar wind with Earth's magnetic field produces the *aurora borealis*, or northern lights—another form of plasma. Plasmas are also the stuff of every spark and lightning bolt.

Plasmas can be created by bringing gases up to a high energy level. The higher the energy, the more atoms will be stripped of their electrons, and the better quality plasma we will have. It's completely possible that one could create a plasma by producing a large enough voltage difference—as with lightning—or a powerful enough laser focus. However, enormous amounts of energy are required with either of these approaches, and it would be extremely difficult to control the plasma's shape. An electrical arc can have wild shifts in direction, and it can hardly be controlled without being surrounded by magnets. A laser will go in a straight line ... but, of course, it doesn't stop. A laser-based lightsaber would require a block or a couple of mirrors floating in midair, moving in sync with the hilt, which is largely impossible. On top of that, they would certainly melt in the presence of such a plasma anyway. Furthermore, all of this says nothing about what the actual quality of the plasma would be and how reliably or quickly it would cut through objects.

So it seems quite impossible to create a lightsaber, as seen in the *Star Wars* films, using existing technologies, materials, and physical laws. But given the enthusiasm of *Star Wars* superfans out there, I wouldn't be surprised if people are trying.

31. The author of this passage would most likely agree with which of the following statements?

A. The authors who invented science fiction never intended for it to depict things like lightsabers.

B. Science-fiction films can give people inaccurate ideas about the world that really surrounds them.

C. One should "never say never," because anything might be possible someday.

D. The content of science-fiction films should be more carefully regulated by the government.

32. The main point of the fifth paragraph (lines 48–58) is that:

F. Real-life crystals are not nearly powerful enough to direct plasma at high temperatures.

G. Studying lightning would be the logical first step in the construction of a lightsaber.

H. The commonness of plasmas in the real world is a good sign for lightsaber technology.

J. The idea of plasma having a predetermined "shape" is inherently absurd.

33. According to the passage, which of the following is an example of a plasma, either real or fictional?

A. The *aurora borealis*

B. A wild electrical arc

C. Earth's magnetic field

D. Diatium crystals

34. As it is used in line 39, the word *convoluted* most nearly means:

F. possible.

G. precise.

H. interesting.

J. confusing.

35. If a new crystal were discovered that might make plasma-lightsaber technology possible, how would the author most likely feel about this discovery?

A. Embarrassed and angry at having been proven wrong

B. Excited that his lifelong dream of owning a lightsaber might be about to come true

C. Interested in the new opportunities promised by such a discovery

D. Concerned that such a discovery will detract from the seriousness of the scientific profession

36. The main purpose of the third paragraph (lines 22–37) is to:

F. establish that the author is not in fact an expert in the type of science being discussed.

G. explain in a humorous fashion that the official explanation of lightsabers borders on nonsense.

H. remind the reader of the important difference between science fiction and fantasy.

J. express disdain for the silliness of the *Star Wars* film series.

37. According to the passage, which of the following would be LEAST likely to be involved in a real-life lightsaber?

A. Crystals

B. Batteries

C. Magnetic fields

D. An ionized gas

38. Which of the following statements about plasmas is accurate, according to information in the passage?

F. They can be directed by magnetic fields.

G. They are rarely visible to the naked eye.

H. They are typically slow moving.

J. They nearly always take up large amounts of space.

39. Which of the following is true about the author's attitude toward the *Star Wars* films?

A. Even by Hollywood standards, they are exceptionally inaccurate in their presentation of science.

B. They have an adoring fan base that retains hope in fanciful scientific ideas despite the odds.

C. They insult their audience by depicting wildly unfeasible technology with little explanation.

D. They have indirectly helped society by making generations of people more enthusiastic about science.

40. Which of the following is NOT mentioned in the passage as an obstacle to the creation of a real lightsaber?

F. The difficulty of developing a sufficiently compact power source

G. The practical impossibility of containing a plasma field in a way that renders it small and portable

H. The likelihood that such "blades" would just pass through each other, making dueling impossible

J. The difficulty of controlling a plasma's shape

If there is still time remaining, you may review your answers.

SCIENCE TEST

Time: 35 Minutes—40 Questions

Directions: There are six passages in this test. Each passage is followed by several questions. After reading a passage, choose the best answer to each question and fill in the corresponding oval on your answer sheet. You may refer to the passages as often as necessary.

You are NOT permitted to use a calculator on this test.

PASSAGE I

Astronomers have found over 400 planets orbiting stars. The discovered planets have a variety of compositions, masses, and orbits. Despite the variety, the universal rules of physics and chemistry allow scientists to broadly categorize these planets into just a few types: Gas Giant, Carbon Orb, Water World, and Rocky Earth. Table 1 shows the composition of the various planet types and typical mass ranges relative to Earth.

Table 1

Planet Classification	Composition	Stars Orbited by Planet Type	Mass Range (Earth = 1)
Gas Giant	Hydrogen/helium Rock	OGLE TR 132 Gliese 777	250–1000
Carbon Orb	Iron/nickel/carbon Diamond Carbon monoxide Silicon carbide	PSR 1257	.5–25
Water World	Silicates Iron Water	Gliese 581	.5–25
Rocky Earth	Silicate Nickel (molten and solid) Rock	Kepler 11 HD 69830	.5–25

Table 2 shows a sampling of planets orbiting various stars described in Table 1. These planets are merely numbered 1–7. Table 2 details the masses and orbital radii of the planets.

Table 2

Planet	Star That the Planet Orbits	Planet Mass (Earth Mass = 1)	Orbital Radius (Earth Orbit = 1)
1	Gliese 777	500	4.0
2	Gliese 581	20	2.0
3	Gliese 581	10	4.0
4	Kepler 11	15	3.5
5	OGLE TR 132	315	.35
6	HD 69830	15	.5
7	PSR 1257	4	.25

1. The data in Table 1 and Table 2 support which of the following statements?
   A. Gas Giant planets have the largest orbital radii.
   B. Orbital radius is directly related to mass.
   C. Orbital radius is inversely related to mass.
   D. The data does not support a correlation between mass and orbital radius.

2. According to Table 1 and Table 2, which of the following stars has the most massive Gas Giant planet orbiting it?
   F. Gliese 777
   G. OGLE TR 132
   H. PSR 1257
   J. Gliese 581

3. If a new planet were discovered, with a mass of 325, an orbital radius of 1.5, and a composition of mostly hydrogen, what would be its most likely classification?
   A. Carbon Orb
   B. Water World
   C. Rocky Earth
   D. Gas Giant

4. All of the following are true about the star Gliese 581 EXCEPT:
   F. Gliese 581 has multiple planets orbiting it.
   G. Gliese 581 has the most massive planet orbiting it.
   H. Gliese 581 has planets orbiting it that are classified as water.
   J. Gliese 581 has only planets with masses less than 50 Earth masses orbiting it.

5. The Rocky Earth planets in Table 2 have what in common?
   A. Their masses are less than 20 Earth masses.
   B. They are only found in deep space.
   C. Hydrogen is a major component of the crust.
   D. Their orbits are all less than 1 Earth radius.

6. Based on the information in Tables 1 and 2, a planet with a mass of 20 and silicate found in its composition, with an orbiting star of Gliese 581, would belong to which planet classification?
   F. Gas Giant
   G. Carbon Orb
   H. Water World
   J. Rocky Earth

PASSAGE II

A group of researchers studied the greenhouse gas (GHG) and energy savings associated with rigid plastic foam sheathing used to insulate single-family housing. The results show the typical annual energy savings for a single house in the United States. Table 1 displays energy savings for various temperature zones, whereas Table 2 shows GHGs avoided.

Table 1

Energy Savings (in million BTUs)	Zone 1 (colder)	Zone 3	Zone 5 (warmer)	U.S. Average
Natural gas	4.2	2.7	0.9	2.37
Petroleum	0.04	0.02	0.22	0.04
Coal	0.81	0.98	0.93	0.76
Hydropower	0.06	0.02	0.03	0.06
Nuclear	0.26	0.26	0.19	0.25
Other	0.03	0.02	0.23	0.03
Total annual	5.41	4.01	2.50	3.51

Table 2

GHGs (in pounds)	Zone 1 (colder)	Zone 3	Zone 5 (warmer)	U.S. Average
Carbon dioxide	609	608	606	599
Methane	101	101	101	101
Nitrous oxide	4.5	4.5	4.5	4.5
HCFC-141b	588	588	588	588
HCFC-142b	1511	1511	1511	1511
Total	2813	2812	2811	2803

There is an initial use of energy and GHG released when the insulation is installed, but large savings result from the use of the product over time. After the "payback" time expires, there is a net savings in energy and GHG emissions for as long as the insulation is in place. Figure 1 displays the payback time in years for energy savings and GHGs avoided.

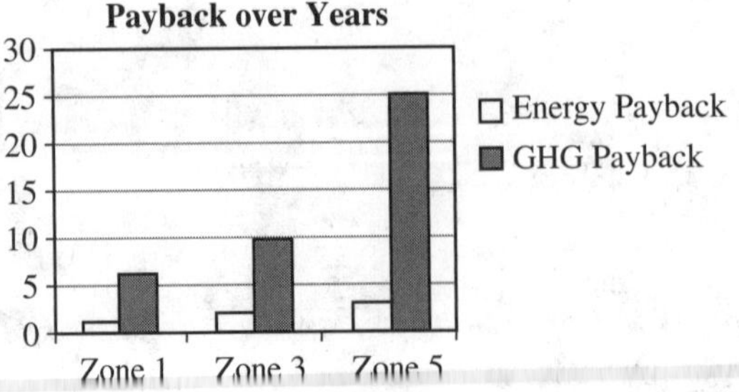

Figure 1

7. Foam sheathing proved to create the highest energy savings in Zone 5 for what type of energy?
   A. Coal
   B. Nuclear
   C. Natural gas
   D. Petroleum

8. According to the data presented in Table 1 and Table 2, which of the following is true?
   F. Foam sheathing prevents more HCFC-141b than HCFC-142b from entering the atmosphere.
   G. The yearly energy savings vary more by zone than the yearly GHGs avoided.
   H. The warmer the zone, the less the energy savings from petroleum.
   J. The U.S. average for GHGs avoided is greatest for carbon dioxide.

9. According to Figure 1, the GHG payback for Zone 3 is approximately:
   A. 12 years.
   B. 2 years.
   C. 13 years.
   D. 9 years.

10. According to Table 1, what zone and fuel combination yield the greatest energy savings after 1 year?
   F. Nuclear in Zone 1
   G. HCFC-142b in Zone 3
   H. Coal in Zone 5
   J. Natural gas in Zone 1

11. Ten years after installing rigid plastic foam sheathing in Zone 3, which of the following is true?
   A. The customer will have produced fewer GHGs, but will not yet have saved money on energy.
   B. The customer will have saved money on energy, but will not yet have produced fewer GHGs.
   C. The customer will have neither saved money on energy nor produced fewer GHGs.
   D. The customer will have both saved money on energy and produced fewer GHGs.

12. Based on the data in Table 1, which of the following lists the fuels that yielded the highest average energy savings, in decreasing order?
   F. Natural gas, coal, and nuclear
   G. Hydropower, nuclear, and other
   H. Coal, natural gas, and nuclear
   J. Nuclear, petroleum, and coal

13. Which of the following statements is FALSE concerning the typical annual energy savings associated with rigid plastic foam sheathing insulation?
   A. Petroleum energy saves the most energy in a warmer zone.
   B. Natural gas energy is most efficient in Zone 1.
   C. Hydropower is the most efficient energy overall.
   D. The U.S. average for natural gas is the highest average savings of all energy types.

PASSAGE III

Ohm's law states that $V = I \times R$ and WRC/L, where V = voltage, I = current, R = resistance, C = cross-sectional area of the wire, W = resistivity of the wire, and L = length of the wire. Using the circuit pictured in Figure 1, a student performed two experiments.

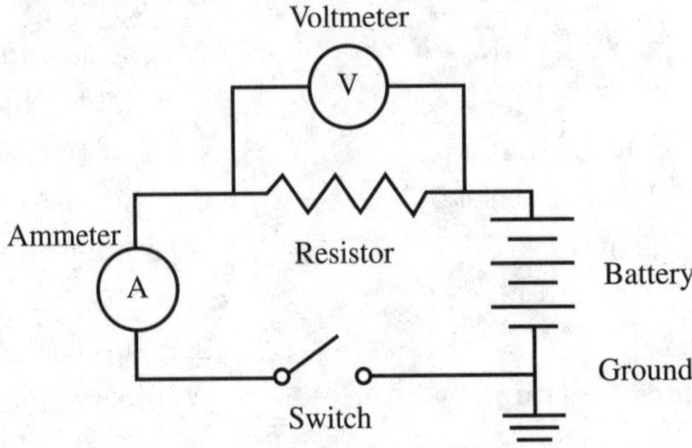

Figure 1

Experiment 1

A 5 V battery was used and the resistance was varied. Table 1 displays the results.

Table 1

Trial	Resistance (ohms)	Current (amperes)
1	2	2.5
2	4	1.25
3	10	0.5
4	20	0.25

Experiment 2

A battery of 1 volt was used and three different wires, each with the same resistivity and length, were used to complete the circuit. Table 2 shows the results and Figure 2 shows the relationship between the diameter of the wire and the measured resistance of each wire.

Table 2

Trial	Diameter (mm)	Resistance (ohms)	Current (amperes)
1	0.22	5.11	0.21
2	0.41	1.51	0.70
3	0.68	0.56	1.84
4	1.04	0.20	4.91

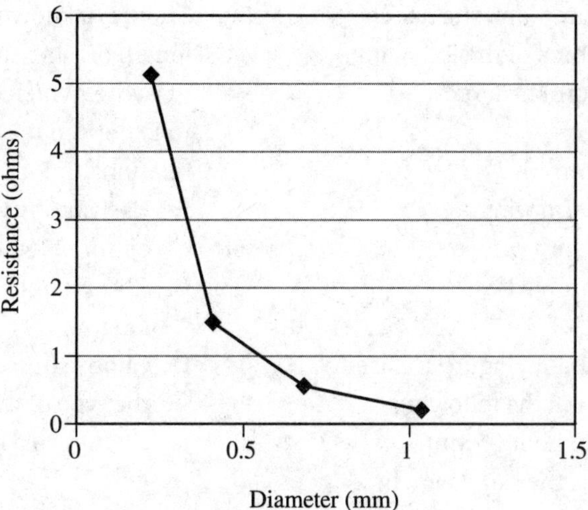

Figure 2

14. In Table 1, what is true about the relationship between current and resistance?
    - **F.** As resistance increased, current increased.
    - **G.** As resistance increased, current was unchanged.
    - **H.** As resistance increased, current decreased.
    - **J.** There is no relationship between current and resistance.

15. Based on Table 2 or Figure 2, it could be determined that a wire with a diameter of 0.5 mm would have a resistance close to
    - **A.** 2.6 ohms.
    - **B.** 1.0 ohms.
    - **C.** 0.5 ohms.
    - **D.** 0.25 ohms.

16. In Experiment 2, which of the following factors was varied?
    - **F.** Voltage of the battery
    - **G.** Diameter of the wire
    - **H.** Length of the wire
    - **J.** The material of the wire

17. The following hypothesis was put forth prior to the experiments: Current is inversely related to resistance. An inverse relationship implies that when one quantity increases, the other decreases. Do Tables 1 and 2 support this hypothesis?
    - **A.** No. Experiment 1 contradicts the hypothesis and shows a direct relationship between current and resistance. The current increases with the resistance.
    - **B.** No. Experiment 2 contradicts the hypothesis and shows a direct relationship between current and resistance. The current increases with resistance.
    - **C.** Yes. The results of both experiments show an inverse relationship between current and resistance. When the resistance increases, current decreases.
    - **D.** No. Neither experiment shows any relationship between current and resistance.

18. Using the circuit in Figure 1 and the results of both experiments, which of the following conditions would result in the largest current?

F. 5-volt battery, 0.5-mm wire
G. 5-volt battery, 0.25-mm wire
H. 2.5-volt battery, 0.5-mm wire
J. 2-volt battery, 0.25-mm wire

19. Consider a circuit like that in Figure 1. Based on Experiment 2, which of the following will produce a current of about 5 amperes (assume the wire used is the same wire in Experiment 2)?

A. 0.22 mm; 5.11 ohms
B. 0.41 mm; 1.51 ohms
C. 1.04 mm; 0.20 ohms
D. 1.04 mm; 0.56 ohms

20. There is a known relationship between the length of wires and the measured resistance of a wire. Which of the following changes to Experiment 2 would permit a test of this relationship?

F. Use varying wire diameter and one common wire length
G. Choose one wire diameter and vary wire length
H. Choose one wire diameter and change the type of wire to copper
J. Change to a battery of 2 volts

PASSAGE IV

Scientists tested a new method of titration, called atomic absorption inhibition titration (AAIT). They ran a series of experiments to determine if AAIT could be used successfully to determine the presence of phosphate, silicate, and sulfate in river and waste water. AAIT involves continually adding magnesium to a stirred sample solution while monitoring the solution for magnesium absorption.

Experiment 1

The scientists conducted an experiment to determine the effect of sulfate on titration of phosphate. Four trials were conducted, varying the concentration of both the sulfate and the magnesium used for the titration. Table 1 displays the results of the AAIT for solutions containing phosphate and sulfate and varying concentrations of magnesium.

Table 1

Trial	PO_4 ppm	SO_4 ppm	Mg		
			2.5 ppm	4.0 ppm	4.5 ppm
1	10	0	0.556	0	0
2	10	5	0.527	0.297	0.244
3	10	10	0.551	0.321	0.263
4	10	15	0.538	0.366	0.289

Experiment 2

Analysis of water from the Milwaukee River was performed. Solutions containing phosphate and sulfate were analyzed using AAIT. Titrations were performed on river water, river water plus the addition of phosphate, and standardized phosphate solution. The endpoint was noted for each trial when the titration reached the conditions under which only silicate would be detected. Table 2 shows the data collected, in ml.

Table 2

Trial	PO_4	River Water	River Water + PO_4
1	0.73	1.50	2.24
2	0.59	1.23	1.80
3	0.50	1.08	1.60
4	0.51	1.05	1.61
5	0.57	1.29	1.84

Experiment 3

Scientists created artificial waste water by adding phosphate, silicate, and sulfate to water and then conducting AAIT to simultaneously determine how much of each substance was in the water. Four titrations were conducted. Table 3 displays the results.

Table 3

	Added μ/ml			Found μ/ml		
Trial	PO_4	SO_4	SiO_2	PO_4	SO_4	SiO_2
1	3.00	20.00	1.50	3.04	20.50	1.44
2	2.00	20.00	1.50	1.56	20.30	1.60
3	2.00	20.00	4.00	2.38	20.30	3.48
4	5.00	20.00	10.00	9.56	20.00	7.30

21. According to the data in Table 2, which trial resulted in the most silicate being detected in river water?
   A. Trial 1
   B. Trial 2
   C. Trial 3
   D. Trial 4

22. Based on the information presented in Table 3, which trial resulted in less PO_4 being found than was initially added?
   F. Trial 1
   G. Trial 2
   H. Trial 3
   J. Trial 4

23. Before conducting Experiment 1, the scientists hypothesized that the higher the concentration of Mg used, the more Mg that would be absorbed. Do the results of the experiment support the hypothesis?
   A. Yes. For each trial as the concentration of Mg used increased from 2.5 to 4.5 ppm, more Mg was absorbed.
   B. Yes. Table 1 shows that the most Mg absorbed was during Trial 1 and with an Mg concentration of 2.5 ppm.
   C. No. The opposite has been shown to be the case. For each trial as the Mg concentration increased, the amount of Mg absorbed decreased.
   D. No. There is not a clear relationship between the Mg concentration and the amount of Mg absorbed.

24. Based on the results of Experiment 2, what type of solution was found to reach the endpoint with the least amount of solution?
   F. Phosphate and sulfate
   G. Standardized phosphate solution
   H. River water
   J. River water plus phosphate

25. The data in Table 1 supports which of the following statements?
   A. The titrations done using Mg with a concentration of 4.0 ppm resulted in the most Mg being absorbed.
   B. The titrations done using Mg with a concentration of 2.5 ppm resulted in the least Mg being absorbed.
   C. With a Mg concentration of 4.5 ppm, as the titrations included more concentrated SO_4, less Mg was absorbed.
   D. With a Mg concentration of 4.5 ppm, as the titrations included more concentrated SO_4, more Mg was absorbed.

26. In Experiment 3 scientists conducted atomic absorption inhibition titration (AAIT) in four separate trials. Which of the following conclusions is FALSE based on the results of those four trials?
   F. All four trials found amounts of sulfate right at or above the amount added.
   G. In all four trials the AAIT method underestimated the amount of silicate in the water.
   H. The same amount of sulfate was added to water in all four trials.
   J. In the fourth trial the amount of phosphate found in the water was almost double the amount initially added.

PASSAGE V

More than 5 percent of Americans have asthma, a chronic disease that affects the airways and lungs, causing shortness of breath, wheezing, and sometimes death. In the United States, rates for asthma have steadily increased, nearly doubling during the past 20 years. There is no cure for asthma. Two researchers discuss factors that cause individuals to develop asthma.

Researcher 1

There has long been an association between the allergen *Dermatophagoides pteronyssinus* (dust mites) and asthma. Evidence for a causal relationship has been supported by bronchial challenge studies and avoidance experiments. Studies have shown that exposure in the child's own house was the primary determinant of sensitization. Research from around the world has provided evidence about other indoor allergens, specifically cats, dogs, and the German cockroach. These studies showed that perennial exposure to allergens was an important cause of inflammation in the lungs and associated nonspecific bronchial hyperreactivity. Children are being exposed to more perennial allergens now than ever before. Houses are built more tightly and are better insulated and have more furnishings and fitted carpets. In addition, children are spending more time indoors. This increased exposure to allergens, including dust mites, has led to increased sensitization, and more cases of asthma.

Since assays for total serum IgE (immunoglobulin E) became available, it has been clear that patients with asthma have, on average, higher total IgE than patients with hay fever or no allergy. Recent work on patients hospitalized for asthma has suggested that the interaction between rhinovirus and allergy occurs predominantly among patients with total IgE > 200 IU/ml. Thus, the different properties of allergens could influence both the prevalence and severity of asthma.

Researcher 2

It is widely accepted that air pollution exacerbates asthma. For example, when traffic controls were put in place during the 1996 Summer Olympic Games in Atlanta, Georgia, morning peak traffic counts declined by 23 percent. This in turn lowered ozone (O_3) concentrations by 13 percent, carbon monoxide (CO) by 19 percent, and nitrogen dioxide (NO_2) by 7 percent. Associated with these declines in ambient air pollution were drops in Medicaid-related emergency room visits and hospitalizations for asthma (down 42 percent), asthma-related care for health maintenance organizations (down 44 percent), and citywide hospitalizations for asthma (down 19 percent). Despite such striking relationships between exposure to air pollution and asthma aggravation, air pollution has not been regarded as a cause of the disease. Increasingly, however, recent studies have been suggesting that air pollution may, indeed, be a cause of asthma.

The Children's Health Study (CHS) followed 3,535 children with no lifetime history of asthma for five years. During that period 265 reported a new physician diagnosis of asthma. Analysis of CHS data has shown that children living in communities with high ozone levels developed asthma more often than those in less polluted areas. The hypothesis that ozone might cause asthma is reinforced by a study of 3,091 nonsmoking adults aged 27 to 87 years who were followed for 15 years. The results of this study showed that 3.2 percent of the men and 4.3 percent of the women reported new doctor-diagnosed asthma. The researchers concluded that there was a connection between ozone concentration and development of asthma.

27. If ozone levels decrease nationwide, Researcher 2 would expect to see what change in asthma rates?

A. An increase in the prevalence of asthma
B. A decrease in the prevalence of asthma
C. No change in the prevalence of asthma
D. First a decrease and then an increase in the prevalence of asthma

28. Researcher 1 would agree with which of the following statements:

F. Asthma rates are lower in rural areas.
G. Men are more likely to have asthma than women.
H. People who have pets are more likely to have asthma.
J. Asthma rates are related to the quality of air.

29. Researcher 1 would most likely agree with which of the following statements about IgE?

A. People who have IgE levels of 400 IU/ml have a high chance of having severe asthma.
B. People who have IgE levels of 100 IU/ml have a high chance of having severe asthma.
C. Most people who have asthma have low levels of IgE: less than 200 IU/ml.
D. There has been no connection made between IgE levels and the prevalence of asthma.

30. If the prevalence of asthma in the United States continues to increase, Researcher 1 would likely cite which of the following as a solution to the problem?

F. People need to spend less time outside.
G. Houses need to be better insulated.
H. People need to be given supplements to increase their IgE levels.
J. Fans need to be added to houses to allow more circulation and to bring more outside air into the house.

31. Researchers 1 and 2 would both agree with which of the following statements?

A. Asthma rates are likely to decline over the next 20 years.
B. Air pollution and high IgE levels are the two leading causes of asthma.
C. Women are more likely to develop asthma than men.
D. Measures can be taken to lower a person's risk of developing asthma.

32. If Researcher 2 is correct, which of the following graphs would best represent the relationship between CO concentrations and cases of asthma?

F.

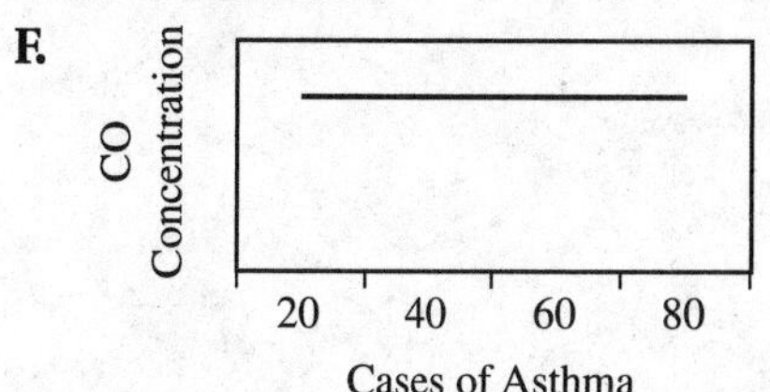

G.

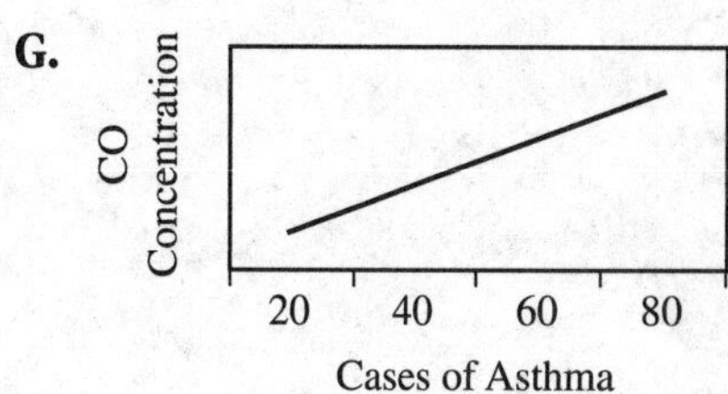

H.

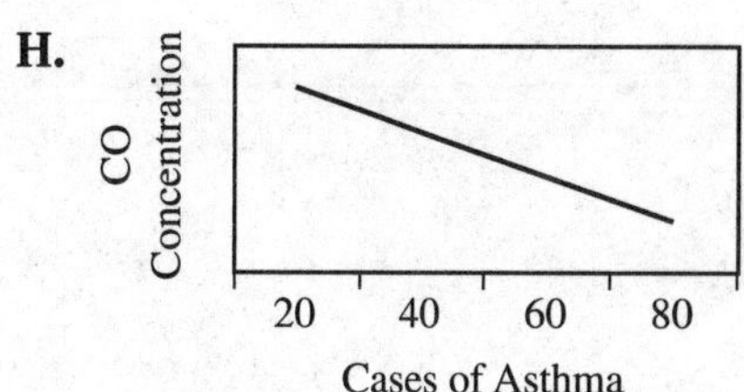

J.

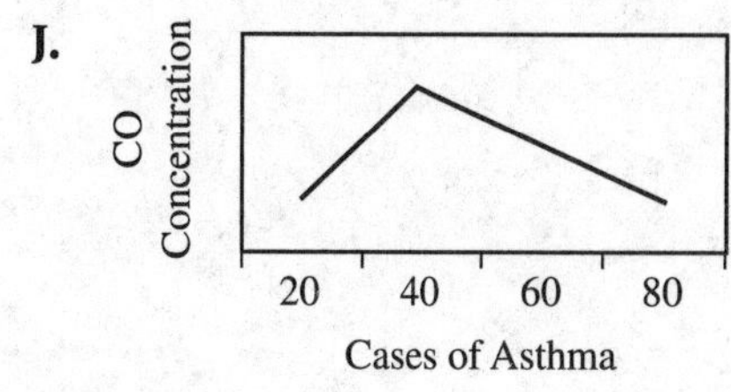

33. Researcher 2 would most likely agree with which of the following statements regarding the prevalence of asthma 20 years ago?

A. There was a higher prevalence of asthma 20 years ago because there was less pollution.

B. There was a lower prevalence of asthma 20 years ago because there were higher ozone levels and less pollution.

C. There was a lower prevalence of asthma 20 years ago because there was less pollution and lower ozone levels.

D. There was a lower prevalence of asthma 20 years ago because people spent more time outside.

PASSAGE VI

Pertussis, commonly known as whooping cough, is a highly infectious disease of the respiratory tract caused by bacteria. The disease spreads by direct contact with secretions from the nose or throat of an infected person, or by breathing in the air when an infected person coughs. Pertussis most easily passes between people in the initial stage of illness, but it can be spread at any time during the course of the illness. Figure 1 depicts the course of pertussis from exposure to recovery.

<table>
<tr><td colspan="6">Incubation Period
5–21 days</td><td colspan="4">Catarrhal Stage
1–2 weeks</td></tr>
<tr><td colspan="2">Weeks: –3</td><td colspan="2">–2</td><td colspan="2">–1</td><td colspan="2">0 + 1
(onset)</td><td colspan="2">2</td></tr>
<tr><td colspan="2">Maximum incubation period 21 days</td><td colspan="4">Average incubation period 7–10 days</td><td colspan="4">*Communicability*
Cold symptoms: rhinorrhea, anorexia, conjunctivitis, lacrimation, malaise, sneezing, and low-grade fever</td></tr>
<tr><td colspan="6">Paroxysmal Stage
1–6 weeks</td><td colspan="4">Convalescent
Stage 2–3 weeks</td></tr>
<tr><td>3</td><td>4</td><td>5</td><td>6</td><td>7</td><td>8</td><td>9</td><td>10</td><td>11</td><td>12</td></tr>
<tr><td colspan="6">Paroxysmal cough, vomiting, cyanosis</td><td colspan="4" rowspan="2">Coughing</td></tr>
<tr><td colspan="3">Communicability ends after 5 days of antibiotics</td><td colspan="3">Communicability ends 3 weeks after onset of cough if no antibiotics taken</td></tr>
</table>

Figure 1

The number of reported cases of pertussis from 1974 through 2004 is depicted in Figure 2.

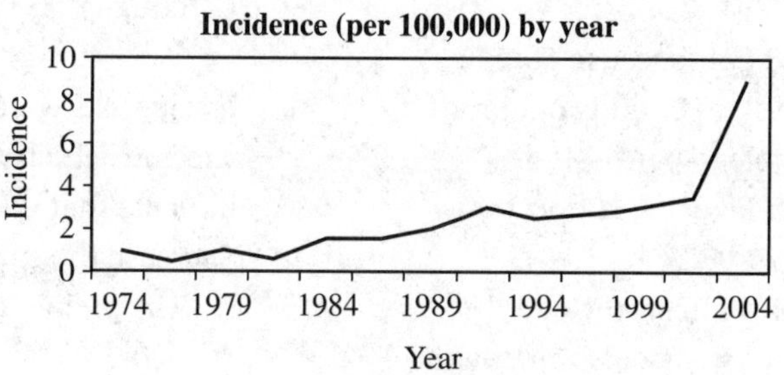

Figure 2

The number of reported cases of pertussis in 2004 by age group is shown in Figure 3.

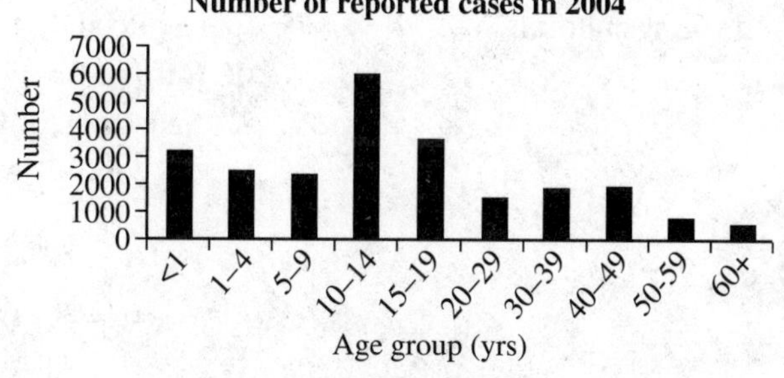

Figure 3

34. A new vaccine for pertussis was introduced in 1991, which claimed to be more effective than the previous vaccine. Do the data in Figure 2 support this claim?
   F. No. Rates of pertussis increased after 1991.
   G. No. Rates of pertussis remained the same after 1991.
   H. Yes. Rates of pertussis decreased after 1991.
   J. Yes. Rates of pertussis increased after 1991.

35. If a person was experiencing a cough, was medicated, and was still contagious, he or she would be in what stage of the disease?
   A. Incubation
   B. Catarrhal
   C. Paroxysmal
   D. Convalescent

36. What is the maximum number of weeks that pertussis can be transmitted?
   F. 1
   G. 3
   H. 8
   J. 12

37. Doctors hypothesized that because of their immature immune systems, young children are the most susceptible to pertussis. Do the data from 2004, in Figure 3, support this theory?
   A. No. Pertussis mostly affects the elderly.
   B. No. Ten- to fourteen-year-olds were the most likely to contract pertussis.
   C. Yes. Infants had the highest rate of pertussis.
   D. Yes. Seven thousand young children contracted pertussis.

38. Which of the following statements could be a plausible explanation for increased incidence of pertussis?
   F. Fewer infants are being vaccinated for pertussis, and are therefore contracting the disease.
   G. Regulations on reporting pertussis are more lax now, so the numbers are inaccurate.
   H. There are more blood transfusions performed now, increasing people's risks of contracting pertussis.
   J. Vaccine immunity wanes after 5–10 years, so more young adults are succumbing to pertussis.

39. Which of the following statements about pertussis is NOT true?
   A. The disease has an incubation period ranging from 1 to 3 weeks.
   B. Symptoms are similar to those of a common cold.
   C. The disease is a virus that cannot be treated with antibiotics.
   D. Pertussis can be communicated via particles left in the air after a person coughs.

40. If scientists were in the testing phase of a new vaccine, which of the following results might indicate that the new vaccine was helping to decrease the spread of pertussis?
   F. The incidence of pertussis in 2007 was 600,000 cases.
   G. Children 5–9 years of age developed more cases of the disease.
   H. The incubation period of the disease was reduced by 4 days.
   J. Antibiotics were more effective in reducing the length of pertussis.

If there is still time remaining, you may review your answers.

WRITING TEST

Time: 40 Minutes

Zoos

The 2013 documentary *Blackfish*, which exposed poor treatment of orcas in captivity, added more fuel to a growing movement arguing that zoos, aquariums, and other venues that keep wild animals in captivity should become a thing of the past. No matter how expensive and modern a facility may be, it is always going to pale in comparison to an animal's natural environment. Even when we treat them well, perhaps we humans don't have the right to keep innocent animals in what is essentially a prison merely for our own amusement.

Read and carefully consider these perspectives. Each suggests a particular way of thinking about the controversy surrounding zoos.

Perspective One	Perspective Two	Perspective Three
We have to look at the big picture. If humans are going to conserve nature and respect animals, we have to learn to love them first, and zoos are the places where most children learn to do so. Additionally, research done on animals in captivity often helps preserve them in the wild, and there are also the species-saving breeding programs for endangered animals to consider.	In this day and age, zoos are hardly the only way for young people to learn to love and respect animals. Kids can watch videos of animals in their natural environments all day long on their computers if they wish. Live video feeds from nature preserves are far more educational than a depressed animal in a cage.	We can't make sweeping statements about "wild animals" as if they're all the same. Large predators like orcas or great white sharks can't thrive in captivity, and imprisoning extremely intelligent animals like the great apes is simply inhuman. But the vast majority of animals—especially prey animals who might end up getting eaten in the wild—are probably happier in well-maintained zoos.

ESSAY TASK

Write a unified, coherent essay concerning the pros and cons of zoos. In your essay, be sure to:

- clearly state your own perspective on the issue and analyze the relationship between your perspective and at least one other perspective
- develop and support your ideas with reasoning and examples
- organize your ideas clearly and logically
- communicate your ideas effectively in standard written English

Your perspective may be in full agreement with any of those given, in partial agreement, or completely different.

Planning Your Response

Your prewriting notes on this page will not be considered in your score.

Use the following space to brainstorm ideas and map out your response. You may want to think about the following as you analyze the given prompt:

Strengths and weaknesses of the three viewpoints

- What good points do they make, and what potential objections do they ignore?
- Why might they be convincing to readers, and why might their perspectives fall short?

Your previous experience, background knowledge, and personal values

- What is your viewpoint on this topic, and what are the pros and cons of this viewpoint?
- How will you craft an argument in support of your point of view?

If there is still time remaining, you may review your answers.

ANSWER KEY
Practice Test 1

English

1. **B**	16. **F**	31. **B**	46. **H**	61. **D**
2. **J**	17. **A**	32. **J**	47. **A**	62. **G**
3. **A**	18. **F**	33. **D**	48. **H**	63. **D**
4. **J**	19. **B**	34. **F**	49. **B**	64. **F**
5. **D**	20. **F**	35. **A**	50. **H**	65. **C**
6. **H**	21. **C**	36. **G**	51. **D**	66. **F**
7. **C**	22. **G**	37. **C**	52. **J**	67. **D**
8. **F**	23. **D**	38. **J**	53. **B**	68. **H**
9. **D**	24. **H**	39. **A**	54. **H**	69. **A**
10. **J**	25. **A**	40. **H**	55. **C**	70. **G**
11. **B**	26. **F**	41. **B**	56. **F**	71. **D**
12. **H**	27. **B**	42. **J**	57. **B**	72. **H**
13. **A**	28. **J**	43. **B**	58. **H**	73. **B**
14. **G**	29. **C**	44. **J**	59. **A**	74. **J**
15. **A**	30. **J**	45. **C**	60. **H**	75. **C**

Mathematics

1. **C**	13. **B**	25. **E**	37. **D**	49. **A**
2. **F**	14. **H**	26. **H**	38. **F**	50. **F**
3. **C**	15. **C**	27. **D**	39. **B**	51. **D**
4. **J**	16. **G**	28. **K**	40. **G**	52. **H**
5. **D**	17. **B**	29. **C**	41. **D**	53. **E**
6. **H**	18. **J**	30. **H**	42. **J**	54. **K**
7. **B**	19. **D**	31. **A**	43. **A**	55. **D**
8. **K**	20. **J**	32. **G**	44. **H**	56. **J**
9. **E**	21. **B**	33. **D**	45. **E**	57. **D**
10. **F**	22. **J**	34. **H**	46. **G**	58. **K**
11. **C**	23. **D**	35. **C**	47. **D**	59. **E**
12. **F**	24. **J**	36. **G**	48. **J**	60. **F**

ANSWER KEY
Practice Test 1

Reading

1. **B**	9. **B**	17. **A**	25. **C**	33. **A**
2. **H**	10. **J**	18. **J**	26. **F**	34. **J**
3. **D**	11. **C**	19. **C**	27. **B**	35. **C**
4. **J**	12. **G**	20. **G**	28. **J**	36. **G**
5. **C**	13. **D**	21. **B**	29. **A**	37. **A**
6. **J**	14. **H**	22. **J**	30. **G**	38. **F**
7. **A**	15. **A**	23. **C**	31. **B**	39. **B**
8. **H**	16. **G**	24. **F**	32. **J**	40. **H**

Science

1. **D**	9. **D**	17. **C**	25. **D**	33. **C**
2. **F**	10. **J**	18. **F**	26. **G**	34. **F**
3. **D**	11. **D**	19. **C**	27. **B**	35. **C**
4. **G**	12. **F**	20. **G**	28. **H**	36. **H**
5. **A**	13. **C**	21. **A**	29. **A**	37. **B**
6. **H**	14. **H**	22. **G**	30. **J**	38. **J**
7. **A**	15. **B**	23. **C**	31. **D**	39. **C**
8. **G**	16. **G**	24. **G**	32. **G**	40. **F**

HOW TO SCORE YOUR PRACTICE TEST

Step 1: Add up the number correct for each section and write that number in the blank under the Raw Score column on the Score Conversion Table. (Your goal is to get more questions correct on each subsequent practice test.)

Step 2: Using the Score Conversion Chart, find your scale score for each section and write it down. Then add up all four sections and divide by 4 to find your overall composite score. (Composite scores are rounded up at .5 or higher.)

SCORE CONVERSION TABLE

Section	Raw Score	Scaled Score
English	(out of 75)	____ / 36
Math	(out of 60)	____ / 36
Reading	(out of 40)	____ / 36
Science	(out of 40)	____ / 36
		Add and divide by 4
Overall Composite =		____ / 36

SCORE CONVERSION CHART

Number Correct					
ACT Score*	English Section	Mathematics Section	Reading Section	Science Section	ACT Score*
36	75	60	40	40	36
35	74	59	39	39	35
34	73	58	38	38	34
33	72	57	37	—	33
32	71	56	36	37	32
31	70	54-55	35	36	31
30	69	53	34	35	30
29	67-68	51-52	33	34	29
28	65-66	49-50	32	33	28
27	64	46-48	31	31-32	27
26	62-63	44-45	30	30	26
25	60-61	41-43	29	28-29	25
24	58-59	39-40	27-28	25-27	24
23	55-57	37-38	25-26	24	23

(continued)

SCORE CONVERSION CHART (*Continued*)

	Number Correct				
ACT Score*	English Section	Mathematics Section	Reading Section	Science Section	ACT Score*
22	53-54	35-36	23-24	22-23	22
21	50-52	33-34	22	20-21	21
20	47-49	31-32	21	18-19	20
19	44-46	28-30	19-20	17	19
18	42-43	25-27	18	15-16	18
17	40-41	22-24	17	14	17
16	37-39	19-21	16	13	16
15	34-36	15-17	15	12	15
14	31-33	11-14	13-14	11	14
13	29-30	09-10	12	10	13
12	27-28	07-08	10-11	09	12
11	25-26	06	08-09	08	11
10	23-24	05	07	07	10
9	21-22	04	06	05-06	9
8	18-20	03	05	—	8
7	15-17	—	—	04	7
6	12-14	02	04	03	6
5	09-11	—	03	02	5
4	07-08	01	02	—	4
3	05-06	—	—	01	3
2	03-04	—	01	—	2
1	00-02	00	00	00	1

**These scores are based on student trials rather than national norms.*

SCORING YOUR ESSAY

As mentioned earlier in this text, two readers will evaluate your essay and each person will then assign it a score from 1 to 6. If, by chance, these two scorers disagree by more than 1 point, a third reader will step in and resolve the discrepancy. Performance on the essay will not affect your English, math, reading, science, or composite scores. You will receive two additional scores on your score sheet—a combined English/writing score (1–36) and a writing test subscore (1–12). Neither of these scores will affect your composite score!

The sample essay that follows reflects higher-level writing. It meets the criteria that ACT has put forth for essays that demonstrate effective writing skills.

- It takes a definite position.
- It addresses and expands on the counterargument.
- It has details that support the topic sentences and is well organized.
- It is not repetitive, and while there may be errors, they do not interfere with the competence of the essay.
- It is consistent and well balanced.
- The essay has a clear introduction and a conclusion that is not just a summary but ends with a significant thought.
- The vocabulary demonstrates good use of language and the sentence structure is varied.

ANSWER EXPLANATIONS

English

1. **(B)** This choice correctly separates two grammatically correct independent clauses into two sentences with a period.

2. **(J)** No comma is necessary. The narrator is saying goodbye to *both* her family and her friends, so the conjunction should not be preceded by a comma—both *family* and *friends* are objects of the preposition *to*. Furthermore, *saying goodbye to my family and friends* acts as one single noun phrase (with *saying* acting as a gerund noun), so no comma is needed between it and the verb *made* (you do not need a comma between the subject and the verb, no matter how long the subject is).

3. **(A)** This is a run-on sentence. Two independent clauses are mashed together with no punctuation. The fact that the conjunction *yet* is present does not make any difference (although the sentence would be correct if there was a comma before *yet*).

4. **(J)** The subsequent sentences mention being afraid to "jinx" something. This implies that the narrator is trying not to think about a desirable outcome, for fear that it will not come true. The idea of winning a gold medal is the only one of the choices that involves a desirable outcome that may or may not happen and is therefore vulnerable to being "jinxed."

5. **(D)** As a general rule, when three of the choices open with a transition word and one does not, the one without a transition word is correct (except in the case of the "*although* trick," where removing *although* would result in a comma splice). Choice D is a correct and comprehensible independent clause, so why mess with it? Besides, none of the proposed transition words makes sense in context.

6. **(H)** This choice explains that the narrator moved to Canada and adds the interesting detail that she did so only 24 hours after graduating, without adding any further details or implications that are unsupported by the text.

7. **(C)** Like the rest of the passage, this sentence is in the past tense (as indicated by the past-tense verb *took*, which appears earlier in the sentence). *I began* is the correct past-tense form.

8. **(F)** This choice correctly presents an independent clause followed by a dependent "afterthought" clause, with the two clauses separated by a comma.

9. **(D)** The national anthem belongs to America, and so the noun *America* needs to be possessive: *America's national anthem.*

10. **(J)** This choice correctly separates multiple adjectives with a comma.

11. **(B)** The phrase *usually jumps have three spins* does not describe the narrator's actions and is not necessary in order to understand the actions mentioned elsewhere in the paragraph, as the fact that jumps usually have three spins is implied by the phrase *a jump with just two spins* in the preceding sentence.

12. **(H)** The cold, unfeeling qualities of ice described in the subsequent sentences render the idea that anyone would love it is unexpected or ironic. Therefore, the rhetorical question, *How can anyone love ice?* is the best introduction.

13. **(A)** *Its* is the possessive form, with no apostrophe.

14. **(G)** Paragraph 3 describes the narrator waiting to perform, and Paragraph 4 describes the medal ceremony. Therefore, Paragraph 5, which describes the narrator's performance, should go in between them.

15. **(A)** The essay centers around the narrator's winning an Olympic gold medal. This certainly qualifies as a "significant event," and none of the details mentioned in choice A are wrong or irrelevant.

16. **(F)** Although the sentence is long, the last several clauses concerning the grandmother's qualities are essentially a list; they are not going to affect the grammar of the beginning of the sentence. We need the first few words here to form an independent clause, and one that is in the past tense, like the rest of the passage: only *She described her grandmother* accomplishes this.

17. **(A)** This choice correctly inserts commas after each item in the list of adjectives, and refrains from inserting any unnecessary commas elsewhere.

18. **(F)** In this choice, two independent clauses are correctly joined with a comma + conjunction (*and*). The fact that the first clause is short and the second is long does not matter; they are both independent clauses.

19. **(B)** The idea we need here is a synonym for *activating,* something like *starting* or *spurring.* The other choices are all synonymous with that idea, but *halting* (which means *stopping*) is the opposite and so the LEAST acceptable.

20. **(F)** The only information contained in the underlined portion deals with who lived in that area before the Civil War. Therefore, the underlined portion contains *details that emphasize the historical importance* of the area.

21. **(C)** The phrase *a genealogist* is a "lift-out" appositive clause containing extra information, inserted in the middle of a single independent clause. It needs to be set off with something, and the only choice that works is a pair of dashes (a pair of commas would also be correct, but is not one of the choices).

22. **(G)** What we are supposed to have here is an adverb modifying an adjective that is modifying a noun: *poorly* (adverb) *preserved* (adjective) *Creole French* (noun phrase).

23. **(D)** The pronoun *who* is used here to introduce a clause containing further information, and *was* is used as part of a passive-voice phrase: *Elisabeth, who was sold.*

24. **(H)** The narrator means to say that *immediately* after finding out this new information, she felt uncontrollably compelled to write her family's history. Of the choices, only *At this point* refers to the *specific moment* in question.

25. **(A)** Both the preceding sentence ("their lives") and the rest of this sentence ("people") demonstrate that we are talking about more than one person. As the people we are talking about have long since passed away, we need the past-tense plural form *They were.*

26. **(F)** The fact that over a thousand documents were used is valuable information, as it demonstrates how hard the author worked and how thorough the resulting account must be.

27. **(B)** Although the sentence is long, everything after the comma is an "afterthought" clause containing extra information, so the part before the comma needs to be an independent clause. Of the choices, only *The result was Cane River* is a grammatically correct independent clause.

28. **(J)** Although some may be made nervous by the fact that this choice results in a very long sentence, it is the only correct one. It combines an independent clause (ending at *Louisiana*) with a dependent clause containing extra information, and separates the two with a comma.

29. **(C)** The beginning of the essay was about the author's great-grandmother Emily. Since this is the only one of the choices that is about her, it is the only one that "ties in" to the beginning.

30. **(J)** Although it may safely be assumed that the experience of writing *Cane River* was personally enriching for the author, the essay is not primarily about the author's feelings or why writing a book is personally beneficial in general. Nothing specific to this effect is said.

31. **(B)** Assuming that they are right next to each other, as they are here, no punctuation is necessary between the subject of a sentence and the main verb. *The different kinds of prairie wildflowers* is our noun phrase (technically, the subject is *kinds*, and *of prairie wildflowers* is a prepositional phrase, but this doesn't make a difference here), and the main verb is *are*.

32. **(J)** This section of the passage is in the present tense, and the subject phrase is *grasses and herbaceous wildflowers*, so the correct form for the main verb is *dominate* (present-tense plural).

33. **(D)** Coneflowers, and how many types there are, are not mentioned anywhere else in this paragraph or the entire passage. The passage is about prairies, not specific types of flowers. Therefore, this sentence would distract from the main idea.

34. **(F)** The entire passage so far has been about the diverse flora found on prairies. The reader would expect that the assertion that prairies are "interesting and colorful" would have something to do with biodiversity.

35. **(A)** This choice correctly results in an independent clause followed by a dependent clause, with the two clauses separated by a comma.

36. **(G)** Old railroads are the rarest of the four environments offered as choices, and so this choice best establishes that black soil prairies are difficult to find today.

37. **(C)** The implication of the sentence in the context of the paragraph is that it is regrettable that the original prairies have been destroyed. Therefore, *Unfortunately* is the appropriate introductory word.

38. **(J)** The main idea of the paragraph concerns the depletion of gravel prairies, and so a guess that some of these prairies are probably new seems out of place.

39. **(A)** Since the noun *they* performs both the verb *are* and the verb *contain*, no comma is necessary after *degraded.* Furthermore, the information presented in this choice is the most relevant to the paragraph. (In this question, the right and wrong answers are determined by a combination of grammatical and stylistic factors—the test does not do this often, but it does happen, so watch out for it!)

40. **(H)** The antecedent of the pronoun *they* is the noun phrase *gravel and dolomite prairies.* Therefore, Sentence 4 should come right after a sentence that makes this apparent. It should also not come between Sentences 3 and 5, as Sentence 5 is clearly supposed to immediately follow Sentence 3. And it makes sense that Sentence 4 should be next to Sentence 2, as both concern the physical characteristics of gravel and dolomite prairies. Of the choices, only H (which places Sentence 4 between Sentences 2 and 3) resolves all of these issues.

41. **(B)** This choice correctly separates two independent clauses into two separate sentences by use of a period.

42. **(J)** This choice correctly uses *that* (with no comma) to attach a grammatically correct essential/limiting clause to the pronoun *those.*

43. **(B)** The subject noun *species* is plural here (although the singular form is identical), and so the plural verb *are* is necessary.

44. **(J)** The adjectives *moist, mesic,* and *dry* constitute a list of three different things that sand prairies can be. Therefore, commas are necessary after *moist* and *mesic.* (Although the comma before the conjunction that separates the final two items in a list is optional when the conjunction is *and*, it is mandatory when the conjunction is *or*!) The word *dry* ends one independent clause, which then needs to be joined to the subsequent one via a comma + conjunction, and so a comma is also necessary after *dry.*

45. **(C)** The question asks for a "colorful image," and choice C offers us the most vivid and specific image: *purple spiderwort, orange butterfly weed, and yellow goldenrod.*

46. **(H)** *Renowned* means "widely known" (by others). The correct construction would be to say that the regions *are renowned* for their beauty. Also, the subject, "regions," is plural, so you need the plural verb "are."

47. **(A)** If the springs are on the islands, then the springs couldn't have been formed before the islands were. So, *later* makes no sense in context.

48. **(H)** Species is singular, and so we need the singular (gender-neutral) possessive pronoun *its* here.

49. **(B)** The sentence in question foreshadows the presence of monkeys, and so could only be used *before* the monkeys are specifically introduced. After that, we would already know about the monkeys.

50. **(H)** *However* is set off with a pair of commas when it is inserted into the middle of a single independent clause.

51. **(D)** The visitors *are encouraged* by others; other people are doing the encouraging to the visitors. The addition of the adverb *strongly* provides additional information.

52. **(J)** *"Are seeking on getting" their money* is an extremely awkward construction in English. It is simply not something we would say.

53. **(B)** The pair of dashes should set off the portion of the sentence that "interrupts" the main independent clause. If that phrase were taken out, the words around it would form a complete correct independent clause. (Parentheses would also be correct, but are not one of the choices.)

54. **(H)** This sentence merely serves to emphasize how weird the situation is, and does not do too much more than that. (Sometimes the least ambitious answer choice is the safe bet.)

55. **(C)** Someone pointed this out *later*, or *after a while*, or *in due time*—in other words, *eventually*.

56. **(F)** *There was no possible way a monkey could get money would be stealing it* does not make sense. (Remember, read the *whole* sentence, not just the part around the underline!)

57. **(B)** This choice correctly precedes an afterthought clause with a single comma.

58. **(H)** *Personally I'm disappointed* is the preferred construction, with *personally* coming before the first-person contraction *I'm*.

59. **(A)** This choice correctly presents the hypothetical *could have motivated me* with the infinitive *to fly*.

60. **(H)** The previous sentence already eloquently ends the passage. The additional aside about whether monkeys like chips is less funny, and also doesn't make much sense, since the author has already established that the monkey problem has been taken care of.

61. **(D)** This choice correctly presents an independent clause (the end of which is a list) preceded by a dependent modifying clause. Because the modifying clause refers to Miró's work, the independent clause correctly begins with "his work" (otherwise it would be a misplaced modifier).

62. **(G)** The sentence, like the rest of the passage, is in the past tense, and the regular past-tense form *expressed* is all that is needed here.

63. **(D)** Even if you don't know what "visual elements" traditional painting involved, this choice clearly refers to Miró *rejecting* something about *established painting*, and so demonstrates his contempt for conventional painting, as the question requests.

64. **(F)** This is the only grammatically correct choice that says what you mean to say: that Miró was *born* to a goldsmith and watchmaker, and that he was *drawn* to the arts community.

65. **(C)** This choice correctly presents an independent clause (*He developed his unique style*) preceded by a dependent clause containing extra information, and followed by a colon and description.

66. **(F)** *Varying* here is correctly used as an adjective to modify *degrees* (*varying degrees* basically means "many ways").

67. **(D)** *The founder of surrealism* is a "lift-out" appositive clause that gives extra information about Andre Breton, and as such, it is set off with a pair of commas.

68. **(H)** Only this choice makes reference to a specific influential technique that Miró developed, thereby demonstrating his importance in the history of painting.

69. **(A)** The fact that Miró chose not to become an official Surrealist is surprising in light of the fact that he helped start the movement, and so the appropriate transition word is *However*, which is used to introduce contrasting information. (It also helps to notice that the other three choices are basically interchangeable.)

70. **(G)** This choice correctly results in an independent clause followed by a dependent participial modifier clause containing extra information.

71. **(D)** The passage is in the past tense, and the regular past-tense form *accelerated* is all we need here.

72. **(H)** This choice correctly makes two independent clauses into two separate sentences, separated by a period.

73. **(B)** The past perfect (the "past of the past") form *had visited* is correct here (the normal past tense would also work, but is not one of the choices).

74. **(J)** This choice correctly presents two independent clauses separated with a semicolon.

75. **(C)** This choice correctly presents a nonessential *which* clause preceded by a comma.

Mathematics

1. **(C)** Substituting $x = 3$ into the equation $x^2 + 2x - 12$ gives $(3)^2 + 2(3) - 12 = 9 + 6 - 12 = 3$.

2. **(F)** $3(2x-1) = 11x + 27 \rightarrow 6x - 3 = 11x + 27 \rightarrow -5x = 30 \rightarrow x = -6$.

3. **(C)** 15% of \$42 is $0.15 \cdot 42 = \$6.30$. This answer is the amount the \$42 jacket is discounted, so to find the discounted price take $\$42 - \$6.30 = \$35.70$.

4. **(J)** $\angle a$ is a same-side exterior angle to the given angle, which is supplementary to 60°. Therefore, $m\angle a = 180 - 60 = 120°$.

5. **(D)** Substituting $x = 3$, $y = 5$, and $w = 4$ into the given expression yields $(3)(4)^3 + \frac{3(4)}{2} - (3)^2(5) = (3)(64) + 6 - 45 = 192 + 6 - 45 = 153$.

6. **(H)** Distributing the given expression gives $(3x-5)(4x+3) = 12x^2 + 9x - 20x - 15$. Combining like terms gives $12x^2 - 11x - 15$.

7. **(B)** $|5-8| - |9-3| = |-3| - |6| = 3 - 6 = -3$. Remember when evaluating absolute values to simplify inside the absolute value bars first, then evaluate the absolute value of the resulting number.

8. **(K)** $\left(5\sqrt{3}\right)^2 = 5\sqrt{3} \cdot 5\sqrt{3} = 25\sqrt{9}$. Evaluating the square root gives $25 \cdot 3 = 75$.

9. **(E)** To calculate probability use the formula $P = \frac{\text{number of successful outcomes}}{\text{total number of outcomes}} = \frac{7+5}{15} = \frac{12}{15}$. Simplifying the fraction gives $\frac{4}{5}$.

10. **(F)** The watch increases by 5%, which is an increase of $100 \cdot 0.05 = \$5$, making the new price of the watch $100 + 5 = \$105$. The necklace decreases by 10%, which is a decrease of $300 \cdot 0.10 = \$30$, making the new price $300 - 30 = \$270$. Adding these two prices together gives the sum of costs as $\$105 + \$270 = \$375$.

11. **(C)** The triangle in the figure is a right triangle given that $\overline{CA}$ is tangent to the circle and $\overline{OT}$ is a radius (all tangents to circles are perpendicular to the radius of the circle at the point of tangency). Using this along with the facts $\overline{TC} = 8$ and $\overline{OC} = 10$ we can set up the Pythagorean Theorem to calculate the leg $\overline{OT}$ as $a^2 + b^2 = c^2 \rightarrow 8^2 + x^2 = 10^2 \rightarrow 64 + x^2 = 100$. Solving for x gives $x^2 = 36 \rightarrow x = 6$. It is also a Pythagorean triple: 6, 8, 10 (3, 4, 5 doubled).

12. **(F)** We are asked to find AB and by looking at the answer choices, we want our answer in terms of x, y, and z. First substituting BC in for A we get $AB = (BC)B$. Now substituting x in for B and yz in for C we get $(BC)B = (xyz)x$, which equals $xyzx$.

13. **(B)** Solving an inequality is almost identical to solving an equation except if you multiply or divide by a negative number you have to switch the direction of the inequality. Solving this inequality for x we get $-5 < -3x - 7 \rightarrow 2 < -3x \rightarrow -\frac{2}{3} > x$, which is equivalent to $x < -\frac{2}{3}$.

14. **(H)** The slope-intercept form is $y = mx + b$. Solving the given equation for y gives $4x - 2y = 12 \rightarrow -2y = -4x + 12$. Dividing both sides by -2 gives $y = 2x - 6$.

15. **(C)** If the solution for x is 6, then we can substitute 6 into the equation for x and solve for a. Plugging 6 in for x gives $3(6) + 3a - 5 = 5(6) - a$. Solving the equation for a gives $18 + 3a - 5 = 30 - a \rightarrow 13 + 3a = 30 - a \rightarrow 4a = 17$. Dividing both sides by 4 gives $a = 4.25$.

16. **(G)** The formula for the circumference of a circle is $C = \pi d$, where d is the diameter of the circle. Using the formula, we can find the diameter of each of the smaller circles by substituting 8π for C and solving for d: $8\pi = \pi d \rightarrow 8 = d$. Therefore, the diameter of each of the small circles is 8 inches. The large circle's diameter is equivalent to all 3 of the smaller circles' diameters combined, which is $8 + 8 + 8 = 24$ inches. Now, using the formula again to find the circumference of a circle with $d = 24$, we get $C = \pi(24) = 24\pi$.

17. **(B)** The length of time needed to cook the turkey is proportional to the weight of the turkey. In other words, $\frac{\text{time}}{\text{weight}} = \frac{\text{time}}{\text{weight}}$. Plugging in 1 hour for time, 3 pounds for the weight, and 19 pounds for the other weight gives: $\frac{1}{3} = \frac{x}{19}$. Cross multiplying gives $1(19) = 3(x)$. Solving for x gives $x = 6\frac{1}{3}$ hours. One-third of an hour is $\frac{1}{3}(60) = 20$ minutes, so the answer is 6 hours and 20 minutes.

18. **(J)** Since the seating was random, Dee would have the same probability for any position. Therefore, the probability of Dee being in the middle is $\frac{1}{5}$.

19. **(D)** The problem states the triangles are similar, so the corresponding parts are proportional. Setting up the ratio as $\frac{\text{big left side}}{\text{big hypotenuse}} = \frac{\text{little left side}}{\text{little hypotenuse}}$ we get $\frac{x}{12} = \frac{4}{5}$. Cross multiplying and solving for x gives $5x = 4(12) \rightarrow x = 9.6$ or $x = 9\frac{3}{5}$.

20. **(J)** To find the area of a rectangle use the formula $A = L \cdot W$. The problem states the length and width are $4x - 3$ and $2x^2 + 7$. Substituting these expressions in for L and W in the formula gives $A = (4x - 3) \cdot (2x^2 + 7)$. Multiplying the expressions together gives $A = 8x^3 + 28x - 6x^2 - 21$. Rewriting in standard form gives $A = 8x^3 - 6x^2 + 28x - 21$.

21. **(B)** Building a prime factor tree for 2,100 gives the prime factorization as $2 \cdot 2 \cdot 3 \cdot 5 \cdot 5 \cdot 7 = 2^2 \cdot 3 \cdot 5^2 \cdot 7$.

22. **(J)** If Jean spent 90% of her vacation money, the percent that remained equals $100 - 90 = 10\%$. Setting up a proportion we get $\frac{\%\text{ remained}}{\text{total }\%} = \frac{\text{amount remained}}{\text{total amount}} \rightarrow \frac{10}{100} = \frac{100}{x}$. Cross multiplying and solving for x we get $10x = 10{,}000 \rightarrow x = 1{,}000$.

23. **(D)** To subtract two fractions we must first have a common denominator. Multiplying the first fraction by $\frac{5}{5}$ gives $\frac{5}{5}\cdot\frac{2x+1}{x}-\frac{x-3}{5x}=\frac{5(2x+1)}{5x}-\frac{x-3}{5x}=\frac{10x+5}{5x}-\frac{x-3}{5x}$. Combining the numerators together gives $\frac{10x+5-(x-3)}{5x}=\frac{9x+8}{5x}$.

24. **(J)** Factoring the equation gives $(2x+5)(x-3)=0$. Setting each factor equal to zero and solving gives $2x+5=0\rightarrow x=-\frac{5}{2}$ and $x-3=0\rightarrow x=3$. Keep in mind there are several ways to solve this problem. You could also use the quadratic formula if factoring is not your strength.

25. **(E)** The figure is made up of 5 congruent squares. Each square has side length 4. To find the area of one square, use the formula $A=s^2$. Substituting in 4 for s gives $A=(4)^2=16$. Since there are 5 squares, the total area is $5\cdot 16=80$.

26. **(H)** The given triangle is a 30°–60°–90° right triangle. Using 30°–60°–90° ratios of x, $x\sqrt{3}$, $2x$, we get $x=3$. The question asks us to find $\overline{BC}$, the side opposite the 60° angle, which has the value $x\sqrt{3}$. Plugging in 3 for x gives $\overline{BC}=3\sqrt{3}$.

27. **(D)** To increase the mean of 5 numbers by 3, each number could be increased by 3. Increasing each of 5 numbers by 3 gives a total increase of $3+3+3+3+3=15$.

28. **(K)** The area the dog is able to roam is the shape of a circle with radius equal to the length of the leash, 12 feet. To find the area of a circle use the formula $A=\pi r^2$. Plugging in 12 for the radius gives $A=\pi(12)^2=144\pi$. Using 3.14 for π gives $144(3.14)\approx 452.16\approx 452$.

29. **(C)** Setting up a proportion gives $\frac{\text{original TV size}}{\text{original car size}}=\frac{\text{new TV size}}{\text{new car size}}=\frac{19}{12}=\frac{32}{x}$. Solving for x gives $19x=12(32)\rightarrow x\approx 20.21\approx 20$.

30. **(H)** We need 120 twice, 90, and 42 (the other 90, less the 48 from the house).

31. **(A)** We need to take $\frac{\text{area of garden}}{\text{area of yard}}=\frac{30\cdot 36}{120\cdot 90}=0.10=10\%$.

32. **(G)** A geometric sequence is a sequence of numbers in which each number is multiplied by some fixed constant r, called a common ratio, to find the next number in the sequence. G is correct because year 1: $60\cdot 2=120$; year 2: $120\cdot 2=240$; year 3: $240\cdot 2=480$.

33. **(D)** The little white triangles in the figure are all right triangles with legs x and $2x$. Since the shaded square has area 25 square feet, each side of the square has measure 5 feet, making the hypotenuse of the right triangles each 5. Setting up the Pythagorean Theorem we get $a^2+b^2=c^2\rightarrow x^2+(2x)^2=5^2$. Solving for x we get $x^2+4x^2=25\rightarrow 5x^2=25\rightarrow x=\sqrt{5}$. To find the area of square $ABCD$ we first need to know the length of one side. Each side is made of $x+2x$, which equals $3x$. Substituting for x gives each side of square $ABCD=3\sqrt{5}$. Now, to find the area, square the length of the side of $ABCD$ to get $(3\sqrt{5})^2=45$. This is quite a lengthy problem, but using your eye to approximate the area could help eliminate 3 of the 5 answers, giving you a 50% chance of guessing and saving several minutes of computations.

34. **(H)** The given equation will simplify by dividing the numerator and the denominator by x giving $y = 4 - 2x$. Graph the linear equation with y-intercept 4 and slope -2 to get choice H as the correct answer. Also, this problem could have been solved using a graphing calculator as long as parentheses are put around the numerator. Remember, since x was divided out, a hole will remain when $x = 0$.

35. **(C)** Dividing a plane using a single line splits the plane into two parts: one part on one side of the plane and another part on the other side of the plane.

36. **(G)** To calculate the number of diagonals in a given polygon, use the formula $D = \frac{n(n-3)}{2}$ where n represents the number of sides of the polygon. Substituting 6 for n gives $D = \frac{6(6-3)}{2} = 9$.

37. **(D)** Using the circle formula $(x-h)^2 + (y-k)^2 = r^2$, the center of circle J is at $(-4, -4)$ putting it in the third quadrant and the radius is $\sqrt{16} = 4$, meaning it just touches the x-axis and y-axis from the center.

38. **(F)** Converting each of the fractions to decimals gives $-\frac{3}{5} = -0.6$, $-\frac{4}{7} \approx -0.57$, $-\frac{5}{6} \approx -0.83$, $-\frac{8}{9} = -0.89$. Order the decimals from least to greatest to get $-0.89 < -0.83 < -0.6 < -0.57$, then substitute the fractions back in to get $-\frac{8}{9} < -\frac{5}{6} < -\frac{3}{5} < -\frac{4}{7}$.

39. **(B)** Slope is the change in y divided by the change in x. Since $\overline{QR}$ goes down 3 units and right 4 units from R to Q, the slope is $-\frac{3}{4}$.

40. **(G)** The midpoint of (0, 5) and (4, 2) is $\left(\frac{0+4}{2}, \frac{5+2}{2}\right) = \left(2, \frac{7}{2}\right)$.

41. **(D)** We divide the opposite side by the adjacent side (relative to $\angle PRQ$), which is the definition of the tangent function.

42. **(J)** When the triangle is rotated about the y-axis, $\overline{PQ}$ becomes the radius and diameter = radius × 2.

43. **(A)** Substituting $L = 4$ and $W = 3$ into the formula gives $p = \frac{\pi}{2}\sqrt{2(4^2 + 3^2)} = \frac{\pi}{2}\sqrt{50}$. Simplifying the square root gives $\frac{\pi}{2} \cdot \sqrt{25} \cdot \sqrt{2} = \frac{\pi}{2} \cdot 5 \cdot \sqrt{2} = \frac{5}{2}\pi\sqrt{2}$.

44. **(H)** x is the common denominator you get when combining the two given fractions. The least common denominator of 28 and 126 is 252 because $28 \cdot 9 = 252$ and $126 \cdot 2 = 252$. Therefore, $x = 252$.

45. **(E)** The circumference of a circle is calculated using the formula $C = 2\pi r$. Substituting R for the radius gives $C = 2\pi R$. Since the runner needs to run 5 laps, multiply the circumference by 5 to get $2\pi R \cdot 5 = 10\pi R$.

46. **(G)** Setting up the law of sines we get $\frac{\sin A}{a} = \frac{\sin C}{c} \rightarrow \frac{\sin(105)}{x} = \frac{\sin(35)}{27}$. Angle A is calculated from $180 - (40 + 35) = 105$. Cross multiplying and solving for x gives $27 \cdot \sin(105) = x \cdot \sin(35) \rightarrow x = \frac{27\sin(105)}{\sin(35)}$.

47. **(D)** $(5 - i)^2 = (5 - i)(5 - i)$. Distributing the expression gives $25 - 5i - 5i + i^2$. Recall that $i^2 = -1$, so the expression becomes $25 - 5i - 5i + (-1)$. Combining like terms gives $24 - 10i$.

48. **(J)** Solving the second equation for y gives $y = 19 - 2x$. Substituting this expression into the inequality for y gives $19 - 2x > 12$. Solve the inequality for x to get $-2x > -7 \rightarrow x < 3.5$. Since the solution for x must be an integer, the inequality becomes $x \leq 3$.

49. **(A)** For the product of pq^3t^4 to be greater than zero it must be positive. The only way the product of three expressions can be positive is if each is positive or if exactly two are negative and the other is positive. Since t^4 is always positive, p and q^3 must either both be positive or both be negative; either way, the product of pq must be positive.

50. **(F)** $3^4 = 81$; therefore, $\log_3 81 = 4$. The equation then becomes $4 = x + 1$. Solve for x to get $x = 3$.

51. **(D)** Setting up an equation for the total charge by the flight instructor gives $C = 75 + k\sqrt[3]{t}$ where C is the cost of the flight, k is the constant of variation, and t is time. Substituting 27 for time and \$120 for cost yields the equation $120 = 75 + k\sqrt[3]{27}$. Solving for k gives $120 = 75 + 3k \rightarrow 45 = 3k \rightarrow k = 15$. Now that we know the constant of variation, use it along with $t = 64$ to find the cost of a 64-minute lesson: $C = 75 + 15\sqrt[3]{64} = 75 + 15(4) = \$135$.

52. **(H)** The ratio for the sine of an angle is $\sin d = \dfrac{\text{opposite}}{\text{hypotenuse}} = \dfrac{\overline{AC}}{6}$. Setting this ratio equal to the ratio given in the problem gives the new equation: $\dfrac{\overline{AC}}{6} = 0.8$. Solve for $\overline{AC}$ to get $\overline{AC} = 4.8$. Now that we know the height of the triangle, calculate the area using the formula $A = \dfrac{1}{2}bh = \dfrac{1}{2}(10)(4.8) = 24$.

53. **(E)** Sometimes the best way to find the correct answer is to plug in values and eliminate incorrect answers. Pick values of x and y such that $2x = 3y$, say $x = 3$ and $y = 2$.

We get $|2(3) + 3(2)| = |2(3) - 3(2)| \rightarrow |12| = |0| \rightarrow 12 = 0$.
This is not true, which eliminates choices B and C.

Then, let $x = 0$ and $y = 1$. We get $|2(0) + 3(1)| = |2(0) - 3(1)| \rightarrow |3| = |-3| \rightarrow 3 = 3$, which is true. This eliminates choices A and D. Therefore, **E** is the correct answer.

54. **(K)** There have to be 20 or more pennies since there are 20 more pennies than quarters. Since the total ends in 3, the number of pennies must end in 3 or 8 because the other coins have 0s or 5s in their ones places and combinations of nickels, dimes, and quarters can only have 0s or 5s in the ones place. Thus, the answer must be K (if the sum of the nickels, dimes, and quarters ended in 0 and there were _5 pennies, the total would end in 8; if the sum of the nickels, dimes, and quarters ended in 5 and there were _3 pennies, the total would end in 8). This problem can also be solved using equations.

55. **(D)** Substituting the given point for x and y into the equation and solving for A gives $11 = (A + 3)(3) + 5 \rightarrow 11 = 3A + 9 + 5 \rightarrow 11 = 3A + 14 \rightarrow A = -1$. Now, to find the slope we need to get the equation into $y = mx + b$ form. Substituting $A = -1$ we get $y = 2x + 5$, so the slope is 2.

56. **(J)** To find the area of a trapezoid we need to know the heights of each of the trapezoids. Draw a strategic line parallel to $\overline{BF}$ to make two special 3-4-5 and 5-12-13 right triangles at the top of the figure. Now that we know the heights of the two trapezoids are 4 and 12, we can use the area of a trapezoid formula: $A=\frac{1}{2}(b_1+b_2)\cdot h$. The area of the smaller trapezoid is $A=\frac{1}{2}(7+4)\cdot 4=22$. The area of the larger trapezoid is $A=\frac{1}{2}(9+4)\cdot 12=78$. The ratio of the two trapezoids is now $\frac{22}{78}=\frac{11}{39}\rightarrow 11{:}39$.

57. **(D)** Substituting $x + 1$ for y in the first equation gives $x + 1 = x^2 - 5$. Solving for x gives $x^2 - x - 6 = 0$. Factor to get $(x-3)(x+2) = 0$. Solve for x: $x - 3 = 0 \rightarrow x = 3$ and $x + 2 = 0 \rightarrow x = -2$. Substitute these values back into either equation for x to solve for y. Solving for y we get $y = (3) + 1 \rightarrow y = 4$ and $y = (-2) + 1 \rightarrow y = -1$, so the two points of intersection are (3, 4) and (–2, –1).

58. **(K)** To find the sum of the interior angles of a septagon, use the formula $(n - 2) \cdot 180$. Substituting 7 for n gives $(7 - 2) \cdot 180 = 900$. Since two of the angles have measures 70° and 115° the remaining angles have a sum of 900 – (70 + 115) = 715°.

59. **(E)** "The product of y and 4 is x" can be represented as the equation $y \cdot 4 = x$. Solving for y gives $y=\frac{x}{4}$. The question asks to find the "sum of y and 4 in terms of x." Writing this as an expression we get $y + 4$. Substitute $\frac{x}{4}$ for y to get $\frac{x}{4}+4$. Add the two fractions to get $\frac{x}{4}+\frac{16}{4}=\frac{x+16}{4}$.

60. **(F)** $\cos\frac{7\pi}{12}=\cos\left(\frac{\pi}{3}+\frac{\pi}{4}\right)$. Using the given formula, the expression becomes $\cos\left(\frac{\pi}{3}\right)\cdot\cos\left(\frac{\pi}{4}\right)-\sin\left(\frac{\pi}{3}\right)\cdot\sin\left(\frac{\pi}{4}\right)$. Substituting the values from the chart gives $\frac{1}{2}\cdot\frac{\sqrt{2}}{2}-\frac{\sqrt{3}}{2}\cdot\frac{\sqrt{2}}{2}=\frac{\sqrt{2}}{4}-\frac{\sqrt{6}}{4}=\frac{\sqrt{2}-\sqrt{6}}{4}$. You can also ignore the chart, set your calculator in radian mode, and get the decimal answer, –0.2588. You would then evaluate all the possible answers as decimals and also arrive at choice F as correct.

Reading

1. **(B)** The fourth paragraph reveals that the narrator met her boyfriend when he was one of the Youth Players that she had gone to see on a school outing, and describes her earliest memories of him. Though it does not explicitly depict their meeting, this is still how she first learned of his existence.

2. **(H)** The last sentence of the first paragraph establishes that the narrator works an office job to pay the bills for both herself and her boyfriend, so that her boyfriend can pursue his music. This means she is *generous* (because she supports him) and *pragmatic* (which means that she is a logical person who does what is necessary to achieve specific goals).

3. **(D)** Paragraph 2, which concerns the narrator's parents, states that they "did not have in their comprehension what it was that she wanted to do." Choice D simply paraphrases this without adding anything further, and so cannot possibly be wrong.

4. **(J)** The narrator's boyfriend is a cellist, and so when the narrator says "the cello is the instrument I love best," she means that she loves him and his playing more than her own comparatively meager musical talent. This is the only one of the four choices where what the narrator says works as a metaphor, whereas the other three are very similar literal paraphrases of one another. (As in so many places on the ACT, "which of these things is not like the others" is a very good strategy here!)

5. **(C)** Although it does not become clear until the last three paragraphs, the main conflict concerns the tension and emotional distance between the narrator and her boyfriend. Everything else serves merely as background to underscore this.

6. **(J)** Although saying that the narrator views her boyfriend as a *talented musician whose opinion she respects* does not tell the whole story, there is certainly nothing in it that is incorrect. (Remember, on the ACT Reading, the right answer is just the one with nothing wrong in it!)

7. **(A)** Although all of the answer choices seem very similar, there are important differences between them, and the line in question most nearly means that *she can tell something is wrong because of the music he plays.* The point of the paragraph is that his feelings are revealed through his music despite his efforts to conceal them.

8. **(H)** It is most directly established in Paragraph 6 (lines 47–57) that the narrator loves listening to her boyfriend play the cello and enjoys the life of a musician's partner.

9. **(B)** The descriptions in Paragraph 6 of the narrator falling asleep to the sound of her boyfriend's playing and smiling unconsciously at his solos are evidence of emotional intimacy. This is all that choice B suggests, and so it is the right answer.

10. **(J)** Lines 40–43 establish that the narrator's boyfriend was honest with her about the fact that her talents would not be sufficient for her to make a living by playing the flute.

11. **(C)** The main idea of the passage is that computer technology is steadily being incorporated into more and more things that are not themselves computers. This can be simply paraphrased as "the changing roles computers have in people's lives," and choice C doesn't assert anything beyond this.

12. **(G)** Nowhere in the passage does the *opinion of a scientist* appear (a clue to this would be the fact that the author never incorporates a single proper name or direct quote).

13. **(D)** *Ubiquitous* means "ever-present" (or "all over the place"). The subsequent sentence deals with the sheer number of transistors and embedded systems being produced, and so it should have been possible to intuit this.

14. **(H)** The passage never hints that more *power and batteries* will be required to run computers, and is in fact explicitly contradicted in lines 79–83, so all of the answer choices are correct EXCEPT this one. And regardless of the passage, the suggestion that computers in the future would need "more batteries" probably sounded funny to you. (It is always

a good idea to *remember real life* on the ACT Reading; although outside knowledge is never necessary, it can reliably be used to eliminate wrong answers!)

15. **(A)** The statement "Computers will be so much a part of everyday life that people will hardly notice them" is essentially a paraphrase of the main idea of the passage, which is stated most directly in the final sentence (lines 96–98). Remembering the right answers to questions 11, 13, and 14 would also be a big help here.

16. **(G)** Yet again, the correct answer is a paraphrase of the main idea: that computers will be so omnipresent that people will hardly notice them. (You may have thought that the fact that choice G is nearly identical to the correct answer on question 15 meant it was a trick, but this is not how the ACT Reading typically works: the main idea is the main idea, and several right answers on a given passage will more or less be paraphrases of the main idea!)

17. **(A)** The *future entertainment system* is described in Paragraph 1, and nothing about a satellite is mentioned. All of the other choices are mentioned EXCEPT this one.

18. **(J)** The subsequent sentence describes how people used to use computers *occasionally for specific tasks*. This is what the author means by *passive appliances*, since it stands in sharp contrast to today's interactive devices that are at the center of so many modern activities, as described throughout the passage.

19. **(C)** Lines 20–27 establish that the number of uses for microprocessors is increasing, and lines 33–38 establish that the number of microprocessors themselves is also dramatically increasing. This is overwhelmingly the main focus and "point" of Paragraph 2.

20. **(G)** All of the choices are mentioned (although not always word-for-word) in Paragraph 1 EXCEPT *power profiles*.

21. **(B)** The passage never brings up science, and never discusses poetry as a source of factual information.

22. **(J)** The "poetical *faculty*" is the *ability* to write poetry.

23. **(C)** The passage mentions how poetry is "to be desired" at such times—i.e., that it can ameliorate the bad influence of selfishness.

24. **(F)** Shelley's famous closing phrase "Poets are the unacknowledged legislators of the world" concerns poetry's influence on society—*legislators* means "lawmakers," and *unacknowledged* means "not openly admitted or known."

25. **(C)** The author mentions *Disobedience* merely as a "very long poem" that she "recently completed"—there is no indication that it is her *most famous* work.

26. **(F)** The quoted snippets of conversation in these lines represent poetry fans trying to characterize the author, something that she regards as pressure coming from society.

27. **(B)** Throughout the passage, the author discusses wanting to prevent her own poetic voice (i.e., her "mode of expression") from being influenced (or "contaminated") by tradition and society.

28. **(J)** Passage A sees poets as serving and channeling some ultimate truth that exists outside themselves (in lines 42–45, for example), whereas the author of Passage B talks only about her own "experience."

29. **(A)** Nothing about reading poetry in books versus hearing it read aloud appears in either passage.

30. **(G)** Despite their differences, both Shelley and Notley agree that poetry can change society for the better, at least when it is done well.

31. **(B)** Although he doesn't seem especially angry about it or necessarily want things to be any different, the author would clearly agree with the simple fact that science-fiction films can misinform people about how certain principles work in real life. (Well, don't they?) The last sentence of Paragraph 1 and the first few sentences of Paragraph 3 make this pretty clear.

32. **(J)** The author opens the paragraph by deriding the idea of a plasma's being "directed" (that's why it's in quotation marks), before going on to explain that this is because a plasma is basically a gas.

33. **(A)** Lines 54–57 explicitly state that the *aurora borealis*, or "northern lights," is composed of plasma.

34. **(J)** *Convoluted* means "hard to follow or make sense of," and if one is speaking casually, then *confusing* works as a synonym (remember, the author's point here is that the explanation makes no sense).

35. **(C)** The author doesn't seem especially emotionally invested in this debate one way or the other (he is simply calmly analyzing the issue), and so it is probably best to say that he would simply be "interested" in the new opportunities in the quest for real lightsabers.

36. **(G)** The author opens the paragraph with a joke about how the explanation in the previous paragraph made no sense, and goes on to mock the idea of compact crystal batteries powerful enough to generate plasma, as well as the fact that even the writers of the extended *Star Wars* universe themselves seem to know how ridiculous this is, since they bothered to specify that the crystals must, in effect, be rendered magical by the mystical Jedi and Sith warriors in some sort of meditation ritual.

37. **(A)** The author spends lines 30–37 mocking the idea that crystals could play any role whatsoever in the generation, direction, or containment of plasma.

38. **(F)** The passage establishes repeatedly in lines 41–52 that plasmas can indeed be contained by magnetic fields.

39. **(B)** The author closes the paragraph by stating that enthusiastic *Star Wars* "superfans" will probably never abandon the quest for a real lightsaber.

40. **(H)** Although the idea that laser or plasma "blades" would just pass through each other like the beams of two flashlights has often been suggested as an obstacle to real lightsabers, this particular passage never brings this up.

Science

1. **(D)** If there were a correlation one way or the other between mass and orbital distance, then the planets in Table 2 would be getting either consistently larger or smaller as the orbital distances increase. But they're not: there are large and small planets all over the place. For example, the two largest planets have orbital distances of 4.0 and 0.35, whereas the two smallest planets have orbital distances of 4.0 and 0.25. Therefore, there is no correlation between mass and orbital distance.

2. **(F)** By looking at Table 1, we know that the answer has to be either OGLE TR 132 or Gliese 777, because those are the two stars with Gas Giants orbiting them. Next, we look at Table 2 and see that the planet orbiting Gliese 777 (500 Earth masses) is bigger than the planet orbiting OGLE TR 132 (315 Earth masses).

3. **(D)** Table 1 establishes the only planet type with a mass over 250 Earth masses and composed of hydrogen is a Gas Giant.

4. **(G)** Table 1 shows the planets orbiting Gliese 581 are Water type with a mass range of 0.5–25 Earth masses. Also, Table 2 shows the most massive planet is orbiting Gliese 777. Therefore, the statement is NOT true and must be correct.

5. **(A)** Every planet shown in Table 2 has a mass less than 20 Earth masses. The Kepler 11 planet has a mass of 15 and the HD 6980 planet has a mass of 15.

6. **(H)** Gliese 581 orbits around Gas Giant and Water planets and with a mass of 20 the planet must be a water type. Water classification also has silicates in its composition.

7. **(A)** All you have to do here is go to Figure 1, look at the (vertical) column for Zone 5, and find the biggest number. The biggest number is 0.93, which is in the (horizontal) column for coal.

8. **(G)** The numbers across zones vary more in Table 1 (energy savings) than they do in Table 2 (GHGs avoided). In Table 2, the numbers for all three zones are often identical, and are still very close even when they are not identical.

9. **(D)** In Figure 1, the black bar representing GHG payback for Zone 3 stops just under the line representing 10 years, and so 9 years is clearly the closest of the answer choices.

10. **(J)** All the question is asking is "Which box in Table 1 has the highest number in it, not counting averages and totals?" The highest number is 4.2, representing the savings for natural gas in Zone 1.

11. **(D)** The bars in Figure 1 represent how long it takes to profit from the installation of plastic foam insulation. Since both the white and black bars in Zone 3 have "run out" by the 10-year mark, this means that at that point the customer will have both saved on energy costs and produced fewer pounds of GHGs.

12. **(F)** In Table 1, the three highest numbers in the U.S. Average column, starting with the highest and decreasing, are for natural gas (2.37), coal (0.76), and nuclear (0.25).

13. **(C)** With some of the lowest BTU, hydropower is one of the least efficient on Table 1, second only to the "other" category.

14. **(H)** In Table 1, the numbers in the Resistance column get bigger trial by trial, and the numbers in the Current column get smaller trial by trial. Therefore, as the resistance increased, the current decreased.

15. **(B)** This is a simple "Go Up, Hit Line, Go Over" question. In Figure 2, a diameter of 0.5 mm would be a little less than halfway between 0.41 and 0.68 mm. Moving upward from this point to the black line, we hit it somewhere around the line representing a resistance of 1 ohm. (The answer can also be gotten by looking at Table 2 and doing math, but getting it from Figure 2 is easier.)

16. **(G)** In Experiment 2, the student uses three different wires of varying diameters.

17. **(C)** Both Table 1 and Table 2 show current decreasing as resistance increases, and vice versa. Remembering the answer to question 12 would be a big help here. (It is often the case on the ACT Science that two questions in the same passage will be closely related!)

18. **(F)** $V = IR$ from the opening paragraph and Experiment 2 establishes that the largest diameter will allow the greatest current. Therefore, the largest voltage from the choices and the largest diameter would be 5 volts and a 0.5-mm diameter.

19. **(C)** We know from Table 2 that as diameter increases and resistance decreases the current increases. The current closest to 5 amperes is 4.91 amperes; therefore, we need a diameter of 1.04 mm and a resistance of 0.20 ohms.

20. **(G)** All other factors must remain constant (control variable) except the factor(s) being tested. Therefore, only wire length should be varied.

21. **(A)** This is correct because of the data presented in Table 2. The third column has the heading "River Water." The largest number in that column is the first one, 1.50. The first row represents Trial 1.

22. **(G)** This is correct because of the data presented in Table 3. To find the correct answer, the values for the columns with the headings PO_4 must be compared—the one on the left side of the table under "Added µg/ml" and the one on the right side of the table under "Found µg/ml." For Trial 2 the amount under "Found µg/ml" is 1.56, whereas the number under "Added µg/ml" is 2.00.

23. **(C)** This is correct because of the data presented in Table 1. Compare the values in the three columns under the heading "Mg." For every trial the value under the concentration 2.5 ppm is the highest, whereas the value under the concentration 4.0 ppm is in the middle, and the value under the concentration 4.5 ppm is the lowest.

24. **(G)** This is correct because of the data presented in Table 2. Find the smallest number in the table. It is 0.50, found in the column for PO_4 and the row for Trial 3, making this the correct answer.

25. **(D)** This is correct because of the data presented in Table 1. For Trials 1–4, each subsequent trial used a higher concentration of SO_4. Compare this to the values in the column with the heading "4.5 ppm" to see that as the SO_4 concentration increased, the amount of Mg absorbed also increased.

26. **(G)** In Trials 1, 3 and 4 the amount of silicate found was below the amount added. However, in Trial 2 the scientists added 1.50 μg/ml and the higher amount of 1.60 μg/ml was found. Therefore, results were inconsistent and not under the amount added.

27. **(B)** In the third sentence of her first paragraph, Researcher 2 mentions ozone as one of the air pollutants that had their concentrations lowered by a decrease in traffic, which also led to a decrease in asthma-related emergencies. Therefore, she would expect a decrease in ozone levels to lead to a decrease in the prevalence of asthma.

28. **(H)** Researcher 1 thinks that asthma is caused by allergens, and mentions dogs and cats as being among these allergens in the middle of her first paragraph. Therefore, she would view pet owners as more likely to have asthma.

29. **(A)** In her second paragraph, Researcher 1 states that high IgE levels and asthma are positively correlated, and that a "high" IgE level is considered to be one above 200 IU/ml. Therefore, she would regard someone with an IgE level of 400 IU/ml as being significantly at risk for asthma.

30. **(J)** In her first paragraph, Researcher 1 names indoor allergens as a cause of asthma, and suggests that less exposure to outside air increased the detrimental effects of these allergens (*Houses are built more tightly and are better insulated*). Therefore, she would expect *more circulation* and *more outside air* to lessen the prevalence of asthma.

31. **(D)** Researcher 1 blames asthma on indoor allergens, and Researcher 2 blames asthma on air pollution. Since these are both things that people can do something about, both researchers would agree that *measures can be taken to lower a person's risk of developing asthma.*

32. **(G)** Researcher 2 names CO as one of the air pollutants linked to high rates of asthma-related emergencies. Therefore, she would expect CO concentration and asthma rates to increase concurrently. Only choice G depicts a graph where CO and cases of asthma increase together, as indicated by the line going steadily upward from left to right.

33. **(C)** Researcher 2 regards air pollution (of which high ozone levels are a component) as a cause of asthma. Therefore, she would expect asthma rates to have been lower 20 years ago when there was less air pollution (including lower ozone levels).

34. **(F)** If the new vaccine introduced in 1991 had really been more effective, then rates of pertussis would have dropped thereafter, but instead they increased (the line starts going upward). Therefore, the data in Figure 2 do not support this claim.

35. **(C)** According to Figure 1, the only stage in which someone would have a cough *and* be contagious is the paroxysmal stage. Although Figure 1 establishes that medication can significantly shorten the period of time that one is contagious, the fact that the person in the question is medicated is superfluous information. (Questions on the ACT Science frequently provide more information than is necessary to answer the question!)

36. **(H)** Figure 1 states that the two stages in which a patient is contagious are the catarrhal and the paroxysmal. It also shows that the maximum amount of time the catarrhal stage can last is 2 weeks, and that the maximum amount of time the paroxysmal stage can last is 6 weeks. Therefore, the maximum amount of time a patient can be contagious is 8 weeks.

37. **(B)** The highest bars in Figure 3 are the ones representing the 10–14 and 15–19 age groups, and so Figure 3 does not support the idea that young children are the most susceptible to pertussis.

38. **(J)** The claim that vaccine immunity wanes after 5–10 years is consistent with the data in Figure 3, which indicates the greatest numbers of pertussis cases are in children ages 10–19.

39. **(C)** Figure 1 states that antibiotics make a big difference in how long pertussis communicability lasts. Therefore, the assertion that pertussis cannot be treated with antibiotics is the one that is NOT true.

40. **(F)** A decrease in the number of cases from approximately 800,000 in 2004 to 600,000 in 2007 may show that the new vaccine is protecting people from the spread of the disease.

Writing Sample

ZOOS

I'll admit that I was a little dismayed to see that the essay prompt concerned zoos, and the question of whether they do good work and should continue to exist or are criminally unfair to the animals and should become a thing of the past. To be perfectly honest, I feel no small amount of hesitation when it comes to writing about this issue—not because I don't feel strongly about it, but because I do.

The Bronx Zoo in New York City is probably my favorite place on the face of the earth. I have gone there every single summer with my father ever since I was too young to even remember, and even though I'm now at an age where most people would be embarrassed to go places with their parents, I still look forward to it every year. I feel like many of the animals are family friends that I've grown up with. Even just seeing commercials for the zoo on TV almost brings a tear to my eye. Because of all this, I feel like I am heavily biased and couldn't possibly be impartial with regard to this issue. If I were a legislator and some sort of resolution concerning the fate of zoos were coming to a vote, I feel I would be honor-bound to recuse myself.

Therefore, it brings me some relief to see Perspective #1 arguing that zoos teach young people to love nature, and that this will in turn make future generations more likely to conserve it. I suppose you could say

I'm living proof that a person knows what he or she is talking about. When it's a friend or relative's birthday, I always get them one of those sponsorships of an endangered animal in their name, and last year I even started a club at my school to raise awareness of climate change and inform people of things they can do to help fight it (melting icecaps are especially hard on my favorites, the polar bears!).

So maybe it's not that I'm "biased" so much as that, in my case, exposure to zoos has done exactly what it's supposed to do: fill me with love, respect, and concern for the animals with whom we humans share (or <u>ought</u> to share) the planet. But although it pains me to consider the possibility, I can't just let myself ignore the idea that zoo animals can be miserable. I couldn't very well say that I "love" the animals in the zoo if they're suffering and I don't care, could I?

All my research and reading on animals over the years backs up the fact one can make the distinction that life in a zoo is much more harmful to certain animals than to others. I support Great Ape Project, which argues that the great apes (chimpanzees, bonobos, gorillas, and orangutans) should be afforded human rights, which in turn would mean that keeping one in a zoo is unlawful imprisonment. And I wholeheartedly agree that trying to keep large ocean predators like orcas or great white sharks in aquariums is unconscionable. No matter how much space they give one of these awesome hunting machines that evolution has spent so many millions of years perfecting, it always dies in a matter of days (I would say of a broken heart, but I can't really back that up scientifically).

But although some animals clearly just weren't meant to be kept in captivity, for other animals it may be the best option at this point. For certain large herbivorous mammals like elephants and rhinos that are frequently the targets of poachers and therefore critically endangered in the wild, well-funded zoos that can give them comfortable homes might be their only chance at this point. Endangered carnivores like the tiger are harder to keep happy in a zoo, but I'm sure both humans and tigers would agree that tigers in zoos would be better than no tigers at all. Ideally, of course, humans would be wise enough to leave them in peace and let them thrive in their natural environments – but we animal lovers have no control over what less enlightened people do, so rescuing certain animals into zoos is the best option that lies within our power.

I hope that in the future there will be no need for zoos, because the human race will have reined in its overpopulation and its destruction of the environment to the point where all my beloved animal friends can naturally do the things they were meant to do in the places they were meant to do them, while interested and appreciative humans of all ages watch them over satellite feeds. But don't see that happening anytime soon—so instead, I hope to see you this summer at the zoo!

ANSWER SHEET
Practice Test 2

Directions: Mark one answer only for each question. Make the mark dark. Erase completely any mark made in error. (Additional or stray marks will be counted as mistakes.)

English

1. Ⓐ Ⓑ Ⓒ Ⓓ
2. Ⓕ Ⓖ Ⓗ Ⓙ
3. Ⓐ Ⓑ Ⓒ Ⓓ
4. Ⓕ Ⓖ Ⓗ Ⓙ
5. Ⓐ Ⓑ Ⓒ Ⓓ
6. Ⓕ Ⓖ Ⓗ Ⓙ
7. Ⓐ Ⓑ Ⓒ Ⓓ
8. Ⓕ Ⓖ Ⓗ Ⓙ
9. Ⓐ Ⓑ Ⓒ Ⓓ
10. Ⓕ Ⓖ Ⓗ Ⓙ
11. Ⓐ Ⓑ Ⓒ Ⓓ
12. Ⓕ Ⓖ Ⓗ Ⓙ
13. Ⓐ Ⓑ Ⓒ Ⓓ
14. Ⓕ Ⓖ Ⓗ Ⓙ
15. Ⓐ Ⓑ Ⓒ Ⓓ
16. Ⓕ Ⓖ Ⓗ Ⓙ
17. Ⓐ Ⓑ Ⓒ Ⓓ
18. Ⓕ Ⓖ Ⓗ Ⓙ
19. Ⓐ Ⓑ Ⓒ Ⓓ
20. Ⓕ Ⓖ Ⓗ Ⓙ
21. Ⓐ Ⓑ Ⓒ Ⓓ
22. Ⓕ Ⓖ Ⓗ Ⓙ
23. Ⓐ Ⓑ Ⓒ Ⓓ
24. Ⓕ Ⓖ Ⓗ Ⓙ
25. Ⓐ Ⓑ Ⓒ Ⓓ
26. Ⓕ Ⓖ Ⓗ Ⓙ
27. Ⓐ Ⓑ Ⓒ Ⓓ
28. Ⓕ Ⓖ Ⓗ Ⓙ
29. Ⓐ Ⓑ Ⓒ Ⓓ
30. Ⓕ Ⓖ Ⓗ Ⓙ
31. Ⓐ Ⓑ Ⓒ Ⓓ
32. Ⓕ Ⓖ Ⓗ Ⓙ
33. Ⓐ Ⓑ Ⓒ Ⓓ
34. Ⓕ Ⓖ Ⓗ Ⓙ
35. Ⓐ Ⓑ Ⓒ Ⓓ
36. Ⓕ Ⓖ Ⓗ Ⓙ
37. Ⓐ Ⓑ Ⓒ Ⓓ
38. Ⓕ Ⓖ Ⓗ Ⓙ
39. Ⓐ Ⓑ Ⓒ Ⓓ
40. Ⓕ Ⓖ Ⓗ Ⓙ
41. Ⓐ Ⓑ Ⓒ Ⓓ
42. Ⓕ Ⓖ Ⓗ Ⓙ
43. Ⓐ Ⓑ Ⓒ Ⓓ
44. Ⓕ Ⓖ Ⓗ Ⓙ
45. Ⓐ Ⓑ Ⓒ Ⓓ
46. Ⓕ Ⓖ Ⓗ Ⓙ
47. Ⓐ Ⓑ Ⓒ Ⓓ
48. Ⓕ Ⓖ Ⓗ Ⓙ
49. Ⓐ Ⓑ Ⓒ Ⓓ
50. Ⓕ Ⓖ Ⓗ Ⓙ
51. Ⓐ Ⓑ Ⓒ Ⓓ
52. Ⓕ Ⓖ Ⓗ Ⓙ
53. Ⓐ Ⓑ Ⓒ Ⓓ
54. Ⓕ Ⓖ Ⓗ Ⓙ
55. Ⓐ Ⓑ Ⓒ Ⓓ
56. Ⓕ Ⓖ Ⓗ Ⓙ
57. Ⓐ Ⓑ Ⓒ Ⓓ
58. Ⓕ Ⓖ Ⓗ Ⓙ
59. Ⓐ Ⓑ Ⓒ Ⓓ
60. Ⓕ Ⓖ Ⓗ Ⓙ
61. Ⓐ Ⓑ Ⓒ Ⓓ
62. Ⓕ Ⓖ Ⓗ Ⓙ
63. Ⓐ Ⓑ Ⓒ Ⓓ
64. Ⓕ Ⓖ Ⓗ Ⓙ
65. Ⓐ Ⓑ Ⓒ Ⓓ
66. Ⓕ Ⓖ Ⓗ Ⓙ
67. Ⓐ Ⓑ Ⓒ Ⓓ
68. Ⓕ Ⓖ Ⓗ Ⓙ
69. Ⓐ Ⓑ Ⓒ Ⓓ
70. Ⓕ Ⓖ Ⓗ Ⓙ
71. Ⓐ Ⓑ Ⓒ Ⓓ
72. Ⓕ Ⓖ Ⓗ Ⓙ
73. Ⓐ Ⓑ Ⓒ Ⓓ
74. Ⓕ Ⓖ Ⓗ Ⓙ
75. Ⓐ Ⓑ Ⓒ Ⓓ

Mathematics

1. Ⓐ Ⓑ Ⓒ Ⓓ Ⓔ
2. Ⓕ Ⓖ Ⓗ Ⓙ Ⓚ
3. Ⓐ Ⓑ Ⓒ Ⓓ Ⓔ
4. Ⓕ Ⓖ Ⓗ Ⓙ Ⓚ
5. Ⓐ Ⓑ Ⓒ Ⓓ Ⓔ
6. Ⓕ Ⓖ Ⓗ Ⓙ Ⓚ
7. Ⓐ Ⓑ Ⓒ Ⓓ Ⓔ
8. Ⓕ Ⓖ Ⓗ Ⓙ Ⓚ
9. Ⓐ Ⓑ Ⓒ Ⓓ Ⓔ
10. Ⓕ Ⓖ Ⓗ Ⓙ Ⓚ
11. Ⓐ Ⓑ Ⓒ Ⓓ Ⓔ
12. Ⓕ Ⓖ Ⓗ Ⓙ Ⓚ
13. Ⓐ Ⓑ Ⓒ Ⓓ Ⓔ
14. Ⓕ Ⓖ Ⓗ Ⓙ Ⓚ
15. Ⓐ Ⓑ Ⓒ Ⓓ Ⓔ
16. Ⓕ Ⓖ Ⓗ Ⓙ Ⓚ
17. Ⓐ Ⓑ Ⓒ Ⓓ Ⓔ
18. Ⓕ Ⓖ Ⓗ Ⓙ Ⓚ
19. Ⓐ Ⓑ Ⓒ Ⓓ Ⓔ
20. Ⓕ Ⓖ Ⓗ Ⓙ Ⓚ
21. Ⓐ Ⓑ Ⓒ Ⓓ Ⓔ
22. Ⓕ Ⓖ Ⓗ Ⓙ Ⓚ
23. Ⓐ Ⓑ Ⓒ Ⓓ Ⓔ
24. Ⓕ Ⓖ Ⓗ Ⓙ Ⓚ
25. Ⓐ Ⓑ Ⓒ Ⓓ Ⓔ
26. Ⓕ Ⓖ Ⓗ Ⓙ Ⓚ
27. Ⓐ Ⓑ Ⓒ Ⓓ Ⓔ
28. Ⓕ Ⓖ Ⓗ Ⓙ Ⓚ
29. Ⓐ Ⓑ Ⓒ Ⓓ Ⓔ
30. Ⓕ Ⓖ Ⓗ Ⓙ Ⓚ
31. Ⓐ Ⓑ Ⓒ Ⓓ Ⓔ
32. Ⓕ Ⓖ Ⓗ Ⓙ Ⓚ
33. Ⓐ Ⓑ Ⓒ Ⓓ Ⓔ
34. Ⓕ Ⓖ Ⓗ Ⓙ Ⓚ
35. Ⓐ Ⓑ Ⓒ Ⓓ Ⓔ
36. Ⓕ Ⓖ Ⓗ Ⓙ Ⓚ
37. Ⓐ Ⓑ Ⓒ Ⓓ Ⓔ
38. Ⓕ Ⓖ Ⓗ Ⓙ Ⓚ
39. Ⓐ Ⓑ Ⓒ Ⓓ Ⓔ
40. Ⓕ Ⓖ Ⓗ Ⓙ Ⓚ
41. Ⓐ Ⓑ Ⓒ Ⓓ Ⓔ
42. Ⓕ Ⓖ Ⓗ Ⓙ Ⓚ
43. Ⓐ Ⓑ Ⓒ Ⓓ Ⓔ
44. Ⓕ Ⓖ Ⓗ Ⓙ Ⓚ
45. Ⓐ Ⓑ Ⓒ Ⓓ Ⓔ
46. Ⓕ Ⓖ Ⓗ Ⓙ Ⓚ
47. Ⓐ Ⓑ Ⓒ Ⓓ Ⓔ
48. Ⓕ Ⓖ Ⓗ Ⓙ Ⓚ
49. Ⓐ Ⓑ Ⓒ Ⓓ Ⓔ
50. Ⓕ Ⓖ Ⓗ Ⓙ Ⓚ
51. Ⓐ Ⓑ Ⓒ Ⓓ Ⓔ
52. Ⓕ Ⓖ Ⓗ Ⓙ Ⓚ
53. Ⓐ Ⓑ Ⓒ Ⓓ Ⓔ
54. Ⓕ Ⓖ Ⓗ Ⓙ Ⓚ
55. Ⓐ Ⓑ Ⓒ Ⓓ Ⓔ
56. Ⓕ Ⓖ Ⓗ Ⓙ Ⓚ
57. Ⓐ Ⓑ Ⓒ Ⓓ Ⓔ
58. Ⓕ Ⓖ Ⓗ Ⓙ Ⓚ
59. Ⓐ Ⓑ Ⓒ Ⓓ Ⓔ
60. Ⓕ Ⓖ Ⓗ Ⓙ Ⓚ

ANSWER SHEET
Practice Test 2

Reading

1. Ⓐ Ⓑ Ⓒ Ⓓ	9. Ⓐ Ⓑ Ⓒ Ⓓ	17. Ⓐ Ⓑ Ⓒ Ⓓ	25. Ⓐ Ⓑ Ⓒ Ⓓ	33. Ⓐ Ⓑ Ⓒ Ⓓ
2. Ⓕ Ⓖ Ⓗ Ⓙ	10. Ⓕ Ⓖ Ⓗ Ⓙ	18. Ⓕ Ⓖ Ⓗ Ⓙ	26. Ⓕ Ⓖ Ⓗ Ⓙ	34. Ⓕ Ⓖ Ⓗ Ⓙ
3. Ⓐ Ⓑ Ⓒ Ⓓ	11. Ⓐ Ⓑ Ⓒ Ⓓ	19. Ⓐ Ⓑ Ⓒ Ⓓ	27. Ⓐ Ⓑ Ⓒ Ⓓ	35. Ⓐ Ⓑ Ⓒ Ⓓ
4. Ⓕ Ⓖ Ⓗ Ⓙ	12. Ⓕ Ⓖ Ⓗ Ⓙ	20. Ⓕ Ⓖ Ⓗ Ⓙ	28. Ⓕ Ⓖ Ⓗ Ⓙ	36. Ⓕ Ⓖ Ⓗ Ⓙ
5. Ⓐ Ⓑ Ⓒ Ⓓ	13. Ⓐ Ⓑ Ⓒ Ⓓ	21. Ⓐ Ⓑ Ⓒ Ⓓ	29. Ⓐ Ⓑ Ⓒ Ⓓ	37. Ⓐ Ⓑ Ⓒ Ⓓ
6. Ⓕ Ⓖ Ⓗ Ⓙ	14. Ⓕ Ⓖ Ⓗ Ⓙ	22. Ⓕ Ⓖ Ⓗ Ⓙ	30. Ⓕ Ⓖ Ⓗ Ⓙ	38. Ⓕ Ⓖ Ⓗ Ⓙ
7. Ⓐ Ⓑ Ⓒ Ⓓ	15. Ⓐ Ⓑ Ⓒ Ⓓ	23. Ⓐ Ⓑ Ⓒ Ⓓ	31. Ⓐ Ⓑ Ⓒ Ⓓ	39. Ⓐ Ⓑ Ⓒ Ⓓ
8. Ⓕ Ⓖ Ⓗ Ⓙ	16. Ⓕ Ⓖ Ⓗ Ⓙ	24. Ⓕ Ⓖ Ⓗ Ⓙ	32. Ⓕ Ⓖ Ⓗ Ⓙ	40. Ⓕ Ⓖ Ⓗ Ⓙ

Science

1. Ⓐ Ⓑ Ⓒ Ⓓ	9. Ⓐ Ⓑ Ⓒ Ⓓ	17. Ⓐ Ⓑ Ⓒ Ⓓ	25. Ⓐ Ⓑ Ⓒ Ⓓ	33. Ⓐ Ⓑ Ⓒ Ⓓ
2. Ⓕ Ⓖ Ⓗ Ⓙ	10. Ⓕ Ⓖ Ⓗ Ⓙ	18. Ⓕ Ⓖ Ⓗ Ⓙ	26. Ⓕ Ⓖ Ⓗ Ⓙ	34. Ⓕ Ⓖ Ⓗ Ⓙ
3. Ⓐ Ⓑ Ⓒ Ⓓ	11. Ⓐ Ⓑ Ⓒ Ⓓ	19. Ⓐ Ⓑ Ⓒ Ⓓ	27. Ⓐ Ⓑ Ⓒ Ⓓ	35. Ⓐ Ⓑ Ⓒ Ⓓ
4. Ⓕ Ⓖ Ⓗ Ⓙ	12. Ⓕ Ⓖ Ⓗ Ⓙ	20. Ⓕ Ⓖ Ⓗ Ⓙ	28. Ⓕ Ⓖ Ⓗ Ⓙ	36. Ⓕ Ⓖ Ⓗ Ⓙ
5. Ⓐ Ⓑ Ⓒ Ⓓ	13. Ⓐ Ⓑ Ⓒ Ⓓ	21. Ⓐ Ⓑ Ⓒ Ⓓ	29. Ⓐ Ⓑ Ⓒ Ⓓ	37. Ⓐ Ⓑ Ⓒ Ⓓ
6. Ⓕ Ⓖ Ⓗ Ⓙ	14. Ⓕ Ⓖ Ⓗ Ⓙ	22. Ⓕ Ⓖ Ⓗ Ⓙ	30. Ⓕ Ⓖ Ⓗ Ⓙ	38. Ⓕ Ⓖ Ⓗ Ⓙ
7. Ⓐ Ⓑ Ⓒ Ⓓ	15. Ⓐ Ⓑ Ⓒ Ⓓ	23. Ⓐ Ⓑ Ⓒ Ⓓ	31. Ⓐ Ⓑ Ⓒ Ⓓ	39. Ⓐ Ⓑ Ⓒ Ⓓ
8. Ⓕ Ⓖ Ⓗ Ⓙ	16. Ⓕ Ⓖ Ⓗ Ⓙ	24. Ⓕ Ⓖ Ⓗ Ⓙ	32. Ⓕ Ⓖ Ⓗ Ⓙ	40. Ⓕ Ⓖ Ⓗ Ⓙ

ENGLISH TEST

Time: 45 Minutes—75 Questions

Directions: In the five passages that follow, certain words and phrases are underlined and numbered. In the right-hand column, you will find alternatives for the underlined part. In most cases, you are to choose the one that best expresses the idea, makes the statement appropriate for standard written English, or is worded most consistently with the style and tone of the passage as a whole. If you think the original version is best, choose "NO CHANGE." In some cases, you will find in the right-hand column a question about the underlined part. You are to choose the best answer to the question.

You will also find questions about a section of the passage, or about the passage as a whole. These questions do not refer to an underlined portion of the passage, but rather are identified by a number or numbers in a box.

For each question, choose the alternative you consider best and fill in the corresponding oval on your answer sheet. Read each passage through once before you begin to answer the questions that accompany it. For many of the questions, you must read several sentences beyond the question to determine the answer. Be sure that you have read far enough ahead each time you choose an alternative.

PASSAGE I

Why I Ride a Bicycle

I waited thirty-two years before I rode a bicycle for the first time, down a tree-lined street in Toronto. I had barely sat on one before, so there were a few false starts as my boyfriend Stephen called out (1) instructions beside me. But then I found I was moving. And since I, more than most objects, seem to obey Newton's first law of motion—an object in motion will remain in motion until acted upon by an external force—off I went, whizzing downhill,

1. A. NO CHANGE
   B. boyfriend, Stephen called
   C. boyfriend Stephen, called
   D. boyfriend, called

weaving like a drunk, and smiled idiotically. I
2

2. F. NO CHANGE
G. smiling
H. had been smiling
J. smiles

didn't stop until three blocks later; where a car was
3
speeding toward the intersection. I'd not yet learned to brake, so I just dropped both feet to the ground inelegantly. Then I got back on the bicycle and did the whole thing again.

3. A. NO CHANGE
B. later. Where
C. later, where
D. later, and—when

I don't know why I'd never learned to ride before, a rite of passage that most people understand
4
somewhere around age six. Clearly, not all middle-

4. F. NO CHANGE
G. experience
H. practice
J. need

class parents in India teach they're children to ride
5
bicycles. Mine certainly didn't. I had singing lessons and, briefly, dancing lessons. I had math tutors and physics tutors. I even had swimming lessons but no bicycles.

5. A. NO CHANGE
B. there
C. their
D. one's

It's strange to come to this mysterious activity as an adult. Most people my age are riding for
6
so long they give little thought to an act that is nothing short of miraculous. But getting on a bike for the first time at thirty-two reveals the triumph of physics and human will that is cycling. Five

6. F. NO CHANGE
G. rode
H. had ridden
J. have been riding

hundred years ago, someone (the tireless Leonardo da Vinci, it was thought) drew a sketch of what was meant to be the world's first bicycle, though both sketch and artist are now disputed. [8] Since then we've had the "walking machine" (Baron von Drais of Sauerbrun's wooden two-wheeled contraption without pedals, designed to aid walkers—a bicycle even I could have ridden), velocipedes, ordinaries, and high-wheel tricycles. They are all results of engineering and machine-age design, but also of something more intangible.

7. A. NO CHANGE
   B. worlds first bicycle
   C. world's first bicycle
   D. worlds first bicycle,

8. The writer is considering adding the following true statement:

   The sketch was done in pencil and charcoal.

   Should the writer make this addition here?

   F. Yes, because it helps support the idea that bicycles have an important place in history.
   G. Yes, because it provides necessary insight into the variety of bicycles that exist.
   H. No, because it is not relevant to the narrative at this point in the essay.
   J. No, because this information has already been presented elsewhere in the essay.

9. Given that all of the choices are true, which one most strongly reinforces the writer's attitude that bicycles are amazing inventions?
   A. Each is a marvel
   B. They are debacles
   C. Each is a creation
   D. Each is a product

The saying that to ride on a bicycle is to balance
10

upon two tubes of rubber and wire, connected by
11
a frame, and to propel them forward with no more than a little foot power and the conviction that you can. We think bicycles carry us forward, but they don't, we carry them. It is largely human will
12
that keep bicycle and rider in motion, as well as
13
that law of Newton's, that it can be adapted into an
14
exhortation: move, because if you are moving, you will keep moving. [15]

10. Which choice provides the most concise and stylistically effective wording here?
   F. NO CHANGE
   G. Operating a bicycle one can say
   H. A person riding a bicycle
   J. To operate a bicycle

11. Which of the following alternatives to the underlined portion would be LEAST acceptable?
   A. NO CHANGE
   B. on top of
   C. atop
   D. on which

12. F. NO CHANGE
   G. don't we must carry
   H. don't: we carry
   J. don't, we are carrying

13. A. NO CHANGE
   B. by keeping
   C. keeps
   D. kept

14. F. NO CHANGE
   G. Newton's Law, which can
   H. Newton's Law which is
   J. Newton's Law and that can

15. The writer is considering concluding the essay with the following statement:

   How much of our lives are lived like this?

   Should the writer end the essay with this statement?

   A. Yes, because it adds to the writer's persuasive goal of convincing the reader to learn to ride a bicycle.
   B. Yes, because it sums up the main points of the essay in a memorable way.
   C. No, because it does not have a meaningful connection to the topic of this essay.
   D. No, because it conflicts with the overall tone and message of this essay.

PASSAGE II

I Give Update

Everyone talks about how social networking sites like Facebook <u>have brought us</u> [16] together and <u>aloud us to</u> [17] connect with friends 24 hours a day. To some people, however, this "connecting" is more complicated than it looks. Sometimes I'll stare at that blank status-update box for half an hour trying to think of what to type, and usually I just give up without typing anything. <u>This strikes me as odd,</u> [18] considering that I'm a professional writer. Back in school, the other kids used to beg me for help with their English papers, so why am I suddenly the only one who <u>can't remember most of the grammatical rules?</u> [19]

<u>I've always hated computers.</u> [20] After all, other people's status updates aren't especially brilliant or interesting, and nobody seems to mind. Sometimes, they don't even make sense. "Sitting in Starbucks LOL?" What the heck is up with that? Are

16. F. NO CHANGE
    G. have brought to us
    H. has brought to us
    J. has brought us

17. A. NO CHANGE
    B. aloud us too
    C. allowed us to
    D. allowed us too

18. Which of the following choices would provide the most logical opening to this sentence?
    F. NO CHANGE
    G. My life has always been like this,
    H. I have everybody fooled,
    J. Nobody is very interested in what I have to say anyway,

19. Which of the following choices would provide the most logical conclusion to this sentence?
    A. NO CHANGE
    B. spends most of his time online?
    C. cares about what other people think?
    D. can't think of anything to say?

20. Given that all of the choices are true, which one would make the most logical opening for this paragraph?
    F. NO CHANGE
    G. Maybe I'm overthinking this.
    H. Obviously, there are more productive things I could be doing with my time.
    J. As everyone knows nowadays, Facebook was developed by Mark Zuckerberg at Harvard in 2003.

you really sitting in a Starbucks, laughing out loud? Doesn't <u>everyone think you're</u> insane?
21

It feels like I'm the only <u>one has</u> figured out that
22
"social networking" is really just a big competition for attention, with success measured in the number of comments other people leave on your updates. <u>Theirs</u> nothing wrong with competition, but some
23
people have such a big advantage in this one that it's not even fun to play. A pretty girl can type "Bought a new swimsuit today!" and get 35 comments in about six minutes. I'm just as interested in pretty <u>girls swimsuits</u> as the next guy, but come on. I didn't
24
get 35 comments when I announced that my first book was being published. Maybe I should have announced it from a Starbucks, in which I was laughing out loud.

<u>It's all so</u> depressing.
25

<u>Being depressed</u> would at least give me something to
26
type, if not for the fact that depressing status updates are looked down upon. Social networking isn't just

21. **A.** NO CHANGE
    B. everyone thinks you're
    C. everyone think your
    D. everyone thinks your

22. **F.** NO CHANGE
    G. one had
    H. one whose
    J. one who's

23. **A.** NO CHANGE
    B. Theres
    C. There's
    D. Their's

24. **F.** NO CHANGE
    G. girl's swimsuits
    H. girls' swimsuits
    J. girl's swimsuit's

25. **A.** NO CHANGE
    B. Its' also
    C. Its all so
    D. Its also

26. **F.** NO CHANGE
    G. It is depressed
    H. It is depressing
    J. I am depressed

about attention; it's also about making other people [27] think, which you're having more fun there then. [28] I'm starting to wonder how many status updates are even true. Did that person really just have "the best day ever" or just get back from "the best party ever," or does he just want everyone to think he did? It would certainly be ironic if a program designed to help us connect with friends has instead forced us to spend all our [29] time lying to them. I've spent so much time thinking about this, I could probably write a book. Unfortunately, nobody would care, so I think instead I'll just go buy a swimsuit.

27. Which of the following alternatives to the underlined portion would NOT be acceptable?

A. attention. It is also
B. attention, you see, it's also
C. attention, you see; it's also
D. attention—it's also

28. **F.** NO CHANGE
G. think that your having more fun than there.
H. think, which your having more fun then theirs.
J. think that you're having more fun than they are.

29. **A.** NO CHANGE
B. is
C. are
D. hour

Question 30 asks about the preceding passage as a whole.

30. Suppose the writer's goal had been to write a brief essay arguing in favor of increased legal regulation of people's online behavior. Would this essay fulfill that goal?

F. Yes, because the author established that other people's online behavior lowers his self-esteem, which constitutes cyberbullying.
G. Yes, because the author clearly doesn't like the way people act on social networking sites, which logically means he must want it to be illegal.
H. No, because the author does not sound angry, and therefore this cannot be an argumentative essay.
J. No, because the essay never mentions legal regulations or implies that the government needs to get involved in the matter.

PASSAGE III

The Rodeo

I could hear their whispers as we <u>begun</u> [31] cantering around the rodeo grounds after our number was called. "I can't believe she's riding that horse in this competition. Look at him!" Monte snorted as if he heard their collective voices in the wind. Yet his head was <u>up, proud as ever and</u> [32] so was mine, hearing a stronger, unwavering voice.

If the truth <u>were told, he</u> [33] wasn't the most beautiful horse in the world. [34]

31. **A.** NO CHANGE
    B. beginning
    C. begin
    D. began

32. **F.** NO CHANGE
    G. up, proud as ever, and
    H. up proud as ever, and
    J. up proud as ever and

33. **A.** NO CHANGE
    B. were, told he
    C. were told; he
    D. were told he,

34. At this point, the writer is considering adding the following sentence:

    His huge workhorse body and thoroughbred legs made him appear clumsy and out of proportion.

    Would this be a relevant addition to make here?

    F. Yes, because it provides clarity about why Monte is so graceful.
    G. Yes, because it adds details relevant to the focus of the paragraph.
    H. No, because it provides a digression that leads the paragraph away from its primary focus.
    J. No, because the information is already provided elsewhere in the passage.

<u>Naturally,</u> Monte had learned a grace that
35
could only have come from sheer spirit and determination.

[1] "No way! No way!" [2] My butt firmly in the saddle, my back straight, and the reins held just right, we smoothly turned into the barrels. [3] Western equitation <u>had been</u> as unfamiliar to
36
Monte and me as five forks in a place setting at an upscale restaurant. [4] The voices in the wind followed us as Monte galloped faster around the ring. [5] Far from the bareback rides across the desert we had cherished over the years, we had <u>learned</u> the
37
rules and were making believers out of the crowd. [6] Monte, now almost on his side, was racing around the barrels as gracefully as if he had wings touched by angels, <u>not grazing even one barrel.</u> [39]
38

35. A. NO CHANGE
B. In fact,
C. Meanwhile,
D. Yet

36. F. NO CHANGE
G. is
H. will be
J. has been

37. Which of the following alternatives to the underlined portion would be LEAST acceptable?
A. NO CHANGE
B. beat
C. mastered
D. grasped

38. If the writer were to delete the underlined portion, placing a period after the word *angels*, the paragraph would primarily lose:
F. an emphasis on how quickly Monte raced.
G. information about how Monte was judged.
H. an explanation for how Monte raced gracefully.
J. an unnecessary detail.

39. For the sake of the logic and coherence of this paragraph, Sentence 4 should be placed:
A. where it is now.
B. before Sentence 2.
C. after Sentence 2.
D. after Sentence 6.

I patted Monte's neck as we cantered out of the ring and suddenly I didn't see or hear anyone
40

accepting my family. "No one will hurt your spirit
41

but you," my grandfather's voice
42

echoed in the gentle wind that kissed my cheeks and my spirit.
43

Monte looked so proud when he and me won first place.
44

40. Given that all of the choices are true, which one most effectively introduces the action in this paragraph while suggesting the writer's nervousness?
   F. NO CHANGE
   G. I proudly held up my head
   H. I dropped the reins
   J. I glanced anxiously at the crowd

41. A. NO CHANGE
   B. accept for
   C. except for
   D. excepting

42. F. NO CHANGE
   G. grandfathers
   H. grandfathers'
   J. grandfather

43. A. NO CHANGE
   B. will echo
   C. echoing
   D. echoes

44. F. NO CHANGE
   G. he and I
   H. him and me
   J. him and I

Question 45 asks about the preceding passage as a whole.

45. Suppose that one of the writer's goals had been to illustrate that spirit and determination are just as important as inborn ability. Would this essay fulfill this goal?
   A. Yes, because Monte was a beautiful racehorse who helped the writer overcome her challenges.
   B. Yes, because the writer was able to win the race riding Monte, even though Monte wasn't born with grace.
   C. No, because the essay doesn't address inborn abilities.
   D. No, because neither Monte nor the writer demonstrated spirit and determination.

PASSAGE IV

Not in Our Stars

I guess I can't blame people from [46] thousands of years ago for believing in astrology—there was simply no way for them to now [47] any better. But it's honestly incredible to me that, after all the knowledge science has given us about how the universe really works, there are still millions of people who eagerly read their horoscopes in the paper every morning and actually expect them [48] to mean anything. [49]

46. Which of the following alternatives to the underlined portion would be LEAST acceptable?
- **F.** in which
- **G.** who lived
- **H.** all those
- **J.** DELETE the underlined portion.

47.
- **A.** NO CHANGE
- **B.** know way for them to now
- **C.** no way for them to know
- **D.** now way for them to no

48.
- **F.** NO CHANGE
- **G.** it
- **H.** themselves
- **J.** DELETE the underlined portion.

49. At this point, the writer is considering adding the following sentence:

> Just imagine if a newspaper ever accidentally printed the horoscopes under the wrong signs—people would be so confused, watching things happen to the wrong people all day!

Should the writer add this sentence here?
- **A.** Yes, because it is a humorous way of illustrating the fact that horoscopes are meaningless.
- **B.** Yes, because this is something that might actually happen, and people deserve to be warned.
- **C.** No, because it is disrespectful to people who work in graphic design for newspapers.
- **D.** No, because it does not offer definitive proof that horoscopes do not accurately predict the future.

Even when I was little, I didn't believe in horoscopes.[50] We're all familiar with the twelve signs of the zodiac and the traits of people supposedly personally[51] born under different signs: a Pisces is emotional, a Taurus is stubborn, an Aquarius is clever. The problem, of course, is that these vague qualities can appear to apply to anyone. Who isn't emotional or stubborn at times? And all people *think* they're clever—even when they aren't! If only astrology made claims which were[52] a little more specific, we might be rid of it by now. For example, if "the stars" predicted that all Sagittarians would be left-handed, or that all Libras would have 20/20 vision, we would be able to test these claims, and astrology would fail. But since the only "test" involves people who *want* to believe in it decide[53] whether to apply broad compliments like "brave"

50. Which of the following would make for the most logical opening to this paragraph?
- **F.** NO CHANGE
- **G.** Modern astronomy first became distinct from astrology in the second century.
- **H.** I do have a few friends who believe in astrology, which has led to some amusing arguments.
- **J.** I'm sure I don't need to explain what astrology is.

51.
- **A.** NO CHANGE
- **B.** personality traits of people supposed to be
- **C.** people's traits supposedly personally
- **D.** supposed personality traits of people

52.
- **F.** NO CHANGE
- **G.** claims, which were
- **H.** claims that were
- **J.** claims, that were

53.
- **A.** NO CHANGE
- **B.** deciding
- **C.** to decide
- **D.** and decided

or "insightful" to <u>their friends and them,</u> astrology 54 probably won't be going away anytime soon.

I can see how people centuries ago <u>would be thinking</u> 55 it was logical for heavenly bodies to "influence" events on Earth, but the funny part is that the math is all wrong. All of the star charts on which astrology is based were drawn up when people still thought that the Earth, rather than the sun, was at the center of the solar system. Plus, as Einstein figured out <u>anyway,</u> 56 the stars' apparent positions aren't really where they are, because the light they emit is bent by gravity before it reaches our eyes. So even if astrology were true, it would be full of mistakes! Luckily for <u>astrologers, it's</u> 57 all a bunch of nonsense, so nobody ever noticed.

I'm not ready for astrology to go away just <u>yet, however, I</u> 58 always enjoy meeting people who believe in it at a party. Once someone brings it up, I know it's only a matter of time before he or she asks me what my sign is, and my answer is always the

54. **F.** NO CHANGE
G. their friends and they,
H. their friends, and themselves,
J. themselves and their friends,

55. **A.** NO CHANGE
B. could've thought
C. should have thought
D. might of thought

56. The best placement for the underlined portion would be:
F. where it is now.
G. after the word *are* (but before the comma).
H. after the word *emit.*
J. after the word *gravity.*

57. **A.** NO CHANGE
B. astrologers are
C. astrologers, and
D. astrologers, and it's

58. **F.** NO CHANGE
G. yet, however I
H. yet, however; I
J. yet—however—I

same. "Well, you've been talking to me all night," <u>I replied.</u> [59] "Shouldn't you be able to tell?" [60]

59. A. NO CHANGE
B. I'll reply.
C. and I replied.
D. and replied:

60. The writer is considering concluding the essay with the following statement:

At the end of the day, though, I don't think anything annoys me as much as going into a bookstore and seeing all the space they waste with books on astrology.

Should the writer end the essay with this statement?

F. Yes, because it is logical for a writer to end an essay with a reference to bookstores.
G. Yes, because unnecessary books are a waste of trees and therefore bad for the environment.
H. No, because this is an essay about people's superstitions, not how bookstores are arranged.
J. No, because the previous sentence makes for a much more pointed and memorable ending.

PASSAGE V

Gut Feelings

<u>Intuitions or gut feelings,</u> [61] are sudden, strong judgments whose origin <u>they can't</u> [62] immediately explain. Although they seem to emerge from an obscure inner force, they actually begin with a perception of something outside—a facial

61. A. NO CHANGE
B. Intuitions, or gut feelings
C. Intuitions, or gut feelings,
D. Intuitions or gut feelings

62. F. NO CHANGE
G. you can't
H. people won't
J. one doesn't

expression, a tone of voice, or a visual inconsistency so fleeting you're not even aware you <u>had noticed</u> it.
63

Think of them as rapid cognition or condensed
64
reasoning that takes advantage of the brain's built-in shortcuts. Or think of intuition as an unconscious associative process. [65]

<u>The best explanation psychologists now offer is</u>
66
that intuition is a mental matching game. The brain <u>takes in a situation, doing a very quick search</u>
67
of its files, and then finds its best analogy among the stored sprawl of memories and knowledge.

63. **A.** NO CHANGE
B. notice
C. felt
D. feel

64. **F.** NO CHANGE
G. Think of intuition
H. Think on it
J. Thinking of them

65. At this point, the writer is considering adding the following sentence:

> Long dismissed as magical or beneath the dignity of science, intuition appears to consist of fast mental operations.

Would this be a relevant addition to make here?

A. Yes, because it provides a needed transition between sentences.
B. Yes, because it finally provides the official definition of *intuition.*
C. No, because it contradicts the idea expressed in the following sentence.
D. No, because it provides a digression that leads the paragraph away from its primary focus.

66. Which phrase best introduces the sentence?
F. NO CHANGE
G. The only thing we know for sure is
H. The only possible explanation is
J. Psychologists now believe

67. **A.** NO CHANGE
B. takes in a situation, does a very quick search
C. took in a situation, doing a very quick search
D. take in a situation, does a very quick search

PRACTICE TEST 2

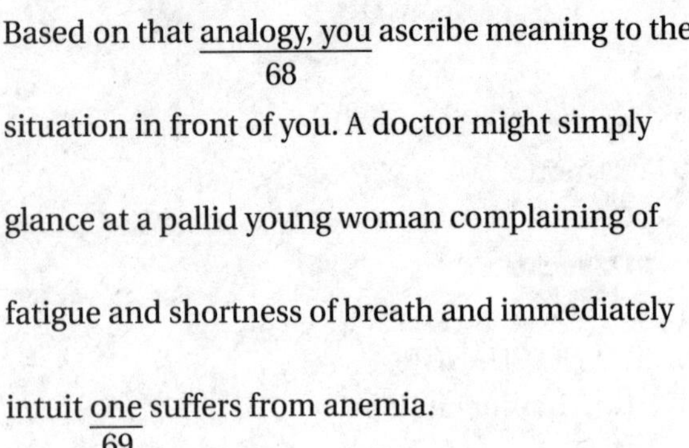

Based on that analogy, you [68] ascribe meaning to the situation in front of you. A doctor might simply glance at a pallid young woman complaining of fatigue and shortness of breath and immediately intuit one [69] suffers from anemia.

68.
F. NO CHANGE
G. analogy: you
H. analogy—you
J. analogy; you

69.
A. NO CHANGE
B. she
C. he
D. her

Experience is encoded In our brains as a web of fact and feeling. [70] When a new experience calls up a similar pattern, it doesn't unleash just stored knowledge but also an emotional state of mind and a predisposition to respond by it [71] in a certain way.

70. Which choice best illustrates how information is stored in our brains?
F. NO CHANGE
G. Everything we do is stored in our brain.
H. Experience is processed by our brain.
J. Our brain remembers all of our experiences.

71.
A. NO CHANGE
B. respond
C. have responded
D. be responding

While endless reasoning in the absence of intuitions is unproductive, some people champion the other extreme—"going with the gut" at all times. [72]

72. The writer is considering deleting this sentence. Should the sentence be kept or deleted?
F. Kept, because it gives an explanation of the usefulness of intuitions.
G. Kept, because it provides a useful introduction to the paragraph.
H. Deleted, because it contradicts the idea that people should pay attention to their intuitions.
J. Deleted, because it is stylistically inconsistent with the rest of the essay.

Accordingly, intuition is best used as the first step in solving a problem or deciding what to do. The more experience you have in a particular domain, the more reliable your intuitions, because they haven't been used many times before. But even in your area of expertise, it's wisest to test out your hunches—you could easily have latched on to the wrong detail and pulled up the wrong web of associations in your brain. So pay attention to your intuition, because the information you received is valid. But it's important to balance this with reason so that you don't make an error of judgment in an impulsive moment.

(73: "Accordingly,"; 74: "because they haven't been used many times before."; 75: "received")

73. A. NO CHANGE
B. Also,
C. For instance,
D. But

74. Which phrase best supports the idea presented in this sentence?
F. NO CHANGE
G. because you haven't formed many situational analogies.
H. because they arise out of the richest array of collected patterns of experience.
J. because you should trust your unconscious mind.

75. A. NO CHANGE
B. have received
C. will be receiving
D. receive

STOP

If there is still time remaining, you may review your answers.

MATHEMATICS TEST

Time: 60 Minutes—60 Questions

Directions: Solve each problem, choose the correct answer, and then fill in the corresponding oval on your answer sheet.

Do not linger over problems that take too much time. Solve as many as you can; then return to the others in the time you have left for this test.

You are permitted to use a calculator on this test. You may use your calculator for any problems you choose, but some of the problems may best be done without using a calculator.

Note: Unless otherwise stated, all of the following should be assumed.

1. Illustrative figures are NOT necessarily drawn to scale.
2. Geometric figures lie in a plane.
3. The word *line* indicates a straight line.
4. The word *average* indicates arithmetic mean.

DO YOUR FIGURING HERE

1. What is the value of the expression $(y-x)^3$ when $x = 5$ and $y = 1$?

A. −64
B. −4
C. 4
D. 16
E. 64

2. What is the smallest positive integer that is divisible by 3, divisible by 5, and divisible by 6 (with no remainders)?

F. 15
G. 30
H. 60
J. 90
K. 180

3. If $[-s + h(t \cdot 3 - w)]r = 1$, then which of the following variables CANNOT equal 0?

A. h
B. r
C. s
D. t
E. w

DO YOUR FIGURING HERE

4. In a certain school district, exactly 30% of the students come from families that have only one child. If there are 7,340 students in the district, how many do NOT come from families with only one child?

F. 220
G. 514
H. 2,202
J. 5,138
K. 7,120

5. What is the slope-intercept form of the equation $3y + 2x = 24$?

A. $y = -\frac{2x}{3} + 8$
B. $y = -\frac{3x}{2} + 12$
C. $3 = 2m + b$
D. $m = 2b + 24$
E. $y = 2x + 24$

6. What is the slope of a line perpendicular to the line $3x + 2y = 19$?

F. $-\frac{3}{2}$
G. $-\frac{2}{3}$
H. $\frac{2}{3}$
J. $\frac{3}{2}$
K. 3

7. The volume of a cone is given by the formula $V = \frac{\pi}{3}r^2h$, where r is the radius of the base of the cone and h is the height of the cone. What is the volume, in cubic centimeters, of a cone with a height of 8 cm that has a base with a radius of 3 cm?

DO YOUR FIGURING HERE

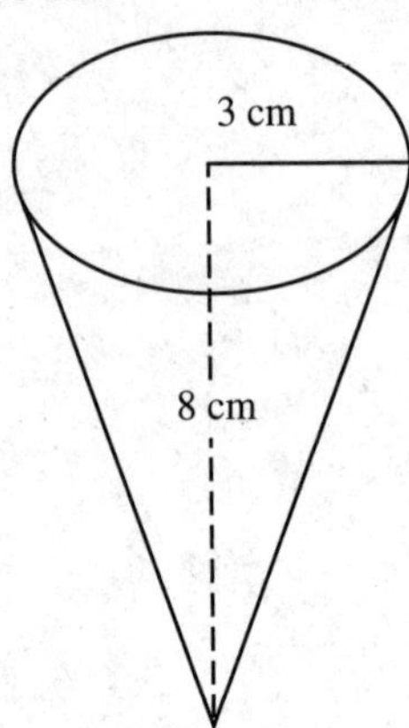

A. 72π
B. 48π
C. 24π
D. 12π
E. 8π

8. Given that m and n are parallel lines, t is a transversal crossing both m and n, and $m\angle b = 100°$, what is the measure of $\angle e$?

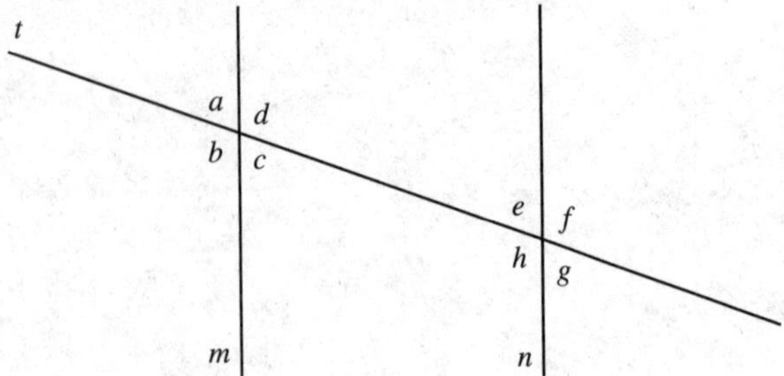

F. 40°
G. 50°
H. 80°
J. 100°
K. 120°

9. In the figure below, 3 lines intersect at the indicated angles.
What is the measure of $\angle x$?
A. 35°
B. 52.5°
C. 65°
D. 70°
E. 75°

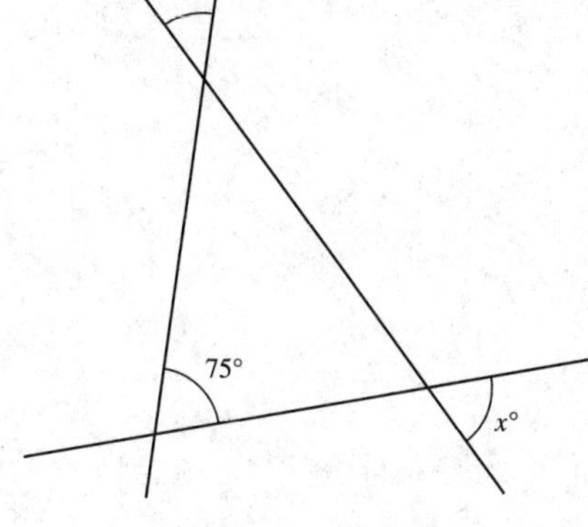

DO YOUR FIGURING HERE

10. Find two numbers between 11 and 26 such that the numbers form an arithmetic sequence.

11, ______, ______, 26

F. 14, 18
G. 15, 20
H. 16, 21
J. 17, 23
K. 18, 24

11. For all real numbers x and y, $(2x + 3y)^2 = ?$
A. $6x^2y^2$
B. $4x^2 + 6y^2$
C. $4x^2 + 9y^2$
D. $4x^2 + 6xy + 6y^2$
E. $4x^2 + 12xy + 9y^2$

12. In a certain town in New Hampshire, there are 7,695 registered voters, 60% of whom are Democrats. How many of the town's registered voters are Democrats?
F. 513
G. 2,565
H. 3,078
J. 4,617
K. 7,695

DO YOUR FIGURING HERE

13. What is the value of tan Y in right triangle $\triangle XYZ$ below?

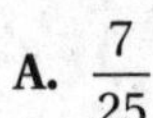

A. $\frac{7}{25}$

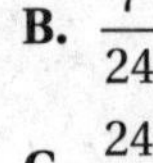

B. $\frac{7}{24}$

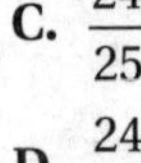

C. $\frac{24}{25}$

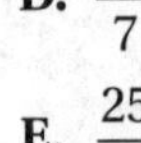

D. $\frac{24}{7}$

E. $\frac{25}{7}$

14. When $\frac{1}{3}w + \frac{2}{5}w = 1$, what is the value of w?

F. $\frac{1}{11}$

G. $\frac{3}{8}$

H. $\frac{11}{15}$

J. $\frac{15}{11}$

K. $\frac{8}{3}$

15. In the figure below, $\overline{AB}$ and $\overline{CD}$ bisect each other at E. The measure of $\angle CAE$ is 80° and the measure of $\angle BDE$ is 60°. What is the measure of $\angle CEA$?

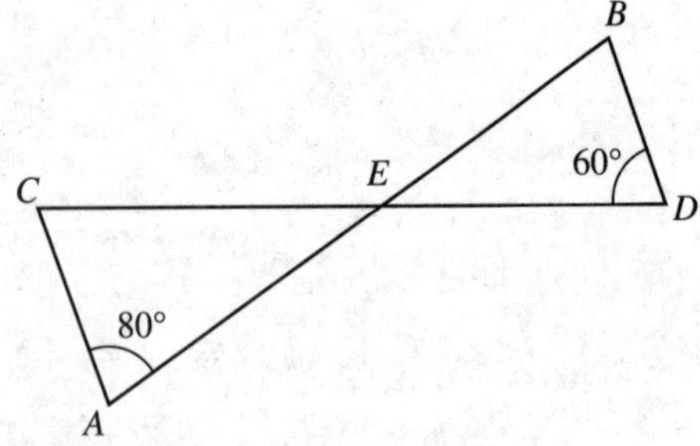

A. 10°
B. 30°
C. 40°
D. 60°
E. Cannot be determined

DO YOUR FIGURING HERE

16. Given that $A = (3, 2)$ and $B = (15, 8)$ in the standard (x, y) coordinate plane, what is the distance from A to B?

F. $5\sqrt{2}$
G. 8
H. $4\sqrt{10}$
J. $6\sqrt{5}$
K. 18

17. For all real numbers a, b, and c such that $a < b$ and $c > 0$, which of the following inequalities, if any, must be true?

A. $a < c$
B. $b < c$
C. $a > c$
D. $b > c$
E. None of the above inequalities must be true.

18. A deli offers 4 types of sandwich meat, 3 kinds of cheese, and 5 bread varieties. When you order a sandwich at the deli, you are allowed to choose 1 meat, 1 cheese, and 1 type of bread. How many different sandwich combinations are possible at the deli?

F. 3
G. 12
H. 15
J. 30
K. 60

19. Alana leaves home to drive to college. She drives 200 miles in 4 hours before stopping for gas. She then drives 10 miles per hour faster than she did on the first part of her trip, and arrives at her dorm in 3 hours. How many miles did she drive in total?

A. 200
B. 300
C. 350
D. 380
E. 430

DO YOUR FIGURING HERE

20. If the monthly payment, M dollars, on a house that costs P dollars is given by the formula $M = \frac{P}{200} - 0.0008P + 40$, what is the monthly payment, to the nearest dollar, on a house that costs $200,000?

F. $868
G. $880
H. $960
J. $1,060
K. $1,200

21. What is the sum of the prime factors of the number 330?

A. 6
B. 19
C. 21
D. 22
E. 43

Use the following information to answer questions 22–24.

Quinn is bowling a series of 3 games. She has bowled 2 of 3 games with scores of 112 and 144. The figure below is a top view of the bowling lane. The *dimensions* for the bowling lane are given in the figure. The *pin deck* is the rectangular region within the bowling lane where the 10 bowling pins are set up.

(Note: The figure is not drawn to scale.)

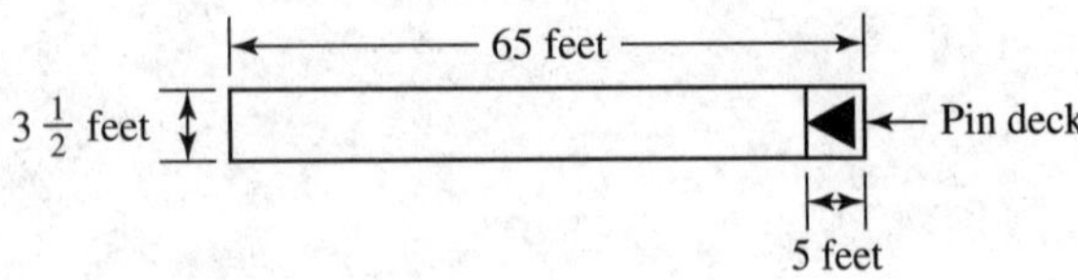

DO YOUR FIGURING HERE

22. In *duckpin* bowling, different balls and pins are used. The diameter of each duckpin at its widest is 4.125 in. When all of the pins are set up, which of the following values is closest to the area, in square inches, that is covered by the widest part of the pins?

F. 130
G. 134
H. 267
J. 535
K. 1,260

23. What is the ratio of the total area of the bowling lane to the area of the lane that is NOT the pin deck?

A. 12:1
B. 13:1
C. 13:12
D. 10:7
E. 120:7

24. What score will Quinn need to earn in her third game to have an average score of 140 for the 3 games?

F. 128
G. 132
H. 140
J. 164
K. 176

---

25. In the standard (x, y) coordinate plane, a line passes through the points $(1, -2)$ and $(5, 10)$. At which of the following points does the line cross the y-axis?

A. $(-8, 0)$
B. $(-5, 0)$
C. $(0, 0)$
D. $(0, -5)$
E. $(0, -8)$

DO YOUR FIGURING HERE

26. The scores below were earned by 10 students on a recent history test. What is the median score?

68, 96, 85, 72, 89, 93, 89, 82, 77, 99

F. 85
G. 86
H. 87
J. 89
K. 91

27. For all positive a, b, and c, $\frac{2^{-1}a^{-3}b^{7}c^{2}}{(5a)^{2}b^{-1}c^{7}} = ?$

A. $\frac{2b^6}{5a^2c^5}$

B. $\frac{2b^8c^9}{2a^5}$

C. $\frac{2b^8c^9}{25a^5}$

D. $\frac{b^8}{10a^5c^5}$

E. $\frac{b^8}{50a^5c^5}$

28. One endpoint of a diameter of a circle with center (2, –3) has coordinates at (5, –2) in the standard (x, y) plane. What are the coordinates of the other endpoint of the diameter?

F. $(2-\sqrt{10}, -3-\sqrt{10})$
G. (–1, –4)
H. (0, –4)
J. $(2+\sqrt{10}, -3+\sqrt{10})$
K. (8, –1)

29. What is the y-coordinate of the point of intersection of the lines $y = 3x - 7$ and $y = 5x + 5$ in the standard (x, y) coordinate plane?

A. –25
B. –11
C. –6
D. 6
E. 11

PRACTICE TEST 2

30. What is the area, in square inches, of the figure shown below?

DO YOUR FIGURING HERE

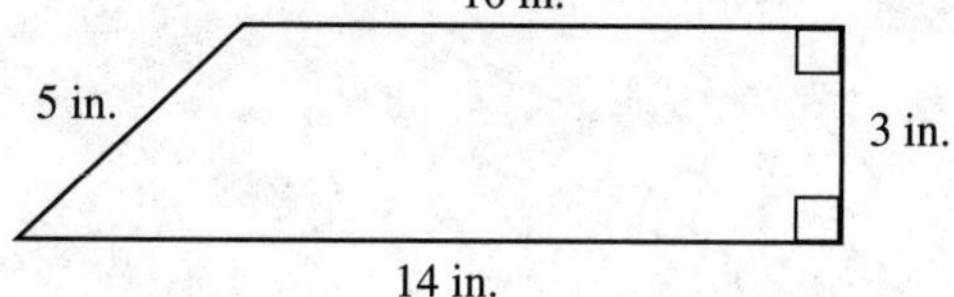

F. 24
G. 32
H. 36
J. 42
K. 72

31. What is the solution set for the inequality $6 - 4(x - 2) > 4x + 5$?

A. $x < -\frac{7}{8}$

B. $x < -\frac{1}{4}$

C. $x < \frac{9}{8}$

D. $x > -\frac{7}{8}$

E. $x > \frac{9}{8}$

PRACTICE TEST 2

DO YOUR FIGURING HERE

Use the following information to answer questions 32–34.

The circle in the standard (x, y) coordinate plane below has center $(6, -7)$ and radius 4 coordinate units.

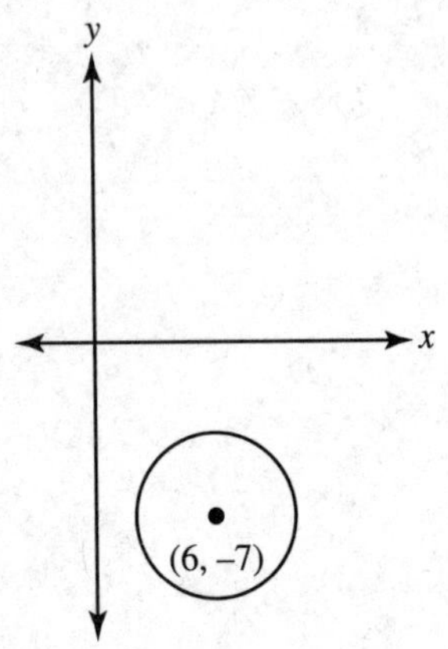

32. Which of the following is an equation for this circle?
    F. $(x-6)^2 + (y+7)^2 = 8$
    G. $(x+6)^2 + (y-7)^2 = 8$
    H. $(x-6)^2 + (y+7)^2 = 16$
    J. $(x-6)^2 + (y-7)^2 = 16$
    K. $(x+6)^2 + (y+7)^2 = 16$

33. The circle will be rotated 90° counterclockwise (↺) about the origin. What will be the coordinates of the image of the center of the circle?
    A. $(-6, 7)$
    B. $(6, 7)$
    C. $(7, 6)$
    D. $(7, -6)$
    E. $(-7, 6)$

34. What is the area, in square coordinate units, of this circle?
    F. 2π
    G. 4π
    H. 8π
    J. 16π
    K. 32π

35. Parallelogram *RSTU* is shown below, with $\overline{UA} = 4$ inches, $\overline{AS} = 7$ inches, and $\overline{ST} = 5$ inches. What is the area of *RSTU* in square inches?

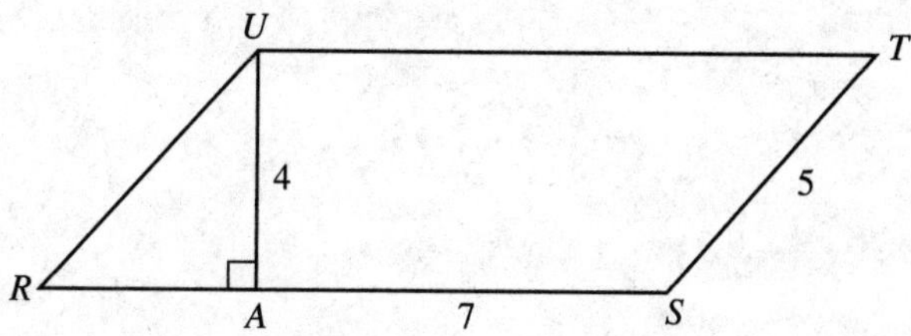

A. 16
B. 20
C. 28
D. 35
E. 40

DO YOUR FIGURING HERE

36. If the lengths of the sides of the triangle below are shown in inches, how many inches long is side $\overline{AB}$?

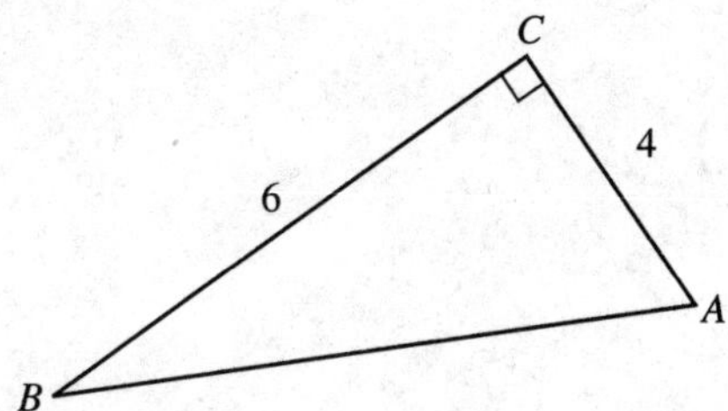

F. $2\sqrt{13}$
G. 10
H. $4\sqrt{13}$
J. 26
K. 42

37. Which of the following comprises all of the values of x for which $\frac{2}{3}x - \frac{1}{2} < \frac{1}{2}x + \frac{2}{3}$?

A. $x < 1$

B. $x < \frac{7}{6}$

C. $x < 7$

D. $x > \frac{7}{3}$

E. $x > 7$

DO YOUR FIGURING HERE

38. A guide wire for a telephone tower makes an angle of 50° with the level ground and is 14 meters from the base of the tower. How many meters long is the guide wire?

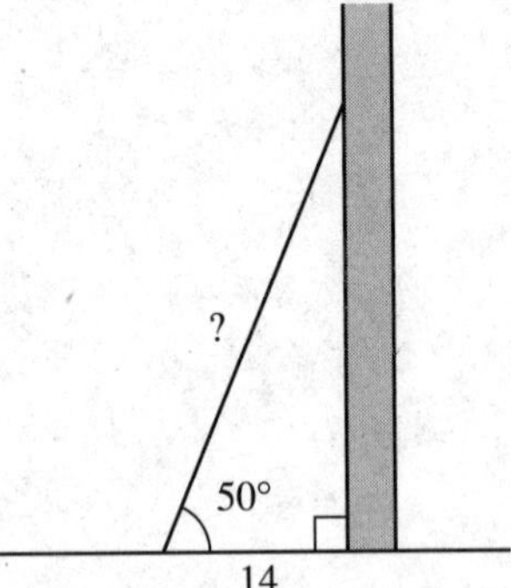

F. 3.80

G. 13.50

H. 16.68

J. 21.78

K. 22.58

39. For all $x^2 \neq 9$, $\frac{(x-3)^2}{x^2-9}$ is equivalent to:

A. -1

B. $\frac{1}{2}$

C. 1

D. $\frac{1}{x+3}$

E. $\frac{x-3}{x+3}$

DO YOUR FIGURING HERE

40. In the standard (x, y) coordinate plane, the midpoint of $\overline{AB}$ is (5, 7) and A is located at (2, 3). If the coordinates of B are (x, y), what is the value of $(x + y)$?

F. 19
G. 17
H. 11
J. 8.5
K. 8

41. If the solutions to the equation $(x + a)(x + b) = 0$ are $x = 8$ and $x = -\frac{3}{2}$, then $a + b = ?$

A. −13
B. −12
C. −6.5
D. 6.5
E. 12

42. In the figure below, all line segments intersect at right angles, and all measurements are given in inches. What is the perimeter of the figure in inches?

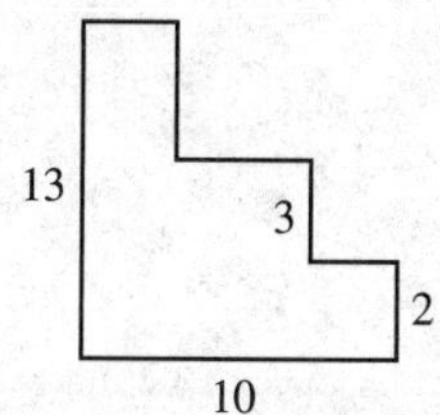

F. 23
G. 28
H. 46
J. 130
K. Cannot be determined

43. A line in the standard (x, y) coordinate plane contains the points (5, 9) and (8, 3). What is the x-intercept of this line?

A. 19
B. $\frac{19}{2}$
C. 0
D. −2
E. $-\frac{19}{2}$

DO YOUR FIGURING HERE

44. Each side of a given cube is a square with an area of 729 square inches. What is the volume of the cube in cubic inches?

F. 3^3
G. 3^9
H. 3^{12}
J. 3^{18}
K. 3^{64}

45. If p and q are positive integers, and $6pq^4$ and $12p^2q^2$ have a greatest common factor of 1,050, then which of the following is a possible value for the sum of p and q?

A. 6
B. 8
C. 12
D. 35
E. 42

46. In the figure shown below, $\triangle ABC$ is a right triangle, $\overline{AB}$ is 8 inches long, and $\overline{BC}$ is 10 inches long. What is the area, in square inches, of square $ACDE$?

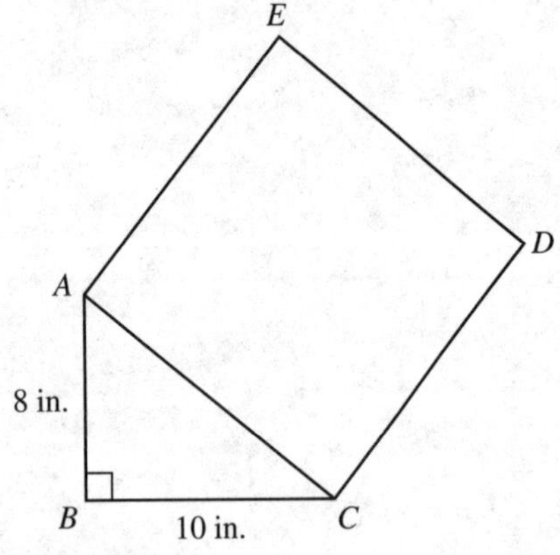

F. $2\sqrt{41}$
G. $\sqrt{164}$
H. 36
J. $8\sqrt{41}$
K. 164

DO YOUR FIGURING HERE

47. The decimal equivalent of $\frac{1}{13}$ is $0.\overline{076923}$. What is the digit in the sixty-third place after the decimal point?

A. 2
B. 3
C. 6
D. 7
E. 9

48. What value must be added to $9x^2 - 30x$ in order to *complete the square* (that is, make it a perfect square trinomial)?

F. -5
G. 5
H. 9
J. 25
K. 45

49. A circle in the standard (x, y) coordinate plane is tangent to the x-axis at $-a$, and tangent to the y-axis at a, with $a > 0$. The radius of the circle is 4 units. What is the equation of the circle?

A. $x^2 + y^2 = 4$
B. $x^2 + y^2 = 16$
C. $(x-4)^2 + (y-4)^2 = 4$
D. $(x+4)^2 + (y+4)^2 = 16$
E. $(x+4)^2 + (y-4)^2 = 16$

50. Compared to the graph of $y = \sin x$, the graph of $y = 2\sin(4x)$ has:

F. 8 times the amplitude and the same period.
G. 2 times the amplitude and 4 times the period.
H. 2 times the amplitude and $\frac{1}{4}$ the period.
J. $\frac{1}{2}$ the amplitude and 4 times the period.
K. $\frac{1}{2}$ the amplitude and $\frac{1}{4}$ the period.

DO YOUR FIGURING HERE

51. Which of the following is the solution set for x such that $3x - 9 \geq -3(9 - x)$?

A. The empty set
B. The set containing only zero
C. The set of negative numbers
D. The set of positive numbers
E. The set of real numbers

52. In the figure below, square *ABCD* has a side length of 6 inches, and squares *AEFG* and *CHIJ* each have a side length of 1 inch. What is the area, in square inches, of the shaded pentagon *DGFIJ*?

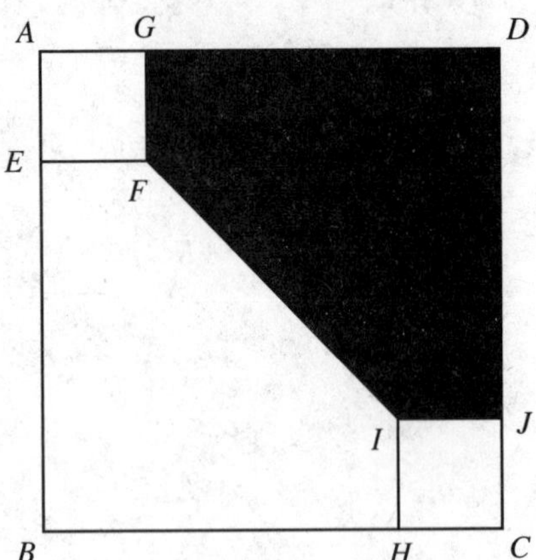

F. 9
G. 12.5
H. 17
J. 18
K. 20.5

53. Consider matrices A, B, C, and D with dimensions as follows:

A = 2 × 2   B = 2 × 3   C = 3 × 2   D = 3 × 3

Which of the following matrix products is NOT defined?

A. AB
B. BC
C. CB
D. CD
E. DC

54. If $x^2 - 36a^2 = 5ax$, what are the two solutions for x in terms of a?

F. $-4a$ and $-9a$
G. $-4a$ and $9a$
H. $-3a$ and $12a$
J. $3a$ and $-12a$
K. $4a$ and $-9a$

DO YOUR FIGURING HERE

55. For all values of θ over which $\sin \theta$ and $\cos \theta$ are positive, $\frac{\sqrt{1 - \cos^2 \theta}}{\sin^2 \theta} \cdot \cos \theta = ?$

A. 1
B. $\tan \theta$
C. $\cot \theta$
D. $\sec \theta$
E. $\csc \theta$

56. If $\log_a x = p$, $\log_a y = q$, and $\log_a z = t$, then $\log_a \left(\frac{x^2 y^3}{\sqrt{z}} \right)$ is equivalent to:

F. $p^2 q^3 - \sqrt{z}$
G. $\frac{p^2 q^3}{\sqrt{z}}$
H. $2p + 3q + \frac{1}{2}t$
J. $2p + 3q - \frac{1}{2}t$
K. $2p + 3q - t^{\frac{1}{2}}$

PRACTICE TEST 2

57. What is the solution set for the equation $|-x| = x$?

A. All real numbers
B. $x \geq 0$
C. $x \leq 0$
D. Only $x = 0$
E. Only $x = -1$

DO YOUR FIGURING HERE

58. For which of the following values of a will there be exactly one real solution to the equation $2x^2 - ax + 8 = 0$?

F. $2\sqrt{3}$
G. 4
H. $4\sqrt{3}$
J. 6
K. 8

59. If $x = 3t + 4$ and $y = 5 - t$, then which of the following equations expresses y in terms of x?

A. $y = \frac{19 - x}{3}$
B. $y = \frac{1 - x}{3}$
C. $y = 9 - x$
D. $y = x + 9$
E. $y = x - 1$

60. In the circle below, radius $\overline{OA}$ has a length of 10 meters, and central angle $\angle AOB$ measures 30°. What is the area, in square meters, of shaded sector *AOB*?

DO YOUR FIGURING HERE

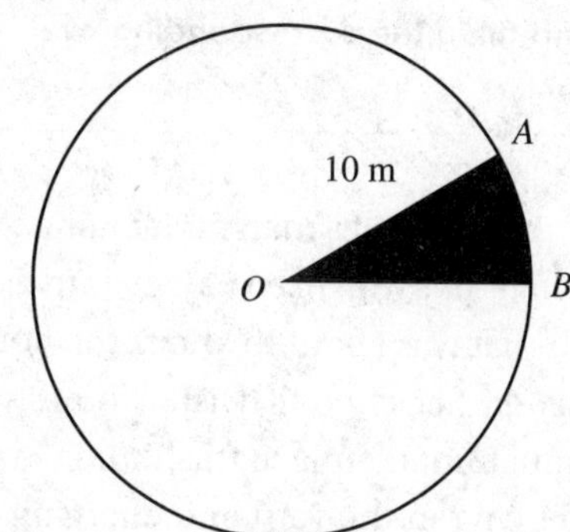

F. $\frac{5\pi}{6}$

G. $\frac{5\pi}{3}$

H. $\frac{10\pi}{3}$

J. $\frac{25\pi}{6}$

K. $\frac{25\pi}{3}$

STOP

If there is still time remaining, you may review your answers.

READING TEST

Time: 35 Minutes—40 Questions

Directions: There are four passages in this test. Each passage is followed by several questions. After reading a passage, choose the best answer to each question and fill in the corresponding oval on your answer sheet. You may refer to the passages as often as necessary.

PASSAGE I—LITERARY NARRATIVE

This passage is adapted from the short story "A Very Old Man With Enormous Wings" by Gabriel Garcia Márquez (© 1971 by Gabriel Garcia Márquez).

The light was so weak at noon that when Pelayo was coming back to the house, it was hard for him to see what it was that was moving and groaning in the rear of the courtyard. He had to go very close to see that it was an old man lying face down in the mud, who, in spite of his tremendous efforts, couldn't get up, impeded by his enormous wings.

Pelayo ran to get Elisenda, his wife, who was putting compresses on the sick child, and he took her to the rear of the courtyard. They both looked at the fallen body with a mute stupor. There were only a few faded hairs left on his bald skull and very few teeth in his mouth, and his pitiful condition took away any sense of grandeur he might have had. And yet, they called in a neighbor woman who knew everything about life and death to see him, and all she needed was one look.

"He's an angel," she told them. "He must have been coming for the child, but the poor fellow is so old that the rain knocked him down."

On the following day everyone knew that a flesh-and-blood angel was held captive in Pelayo's house. With the first light of dawn, they found the whole neighborhood in front of the chicken coop having fun with the angel, tossing him things to eat through the openings in the wire.

The news of the captive angel spread with such rapidity that after a few hours the courtyard had the bustle of a marketplace and they had to call in troops with fixed bayonets to disperse the mob that was about to knock the house down. Elisenda, her spine all twisted from sweeping up so much marketplace trash, then got the idea of fencing in the yard and charging five cents admission to see the angel.

The curious came from far away. The most unfortunate invalids on earth came in search of health: a poor woman who since childhood has been counting her heartbeats and had run out of numbers; a Portuguese man who couldn't sleep because the noise of the stars disturbed him; a sleepwalker who got up at night to undo the things he had done while awake; and many others with less serious ailments. Pelayo and Elisenda were happy with fatigue, for in less than a week they had crammed their rooms with money and the line of pilgrims waiting their turn to enter still reached beyond the horizon.

The angel was the only one who took no part in his own act. He spent his time trying to get comfortable in his borrowed nest, befuddled by the heat of the oil lamps and sacramental candles that had been placed along the wire. At first they tried to make him eat some mothballs, which, according to the wisdom of the wise neighbor woman, were the food prescribed for angels. But he turned them down. His only supernatural virtue seemed to be patience. Especially during the first days, when the hens pecked at him, searching for the stellar parasites that proliferated in his wings, and even the most merciful threw stones at him, trying to get him to rise so they could see him standing.

It so happened that during those days there arrived in the town the traveling show of the woman who had been changed into a spider for having disobeyed her parents. The admission to see her was not only less than the admission to see the angel, but people were permitted to ask her all manner of questions and to examine her up and down. While still practically a child she had sneaked out of her parents' house to go to a dance, and while she was coming back through the woods after having danced all night without permission, a fearful thunderclap rent the sky in two and through the crack came the lightning bolt of brimstone that changed her into a spider. A spectacle like that, with such a fearful lesson, was bound to defeat that of a haughty angel who scarcely deigned to look at mortals. Pelayo's courtyard went back to being as empty as during the time it had rained for three days and crabs walked through the bedrooms.

With the money they saved they built a two-story mansion with iron bars on the windows so that angels wouldn't get in. Pelayo also set up a rabbit warren close to town and gave up his job as a bailiff for good, and Elisenda bought some satin pumps with high heels and many dresses of iridescent silk, the kind worn on Sunday by the most desirable women in those times.

One morning Elisenda was cutting some bunches of onions for lunch when a wind that seemed to come from the high seas blew into the kitchen. Then she went to the window and caught the angel in his first attempts at flight. He was on the point of knocking the shed down with the ungainly flapping that slipped on the light and couldn't get a grip on the air. But he did manage to gain altitude. Elisenda let out a sigh of relief, for herself and for him, when she watched him pass over the last houses. She kept watching him even when she was through cutting the onions, until it was no longer possible for her to see him, because then he was no longer an annoyance in her life but an imaginary dot on the horizon of the sea.

1. The inhabitants of the town in which the story takes place are depicted as:
   A. proud and stubborn people who are always arguing about religion.
   B. laid-back people who react to odd events with less surprise than one might expect.
   C. wise people who are always constructing elaborate theories about the universe.
   D. devious people who will do anything to make money.

2. The "neighbor woman" believes that the angel is a (an):
   F. angel of death.
   G. angel of good fortune.
   H. warrior angel.
   J. angel who can predict the future.

3. All of the following are described in detail EXCEPT:
   A. the ailments of the invalids.
   B. the girl who disobeyed her parents.
   C. the clothes bought by Elisenda.
   D. the crabs brought by the rainstorm.

4. The character of the angel can best be described as
   F. wise and loving.
   G. powerful but unforgiving.
   H. baffling and mysterious.
   J. pessimistic but determined.

5. Elisenda's idea to start charging people admission to see the angel is a (an):
   A. disrespectful decision motivated by greed.
   B. understandable decision motivated by necessity.
   C. risky decision motivated by poor business sense.
   D. weak decision motivated by her tendency to be influenced by others.

6. When they first encounter him, the townspeople treat the angel as if he is a (an):
   F. animal.
   G. impostor.
   H. impartial judge.
   J. bad omen.

7. All of the following are reasons why people became more interested in the spider girl than they had been in the angel EXCEPT:
   A. it is more obvious what moral they are supposed to learn from her.
   B. she is more willing to interact with her audience.
   C. she has been officially approved by local religious authorities.
   D. it is less expensive to see her.

8. Which of the following phrases indicates that the appearance of the angel is regarded as a somewhat normal occurrence?
   F. "They both looked at the fallen body with a mute stupor." (lines 11–12)
   G. "The most unfortunate invalids on earth came in search of health." (lines 38–40)
   H. "The angel was the only one who took no part in his own act." (lines 51–52)
   J. "they built a two-story mansion with iron bars on the windows so that angels wouldn't get in." (lines 87–89)

9. At the beginning of the story, Pelayo is employed as a (an):
   A. farmer.
   B. fisherman.
   C. bailiff.
   D. architect.

10. The main point of the last paragraph is that after the departure of the angel, Elisenda feels:
   F. remorseful about how poorly the townspeople treated the angel.
   G. frightened about what the angel might do if he ever comes back.
   H. optimistic about the new lifestyle that was made possible for her by the angel.
   J. unburdened now that she doesn't have to worry about the angel anymore.

PASSAGE II—SOCIAL SCIENCE

Passage A is adapted from "Whether Toleration Is Dangerous" by Voltaire. Passage B is adapted from *Civilization and Its Discontents* by Sigmund Freud.

Passage A by Voltaire

There are some who say that, if we treated with paternal indulgence those erring brethren who pray to God in bad French (instead of bad Latin), we should be putting weapons in their hands, and would once more witness the battles of Jarnac, Moncontour, Coutras, Dreux, and St. Denis. I do not know anything about this, as I am not a prophet; but it seems to me an illogical piece of reasoning to say "These men rebelled when I treated them ill; therefore, they will rebel when I treat them well."

I would venture to take the liberty to invite those who are at the head of the government, and those who are destined for high positions, to reflect carefully whether one really has ground to fear that kindness will lead to the same revolts as cruelty; whether what happened in certain circumstances is sure to happen in different circumstances; if the times, public opinion, and morals are unchanged.

The Huguenots, it is true, have been as inebriated with fanaticism and stained with blood as we. But are this generation as barbaric as their fathers? Have not time, the progress of reason, good books, and the humanising influence of society had an effect on the leaders of these people? And do we not perceive that the aspect of nearly the whole of Europe has been changed within the last fifty years? Government is stronger everywhere, and morals have improved. Different times have different needs. It would be absurd to decimate the Sorbonne today because it once presented a demand for the burning of the Maid of Orleans, as stupid as to purge all the inhabitants of Marseilles because they had the plague in 1720.

Toleration never led to civil war; intolerance has covered the earth with carnage. I speak here only of the interest of nations. While respecting theology, as I do, I regard in this article only the physical and moral well-being of society. I beg every impartial reader to weigh these truths, verify them, and add to them. Attentive readers, who restrain not their thoughts, always go farther than the author.

Passage B by Sigmund Freud

The clue may be supplied by one of the ideal demands, as we have called them, of civilized society. It runs: "Thou shall love thy neighbour as thyself." Let us adopt a naive attitude towards it, as though we were hearing it for the first time; we shall be unable to suppress a feeling of bewilderment. Why should we do it? What good will it do us? My love is something valuable to me which I ought not to throw away without reflection. It imposes duties on me for whose fulfilment I must be ready to make sacrifices. If I love someone, he must deserve it in some way. He deserves it if he is so like me in important ways that I can love myself in him; and he deserves it if he is so much more perfect than myself that I can love my ideal of my own self in him. I have to love him if he is my friend's son, since the pain my friend would feel if any harm came to him would be my pain too. But if he is a stranger to me and cannot attract me by any worth of his own, it will be hard for me to love him. Indeed, I should be wrong to do so, for my love is valued by all my own people, and it is an injustice to them if I put a stranger on a par with them. What is the point of a precept enunciated with so much solemnity if its fulfilment cannot be recommended as reasonable?

On closer inspection, I find still further difficulties. Not merely is this stranger in general unworthy of my love; I must honestly confess that he has more claim to my hostility and even my hatred. He seems not to have the least trace of love for me and shows me not the slightest consideration. If it will do him any good he has no hesitation in injuring me, nor does he ask himself whether the amount of advantage he gains bears any proportion to the extent of the harm he does to me. Indeed, he need not even obtain an advantage; if he can satisfy any sort of desire by it, he thinks nothing of jeering at me, insulting me, slandering me and showing his superior power; and the more secure he feels and the more helpless I am, the more certainly I can expect him to behave like this to me. If he behaves differently, I am ready to treat him in the same way. Indeed, if this grandiose commandment had run "Love thy neighbour as thy neighbour loves thee," I should not take exception to it.

The truth behind all this, which people are so ready to disavow, is that men are not gentle creatures who merely defend themselves if attacked; they are, on the contrary, creatures among whose instinctual endowments is a powerful share of aggressiveness. As a result, their neighbour is someone who tempts them to satisfy their aggressiveness on him, to humiliate him, to cause him pain, to torture and to kill him. Who, in the face of all his experience of life and of history, will have the courage to dispute this assertion?

Questions 11–13 ask about Passage A.

11. Which of the following inferences would be most strongly supported by a reading of Passage A?
   A. The Huguenots were a French religious minority that had violently revolted in the past, but not recently as of the time of the passage's composition.
   B. The battles referenced by the author in line 5 were not real historical events, but legendary battles that have great symbolic significance in French culture.
   C. The author believes praying in Latin to be absurd and self-important but praying in French to be an admirable mark of humility.
   D. Marseilles was a French ghost town, all of its former inhabitants having perished in the year 1720.

12. Based on an understanding of the passage as a whole, it is most logical to assume that, in his discussion upon how much Europe has improved in the recent past (lines 24–35), the author of Passage A is:
   F. being sarcastic.
   G. being completely serious.
   H. seeking to prompt discussion of complex questions to which he genuinely does not know the answers.
   J. testing the reader's knowledge.

13. Based on the contexts of the passage as a whole and of the closing paragraph specifically, the concluding sentence of Passage A ("Attentive readers ... the author") was most likely intended by Voltaire to be a:
   A. clue to the fact that the essay contains some sort of hidden message that was too controversial for him to state openly.
   B. subtle foreshadowing of the fact that Voltaire was dying, suspected that this might be his final essay, and wished his readers to carry on his work.
   C. genuine compliment to his readers, made in the hopes of enlisting the aid of as many of them as possible in a worthy cause.
   D. biting joke at the expense of readers who would seek to imply that his authorship of this essay implicates Voltaire as a party to some Huguenot conspiracy.

Questions 14–17 ask about Passage B.

14. Which of the following statements best captures how Passage B characterizes the obstacle(s) to "Love thy neighbor as thyself" ever being widely practiced?
   F. Human beings are simply biologically predisposed to regular acts of unprovoked aggression.
   G. The expression has become so familiar by now that it is difficult for people to stop and think about what it truly means, as though hearing it for the first time.
   H. Mankind's long history of violence means that different groups of people have built up too much resentment for each other at this point to ever get over it.
   J. Psychologists and philosophers have historically always failed in their attempts to establish that the advice is reasonable.

15. In lines 52–72, the author of Passage B presents:
   A. his own personal argument for why "Love thy neighbor" is flawed advice.
   B. his approximation of what he deems the average person's true inner reaction to "Love thy neighbor" to be, on an unspoken emotional level.
   C. a deliberately bad argument against "Love thy neighbor," the flaws of which he will explain later in the passage.
   D. a lament for the sad act that "Love thy neighbor" is impossible because humans do not have any control over who they love.

16. As it is used in line 91, the word *grandiose* is most nearly synonymous with which of the following phrases?
   F. "A wolf in sheep's clothing"
   G. "The canary in the coal mine"
   H. "Full of hot air"
   J. "As clear as mud"

17. In light of Sigmund Freud's status as one of the most innovative thinkers in human history, the style and structure of Passage A is unexpected and ironic because:
   A. nearly every claim it makes is presented as something that everybody already knows.
   B. it analyzes a religious proverb as though it were a scientific hypothesis.
   C. Freud concludes it with a pessimistic and overdramatic prophecy about how nobody will believe him.
   D. most of its assertions are supported solely by personal anecdotes from Freud's own life.

Questions 18–20 ask about both passages.

18. The potential rebuttal to Passage A that is implicit in the conclusions of Passage B would most nearly be that:
   F. policies of tolerance will not end violence, as people will find excuses to hate one another no matter what.
   G. tolerance could only ever be proposed by someone who sees his own position as weak—if he were confident of his strength, he would seek to oppress his enemies.
   H. people only preach tolerance as a means of distracting themselves from truths they are unwilling to admit.
   J. the fact that revenge is a moral obligation means that tolerance itself is an injustice.

19. Based on the two passages, the question that the author of Passage A would presumably be most eager to ask the author of Passage B would concern whether:
   A. increasingly fair and just laws are at least capable of significantly decreasing violence, even if the aggressive instinct must forever remain with us.
   B. he is willing to admit the fact that the world has been improved by unreasonable things occasionally.
   C. there is a chance that, rather than human nature being inherently bad, human beings are merely reinforcing the worst parts of it by concentrating on the past.
   D. he believes that human beings' treatment of one another has been getting steadily better throughout history, or whether this assessment is just an illusion.

20. Which of the following is the most accurate and thought-provoking comparison of the two passages' closing paragraphs?
   F. Both authors take it for granted that violence is a bad thing, despite admitting that it has been common at all times in all places.
   G. Though Passage B primarily seeks to rebut a religious concept, it is Passage A that sees theology as being inherently at odds with the interest of nations.
   H. Neither author draws a distinction between humans and the rest of the animal kingdom, despite the fact that both closing paragraphs demand one.
   J. Though the passages' claims contradict each other, both authors expect all readers to assess their points as self-evident and undeniable.

PASSAGE III—HUMANITIES

This passage is adapted from the essay "My Father's Suitcase" by Orhan Pamuk (© 2006 Orhan Pamuk).

Two years before my father died, he gave me a small suitcase filled with his manuscripts and notebooks. Assuming his usual jocular, mocking air, he told me that he wanted me to read them after he was gone, by which he meant after his death.

"Just take a look," he said, slightly embarrassed. "See if there's anything in there that you can use. Maybe after I'm gone you can make a selection and publish it." We were in my study, surrounded by books. My father was searching for a place to set down the suitcase, wandering around like a man who wished to rid himself of a painful burden. In the end, he deposited it quietly, unobtrusively, in a corner.

For several days after that, I walked back and forth past the suitcase without ever actually touching it. I knew what was inside some of the notebooks it held. I had seen my father writing in them. In his youth, he had wanted to be an Istanbul poet, but he had not wanted to live the sort of life that came with writing poetry in a poor country where there were few readers.

The first thing that kept me away from my father's suitcase was, of course, a fear that I might not like what I read. Because my father understood this, he had taken the precaution of acting as if he did not take the contents of the case seriously. By this time, I had been working as a writer for twenty-five years, and his failure to take literature seriously pained me. But my real fear—the crucial thing that I did not wish to discover—was that my father might be a good writer. If great literature emerged from my father's suitcase, I would have to acknowledge that inside my father there existed a man entirely different from the one I knew. This was a frightening possibility. Even at my advanced age, I wanted my father to be my father and my father only—not a writer.

A writer is someone who spends years patiently trying to discover the second being inside him, and the world that makes him who he is. To write is to transform that inward gaze into words, to study the worlds into which we pass when we retire into ourselves, and to do so with patience, obstinacy, and joy. As I sit at my table, for days, months, years, slowly adding words to empty pages, I feel as if I were bringing into being that other person inside me, in the same way that one might build a bridge or a dome, stone by stone.

I was afraid of opening my father's suitcase and reading his notebooks because I knew that he would never have tolerated the difficulties that I had tolerated, that it was not solitude he loved but mixing with friends, crowds, company. I would have to remember that my father enjoyed being alone with his books and his thoughts—and not pay too much attention to the literary quality of his writing. But as I gazed so anxiously at the suitcase he had bequeathed to me I also felt that this was the very thing I would not be able to do.

In fact, I was angry at my father because he had not led a life like mine—because he had never quarreled with his life, and had spent it happily laughing with his friends and his loved ones. But part of me also knew that I was not so much "angry" as "jealous," and this, too, made me uneasy. What is happiness? Is happiness believing that you live a deep life in your lonely room? Or is happiness leading a comfortable life in society, believing in the same things as everyone else, or, at least, acting as if you did? Is it happiness or unhappiness to go through life writing in secret, while seeming to be in harmony with all that surrounds you?

On some deeper level, I was able to become a writer because my father, in his youth, had also wished to be one. I would have to read him with tolerance—to seek to understand what he had written in those hotel rooms. It was with these hopeful thoughts that I walked over to the suitcase, which was still sitting where my father had left it. Using all my will power, I read through a few manuscripts and notebooks. What had my father written about? I recall a few views from the windows of Paris hotels, a few poems, paradoxes, analyses ...

A week after he left me his suitcase, my father paid me another visit; as always, he brought me a bar of chocolate (he had forgotten that I was forty-eight years old). As always, we chatted and laughed about life, politics, and family gossip. A moment arrived when my father's gaze drifted to the corner where he had left his suitcase, and he saw that I had moved it. We looked each other in the eye. There followed a pressing silence. I did not tell him that I had opened the suitcase and tried to read its contents; instead, I looked away. But he understood. Just as I understood that he had understood. Because my father was a happy, easygoing man who had faith in himself, he smiled at me the way he always did. And, as he left the house, he repeated all the lovely and encouraging things he always said to me, like a father.

As always, I watched him leave, envying his happiness, his carefree and unflappable temperament. But I remember that on that day there was also a flash of joy inside me that made me ashamed. It was prompted by the thought that maybe I wasn't as comfortable in life as he was, maybe I had not led as happy or footloose a life as he had, but at least I had devoted mine to writing. I was ashamed to be thinking such things at my father's expense—of all people, my father, who had never been a source of pain to me, who had left me free. All this should remind us that writing and literature are intimately linked to a void at the center of our lives, to our feelings of happiness and guilt.

21. The author of the passage would most strongly agree with which of the following statements?

A. Happiness can only be found through others.

B. The paths that children take can be predicted by anyone who knows their parents well.

C. Good writing is actually the opposite of what has traditionally been viewed as "great literature."

D. Writing is largely a solitary endeavor.

22. All of the following are reasons why the author is afraid to open the suitcase and read its contents EXCEPT:

F. he fears that he will come to see his father as a writer, rather than as just his father.

G. he suspects that the notebooks might contain painful secrets about his parents' relationship.

H. he suspects that his father's writing will force him to examine his own ideas about happiness.

J. he is afraid that his father's writing will be very good.

23. In the context of the passage, the statement "he had forgotten that I was forty-eight years old" (lines 91–92) suggests that the:
A. author's father is becoming absent-minded in his old age.
B. author's father was absent for most of his childhood.
C. author's father still treats him like a child in some small ways.
D. author may have been adopted.

24. When the author says that his father "would never have tolerated the difficulties that I had tolerated" (lines 54–55), he means that his father:
F. prioritized making money when he was a younger man.
G. could not have endured the solitude that real writing demands.
H. tended toward orthodoxy in his political and religious opinions.
J. fled their native country rather than trying to improve it from within.

25. As it is used in line 15, *unobtrusively* most nearly means:
A. inconspicuously.
B. rudely.
C. painfully.
D. ashamedly.

26. The author mentions feeling all of the following emotions concerning his father EXCEPT:
F. anger.
G. joy.
H. jealousy.
J. suspicion.

27. The main point of paragraph 7 (lines 63–76) is that:
A. the author is jealous of his father for being able to make friends so easily wherever he goes.
B. happiness means being in harmony with all that surrounds you.
C. it is unclear whether the author's approach to life or his father's is ultimately more satisfying.
D. there is really no such thing as true happiness.

28. Writing, according to the author, is a lifelong process of discovering:
F. an alternate version of oneself.
G. one's relationship to one's native country.
H. one's true feelings about one's family.
J. the true nature of happiness.

29. When the author's father was young, he aspired to write:
A. novels.
B. poetry.
C. plays.
D. comedy.

30. The point of the last paragraph (lines 107–121) is that:
F. the author did not realize until that day that his father truly loved him.
G. the author is ashamed of his father.
H. writing draws on negative emotions as well as positive ones.
J. the author has finally decided to have children of his own.

PASSAGE IV—NATURAL SCIENCE

This passage is adapted from *The Selfish Gene* by Richard Dawkins (© 1976 Oxford University Press).

Most of what is unusual about man can be summed up in one word: "culture." I use the word not in its snobbish sense, but as a scientist uses it. Cultural transmission is analogous to genetic transmission in that, although basically conservative, it can give rise to a form of evolution. Geoffrey Chaucer could not hold a conversation with a modern Englishman, even though they are linked to each other by an unbroken chain of some twenty generations of Englishmen, each of whom could speak to his immediate neighbors in the chain as a son speaks to his father. Language seems to "evolve" by non-genetic means, and at a rate which is orders of magnitude faster than genetic evolution.

As an enthusiastic Darwinian, I have been dissatisfied with explanations that my fellow-enthusiasts have offered for human behavior. They have tried to look for "biological advantages" in various attributes of human civilization. These ideas are plausible as far as they go, but I find that they do not begin to square up to the formidable challenge of explaining culture, cultural evolution, and the immense differences between human cultures around the world. I think we have got to start again and go right back to first principles. The argument I shall advance is that, for an understanding of the evolution of modern man, we must begin by throwing out the gene as the sole basis of our ideas on evolution.

What, after all, is so special about genes? The answer is that they are replicators. But do we have to go to distant worlds to find other kinds of replicators and other kinds of evolution? I think that a new kind of replicator has recently emerged on this very planet. It is staring us in the face. It is still in its infancy, still drifting clumsily about in its primeval soup, but already it is achieving evolutionary change at a rate that leaves the old gene panting far behind.

The new soup is the soup of human culture. We need a name for the new replicator, a noun that conveys the idea of a unit of cultural transmission, or a unit of *imitation*. "Mimeme" comes from a suitable Greek root, but I want a monosyllable that sounds a bit like "gene." I hope my classicist friends will forgive me if I abbreviate "mimeme" to *meme*. Examples of memes are tunes, ideas, catch-phrases, clothes fashions, ways of making pots or of building arches. Just as genes propagate themselves in the gene pool by leaping from body to body, so memes propagate themselves in the meme pool by leaping from brain to brain. If a scientist hears, or reads about, a good idea, he passes it on to his colleagues and students. He mentions it in his articles and his lectures. If the idea catches on, it can be said to propagate itself, spreading from brain to brain.

Imitation, in the broad sense, is how memes *can* replicate. But just as not all genes that can replicate do so successfully, so some memes are more successful in the meme-pool than others. The longevity of any one copy of a meme is probably relatively unimportant, as it is for any one copy of a gene. The copy of the tune "Auld Lang Syne" that exists in my brain will last only for the rest of my life. But I expect there will be copies of the same tune on paper and in people's brains for centuries to come. If the meme is a scientific idea, its spread will depend on how acceptable it is to the population of individual scientists; a rough measure of its survival value could be obtained by counting the number of times it is referred to in successive years in scientific journals. If it is a popular tune, its spread through the meme pool may be gauged by the number of people heard whistling it in the streets. If it is a style of women's shoe, the population memeticist may use sales statistics from shoe shops.

Some memes, like some genes, achieve brilliant short-term success in spreading rapidly, but do not last long in the meme pool. Popular songs and stiletto heels are examples. Others may continue to propagate themselves for thousands of years, usually because of the great potential permanence of written records.

When we die there are two things we can leave behind us: genes and memes. We were built as gene machines, created to pass on our genes. But that aspect of us will be forgotten in three generations. Your child, even your grandchild, may bear a resemblance to you, perhaps in facial features, in a talent for music, in the color of her hair. But as each generation passes, the contribution of your genes is halved. It does not take long to reach negligible proportions. We should not seek immortality in reproduction.

But if you contribute to the world's culture, if you have a good idea, compose a tune, invent a sparking plug, write a poem, it may live on, intact, long after your genes have dissolved in the common pool. Socrates may or may not have a gene or two alive in the world today, but who cares? The meme-complexes of Socrates, Leonardo, Copernicus and Marconi are still going strong.

31. The author's motivation in writing the passage is his belief that:

A. genes actually have nothing to do with human evolution.
B. genetics does not sufficiently explain human culture.
C. culture is too obsessed with trivial things like fashion and pop songs.
D. humans are too concerned with seeking immortality.

32. When the author says that he uses the word *culture* "not in its snobbish sense, but as a scientist uses it" (lines 3–4), he means that he:

F. plans to honestly admit what aspects of culture he really likes, rather than pretending he only likes the critically respected things.
G. does not believe that there is really such a thing as culture at all.
H. thinks that culture can be completely explained by Darwinian evolution.
J. does not distinguish between "good" and "bad" culture, but refers merely to the facts of human civilization.

33. The author argues that all of the following would constitute examples of *memes* EXCEPT:

A. a word.
B. a piece of music.
C. a particular hair color.
D. a fashion item.

34. According to the author, one thing that genes and memes have in common is that they are both:

F. examples of replicators.
G. still only unproven theories rather than facts.
H. ideas that people in the future will only know about because of written records.
J. capable of inspiring great art.

35. The author mentions Geoffrey Chaucer in the first paragraph as an example of:
A. a pioneer in the field of mimetics.
B. one of the first major poets to write in English.
C. someone who would not have understood modern science, even though he was a genius for his time.
D. a speaker of English as it existed twenty generations ago.

36. As it is used in lines 52, 54, 59, and 86, the word *propagate* most nearly means:
F. multiply.
G. change.
H. prove.
J. conceal.

37. According to the passage, the word *memes* was invented by:
A. the ancient Greeks.
B. friends of the author.
C. the author's former teacher.
D. the author himself.

38. The author states that "[t]he copy of the tune 'Auld Lang Syne' that exists in my brain will last only for the rest of my life" (lines 67–69) in order to demonstrate that:
F. no two people's brains are alike.
G. memories do not survive death.
H. no one copy of an idea is vital, as long as the idea survives.
J. he is older than he imagines most of his readers will be, and accordingly has memories of older songs.

39. According to the author, the "survival value" of a meme is expressed by:
A. how widespread the meme itself becomes.
B. how it contributes to the survival of the people who have memories of it.
C. whether it makes the people who have memories of it into better people or worse people.
D. whether scientists believe that it is true or false.

40. The author mentions "Socrates, Leonardo, Copernicus and Marconi" in the closing paragraph because they are:
F. people whose genes have become extremely widespread.
G. people whose ideas have become extremely influential.
H. the four most complex thinkers in the history of science.
J. the people who made the biggest contributions to the field of memetics.

If there is still time remaining, you may review your answers.

SCIENCE TEST

Time: 35 Minutes—40 Questions

Directions: There are six passages in this test. Each passage is followed by several questions. After reading a passage, choose the best answer to each question and fill in the corresponding oval on your answer sheet. You may refer to the passages as often as necessary.

You are NOT permitted to use a calculator on this test.

PASSAGE I

Scientists examined several ingredients commonly used as active agents in sunscreen. The goal of the study was to determine which ingredients are most effective at blocking harmful UV rays.

Scientists used PABA, oxybenzone, octyl salicylate, and a broad-spectrum commercial sunscreen (SPF 45). The samples were exposed to sunlight with wavelengths ranging from 240 to 440 nm. The percent transmittance of UV rays at each wavelength was recorded. The data was collected manually using a spectrophotometer. The results, in 20-nm increments, are shown in Table 1.

Table 1

nm	PABA	Oxybenzone	Octyl Salicylate	Commercial Sunscreen
240	38.2	15.7	12.7	15.2
260	2.9	19.2	83.5	24.5
280	1.7	3.2	33.1	4.2
300	9	4.2	3	1.5
320	82.9	6	10.8	2.5
340	99.2	9.7	93.5	25.5
360	100	45.3	100	67.6
380	100	92.6	100	96.8
400	100	100	100	99.8
420	100	100	100	100
440	100	100	100	100

Figure 1 displays the intensity of sunlight across the spectrum.

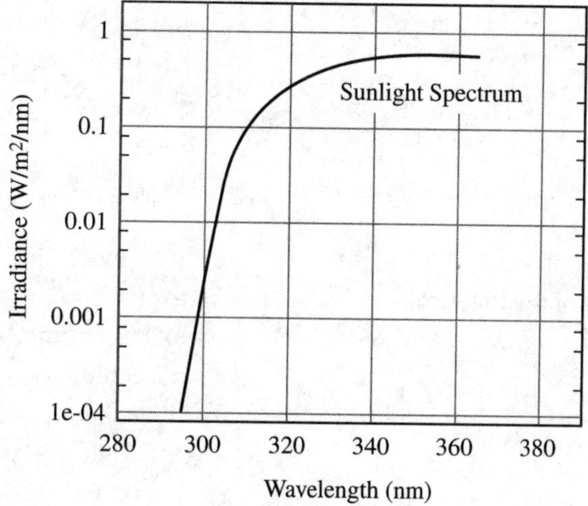

Figure 1

In 1975, Thomas B. Fitzpatrick, MD, Ph.D., of Harvard Medical School, developed a classification system for skin type. This system was based on a person's complexion and responses to sun exposure. Table 2 lists the skin types and their characteristics.

Table 2

Skin Type	Color	Reaction to UVA	Reaction to Sun
Type I	Very fair skin tone	Very sensitive	Always burns easily, never tans
Type II	Fair skin tone	Very sensitive	Usually burns easily, tans with difficulty
Type III	Fair to medium skin tone	Sensitive	Burns moderately, tans gradually
Type IV	Medium skin tone	Moderately sensitive	Rarely burns, always tans well
Type V	Olive or dark skin tone	Minimally sensitive	Very rarely burns, tans very easily
Type VI	Very dark skin tone	Least sensitive	Never burns, deeply pigmented

1. According to Table 1, which substance had the highest percent transmittance of UV rays for sunlight with a wavelength of 260 nm?
   A. Octyl salicylate
   B. PABA
   C. Oxybenzone
   D. Commercial sunscreen

2. Based on the information in Figure 1, sunlight is most intense at which of the following wavelengths?
   F. 290 nm
   G. 300 nm
   H. 320 nm
   J. 340 nm

3. A person with fair skin tone, whose skin burns but also tans slowly, likely has which of the following skin types?
   A. Type I
   B. Type II
   C. Type III
   D. Type IV

4. Experts state that anyone whose skin is sensitive or very sensitive to UVA should always wear sunscreen. According to Table 2, people with which skin types should always wear sunscreen?
   F. Types I and II
   G. Types I, II, and III
   H. Types II, III, and IV
   J. Types V and VI

5. In sunlight with an irradiance of 0.01 $W/m^2/nm$, oxybenzone would be expected to have a UV ray percent transmittance of:
   A. 3.8
   B. 5
   C. 9.7
   D. 100

6. If an individual with Type II skin type was exposed to the sun at a wavelength of 320 nm immediately after applying commercial sunscreen SPF 45, how would their skin most likely be affected?
   F. Their skin would burn because Type II skin is sensitive and sunscreen SPF 45 does not block most of the sun's harmful rays at 320 nm wavelength.
   G. Their skin would burn because 320 nm wavelength is very damaging and would burn any skin type.
   H. Their skin would not burn because though they have sensitive skin, sunscreen SPF 45 blocks most of the sun's rays at 320 nm.
   J. Their skin would not burn because Type II skin is not sensitive enough to cause a burn at 320 nm.

PASSAGE II

The most common type of red-green color perception defect is caused by a mutation on the X chromosome. X-linked red color blindness is a recessive trait. The eggs of the mother will contain either a normal X chromosome (X^R) or an X chromosome with the mutation (X^r) causing red-green color blindness. The sperm of the father will contain the normal X chromosome, the X chromosome with the mutation, or the Y chromosome. Females *heterozygous* (one normal gene, one mutated gene) for this trait have normal vision. The color perception defect manifests itself in females only when it is inherited from both parents. By contrast, males inherit their sole X chromosome from their mothers, and become red-green color blind when this one X chromosome has the color perception defect.

Genotype refers to the combination of alleles that an individual has for a gene. Table 1 lists the possible genotypes for red-green color perception and their corresponding effects on vision.

Table 1

Female Genotype	Vision
$X^R X^R$	normal
$X^R X^r$	normal, carrier
$X^r X^r$	red-green color blind
Male Genotype	**Vision**
$X^R Y$	normal
$X^r Y$	red-green color blind

Students interviewed members of the Allen family to investigate the inheritance of red-green color blindness. Figure 1 displays the family tree of the Allen family.

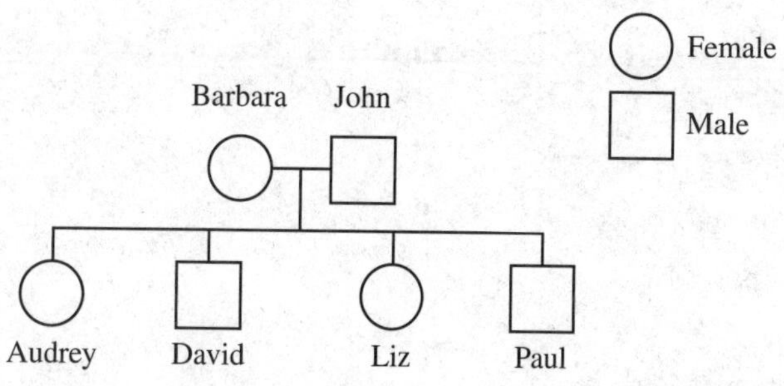

Figure 1

Study 1

Students interviewed Barbara and John and learned that Barbara is red-green color blind, while John is not. Based on this information, the students deduced that their four children have the following genotypes:

Females:	$X^R X^r$
Males:	$X^r Y$

Figure 2

Study 2

Students assumed that Liz would have children with a man who has normal vision, and using a Punnett square calculated all of the possible genotypes for their children:

$X^R X^R$	$X^R X^r$
$X^R X^r$	$X^r Y$

Figure 3

Study 3

Students assumed that David would have children with a woman who has red-green color blindness, and using a Punnett square calculated all of the possible genotypes for their children:

$X^r X^r$	$X^r Y$

Figure 4

7. A female who has normal vision but is a carrier of red-green color blindness must have which of the following genotypes?
   A. $X^R X^R$
   B. $X^R X^r$
   C. $X^r X^r$
   D. $X^R Y$

8. For a couple to produce only red-green color-blind children, regardless of the child's sex, they would need to have which of the following pairs of genotypes?
   F. $X^R X^R$ and $X^r Y$
   G. $X^r X^r$ and $X^R Y$
   H. $X^R X^r$ and $X^r Y$
   J. $X^r X^r$ and $X^r Y$

9. All of the male offspring exhibited red-green color blindness in Studies:
   A. 1 and 3.
   B. 1, 2, and 3.
   C. 2 and 3.
   D. 1 and 2.

10. Suppose that Barbara and John have 4 daughters. According to the information in Study 1 and the passage, how many of their daughters will manifest the color blind defect?
    F. 0
    G. 1
    H. 2
    J. 4

11. The ratio of Barbara and John's offspring with normal vision to offspring with red-green color blindness is:
    A. 1:2
    B. 2:1
    C. 1:1
    D. 3:1

12. Barbara's parents could have had which of the following pairs of genotypes?
    F. $X^r X^r$ and $X^R Y$
    G. $X^R X^r$ and $X^r Y$
    H. $X^R X^R$ and $X^r Y$
    J. $X^R X^R$ and $X^R Y$

13. Using the information in Study 1, if Barbara and John had a daughter who married a man with a genotype of X^rY, what is the chance that the two would produce an offspring that is a carrier for red-green color blindness, but has normal vision?
    A. 25%
    B. 50%
    C. 75%
    D. 100%

PASSAGE III

Crude oil contains many different types of carbons. Different carbon chain lengths have different boiling points, so they can be separated using *distillation*—the process of boiling and then condensing a liquid in order to separate and purify its components (see Figure 1).

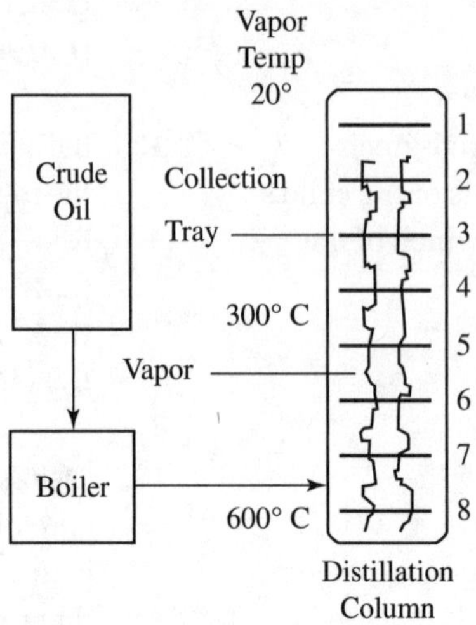

Figure 1

Crude oil is put into a boiler. The boiler is connected to a distillation column filled with collection trays. As the heated oil boils, the vapors released enter the distillation column and rise to the top. When a substance in the vapor reaches a height where the temperature of the column is equal to that substance's boiling point, it will condense to form a liquid. The liquid is gathered on the collection trays.

Experiment 1

Students determined the boiling points of various components of crude oil by recording the temperature of the vapor at various heights in the distillation column, then determining which component was collected in each of the eight collection trays. See Table 1 and Table 2.

Table 1

Boiling Point	Tray #
20°C	1
40°C	2
120°C	3
200°C	4
350°C	5
400°C	6
500°C	7
600°C	8

PRACTICE TEST 2

Table 2

Crude Oil Component	Tray #
Gas	1
Naphtha	2
Gasoline	3
Kerosene	4
Diesel	5
Lubricating oil	6
Heavy gas oil	7
Residual oil	8

The students distilled one barrel of crude oil. Figure 2 shows the breakdown of that barrel, in terms of which components were collected.

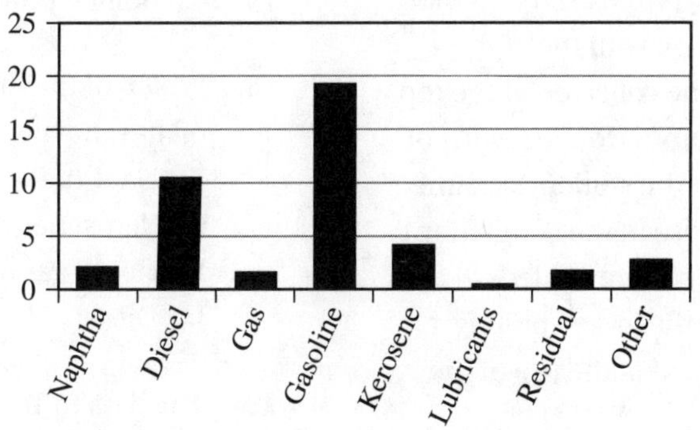

Figure 2

Experiment 2

Students determined the number of carbons in each component of crude oil and recorded the data in Table 3.

Table 3

Crude Oil Component	# of Carbons
Diesel	12+
Gas	1–4
Gasoline	5–12
Heavy gas oil	20–70
Kerosene	10–18
Lubricating oil	20–50
Naphtha	5–9
Residual oil	70+

14. Based on the results of Experiment 1, the boiling temperature of naphtha is:
F. 20°C
G. 40°C
H. 120°C
J. 200°C

15. According to the results of Experiment 1, one barrel of crude oil contains about how many gallons of diesel?
A. 2
B. 6
C. 11
D. 29

16. One of the students hypothesized that the components of crude oil with the highest boiling points would be collected at the top of the distillation column. Do the results of Experiment 1 support the student's claim?
F. No. As the vapor rose in the distillation column, the temperature cooled, so the components with the lowest boiling points were collected at the top of the column.
G. No. There was no correlation between boiling point and location in the distillation column.
H. Yes. Gasoline and diesel had the highest boiling points, and they were collected in the top two trays.
J. Yes. The lower the collection tray was in the distillation column, the lower the component's boiling point.

17. A scientist claimed that the more carbons a substance has, the higher its boiling point will be. Do the results of Experiment 1 and Experiment 2 support this claim?
A. No. There is no relationship between the number of carbons and the boiling point.
B. No. Diesel has more carbons than gasoline, yet its boiling point is lower.
C. Yes. Residual oil has the most carbons and the lowest boiling point, whereas gas has the fewest carbons and the highest boiling point.
D. Yes. Residual oil has the most carbons and the highest boiling point, whereas gas has the fewest carbons and the lowest boiling point.

18. Which of the following components of crude oil has the highest boiling point?
F. Naphtha
G. Kerosene
H. Heavy gas oil
J. Diesel

19. The data in Table 1 and Figure 2 support which of the following?
A. Components with the highest boiling points are collected in greatest quantity.
B. Components with the lowest boiling points are collected in greatest quantity.
C. Components with medium boiling points are collected in greatest quantity.
D. Components with higher boiling points are collected in the same quantities as those with medium boiling points.

20. A scientist conducting studies on crude oil discovered another substance contained in the oil with a boiling point of 300 degrees. How many carbons would it likely have in its composition?
F. 12–18
G. 5–9
H. 70+
J. 20–50

PASSAGE IV

Solubility refers to the ability of one substance, the solute, to dissolve in another (the *solvent*). The balance of molecules between the solvent and the solute determines the solubility of one substance in another. Factors such as temperature and pressure will alter this balance, thus changing the solubility.

Experiments to determine the solubility of methane and carbon dioxide in polyamide (PA-11) were performed in the temperature range 50–90°C, and the pressure range 50–150 atm for methane and 20–40 atm for carbon dioxide. Table 1 displays the solubility (sol) of methane in PA-11. Table 2 shows the solubility (sol) of carbon dioxide in PA-11.

$$\text{Solubility} = (g\ \text{gas}/g\ \text{PA-11}) \times 10^3$$

Table 1—Methane

T = 50°C		T = 70°C		T = 90°C	
Pressure (atm)	Sol	Pressure (atm)	Sol	Pressure (atm)	Sol
51.2	3.18	55.3	2.61	53.1	2.38
107.2	4.51	104.0	4.97	106.5	5.14
156.6	3.45	158.1	5.33	144.4	6.52

Table 2—Carbon Dioxide

T = 50°C		T = 70°C		T = 90°C	
Pressure (atm)	Sol	Pressure (atm)	Sol	Pressure (atm)	Sol
22.1	12.8	20.3	11.8	20	6.93
31.1	18.9	26.4	14.3	30.4	12.0
39.8	23.1	37.5	18.7	42.4	14.0

Figure 1 shows the pressurization cycle for methane at 100 atm and 50°C. The mass gain divided by the net polyamide mass determines the solubility of the gas.

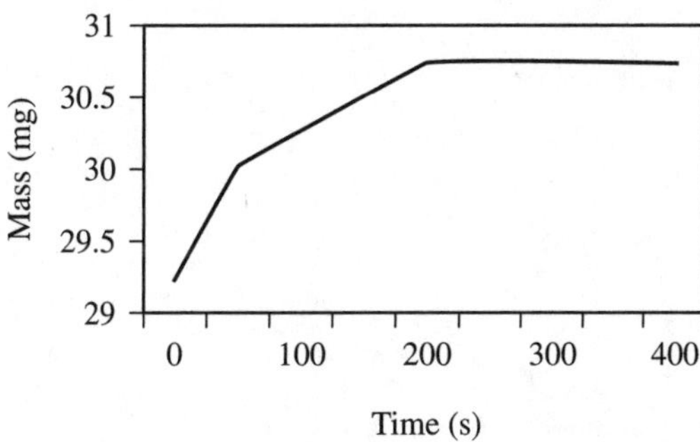

Figure 1

PRACTICE TEST 2

21. Which of the following substances did NOT become more soluble as pressure increased?
    A. Methane at 70°C
    B. Methane at 50°C
    C. Carbon dioxide at 50°C
    D. Carbon dioxide at 90°C

22. According to Table 2, at which temperature was carbon dioxide the most soluble under pressure of 31.1 atm?
    F. 50°C
    G. 70°C
    H. 90°C
    J. 100°C

23. Figure 1 supports which of the following claims about polyamide mass gain over time?
    A. The polyamide steadily gained mass.
    B. The polyamide lost mass over time.
    C. The polyamide gained mass at first, and then lost mass.
    D. The polyamide quickly gained mass and then leveled off.

24. If the experiment was repeated at a temperature of 90°C and a pressure of 80 atm, the solubility of methane would be closest to:
    F. 2.61 atm.
    G. 3.75 atm.
    H. 5.08 atm.
    J. 14.0 atm.

25. Based on the results shown in Table 2, which of the following conclusions can be drawn regarding the relationship between pressure and solubility?
    A. Solubility increases with pressure only above 70°C.
    B. As pressure increases, solubility decreases.
    C. As pressure increases, so does solubility.
    D. There is no correlation between pressure and solubility.

26. In this experiment, which substance functioned as the *solvent*?
    F. Methane
    G. Carbon dioxide
    H. Mass
    J. Polyamide

27. Scientists wanted to conduct further tests and needed to ensure that experimental conditions were ideal for the solubility of methane. What temperature and pressure would they have to maintain in their experiment?
    A. Temperature of 70 degrees; pressure of 104 atm
    B. Temperature of 90 degrees; pressure of 144.4 atm
    C. Temperature of 50 degrees; pressure of 39.8 atm
    D. Temperature of 70 degrees; pressure of 158.1 atm

PASSAGE V

Ever since Darwin proposed his theory of natural selection in 1859, biologists have regarded the gene as the sole unit of inheritance, and the discovery of DNA in the twentieth century only served to reinforce this view, known as "hard inheritance." The idea that environmental factors could produce heritable changes in an organism without altering the organism's DNA (as occurs in gene mutation due to radiation exposure, for example), known as "soft inheritance," had long been written off as an impossibility. "Inheritance of acquired traits" became a biological fallacy associated with pre-Darwinians like Jean-Baptiste Lamarck and fanatical Soviet scientists like Trofim Lysenko. But the very recent discovery of what has been termed *epigenetics*—biological mechanisms that leave DNA unchanged but can alter the ways in which individual genes express themselves—has opened the door on the possibility of "soft inheritance" once again, although many biologists remain skeptical.

Scientist 1

Although study of the so-called "epigenome" is worthwhile and possesses the potential to answer questions about a host of problems from diabetes to cancer, it would be premature to call true "soft inheritance" a reality, at least in animal species. Isolated situations in which environmental factors could affect an organism's immediate descendants—a mother with a zinc deficiency producing children and grandchildren with weakened immune systems, for example—had already been documented without anyone ever suggesting that there was more to heritability than the gene. Immediate successive generations may exhibit observable effects, but the bloodline always reverts to the true expression of its DNA. A map with dust on it may be hard to read, but the information on the map remains unchanged, and it is simply a matter of how long it takes for a strong wind to blow away the dust.

Scientist 2

Someone who is determined never to see "true soft inheritance" will never see it, but that doesn't change the fact that it occurs, and indeed has been occurring all along without our realizing it. Epigenetic mechanisms may not alter DNA, but they possess the ability to turn genes "on" or "off" for the duration of an organism's bloodline, at least until such time as the genes are affected by another epigenetic mechanism. There is already compelling evidence, for example, that tobacco smoking poses risks not only to the individual smoker, but to all of his or her descendants. Imagine a three-way lightbulb with three possible brightness settings being put into a three-way lamp on which one of the settings is broken. The fact that the bulb still possesses three settings is immaterial if it is permanently set into a broken lamp. It will continue to "express itself" in a limited way. And the same thing can happen to a gene. If environmental factors can permanently alter the way in which an unaltered gene expresses itself down along a bloodline, resulting in observable effects in the members of that bloodline, then what can we possibly call this other than true soft inheritance?

28. According to the information in the passage, which of the following might constitute an example of true soft inheritance?
   F. Inherited gene damage due to a parent's heavy radiation exposure
   G. A susceptibility to diabetes as the result of a malnourished grandparent
   H. A left-handed parent producing predominantly left-handed offspring
   J. A parent who loves books teaching her children to love books

29. Who first proposed the theory of epigenetics?
   A. Charles Darwin
   B. Trofim Lysenko
   C. Scientist 2
   D. The information is not included in the passage.

30. In the offspring of which of the following organisms might Scientist 1 currently be willing to concede the documented existence of true soft inheritance?
   F. A rhinoceros
   G. A radiation-exposed human being
   H. An apple tree
   J. A zinc-deficient human being

31. Scientist 2 would most likely *disagree* with the suggestion that genes:
   A. are the primary units of inheritance.
   B. act in isolation to produce traits.
   C. possess the ability to express themselves.
   D. are made up of stretches of DNA.

32. Scientist 1 would be most likely to predict that any ill effects on the grandchildren of a tobacco smoker:
   F. have nothing to do with the epigenome.
   G. are probably psychological rather than biological in origin.
   H. must be the result of tobacco use having altered the smoker's DNA.
   J. will cease to be expressed in the bloodline given enough time.

33. *Histones* are proteins that attach themselves to sequences of DNA and can alter the expression of genes depending on whether they are *acetylated* or *methylated*. Given this information, it would appear that *histones* are analogous to the:
   A. sole unit of inheritance.
   B. zinc-deficient mother mentioned by Scientist 1.
   C. map mentioned by Scientist 1.
   D. lamp mentioned by Scientist 2.

34. A study of what would be most likely to resolve the disagreement between Scientist 1 and Scientist 2?
   F. the length of time that epigenetic mechanisms tend to remain in a bloodline
   G. the unpublished work of Jean-Baptiste Lamarck
   H. a comparison of cancer rates among identical twins
   J. the inner workings of three-way lightbulbs

PASSAGE VI

Figure 1 shows the average sleep pattern of a child, Figure 2 shows the average sleep pattern of a young adult, and Figure 3 shows the average sleep pattern of an elderly person. At Stage 0, the person is awake. As sleep moves from Stage 1 to Stage 4, it grows progressively deeper. REM sleep, commonly associated with dreaming, is predominant in the final third of a sleep cycle.

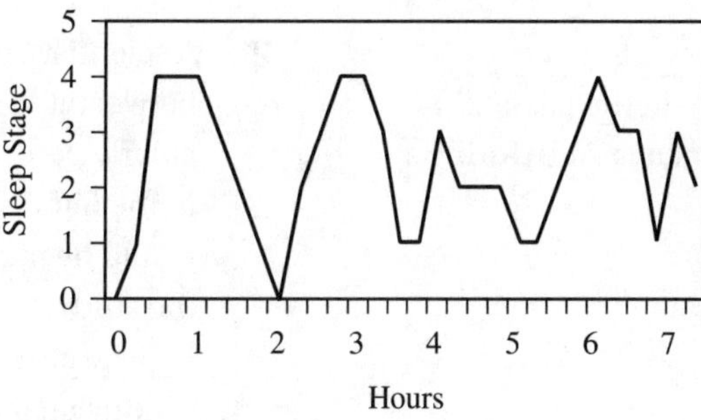

Figure 1

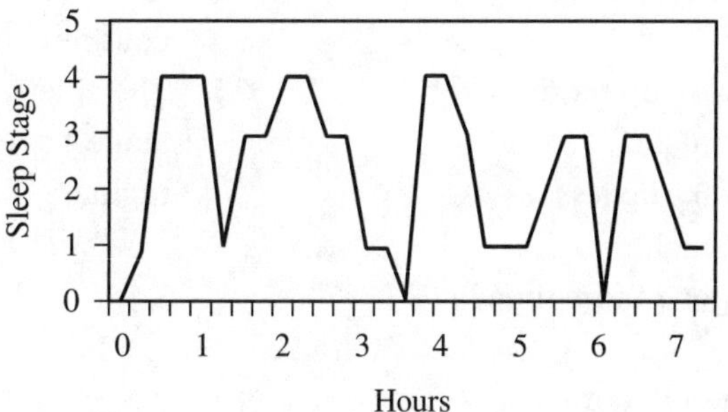

Figure 2

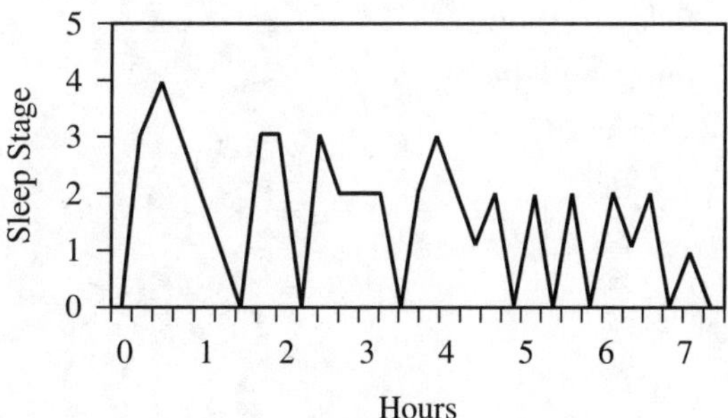

Figure 3

35. According to Figure 2, a young adult who has been asleep for 5 hours will most likely be in which sleep stage?
    A. Stage 0
    B. Stage 1
    C. Stage 3
    D. Stage 5

36. Based on the information in the passage, a child will wake up how many times during a 7-hour stretch of sleep?
    F. 7
    G. 2
    H. 1
    J. 0

37. Based on the data presented in Figures 1, 2, and 3, which of the following conclusions can be properly drawn?
    A. As people age, they wake up more frequently during the night.
    B. As people age, they wake up less frequently during the night.
    C. As people age, they spend more time in deep sleep.
    D. As people age, they spend more consecutive time in each sleep stage.

38. Based on the information in the passage and in Figure 2, at which of the following hours into a sleep interval will a young adult be most likely to experience REM sleep?
    F. 0
    G. 1
    H. 2
    J. 7

39. At which of the following hours of sleep will a child most likely be in the deepest sleep?
    A. 2
    B. 3
    C. 5
    D. 7

40. A scientist decided to do a comparative study between the sleep cycles of a child and an elderly person. From the information given in the figures, which of the following results would he most likely NOT find at the end of the study?
    F. The elderly generally wake up more often during the night.
    G. The elderly and children generally reach Stage 4 within the first hour of sleep.
    H. The elderly wake more often than children in the last two hours of sleep.
    J. The elderly and children generally reach Stage 4 at least three times during the night.

If there is still time remaining, you may review your answers.

WRITING TEST

Time: 40 Minutes

Online Culture

The Internet enables people all over the world to express themselves to one another directly, but the nature of this interaction is often antagonistic. Online anonymity, combined with the absence of the emotional recognition that comes with face-to-face communication, has created an Internet culture in which many people will say anything they can think of to hurt someone else's feelings, or even to threaten them with real-life harm, often over the slightest of disagreements. "Diversity," in the form of exposure to viewpoints other than our own, is usually hailed as a desirable goal, but when diverse environments are both anonymous and unpoliced, the result can be insults and hurt feelings, or even threats and fear.

Read and carefully consider these perspectives. Each suggests a particular way of thinking about online culture.

Perspective One	Perspective Two	Perspective Three
When people are able to communicate anonymously, they will behave like jerks. And when most people are communicating anonymously most of the time, most communication will be combative and unnecessarily cruel.	Before the Internet, people were mostly only exposed to the viewpoints of others who were like them. The amazing ability to interact with someone of a completely different background and experience at the click of a button is bound to cause some tensions, but overall it is moving humanity forward.	The Internet hasn't replaced the real world, but only extended it. The groups of people who have privilege and power in real life have merely transferred their bullying and oppression into the virtual world. Their targets aren't just afraid for their online selves, but for their physical selves as well—just like they already were before the web was invented.

ESSAY TASK

Write a unified, coherent essay about online culture. In your essay, be sure to:

- clearly state your own perspective on the issue and analyze the relationship between your perspective and at least one other perspective
- develop and support your ideas with reasoning and examples
- organize your ideas clearly and logically
- communicate your ideas effectively in standard written English

Your perspective may be in full agreement with any of those given, in partial agreement, or completely different.

Planning Your Response

Your prewriting notes on this page will not be considered in your score.

Use the following space to brainstorm ideas and map out your response. You may want to think about the following as you analyze the given prompt:

Strengths and weaknesses of the three viewpoints

- What good points do they make, and what potential objections do they ignore?
- Why might they be convincing to readers, and why might their perspectives fall short?

Your previous experience, background knowledge, and personal values

- What is your viewpoint on this topic, and what are the pros and cons of this viewpoint?
- How will you craft an argument in support of your point of view?

If there is still time remaining, you may review your answers.

ANSWER KEY
Practice Test 2

English

1. **A**	16. **F**	31. **D**	46. **F**	61. **C**
2. **G**	17. **C**	32. **G**	47. **C**	62. **G**
3. **C**	18. **F**	33. **A**	48. **F**	63. **B**
4. **G**	19. **D**	34. **G**	49. **A**	64. **G**
5. **C**	20. **G**	35. **D**	50. **J**	65. **A**
6. **J**	21. **A**	36. **F**	51. **D**	66. **J**
7. **A**	22. **J**	37. **B**	52. **H**	67. **B**
8. **H**	23. **C**	38. **H**	53. **B**	68. **F**
9. **A**	24. **H**	39. **B**	54. **J**	69. **B**
10. **J**	25. **A**	40. **J**	55. **B**	70. **F**
11. **D**	26. **F**	41. **C**	56. **G**	71. **B**
12. **H**	27. **B**	42. **F**	57. **A**	72. **G**
13. **C**	28. **J**	43. **A**	58. **H**	73. **D**
14. **G**	29. **A**	44. **G**	59. **B**	74. **H**
15. **C**	30. **J**	45. **B**	60. **J**	75. **D**

Mathematics

1. **A**	13. **D**	25. **D**	37. **C**	49. **E**
2. **G**	14. **J**	26. **H**	38. **J**	50. **H**
3. **B**	15. **C**	27. **E**	39. **E**	51. **E**
4. **J**	16. **J**	28. **G**	40. **F**	52. **H**
5. **A**	17. **E**	29. **A**	41. **C**	53. **D**
6. **H**	18. **K**	30. **H**	42. **H**	54. **G**
7. **C**	19. **D**	31. **C**	43. **B**	55. **C**
8. **H**	20. **G**	32. **H**	44. **G**	56. **J**
9. **C**	21. **C**	33. **C**	45. **C**	57. **B**
10. **H**	22. **G**	34. **J**	46. **K**	58. **K**
11. **E**	23. **C**	35. **E**	47. **C**	59. **A**
12. **J**	24. **J**	36. **F**	48. **J**	60. **K**

ANSWER KEY
Practice Test 2

Reading

1. **B**	9. **C**	17. **A**	25. **A**	33. **C**
2. **F**	10. **J**	18. **F**	26. **J**	34. **F**
3. **D**	11. **A**	19. **A**	27. **C**	35. **D**
4. **H**	12. **G**	20. **J**	28. **F**	36. **F**
5. **B**	13. **C**	21. **D**	29. **B**	37. **D**
6. **F**	14. **F**	22. **G**	30. **H**	38. **H**
7. **C**	15. **B**	23. **C**	31. **B**	39. **A**
8. **J**	16. **H**	24. **G**	32. **J**	40. **G**

Science

1. **A**	9. **A**	17. **D**	25. **C**	33. **D**
2. **J**	10. **F**	18. **H**	26. **J**	34. **F**
3. **C**	11. **C**	19. **C**	27. **B**	35. **B**
4. **G**	12. **G**	20. **F**	28. **G**	36. **H**
5. **B**	13. **A**	21. **B**	29. **D**	37. **A**
6. **H**	14. **G**	22. **F**	30. **H**	38. **J**
7. **B**	15. **C**	23. **D**	31. **B**	39. **B**
8. **J**	16. **F**	24. **G**	32. **J**	40. **J**

HOW TO SCORE YOUR PRACTICE TEST

Step 1: Add up the number correct for each section and write that number in the blank under the Raw Score column on the Score Conversion Table. (Your goal is to get more questions correct on each subsequent practice test.)

Step 2: Using the Score Conversion Chart, find your scale score for each section and write it down. Then add up all four sections and divide by 4 to find your overall composite score. (Composite scores are rounded up at .5 or higher.)

SCORE CONVERSION TABLE

Section	Raw Score	Scaled Score
English	(out of 75)	____ / 36
Math	(out of 60)	____ / 36
Reading	(out of 40)	____ / 36
Science	(out of 40)	____ / 36
		Add and divide by 4
Overall Composite =		____ / 36

SCORE CONVERSION CHART

		Number Correct			
ACT Score*	English Section	Mathematics Section	Reading Section	Science Section	ACT Score*
36	75	60	40	40	36
35	74	59	39	39	35
34	73	58	38	38	34
33	72	57	37	—	33
32	71	56	36	37	32
31	70	54-55	35	36	31
30	69	53	34	35	30
29	67-68	51-52	33	34	29
28	65-66	49-50	32	33	28
27	64	46-48	31	31-32	27
26	62-63	44-45	30	30	26
25	60-61	41-43	29	28-29	25
24	58-59	39-40	27-28	25-27	24
23	55-57	37-38	25-26	24	23

(continued)

SCORE CONVERSION CHART (*Continued*)

	Number Correct				
ACT Score*	English Section	Mathematics Section	Reading Section	Science Section	ACT Score*
22	53-54	35-36	23-24	22-23	22
21	50-52	33-34	22	20-21	21
20	47-49	31-32	21	18-19	20
19	44-46	28-30	19-20	17	19
18	42-43	25-27	18	15-16	18
17	40-41	22-24	17	14	17
16	37-39	19-21	16	13	16
15	34-36	15-17	15	12	15
14	31-33	11-14	13-14	11	14
13	29-30	09-10	12	10	13
12	27-28	07-08	10-11	09	12
11	25-26	06	08-09	08	11
10	23-24	05	07	07	10
9	21-22	04	06	05-06	9
8	18-20	03	05	—	8
7	15-17	—	—	04	7
6	12-14	02	04	03	6
5	09-11	—	03	02	5
4	07-08	01	02	—	4
3	05-06	—	—	01	3
2	03-04	—	01	—	2
1	00-02	00	00	00	1

**These scores are based on student trials rather than national norms.*

SCORING YOUR ESSAY

As mentioned earlier in this text, two readers will evaluate your essay and each person will then assign it a score from 1 to 6. If, by chance, these two scorers disagree by more than 1 point, a third reader will step in and resolve the discrepancy. Performance on the essay will not affect your English, math, reading, science, or composite scores. You will receive two additional scores on your score sheet—a combined English/writing score (1–36) and a writing test subscore (1–12). Neither of these scores will affect your composite score!

The sample essay that follows reflects higher-level writing. It meets the criteria that ACT has put forth for essays that demonstrate effective writing skills.

- It takes a definite position.
- It addresses and expands on the counterargument.
- It has details that support the topic sentences and is well organized.
- It is not repetitive, and while there may be errors, they do not interfere with the competence of the essay.
- It is consistent and well balanced.
- The essay has a clear introduction and a conclusion that is not just a summary but ends with a significant thought.
- The vocabulary demonstrates good use of language and the sentence structure is varied.

ANSWER EXPLANATIONS

English

1. **(A)** Although it would also be correct to turn the name *Stephen* into an appositive clause set off with commas on both sides (since you could take out the name and it would still be a complete sentence), when the appositive clause is *just the person's name and nothing else* it is fine to leave out the commas. (For example, you could write *My friend Adam has a car* without having to put commas before and after *Adam*.) But remember, *only one* comma in this situation is wrong; you have to either have two or none.

2. **(G)** This is a parallel phrasing question. The end of the sentence presents a list of three actions, and the previous two verbs (*whizzing* and *weaving*) are in the progressive tense (meaning they end in *-ing*, to signify an ongoing action), so this verb has to be too.

3. **(C)** The first clause is an independent one, and then the clause beginning with the relative pronoun *where* is a dependent descriptive one, and so all we need is a comma. Although the second clause would be an independent one if you got rid of the *where*, with the *where* it is not. (Remember, when you see that two of the choices are a semicolon and a period, it is almost always the case that they cancel each other out and the right answer is a comma!)

4. **(G)** A *rite of passage* is an event or ceremony you go through that changes you in some important way and makes you part of something. So, *experience* would be the right verb here, because you *go through* it.

5. **(C)** The third-person plural possessive pronoun is spelled *their*. You can remember that this is the possessive one because it contains the word *heir* (as in a person who eventually *possesses* something), and distinguish it from the other spellings by memorizing the sentence *They're in there with their bear.*

6. **(J)** What we need here is *have been riding*, which is in the present perfect continuous tense. That sounds complicated, but all it means is that someone is currently in the state of having been doing something for a long time—in other words, the verb needs to include both the present *and* the past, and choice J is the only option that does. (Remember, you don't need to know what tenses are *called* to get tense questions right!)

7. **(A)** *How many* worlds are there here? One. And does it *possess* something? Yes (the first bicycle). So, what we need is the singular possessive *world's*. The sentence is an independent clause up through the word *bicycle*, and the clause beginning with though is an "afterthought clause" that adds extra information, so it needs to be preceded by a comma.

8. **(H)** The essay is about the narrator and her relationship to bicycles, not about da Vinci or the history of bicycles themselves, and so specifics about da Vinci's bicycle sketch are unnecessary and distracting.

9. **(A)** The question asks for the phrase that reinforces the idea that bicycles are *amazing inventions*, and so you want the one that is extremely complimentary. The best choice is A, which refers to bicycles as a *marvel*.

10. **(J)** Since the underlined part is followed by *is*, we know that the right answer has to be a noun phrase, because it will function as the subject of the sentence. The infinitive form of a verb represents a concept, and so can work like a noun (as in *To err is human*). It also

PRACTICE TEST 2

matches the infinitive *to balance* that comes after the *is*, and so obeys the rule of parallel phrasing. That is pretty complicated, but hopefully the wrong answers all "sounded strange," even if you couldn't explain why. (Remember, when in doubt on the ACT English, always go with the shortest answer, as long as it makes a complete sentence and doesn't sound strange!)

11. **(D)** All of the choices are prepositions or prepositional phrases that simply mean "on" and can be used in its place, except for *on which*, which would be used to introduce extra information and would precede the thing that is on something else: *The dog, on which there were fleas, was brown.*

12. **(H)** Every answer choice involves how to separate two independent clauses. A colon can be used to separate two independent clauses, although it does not always have to.

13. **(C)** The earlier *is* establishes that the sentence is in the present tense, and *human will* is singular. So, what we need here is the present third-person singular form of the verb, which is *keeps.*

14. **(G)** This is the only choice that efficiently completes the preceding independent clause and appropriately introduces the subsequent dependent clause with a comma and *which.*

15. **(C)** The proposed sentence doesn't have anything directly to do with the subject of the essay, and the previous sentence conveyed a much more forceful "sense of an ending."

16. **(F)** The plural verb *have* agrees with the plural noun *sites. Like* acts as a preposition here, and the prepositional phrase *like Facebook* must be "jumped over." As the pronoun *us* is the object of *have*, there is no reason to add the preposition *to* (no object is being brought *to* us; rather, *we* are being brought together).

17. **(C)** What we need here is the adjective *allowed*, which means "permitted" (rather than the adverb *aloud*, which means "out loud"), and the preposition *to*, which introduces infinitives (rather than the adverb *too*, which means "also").

18. **(F)** The fact that the author is a professional writer means that he would find it odd or ironic that he is having more trouble writing something simple than nonwriters are having.

19. **(D)** The preceding paragraph has been about how the author has difficulty thinking of Facebook status updates. Although being good at writing English papers involves many different skills, the one that is relevant in context is the ability to think of things to say.

20. **(G)** The subsequent sentences joke about how no one cares that other people's status updates are boring, and yet the author is still agonizing over making his perfect. Therefore, *Maybe I'm overthinking this* is a logical opening.

21. **(A)** We need the contraction *you're* here ("you are"), rather than the possessive pronoun *your.* Additionally, although normally *thinks* would be required by the noun *everyone* (which is singular, despite the fact that it refers to many people), the fact that this is a question beginning with *doesn't* changes things. It's "everyone *thinks*," but "everyone does/doesn't *think*." That may sound complicated, but it's easy if you just remain calm and think about what *sounds* right.

22. **(J)** The author is calling himself the only one *who has* figured this out, and *who's* is a contraction for "who has" (or "who is").

23. **(C)** What we need here is the contraction *there's*, for "there is" ("There is nothing wrong with ...").

24. **(H)** We are talking about girls in general, and so we need the plural possessive *girls'* (with the apostrophe after the *s*). *Swimsuits* is not possessive, and does not need an apostrophe anywhere.

25. **(A)** The author means to say *It's* ("It is") *all* (meaning the "whole situation") *so* (as in "very") *depressing*. This is the only one of the choices that presents a comprehensible sentence. ("It's also depressing" would also be a comprehensible sentence, but it is not one of the choices.)

26. **(F)** *Being* is a gerund here, and *being depressed* is the subject clause of the sentence. None of the other choices make sense. (Remember, just because the test tries to trick you with *being* a lot, that doesn't mean that it's *never* the right answer!)

27. **(B)** This is a comma splice, albeit a comma splice in disguise. The clauses before and after "you see" are both independent clauses, and putting "you see" between them doesn't change this. Remember, you can't fix a comma splice by just inserting *any* words—the words you add have to render one of the independent clauses dependent! The other choices are all correct, but this one is NOT acceptable.

28. **(J)** The clause is an essential one (it is not "extra") and so we need to begin it with *that*, not with comma + *which*. Furthermore, we need the contraction *you're* ("you are"), not the possessive pronoun *your*. We also need the comparative conjunction *than*, rather than the time-related adverb *then*. Finally, we need the pronoun + verb *they are*, rather than the possessive pronoun *theirs* or adverb/pronoun *there*. That sounds complicated, but the clause we're trying to construct here is perfectly straightforward: "making people think *that you're* having more fun *than they are*." None of the other choices make even a little bit of sense.

29. **(A)** What we need here is the possessive pronoun *our*.

30. **(J)** An argument that something should be legally regulated would have to mention the law or the government at some point, and this passage does not.

31. **(D)** The other verb phrases in the sentence (*could hear, was called*) establish that it is in the past tense. Therefore, the past tense form *we began* is what is needed.

32. **(G)** The descriptive phrase *proud as ever* is an "extra" clause providing additional information that could be lifted out of the sentence. Therefore, it should be set off with commas on both sides.

33. **(A)** *He wasn't the most beautiful horse in the world* is an independent clause, and *If the truth were told* is a dependent introductory clause that needs to be followed by a comma.

34. **(G)** As the preceding and subsequent sentences indicate, the paragraph is about how Monte is a fine horse despite not being beautiful. This sentence offers a physical description of the ways in which he is not beautiful, and so it is relevant and necessary here. Furthermore, without it the paragraph would only have two sentences and seem bizarrely short, further indicating that you are probably supposed to include it.

35. **(D)** The information in this sentence stands in opposition or contrast to the information contained in the previous sentence. Therefore, the appropriate transition phrase is *Yet,* which implies contrast or counterpoint; the other choices do not. (As with so many places on the ACT, "which of these things is not like the others" is a very good strategy here!)

36. **(F)** The idea is that once upon a time Western equitation was unfamiliar to them, but it is not now. Therefore, what is needed is the past perfect tense *had been.* The regular past tense might be acceptable too, but it is not one of the choices; the past perfect is the only type of past tense that is an option.

37. **(B)** All of the answers are synonyms for *learned* or *understood* except for *beat,* which means "overcome." Therefore, *beat* is the LEAST acceptable alternative to the underlined portion. An athlete might say that they beat their competition, but not that they beat the *rules* of the sport themselves. (As with so many places on the ACT, "which of these things is not like the others" is a very good strategy here!)

38. **(H)** The fact that Monte did not touch any of the barrels provides more specific information about the nature of his graceful racing; it explains that he was not just good, but perfect.

39. **(B)** This sentence concerns the portion of the race *before* the narrator and Monte entered the barrels. Therefore, it needs to come before Sentence 2, where they enter the barrels.

40. **(J)** The question asks for a phrase that suggests the narrator's nervousness. Only choice J, which includes the word *anxiously,* does so. The others all make her seem satisfied and confident. (Remember, even when it seems obvious what a question on the ACT English is asking for, always carefully read the little directions in their entirety, because they usually give a fairly big hint!)

41. **(C)** What you need here is a phrase that means *besides,* and *except for* is the only one of the choices that does.

42. **(F)** *How many* grandfathers are we talking about? One. And does he *possess* anything? Yes (his voice). So, what we need is the singular possessive, which is *grandfather's.* It is just that simple.

43. **(A)** The story is in the past tense, and the past tense verb *kissed* in the same sentence reminds us of this. The form we need here is the past tense *echoed.*

44. **(G)** The underlined portion is followed by the verb *won,* which means that the pronouns in the underlined portion are performing a verb. Therefore, they should both be in the subjective case, which means what we need is *he and I* (you wouldn't say *him won* or *me won*; you would say *he won* and *I won*).

45. **(B)** The point of the story is that Monte was able to win the race even though he wasn't a natural-born athlete. This successfully fulfills the question's requirement about spirit and determination being just as important as inborn ability.

46. **(F)** The phrase "people *in which* thousands of years ago" makes no sense. It would mean that "thousands of years ago" is a subject phrase that *did* something *inside* people. All of the other choices make sense.

47. **(C)** This choice correctly uses *no* (i.e., "not any") and *know* (i.e., "to understand").

48. **(F)** This choice correctly uses the plural pronoun *them* to stand in for the plural noun *horoscopes.*

49. **(A)** The phrase is indeed humorous, and does indeed illustrate the fact that horoscopes are meaningless (i.e., they are so vague that there would be no way to know they are wrong, even if they had been misprinted).

50. **(J)** The next sentence continues the idea that the reader already knows what astrology is ("We're all familiar with ....").

51. **(D)** This results in a comprehensible sentence with the clauses in the right order. The *supposed personality traits* are what we're all familiar with, and these traits allegedly belong to *people* (who were) born under certain signs.

52. **(H)** The issue is *essential* versus *nonessential* clauses. We already know that astrology makes claims; the issue is whether it makes sufficiently specific claims. Therefore, the part about whether the claims are specific is not "extra," but essential, and should be introduced with *that* (and no comma).

53. **(B)** The so-called test involves *people* (who are) *deciding.* The test involves *people deciding whether to apply* terms. The present progressive *-ing* form is necessary, as this is an *ongoing* state. This is easy to see if you just "jump over" the extra descriptive clause *who want to believe.*

54. **(J)** The people in question are self-applying the terms, and so the reflexive *themselves* is needed, rather than the nominative *they* or objective *them.* Since the preposition *to* extends to both objects, no comma before the conjunction is necessary. Though it is a polite convention to name oneself after others, it is not a grammatical rule, and so the fact that *themselves* comes before *their friends* is not enough to make this choice wrong, especially in light of the serious errors in the other choices.

55. **(B)** *Could've* is a contraction of *could have,* and so makes perfect sense in context.

56. **(G)** *Anyway* (here acting like "in the first place") makes the most sense after *are*: "the stars' apparent positions aren't really where they are *in the first place.*"

57. **(A)** *It's all a bunch of nonsense* is the main independent clause. *Luckily for astrologers* is a dependent introductory clause followed by a comma, and *so nobody ever noticed* is a dependent clause preceded by a comma.

58. **(H)** The semicolon correctly separates two independent clauses. This is a deliberate trick question. Although *however* is typically inserted into the middle of a single independent clause and set off with a pair of commas, it can also appear as the first word of an independent clause (meaning "on the other hand") or the last word of an independent clause (meaning "though" or "despite this"), set off with a single comma. In this sentence, an independent clause that *happens to end* with *however* is followed by a semicolon and a second independent clause. Although this would hardly ever happen in real life because it's so confusing, it is technically grammatically correct, and so the ACT English does it occasionally to trick you. If you see *however* set off with two commas, make sure that a *single* independent clause exists *around* it—not one on each side.

59. **(B)** As the preceding sentence implies ("my answer is always the same"), this describes a *habitual* practice, and so the future tense ("I'll reply") is used.

60. **(J)** In addition to being funny and memorable, the previous sentence sums up what the entire final paragraph was about. Adding the bit about bookstores would be a weaker ending and randomly introduces a new idea.

61. **(C)** The subject of the sentence is *Intuitions* and the verb is *are.* The phrase *or gut feelings* is extra information that can be lifted out of the sentence, and so should be set off with commas.

62. **(G)** Although there has been no indication of this so far, by the end of the subsequent sentence it is established that the passage is written in the second person. Therefore, what we need here is *you can't.* (Remember, person and tense questions on the ACT English frequently necessitate reading ahead, especially when they appear early in a passage!)

63. **(B)** The passage is in the present tense, as indicated in this sentence by the verbs *emerge* and *begin,* and by the contraction *you're* ("you are"). And the antecedent of *it* is *visual inconsistency,* which you would *notice* rather than *feel.* Therefore, what we need is the second-person present tense form *notice.*

64. **(G)** As the first sentence of the first paragraph establishes, what is being referred to here is *intuition.* You must be clear. "It" has no reference.

65. **(A)** The proposed sentence explains that intuition is now acknowledged by science, and therefore provides a needed transition between the previous sentence and the following one, which involves psychologists studying intuition.

66. **(J)** *Psychologists now believe* is the most direct way of saying what you want to say here. (Remember, on the ACT English, when a question presents alternate ways of arranging a phrase, and the question does not ask for something specific such as "the most vivid description," the right answer is almost always the shortest one as long as it results in a complete sentence!)

67. **(B)** The rule of parallel phrasing dictates that the other verbs in the series need to match the third-person singular present tense form *finds* (which is in that form because the sentence is in the present tense and the subject is *brain*). Therefore, the forms we need for the other verbs are *takes* and *does.*

68. **(F)** *You ascribe meaning to the situation in front of you* is the independent clause, and *Based on that analogy* is the introductory dependent clause. They should be separated with a comma.

69. **(B)** The antecedent of the pronoun is the *young woman,* and so the pronoun needed here is *she.*

70. **(F)** The question asks for the best illustration of how information is stored in our brain; only choice A, which includes the phrase *as a web of fact and feeling,* offers an *illustration* of this.

71. **(B)** The sentence is in the present tense, and there is no indication that we need anything other than the simplest form of the infinitive: a new experience unleashes a predisposition *to respond.*

72. **(G)** The sentence provides a useful introduction to the closing paragraph by contextualizing intuition alongside another means of arriving at knowledge. You would also do well to notice that, regardless of how you answer question 73, the subsequent sentence is going to begin with a transition phrase that suggests it is not the first sentence of the paragraph (which means you are supposed to keep this one).

73. **(D)** The sentence suggests a third option different from the two explored in the previous sentence. A simple *But* is the most effective transition phrase. (Remember, although you may have been told in grade school not to begin a sentence with a conjunction such as *and* or *but*, it is actually acceptable to begin a sentence with a conjunction under certain circumstances, and so an answer choice on the ACT English cannot be eliminated solely because it begins a sentence with a conjunction!)

74. **(H)** The question asks for a phrase supporting the idea that intuitions are reliable in an area where one is experienced. Only choice H, which points out that such intuitions *arise out of the richest array of collected patterns of experience,* gets the job done.

75. **(D)** The sentence, along with the rest of the passage, is in the present tense. There is no indication that anything other than the regular present tense *receive* is what is needed here.

PRACTICE TEST 2

Mathematics

1. **(A)** $(1-5)^3 = (-4)^3 = -64$.

2. **(G)** 30 is divisible by 3, 5, and 6. It is the lowest common multiple.

3. **(B)** If $r = 0$, $[-s + h(t \cdot 3 - w)](0) = 0$, not 1.

4. **(J)** If 30% come from families that have only one child, then 70% come from families that do not have one child. 70% of 7,340 = 0.70(7,340) = 5,138.

5. **(A)** $3y + 2x = 24$ is $3y = -2x + 24$ when we subtract $2x$ from both sides. Finally, dividing each term by 3 gives $y = \frac{-2}{3}x + 8$.

6. **(H)** The equation $3x + 2y = 19$ is equivalent to $y = \frac{-3}{2}x + \frac{19}{2}$. The slopes of perpendicular lines are opposite reciprocals. Therefore, the slope would be $\frac{2}{3}$.

7. **(C)** $V = \frac{\pi}{3}(3)^2(8) = \frac{\pi}{3}(9)(8) = 24\pi$.

8. **(H)** $\angle b \cong \angle d$ by vertical angles. $\angle d$ and $\angle e$ are supplementary because they are interior angles on the same side of the transversal. Since $m\angle d = m\angle b = 100°$, $m\angle e = 80°$.

9. **(C)** In the diagram $m\angle 1 = 40°$ by vertical angles. Then, $m\angle 2 = 65°$, since the angles of a triangle add to 180°. By vertical angles $x = 65$.

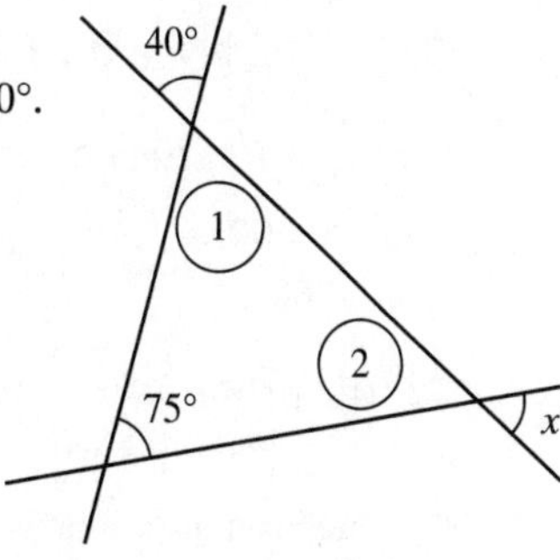

10. **(H)** 11, 16, 21, 26 is an arithmetic sequence with a common difference equal to 5.

11. **(E)** $(2x + 3y)^2$ means $(2x + 3y)(2x + 3y) = 2x(2x) + 2x(3y) + 3y(2x) + (3y)(3y)$. This simplifies to $4x^2 + 6xy + 6xy + 9y^2$ and finally to $4x^2 + 12xy + 9y^2$.

12. **(J)** 60% are Democrats translates to $(0.60)(7{,}695) = 4{,}617$. This problem can also be done by using the proportion: $\frac{60}{100} = \frac{x}{7{,}695}$.

13. **(D)** The tangent of an angle in a right triangle is defined as the length of the opposite side divided by the length of the adjacent side.

14. **(J)** $\frac{1}{3}w + \frac{2}{5}w = 1$ equals $\frac{5}{15}w + \frac{6}{15}w = 1$ when we get a common denominator. (You could also add $\frac{1}{3} + \frac{2}{5}$ on your calculator.) Combining like terms we have $\frac{11}{15}w = 1$. Either multiply by $\frac{15}{11}$ or divide by $\frac{11}{15} \cdot \frac{15}{11} \cdot \frac{11}{15}w = \frac{15(1)}{11} \cdot w = \frac{15}{11}$.

15. **(C)** $\triangle CEA \cong \triangle DEB$. To see this we have $\overline{CE} \cong \overline{DE}$ and $\overline{AE} \cong \overline{BE}$ and $\angle CEA \cong \angle DEB$. The segments are congruent since $\overline{AB}$ and $\overline{CD}$ bisect each other. The angles are vertical angles. So, the triangles are congruent by SAS. By CPCTC, $\angle C \cong \angle D$. That means $m\angle C = 60°$. In $\triangle CEA$ we have a 60° and an 80° angle, so the third angle ($\angle CEA$) must be 40° since the three angles of a triangle must add up to 180°.

16. **(J)** The distance formula is $\sqrt{(x_2 - x_1)^2 + (y_2 - y_1)^2}$. For $A(3, 2)$ and $B(15, 8)$, we have $\sqrt{(15-3)^2 + (8-2)^2} = \sqrt{144+36} = \sqrt{180} = \sqrt{36}\sqrt{5} = 6\sqrt{5}$.

17. **(E)** Although we are not told that a and b are positive, we can use positive values to help us eliminate incorrect choices. Let $a = 2$ and $b = 3$. c can be any number greater than zero. Now we can eliminate answers. We see that A, B, C, and D can be eliminated, which leaves E. So, E must be correct because the others cannot be correct.

18. **(K)** This problem is done by using the fundamental counting principle that if Event 1 can be done in M ways and Event 2 can be done in N ways, then the total number of ways that we can do both events is M(N). Applying this we have $(4)(3)(5) = 60$ ways of choosing meat, cheese, and bread.

19. **(D)** We will use the equation $d = rt$, where d = distance, r = rate, and t = time. $200 = (4)r$, which gives $r = 50$ mph before stopping for gas. She then drives 10 mph faster for 3 hours. $50 + 10 = 60$ mph. $d = 60(3) = 180$ miles. The total number of miles equals $200 + 180 = 380$ miles.

20. **(G)** We are given the formula $M = \frac{P}{200} - 0.0008P + 40$, where M is the monthly payment and P is the cost of the house. Since the house costs \$200,000, $P = 200{,}000$ and $M = \frac{200{,}000}{200} - 0.0008(200{,}000) + 40.$ $M = \$880.$

21. **(C)** The prime factorization of 330 is 2(3)(5)(11). The sum is $2 + 3 + 5 + 11 = 21$.

22. **(G)** The area of a circle is πr^2. There are 10 pins and the radius is half of the given diameter of 4.125 in.

23. **(C)** The entire lane is 65 feet long and the part of the lane that is NOT the pin deck is 60 feet long. Since the width is the same, it does not matter. 65:60 reduces to 13:12.

24. **(J)** $3 \times 140 = 420$ points are needed in order to average 140. Quinn has $112 + 144 = 256$ points already, so she needs $420 - 256 = 164$ more points in the third game.

25. **(D)** If you sketch the points and draw the line that contains the two points, it appears that it crosses the y-axis at –5. Mathematically, the slope of the line is $\frac{10-(-2)}{5-1} = \frac{12}{4} = 3$. Using $y = mx + b$ and the point (5, 10), we have $10 = 3(5) + b$. Thus, $b = -5$. The y-intercept is –5, so the point is (0, –5).

26. **(H)** The median is the middle number of a data set when the numbers are written in order. When there are an even number of data, take the average of the middle two numbers. Since the middle two numbers are 85 and 89, we take the average of those, which is 87.

27. **(E)** $\frac{2^{-1}a^{-3}b^7c^2}{(5a)^2b^{-1}c^7}$ can be rewritten as $\frac{2^{-1}a^{-3}b^7c^2}{25a^2b^{-1}c^7}$ by squaring $(5a)$, then as $\frac{b \cdot b^7c^2}{2 \cdot 25a^2a^3c^7}$ by eliminating the negative exponents, and, finally, $\frac{b^8}{50a^5c^5}$.

28. **(G)** The center of the circle is the midpoint of any diameter. Thus, if we say the other endpoint is (a, b) and use the midpoint formula we have $\left(\frac{a+5}{2}, \frac{b+-2}{2}\right) = (2, -3)$. The x-coordinates must be equal. $\frac{a+5}{2} = 2 \rightarrow a + 5 = 4$, so $a = -1$. There is only one answer choice with $x = -1$, so we really don't need to find y. But $\frac{b-2}{2} = -3 \rightarrow b - 2 = -6$, so $b = -4$.

29. **(A)** This can be solved easily by the substitution method. $5x + 5 = 3x - 7$ is equivalent to $2x = -12$. Therefore, $x = -6$. But we were asked for the y-coordinate. Using the equation $y = 3x - 7$ and substituting (–6) for x we find that $y = 3(-6) - 7 = -25$.

30. **(H)** The figure is a trapezoid. The area formula is $A = \frac{h(b_1 + b_2)}{2}$, where h is the height and b_1 and b_2 are the bases. $A = \frac{3(10+14)}{2} = \frac{72}{2} = 36$.

31. **(C)** $6 - 4(x - 2) > 4x + 5$ is equivalent to $6 - 4x + 8 > 4x + 5$. $14 - 4x > 4x + 5$ is equivalent to $-8x > -9$. Now, we divide by (–8). When dividing an inequality by a negative number, the inequality sign must be switched. The answer then is $x < \frac{9}{8}$.

32. **(H)** $(x-h)^2+(y-k)^2=r^2$ is the equation for a circle with center (h, k) and radius r.

33. **(C)** When a 90 degree counterclockwise rotation is performed, the point (x, y) becomes $(-y, x)$.

34. **(J)** The area of a circle is πr^2 and the radius was given as 4.

35. **(E)** The area of a parallelogram is base times height. The base is $\overline{RS}$, so we must find $\overline{RA}$. $\overline{UR}$ is 5 since opposite sides of a parallelogram are congruent. Either by the Pythagorean Theorem or by a 3–4–5 right triangle, $\overline{RA}=3$. So, $\overline{RS}=3+7=10$. Height of $\overline{UA}=4$. $A=10(4)=40$.

36. **(F)** We have a right triangle and are given the lengths of two sides. Therefore, we use the Pythagorean Theorem: $a^2+b^2=c^2$. $6^2+4^2=c^2 \to c^2=52$. Taking square roots gives us $c=\sqrt{52}=2\sqrt{13}$.

37. **(C)** If we multiply both sides of the inequality by 6 (the lowest common denominator), we get an inequality with no fractions. $4x-3<3x+4$, which is equivalent to $x<7$.

38. **(J)** For this problem we have a right triangle shown with x (the hypotenuse) representing the length of the guide wire and 14 representing the base. Since $\cos 50° = \frac{\text{adj}}{\text{hyp}}$, we have $\cos 50° = \frac{14}{x}$. So, $x=\frac{14}{\cos 50°}$, which is 21.78 (to the nearest hundredth).

39. **(E)** $x^2-9=(x-3)(x+3)$. This gives $\frac{(x-3)(x-3)}{(x-3)(x+3)}=\frac{x-3}{x+3}$. Another method that will work on a problem such as this is to pick a value for x such that $x^2 \neq 9$, say $x=2$. Then, $\frac{(2-3)^2}{2^2-9}=\frac{1}{-5}=\frac{-1}{5}$. Now, put $x=2$ in for x in the answer choices and see which one equals $\frac{-1}{5}$. Only choice E yields this value.

40. **(F)** We know the midpoint is (5, 7) and A (2, 3) with B (x, y) as endpoints. By the midpoint formula $\left(\frac{x+2}{2}, \frac{y+3}{2}\right)=(5,7)$. Thus, $\frac{x+2}{2}$ must equal 5 and $\frac{y+3}{2}$ must equal 7. Solving these two equations $\frac{x+2}{2}=5$ and $\frac{y+3}{2}=7$, we get $x=8$ and $y=11$. Therefore, $x+y=19$.

41. **(C)** $(x+a)(x+b)=x^2+(a+b)x+ab$. Since the solutions are $x=8$ and $x=\frac{-3}{2}$, we have $(x-8)(x-\frac{-3}{2})=0$. This multiplies to $x^2-8x+\frac{3}{2}x-12=0$ and simplifies to $x^2-6.5x-12=0$. Therefore, $a+b=-6.5$. Or we could use the theorem that says for quadratic equations of the type $x^2+Bx+C=0$ that the sum of the solutions equals $(-B)$. Therefore, $8+\frac{-3}{2}=-B \to 6.5=-B$ or $B=-6.5$.

42. **(H)** We do not have enough information to find the lengths of the three horizontal segments but we know their sum is 10. The missing vertical segment is 8. So, the perimeter is $10+13+10+8+3+2=46$. If we make a rectangle out of the figure, the perimeter

is the same as the perimeter of the original figure. So, the perimeter of the figure is 13 + 10 + 13 + 10 = 46.

43. **(B)** If you graph the two points, it should be clear that the x-intercept should be greater than 8, leaving two options: 19 and $\frac{19}{2}$. Since 19 is too large, that leaves $\frac{19}{2}$. The slope of the line is $\frac{3-9}{8-5} = \frac{-6}{3} = -2$. From $y = mx + b$ and the point (5, 9), we have $9 = -2(5) + b$. Therefore, $b = 19$. The equation of the line is $y = -2x + 19$. To find the x-intercept, let $y = 0$. $0 = -2x + 19$ and $x = \frac{19}{2}$. For a problem with coordinates, we can often find the answer from a sketch. Clearly, the x-intercept cannot be zero or negative. That leaves only (A) 19 and (B) $\frac{19}{2}$. 19 is not a reasonable answer.

44. **(G)** If a square has an area of 729, the length of a side is $\sqrt{729} = 27 = 3^3$. The volume of a cube is s^3, where s is the length of a side. Thus, in this problem $V = (3^3)^3 = 3^9$.

45. **(C)** The GCF of $6pq^4$ and $12p^2q^2$ is $6pq^2$. Thus, $6pq^2 = 1{,}050$ or $pq^2 = 175$. It asks for a possible value of p and q. One way of finding p and q is to find the prime factorization of 175. It is $7(5)^2$. Comparing pq^2 to $7(5)^2$, we see that $p = 7$ and $q = 5$. So, $p + q = 7 + 5 = 12$.

46. **(K)** $AC = \sqrt{164}$. We get this value by using the Pythagorean Theorem on $\triangle ABC$. $8^2 + 10^2 = (AC)^2$, $(AC)^2 = 64 + 100 = 164$. Taking square roots leaves $AC = \sqrt{164}$. $\overline{AC}$ is a side of square $ACDE$. Therefore, the area of square $ACDE$ is $(\sqrt{164})^2 = 164$. You could also get this value by taking $\sqrt{164}$ on your calculator and squaring the answer.

47. **(C)** Since there are 6 digits that repeat, we will want to know how many complete cycles of 6 there are that are less than 63. 60 is the largest multiple of 6 that is less than 63. Therefore, the 61st digit will be the start of a new cycle. So, the digit in the sixty-third place will be the third in the cycle, which is C.

48. **(J)** A perfect square trinomial will factor to a binomial squared: $(x + y)^2 = x^2 + 2xy + y^2$. This tells us that the number to be added must be a perfect square. If we add 9, it would have to factor to $(3x - 3)^2$. But this equals $9x^2 - 18x + 9$, and we need $(-30x)$. Adding 25, we have $9x^2 - 30x + 25 = (3x - 5)^2$.

49. **(E)** From the data given in the problem, we can conclude that the center of the circle is $(-a, a)$. Since the radius of the circle is 4, a must equal 4. Therefore, the center is $(-4, 4)$. The formula for a circle with center (h, k) and radius r is $(x - h)^2 + (y - k)^2 = r^2$. Substituting in the formula, we get $(x + 4)^2 + (y - 4)^2 = 16$.

50. **(H)** In the equation $y = A \sin Bx$, the amplitude is $|A|$ and the period is $\frac{2\pi}{|B|}$. From $y = \sin x$ to $y = 2\sin(4x)$, the amplitude increases from 1 to 2 and the period decreases from $\frac{2\pi}{1} = 2\pi$ to $\frac{2\pi}{4} = \frac{1}{2}\pi$.

51. **(E)** Applying the Distributive Property to $3x - 9 \geq -3(9 - x)$ is equivalent to $3x - 9 \geq -27 + 3x$. Subtracting $3x$ from both sides leaves $-9 \geq -27$. This is true and since there is no x in the inequality, it is true for all real numbers.

52. **(H)** Extend $\overline{GF}$ and $\overline{IJ}$ to intersect at a new point *P*. *GDJP* is a square with side length of 5. Its area is $5^2 = 25$. The area of the shaded pentagon equals the area of *GDJP* minus the area of $\triangle FIP$. Area of $\triangle FIP = \frac{1}{2}(4)(4) = 8$. Therefore, the area of pentagon *DGFIJ* is $25 - 8 = 17$.

53. **(D)** In order for the product of 2 matrices to be defined, the inner dimensions of the matrices must match. Since CD would be a 3×2 matrix and a 3×3 matrix, this will not work because the 2 from matrix C and the first 3 from matrix D are not equal.

54. **(G)** This is a quadratic equation. To solve, we must get one side equal to zero. So, we come up with $x^2 - 5ax - 36a^2 = 0$. This factors to $(x - 9a)(x + 4a) = 0$. Now, we use the zero product property and set each factor equal to zero.

$$x - 9a = 0 \qquad x + 4a = 0$$
$$x = 9a \qquad x = -4a$$

55. **(C)** To simplify this we will use the identity $\sin^2\theta + \cos^2\theta = 1$. From this we have $1 - \cos^2 = \sin^2$. Substituting, we now have $\frac{\sqrt{\sin^2\theta}}{\sin^2\theta} \cdot \cos\theta = \frac{\sin\theta}{\sin^2\theta} \cdot \cos\theta$. This simplifies to $\frac{\cos\theta}{\sin\theta}$, which is equivalent to $\cot\theta$.

56. **(J)** By multiplication and division properties of logarithms, $\log_a\left(\frac{x^2y^3}{\sqrt{z}}\right) = \log_a x^2 + \log_a y^3 - \log_a \sqrt{z}$. By power rule, $\log_a x^2 + \log_a y^3 - \log_a z^{\frac{1}{2}}$ equals $2\log_a x + 3\log_a y - \frac{1}{2}\log_a z = 2p + 3q - \frac{1}{2}t$. So, choice J is the correct answer.

57. **(B)** We know that the absolute value of a number is non-negative. Since $|-x| = x$, x must be non-negative, which means $x \geq 0$. Mathematically, $|x| = x$ if $x \geq 0$ and $|x| = -x$ if $x \leq 0$. We could also substitute numbers in for *x*.

58. **(K)** When a quadratic equation has exactly one real solution, the discriminant "$b^2 - 4ac$" must equal zero. This gives us the equation $(-a)^2 - 4(2)(8) = 0$ OR $a^2 - 64 = 0$ OR $a^2 = 64$. Taking the square root we get $a = \pm 8$. We could also plug 8 (or another number) into the equation. $2x^2 - 8x + 8 = 0 \rightarrow 2(x^2 - 4x + 4) = 0$. $2(x - 2)^2 = 0$.

59. **(A)** Because all the possible answers only contain *x* and *y*, we want to eliminate *t*. Solve $y = 5 - t$ for *t* and substitute into the other equation. $t = 5 - y$, so $x = 3(5 - y) + 4 \rightarrow x = 15 - 3y + 4$. Solving for *y*, we first combine the 15 and 4. $x = 19 - 3y \rightarrow x - 19 = -3y$. Multiply both sides by (–1) to get $19 - x = 3y$. Divide by 3 and $y = \frac{19 - x}{3}$. If you had solved the other equation for *t*, the work would look like this: $t = \frac{x - 4}{3}$ and $y = 5 - \frac{x - 4}{3} \rightarrow y = \frac{15}{3} - \frac{x - 4}{3}$ and $y = \frac{15 - (x - 4)}{3} = \frac{15 - x + 4}{3} = \frac{19 - x}{3}$.

60. **(K)** To find the area of a sector we use this formula: $\frac{\text{central angle}}{360}$ (area of circle). Substituting the given values, we get $\frac{30}{360}(\pi(10)^2)$. Simplify to get $\frac{25\pi}{3}$.

PRACTICE TEST 2

Reading

1. **(B)** The cavalier reaction of the townspeople to the angel in lines 23–28, as well as Elisenda's casual reaction to his departure at the end, establish that the appearance of an angel was not a terribly big deal to these people. In other words, they are *laid-back* and *react with less surprise* than others would to such things.

2. **(F)** In light of the child's illness (line 10), it is safe to assume that when the neighbor woman says the angel was "coming for the child" (line 21), she means that he is an angel of death.

3. **(D)** The crabs from the rainstorm are mentioned in line 86, but only mentioned, and not described.

4. **(H)** This angel never really does much of anything. We know basically nothing about him other than the fact that he has wings. He may not even be an angel, for all anyone knows. Therefore, the only possible answer is that he is *baffling and mysterious.*

5. **(B)** Right before she gets the idea to charge admission, we are told that Elisenda is practically crippled from the hard work she is compelled to do (lines 34–37). We are supposed to feel pity for her, and regard her idea to charge admission as *understandable and motivated by necessity.*

6. **(F)** In lines 27–28, the first reaction of the townspeople to the angel involves *tossing him things to eat through ... the wire.* This is clearly supposed to mirror the behavior of humans toward an *animal* at the zoo.

7. **(C)** Nowhere is it stated or implied that the spider girl had the approval of any religious authority of any kind.

8. **(J)** Building a mansion with bars to keep out angels implies that Pelayo and Elisenda considered it likely that more angels would show up someday—that is, that the appearance of angels is *somewhat normal.*

9. **(C)** The question is structured in a tricky way: it refers to *the beginning of the story,* but the fact that Pelayo had been employed as a *bailiff* is not mentioned until line 91.

10. **(J)** Elisenda's sigh of relief (line 103) and the statement that the angel was no longer an annoyance in her life (line 108) both imply that she feels unburdened by not having to deal with him anymore. (Remember, on a question like this, you have to look at the *emotion words*!)

11. **(A)** The first three sentences of Paragraph 3 (lines 21–27) definitively establish all of this information, albeit a bit indirectly.

12. **(G)** It would not support Voltaire's point about the wisdom of tolerance very effectively if he didn't mean it when he says here that Europe has gotten less violent and more civilized in recent decades (the point being that you can trust people not to take advantage of your tolerance now, because things aren't like they were in the past).

13. **(C)** Once again, the answer is that Voltaire is wearing his heart on his sleeve here and saying exactly what he means—his goal in this piece is to rally as many readers as possible to a political cause, rather than to showcase his wit to the sharpest of them.

14. **(F)** Lines 98–100 explicitly state this very theory, albeit in more flowery and challenging language.

15. **(B)** The basic, nonspecific universality of the thoughts narrated here, as well as the fact that Freud employs the plural "we" for the first few questions, all implies that Freud is presenting this as a generic "everyman's" private reaction to the command to love his neighbor as himself, rather than the particular reaction of some specific person or type of person.

16. **(H)** *Grandiose* means "pretentiously self-important," and when we say that someone is "full of hot air," we mean that they speak much, and assign great value to their own words, but that their speech is ultimately of little value. The former word and the latter phrase are not exactly synonymous, but this phrase is by far the closest to *grandiose* of the four choices.

17. **(A)** Freud spends most of the first two paragraphs assuming the voice of the "average" person, and he sums up his assertions in the last paragraph by pointing out that anyone else's life experience would have shown him the same things too. Though his writing was often at odds with, or even offensive to, popular opinion, in this case Freud seems to be trying to make an entire essay out of common knowledge—or at least, what he presents as common knowledge.

18. **(F)** Throughout Passage A, Voltaire argues as though violence is typically a response to injustice—Freud, meanwhile, posits that human beings are just naturally aggressive, and would therefore presumably seek out excuses to hate and to do violence even in a perfectly just society.

19. **(A)** Freud clearly argues that "man's inhumanity to man" is here to stay, but he never addresses the extent to which its prevalence might be lessened, and by what means. Voltaire states a number of facts about European society becoming markedly less violent over the course of the few generations preceding his own time—so presumably something must be capable of at least making people *less* mean, if not altogether altruistic.

20. **(J)** As has already been established in previous questions, these essays are unusual for both Voltaire and Freud in that they aim to present only ideas that the authors figure as self-evident and undeniable. And what's really interesting is that, although both arguments do indeed seem undeniable based on lived experience when one first reads them, they largely present mutually exclusive views of human nature. How can two ideas that contradict each other *both* be self-evidently true?!

21. **(D)** In lines 40–45, the author characterizes a writer as someone who tries to *discover the second being inside him,* who tries to *transform that inward gaze into words,* and who studies *the worlds into which we pass when we retire into ourselves.* These phrases clearly characterize writing as a solitary activity.

22. **(G)** The author never mentions anything at all about his parents' relationship, and certainly doesn't hint that the suitcase might hold painful secrets about it.

23. **(C)** Since the author says this in response to his father's having brought him a candy bar, it is clear in context that he is merely making a joke about how his father still sees him as a child in some ways—that is, his father has not *really* forgotten his age.

24. **(G)** Immediately after this statement, the author goes on to say that his father was a very social man who disliked solitude and loved company—that is, he could not have endured the solitude that is necessary in order to be a real writer.

25. **(A)** The fact that the author's father put the suitcase quietly in a corner implies that he is depositing it shyly and without fanfare: *unobtrusively* means "inconspicuously."

26. **(J)** The author never mentions being *suspicious* of his father about anything, for any reason.

27. **(C)** The series of rhetorical questions that ends the paragraph makes it clear that the point is ultimately about the true source of happiness.

28. **(F)** Lines 40–46 establish that, according to the author, writing is a long process of self-discovery.

29. **(B)** It is mentioned in lines 20–21 that the author's father had wanted to write poetry as a young man.

30. **(H)** The linkage of opposites in the final paragraph (*a flash of joy inside me that made me ashamed ... our feelings of happiness and guilt*) establishes that the author sees writing as wrapped up in both positive and negative emotions.

31. **(B)** The first paragraph establishes something to do with "culture" as our topic, and the end of the second and beginning of the third paragraphs (lines 30–35) establish that the author feels that something besides genes is necessary to explain culture.

32. **(J)** The remainder of the first paragraph (as well as the passage itself) establishes that the author's goal is to dispassionately analyze the means by which culture changes—that is, he is using the word *culture* to mean everything about society, rather than to distinguish between the good and bad things about it.

33. **(C)** A hair color is not an *idea* (though a hair*style* is), and thus could not succeed or fail as a meme.

34. **(F)** Lines 33–49 explain that, just as genes are replicators of DNA, memes are replicators of ideas.

35. **(D)** Chaucer is mentioned merely as an example of someone who spoke English as it existed twenty generations ago (lines 7–12).

36. **(F)** It is clear in all four contexts that *propagate* means something like "spread," or *multiply* (in the sense that living beings *multiply* by reproduction).

37. **(D)** Lines 43–49 establish that the author is making up the word *meme* himself ("*if I abbreviate 'mimeme' to meme*").

38. **(H)** In the sentence immediately following, the author explains that other copies of the same tune will continue to exist on paper or in other people's brains—that is, no one copy of an idea is the "real" one, as long as the idea continues to exist somewhere.

39. **(A)** The examples in lines 76–81 (immediately following the term *survival value*) all concern possible ways to measure how widespread a particular concept has become.

PRACTICE TEST 2

40. **(G)** When the author says that their *meme-complexes ... are still going strong* (lines 106–107), he means that the ideas these people came up with are continuing to thrive after their deaths.

Science

1. **(A)** All this question is asking you to do is look at Table 1 and find the biggest number in the (horizontal) 260 nm row. The biggest number in that row by a wide margin is 83.5, which falls in the (vertical) Octyl Salicylate column. The fact that the numbers represent *percent transmittance of UV rays* is explained in the text, rather than in Table 1 itself, but this is the only thing Table 1 measures, and the question tells you that the answer is in Table 1.

2. **(J)** This is a simple "Go Up, Hit Line, Go Over" question. The black line in Figure 1 is higher at the point on the *x*-axis (horizontal) representing a wavelength of 340 nm than it is at the points representing any of the other choices. Since the line in Figure 1 only increases (it goes up and up but never down), another reliable method of getting the answer would be to just look at the choices and pick the highest number.

3. **(C)** The question asks about someone whose skin *burns but also tans slowly.* "Gradually" is a synonym for "slowly," and so the question is likely asking about Skin Type III, which Table 2 says *Burns moderately, tans gradually.* Although the person *could possibly* have Skin Type II, the question is clearly indicating Skin Type III as the preferable answer.

4. **(G)** All you have to do here is look at Table 2 and list all the skin types identified as *sensitive* or *very sensitive.* Skin Types I and II are identified as *very sensitive,* and Skin Type III is identified as *sensitive.* You probably also already know from real life that sunscreen should be worn by pale people, and so the answer is going to be the people on the paler half of the table. (Remember, although the ACT Science <u>does not require</u> real-life knowledge, the questions are always accurate, and so any real-life knowledge you <u>happen to have</u> can be useful!)

5. **(B)** This is one of those questions that require looking in two places. Figure 1 establishes that sunlight with an irradiance of 0.01 $W/m^2/nm$ would have a wavelength of *a little more than* 300 nm (because the black line at the 0.01 point on the *y*-axis is a little past the 300 point on the *x*-axis). Then you look in Table 1 and see that the percent transmittance for oxybenzone at a wavelength of 300 nm would be 4.2, and so the answer is *a little more than* 4.2, in other words 5%.

6. **(H)** According to Table 1, sunscreen SPF 45 blocks all but 2.5% of UV rays. Even though Type II skin is very sensitive to UV rays, at 320 nm skin Type II would not burn easily using SPF 45 sunblock.

7. **(B)** Table 1 establishes that a female who has normal vision but is a carrier of red-green color blindness would have one normal X chromosome and one mutated X chromosome. (It is also entirely possible to figure this out without Table 1, assuming you knew that women have two X chromosomes and a bit about how heritability works.)

PRACTICE TEST 2

8. **(J)** For a couple to be assured of producing only red-green color-blind children, both parents would have to be red-green color blind. The genotypes in choice J represent a red-green color-blind female and a red-green color-blind male.

9. **(A)** The top right corner of the Punnett square in Figure 3 (Study 2) represents a male with normal vision. All of the males represented in Figures 2 and 4 (in Studies 1 and 3) are red-green color blind.

10. **(F)** The information in the passage states that the defect appears in women only when both parents possess the gene.

11. **(C)** Study 1 establishes that all of Barbara and John's male children are red-green color blind, while none of their female children are (though they all carry the mutated gene). Figure 1 establishes that Barbara and John have two girls and two boys; that is, they have an equal number of red-green color-blind children and children with normal vision, for a ratio of 1:1 (2:2 reduced).

12. **(G)** A red-green color-blind female would have to have had a red-green color-blind father and a mother who was either red-green color-blind herself or a carrier. Only choice G presents one of these options (red-green color-blind father and carrier mother).

13. **(A)** Based on Study 1, the daughter of Barbara and John would have a genotype of X^RX^r. Combining the daughter's genotype with a man of genotype X^rY would produce the following offspring:

	X^R	X^r
X^r	X^RX^r	X^rX^r
Y	X^RY	X^rY

According to Table 1, only a genotype of X^RX^r is a genotype that is a carrier with normal vision. One of the squares above shows the needed genotype and one out of four is represented as 25%.

14. **(G)** This is one of those questions that requires you to look in two places. Table 2 indicates that naphtha is in Tray 2, and Table 1 indicates that the boiling point of whatever is in Tray 2 is 40°C.

15. **(C)** In Figure 2, the bar representing diesel goes up to 11, indicating 11 gallons of diesel per barrel of crude oil.

16. **(F)** This question involves looking in <u>three</u> places, but still is not really that hard (technically, getting the right answer only requires looking in two places, but eliminating some of the wrong answers requires looking in three). Figure 1 establishes that the trays are arranged from 1 to 8 from the top to the bottom of the Distillation Column, Table 2 indicates which substances are in which trays, and Table 1 indicates their boiling points. All together, these data indicate that the substances with the lowest boiling points are at the top of the column, and so the student's hypothesis is wrong (it is not necessary to understand the explanation in choice F about the rising vapor and all that, only to see that the substances with the lowest boiling points are on top).

17. **(D)** A comparison of Table 3 with Tables 1 and 2 establishes that the greater the number of carbons in a substance, the higher the boiling point, in decreasing order from residual oil to gas.

18. **(H)** Tables 1 and 2 establish that heavy gas oil has a boiling point of 500°C, higher than that of any of the components except residual oil, which is not one of the choices.

19. **(C)** Components with medium boiling points on Table 1 in a range of 120 to 350 degrees correspond to the gasoline, kerosene, and diesel on Figure 2, which are collected in greatest quantity.

20. **(F)** Tables 1 and 2 show you that kerosene has a boiling point of 200 degrees and diesel has a boiling point of 350 degrees, so the new substance would have a number of carbons that fall somewhere in the range of carbons for kerosene and diesel. Diesel has 12+ carbons and kerosene has carbons in a range of 10–18. Therefore, the new substance should have a number of carbons between 12 and 18.

21. **(B)** Table 1 indicates that the solubility of methane at 50°C *increases and then decreases* as pressure is increased. All of the other choices involve substances that steadily increased in solubility as pressure increased, but NOT this one.

22. **(F)** At 50°C, the solubility is 18.9.

23. **(D)** The line in Figure 1 climbs until about the 200-second mark and then levels off. It is not necessary to understand the paragraph above Figure 1 in order to answer the question: all you need to know is that the graph is measuring an increase in the PA-11 mass over time.

24. **(G)** In Table 1, we see that the solubility of methane at 90°C and 53.1 atm is 2.38. At a pressure of 106.5, the solubility is 5.14. Since 3.75 is halfway between 2.38 and 5.14 and 80 is roughly halfway between 53.1 and 106.5, the best answer is 3.75.

25. **(C)** Table 2 establishes that the solubility of carbon dioxide increases as pressure increases, at all three temperatures.

26. **(J)** The first paragraph states that the *solvent* is the substance that another substance is being dissolved in. The second paragraph states that methane and carbon dioxide are being dissolved in polyamide. Therefore, polyamide is the solvent and carbon dioxide and methane are the solutes.

27. **(B)** According to Table 1, methane has the highest solubility reading of 6.52 at a temperature of 90 degrees and pressure of 144.4 atm.

28. **(G)** Nutrition or the lack thereof is an environmental factor, and does not alter an individual's DNA, so if ill effects due to a grandparent's malnutrition are turning up in grandchildren, then this would be an example of "soft inheritance."

29. **(D)** The passage does not say who proposed the theory of epigenetics. It only mentions that the discovery was "very recent."

30. **(H)** Scientist 1 states that it would be premature to acknowledge true soft inheritance *in animal species.* This implies that she might be willing to concede its existence in plant

PRACTICE TEST 2

species (as many otherwise skeptical biologists indeed do). An apple tree is the only one of the choices that is a plant.

31. **(B)** A believer in epigenetic soft inheritance would disagree with the idea than genes *act in isolation* to produce traits. In other words, he or she would believe that an organism's expressed traits are the result partly of genes and partly of other factors.

32. **(J)** Scientist 1 dismisses apparent evidence for epigenetic theory by arguing that the inherited acquired traits would work themselves out of the bloodline in time ("the bloodline always reverts to the true expression of its DNA," and the map and wind analogy).

33. **(D)** If *histones* are the modules through which genes express themselves, and Scientist 2 figures genes (i.e., "sequences of DNA") as lightbulbs, then it follows that histones would be analogous to the lamp.

34. **(F)** Scientist 1's defense against all epigenetic arguments is to imply that all apparently epigenetic effects are only temporary. And Scientist 2 appears to have no proof so far that they are not. Only a conclusive study of how long the "altered expression" of a gene truly lasts (which would take a pretty long time) can settle the matter for good.

35. **(B)** This is a simple "Go Up, Hit Line, Go Over" question. In Figure 2, right above the 5-hour mark on the *x*-axis (horizontal), the line representing sleep stages is at a height of around 1 on the *y*-axis (vertical).

36. **(H)** The line in Figure 1, which represents the sleep pattern of a child, hits the bottom of the graph (Stage 0, or being awake) only once. The 0 at the left of the graph is not included because this represents the beginning of sleep.

37. **(A)** The subjects of the figures get increasingly older, and the line in Figure 3 hits bottom more than the lines in the other figures do. Therefore, the conclusion that people wake up more frequently as they age is supported by the data. Remember, each touch at the bottom is Stage 0 and Stage 0 indicates awake.

38. **(J)** The introductory paragraph states that REM sleep is associated with the final third of a sleep cycle. Of the answer choices, only the 7-hour mark is in the final third of the sleep cycle depicted in Figure 2, which represents a young adult (although since the passage states that REM sleep occurs in the final third of a sleep cycle for everyone, it wouldn't matter which figure you looked at).

39. **(B)** The introduction says sleep gets deeper as it moves from Stage 1 to Stage 4.

40. **(J)** Though the child reached Stage 4 during hours 1, 3, and 6, the elderly chart shows that the sleep cycle reaches Stage 4 only in hour one.

Writing Sample

Online Culture

Are we losing the Internet to the culture of hate? A recent Time magazine cover suggests that, at least in the U.S., the answer to this question is a gloomy "Yes." The very characteristics that make online communication (via Twitter, Snapchat, Reddit, and other media) so appealing also provide fertile ground for everything from harmless pranking to harassment and even violent threats against society's most vulnerable, including women, religious and ethnic minorities, and young people. Although online anonymity can bring out the worst in people, Perspective 3, in arguing for the Internet's "moving humanity forward," correctly sees the plentiful, if less sensational, positives of virtual communication. Despite its considerable drawbacks, the Internet provides young people unparalleled opportunities to connect their important causes to larger audiences, empowering them to use their wide social networks for good on a global scale.

Daily news stories of cyberbullying suggest that the culture of hate just might be winning. Perspective 1 points out that the Internet emboldens people to be "combative and cruel," and such combativeness shows up even among Facebook friends. Perspective 2 mentions the very real threats to "online" and "physical" selves that tormentors pose. At my suburban high school, bullying doesn't stop when the last bell rings. Overweight kids, skinny kids, kids with acne, kids with accents —they all become easy targets in cyberspace. Online discussion board Reddit recently revealed that the group with the largest user base happens to be "fatpeoplehate," just one forum where "trolls" are free to body shame unsuspecting victims, sending images and rude comments through the Web while preserving their own anonymity. Most disturbing

PRACTICE TEST 2

of all are instances where already depressed teens are bullied into taking their own lives, clear examples of the "game" of hate taken to extremes.

Such horrific stories of hate and intolerance steal attention away from the myriad ways young people create meaningful, constructive change through their online presence. Many kids my age, either unwilling or unable to confide in parents or relatives, rightly or wrongly turn to Facebook or other social media for solace, advice, or support. But teens are also more outward thinking and philanthropic than adults give them credit for, using the Internet to raise money and awareness and to spread their inspirational stories. GoFundMe and other crowdfunding platforms raise money for teens' charitable projects like my World History class's efforts to aid schools in Ghana and Costa Rica. Everyone knows about YouTube, but how many people are familiar with its nonprofit program that allows charitable organizations to post videos with a "donate now" button? My cousin recently made me aware of Dosomething.org, which integrates with Facebook and is specifically designed to get teens involved in social causes, tapping into young people's large social networks, but for the betterment of society. Finally, teen TedTalks include the stories of kids who have done amazing things, including building nuclear fusion reactors, honestly dealing with depression, or something seemingly simple as "just trying to figure it out." Judging by the popularity of these sites and the reach of their messages, charitable works can be just as contagious as hateful acts.

Touting the unlimited potential of Internet communication to do good does not in any way downplay its sinister side, particularly when it comes to my peers and their brutal online assessments of each other. But the words "online culture" do not have to be oxymoronic. Even as some argue that we have not yet lost the battle against hate, we face the challenge of balancing First Amendment rights against the right of every American to safety and security. With unbridled free speech come abuses of that privilege, but the benefits of harnessing the power of multitudes outweigh the more sensationalized harmful effects.

ANSWER SHEET
Practice Test 3

Directions: Mark one answer only for each question. Make the mark dark. Erase completely any mark made in error. (Additional or stray marks will be counted as mistakes.)

English

1. Ⓐ Ⓑ Ⓒ Ⓓ	**16.** Ⓕ Ⓖ Ⓗ Ⓙ	**31.** Ⓐ Ⓑ Ⓒ Ⓓ	**46.** Ⓕ Ⓖ Ⓗ Ⓙ	**61.** Ⓐ Ⓑ Ⓒ Ⓓ
2. Ⓕ Ⓖ Ⓗ Ⓙ	**17.** Ⓐ Ⓑ Ⓒ Ⓓ	**32.** Ⓕ Ⓖ Ⓗ Ⓙ	**47.** Ⓐ Ⓑ Ⓒ Ⓓ	**62.** Ⓕ Ⓖ Ⓗ Ⓙ
3. Ⓐ Ⓑ Ⓒ Ⓓ	**18.** Ⓕ Ⓖ Ⓗ Ⓙ	**33.** Ⓐ Ⓑ Ⓒ Ⓓ	**48.** Ⓕ Ⓖ Ⓗ Ⓙ	**63.** Ⓐ Ⓑ Ⓒ Ⓓ
4. Ⓕ Ⓖ Ⓗ Ⓙ	**19.** Ⓐ Ⓑ Ⓒ Ⓓ	**34.** Ⓕ Ⓖ Ⓗ Ⓙ	**49.** Ⓐ Ⓑ Ⓒ Ⓓ	**64.** Ⓕ Ⓖ Ⓗ Ⓙ
5. Ⓐ Ⓑ Ⓒ Ⓓ	**20.** Ⓕ Ⓖ Ⓗ Ⓙ	**35.** Ⓐ Ⓑ Ⓒ Ⓓ	**50.** Ⓕ Ⓖ Ⓗ Ⓙ	**65.** Ⓐ Ⓑ Ⓒ Ⓓ
6. Ⓕ Ⓖ Ⓗ Ⓙ	**21.** Ⓐ Ⓑ Ⓒ Ⓓ	**36.** Ⓕ Ⓖ Ⓗ Ⓙ	**51.** Ⓐ Ⓑ Ⓒ Ⓓ	**66.** Ⓕ Ⓖ Ⓗ Ⓙ
7. Ⓐ Ⓑ Ⓒ Ⓓ	**22.** Ⓕ Ⓖ Ⓗ Ⓙ	**37.** Ⓐ Ⓑ Ⓒ Ⓓ	**52.** Ⓕ Ⓖ Ⓗ Ⓙ	**67.** Ⓐ Ⓑ Ⓒ Ⓓ
8. Ⓕ Ⓖ Ⓗ Ⓙ	**23.** Ⓐ Ⓑ Ⓒ Ⓓ	**38.** Ⓕ Ⓖ Ⓗ Ⓙ	**53.** Ⓐ Ⓑ Ⓒ Ⓓ	**68.** Ⓕ Ⓖ Ⓗ Ⓙ
9. Ⓐ Ⓑ Ⓒ Ⓓ	**24.** Ⓕ Ⓖ Ⓗ Ⓙ	**39.** Ⓐ Ⓑ Ⓒ Ⓓ	**54.** Ⓕ Ⓖ Ⓗ Ⓙ	**69.** Ⓐ Ⓑ Ⓒ Ⓓ
10. Ⓕ Ⓖ Ⓗ Ⓙ	**25.** Ⓐ Ⓑ Ⓒ Ⓓ	**40.** Ⓕ Ⓖ Ⓗ Ⓙ	**55.** Ⓐ Ⓑ Ⓒ Ⓓ	**70.** Ⓕ Ⓖ Ⓗ Ⓙ
11. Ⓐ Ⓑ Ⓒ Ⓓ	**26.** Ⓕ Ⓖ Ⓗ Ⓙ	**41.** Ⓐ Ⓑ Ⓒ Ⓓ	**56.** Ⓕ Ⓖ Ⓗ Ⓙ	**71.** Ⓐ Ⓑ Ⓒ Ⓓ
12. Ⓕ Ⓖ Ⓗ Ⓙ	**27.** Ⓐ Ⓑ Ⓒ Ⓓ	**42.** Ⓕ Ⓖ Ⓗ Ⓙ	**57.** Ⓐ Ⓑ Ⓒ Ⓓ	**72.** Ⓕ Ⓖ Ⓗ Ⓙ
13. Ⓐ Ⓑ Ⓒ Ⓓ	**28.** Ⓕ Ⓖ Ⓗ Ⓙ	**43.** Ⓐ Ⓑ Ⓒ Ⓓ	**58.** Ⓕ Ⓖ Ⓗ Ⓙ	**73.** Ⓐ Ⓑ Ⓒ Ⓓ
14. Ⓕ Ⓖ Ⓗ Ⓙ	**29.** Ⓐ Ⓑ Ⓒ Ⓓ	**44.** Ⓕ Ⓖ Ⓗ Ⓙ	**59.** Ⓐ Ⓑ Ⓒ Ⓓ	**74.** Ⓕ Ⓖ Ⓗ Ⓙ
15. Ⓐ Ⓑ Ⓒ Ⓓ	**30.** Ⓕ Ⓖ Ⓗ Ⓙ	**45.** Ⓐ Ⓑ Ⓒ Ⓓ	**60.** Ⓕ Ⓖ Ⓗ Ⓙ	**75.** Ⓐ Ⓑ Ⓒ Ⓓ

Mathematics

1. Ⓐ Ⓑ Ⓒ Ⓓ Ⓔ	**16.** Ⓕ Ⓖ Ⓗ Ⓙ Ⓚ	**31.** Ⓐ Ⓑ Ⓒ Ⓓ Ⓔ	**46.** Ⓕ Ⓖ Ⓗ Ⓙ Ⓚ
2. Ⓕ Ⓖ Ⓗ Ⓙ Ⓚ	**17.** Ⓐ Ⓑ Ⓒ Ⓓ Ⓔ	**32.** Ⓕ Ⓖ Ⓗ Ⓙ Ⓚ	**47.** Ⓐ Ⓑ Ⓒ Ⓓ Ⓔ
3. Ⓐ Ⓑ Ⓒ Ⓓ Ⓔ	**18.** Ⓕ Ⓖ Ⓗ Ⓙ Ⓚ	**33.** Ⓐ Ⓑ Ⓒ Ⓓ Ⓔ	**48.** Ⓕ Ⓖ Ⓗ Ⓙ Ⓚ
4. Ⓕ Ⓖ Ⓗ Ⓙ Ⓚ	**19.** Ⓐ Ⓑ Ⓒ Ⓓ Ⓔ	**34.** Ⓕ Ⓖ Ⓗ Ⓙ Ⓚ	**49.** Ⓐ Ⓑ Ⓒ Ⓓ Ⓔ
5. Ⓐ Ⓑ Ⓒ Ⓓ Ⓔ	**20.** Ⓕ Ⓖ Ⓗ Ⓙ Ⓚ	**35.** Ⓐ Ⓑ Ⓒ Ⓓ Ⓔ	**50.** Ⓕ Ⓖ Ⓗ Ⓙ Ⓚ
6. Ⓕ Ⓖ Ⓗ Ⓙ Ⓚ	**21.** Ⓐ Ⓑ Ⓒ Ⓓ Ⓔ	**36.** Ⓕ Ⓖ Ⓗ Ⓙ Ⓚ	**51.** Ⓐ Ⓑ Ⓒ Ⓓ Ⓔ
7. Ⓐ Ⓑ Ⓒ Ⓓ Ⓔ	**22.** Ⓕ Ⓖ Ⓗ Ⓙ Ⓚ	**37.** Ⓐ Ⓑ Ⓒ Ⓓ Ⓔ	**52.** Ⓕ Ⓖ Ⓗ Ⓙ Ⓚ
8. Ⓕ Ⓖ Ⓗ Ⓙ Ⓚ	**23.** Ⓐ Ⓑ Ⓒ Ⓓ Ⓔ	**38.** Ⓕ Ⓖ Ⓗ Ⓙ Ⓚ	**53.** Ⓐ Ⓑ Ⓒ Ⓓ Ⓔ
9. Ⓐ Ⓑ Ⓒ Ⓓ Ⓔ	**24.** Ⓕ Ⓖ Ⓗ Ⓙ Ⓚ	**39.** Ⓐ Ⓑ Ⓒ Ⓓ Ⓔ	**54.** Ⓕ Ⓖ Ⓗ Ⓙ Ⓚ
10. Ⓕ Ⓖ Ⓗ Ⓙ Ⓚ	**25.** Ⓐ Ⓑ Ⓒ Ⓓ Ⓔ	**40.** Ⓕ Ⓖ Ⓗ Ⓙ Ⓚ	**55.** Ⓐ Ⓑ Ⓒ Ⓓ Ⓔ
11. Ⓐ Ⓑ Ⓒ Ⓓ Ⓔ	**26.** Ⓕ Ⓖ Ⓗ Ⓙ Ⓚ	**41.** Ⓐ Ⓑ Ⓒ Ⓓ Ⓔ	**56.** Ⓕ Ⓖ Ⓗ Ⓙ Ⓚ
12. Ⓕ Ⓖ Ⓗ Ⓙ Ⓚ	**27.** Ⓐ Ⓑ Ⓒ Ⓓ Ⓔ	**42.** Ⓕ Ⓖ Ⓗ Ⓙ Ⓚ	**57.** Ⓐ Ⓑ Ⓒ Ⓓ Ⓔ
13. Ⓐ Ⓑ Ⓒ Ⓓ Ⓔ	**28.** Ⓕ Ⓖ Ⓗ Ⓙ Ⓚ	**43.** Ⓐ Ⓑ Ⓒ Ⓓ Ⓔ	**58.** Ⓕ Ⓖ Ⓗ Ⓙ Ⓚ
14. Ⓕ Ⓖ Ⓗ Ⓙ Ⓚ	**29.** Ⓐ Ⓑ Ⓒ Ⓓ Ⓔ	**44.** Ⓕ Ⓖ Ⓗ Ⓙ Ⓚ	**59.** Ⓐ Ⓑ Ⓒ Ⓓ Ⓔ
15. Ⓐ Ⓑ Ⓒ Ⓓ Ⓔ	**30.** Ⓕ Ⓖ Ⓗ Ⓙ Ⓚ	**45.** Ⓐ Ⓑ Ⓒ Ⓓ Ⓔ	**60.** Ⓕ Ⓖ Ⓗ Ⓙ Ⓚ

ANSWER SHEET
Practice Test 3

Reading

1. Ⓐ Ⓑ Ⓒ Ⓓ	9. Ⓐ Ⓑ Ⓒ Ⓓ	17. Ⓐ Ⓑ Ⓒ Ⓓ	25. Ⓐ Ⓑ Ⓒ Ⓓ	33. Ⓐ Ⓑ Ⓒ Ⓓ
2. Ⓕ Ⓖ Ⓗ Ⓙ	10. Ⓕ Ⓖ Ⓗ Ⓙ	18. Ⓕ Ⓖ Ⓗ Ⓙ	26. Ⓕ Ⓖ Ⓗ Ⓙ	34. Ⓕ Ⓖ Ⓗ Ⓙ
3. Ⓐ Ⓑ Ⓒ Ⓓ	11. Ⓐ Ⓑ Ⓒ Ⓓ	19. Ⓐ Ⓑ Ⓒ Ⓓ	27. Ⓐ Ⓑ Ⓒ Ⓓ	35. Ⓐ Ⓑ Ⓒ Ⓓ
4. Ⓕ Ⓖ Ⓗ Ⓙ	12. Ⓕ Ⓖ Ⓗ Ⓙ	20. Ⓕ Ⓖ Ⓗ Ⓙ	28. Ⓕ Ⓖ Ⓗ Ⓙ	36. Ⓕ Ⓖ Ⓗ Ⓙ
5. Ⓐ Ⓑ Ⓒ Ⓓ	13. Ⓐ Ⓑ Ⓒ Ⓓ	21. Ⓐ Ⓑ Ⓒ Ⓓ	29. Ⓐ Ⓑ Ⓒ Ⓓ	37. Ⓐ Ⓑ Ⓒ Ⓓ
6. Ⓕ Ⓖ Ⓗ Ⓙ	14. Ⓕ Ⓖ Ⓗ Ⓙ	22. Ⓕ Ⓖ Ⓗ Ⓙ	30. Ⓕ Ⓖ Ⓗ Ⓙ	38. Ⓕ Ⓖ Ⓗ Ⓙ
7. Ⓐ Ⓑ Ⓒ Ⓓ	15. Ⓐ Ⓑ Ⓒ Ⓓ	23. Ⓐ Ⓑ Ⓒ Ⓓ	31. Ⓐ Ⓑ Ⓒ Ⓓ	39. Ⓐ Ⓑ Ⓒ Ⓓ
8. Ⓕ Ⓖ Ⓗ Ⓙ	16. Ⓕ Ⓖ Ⓗ Ⓙ	24. Ⓕ Ⓖ Ⓗ Ⓙ	32. Ⓕ Ⓖ Ⓗ Ⓙ	40. Ⓕ Ⓖ Ⓗ Ⓙ

Science

1. Ⓐ Ⓑ Ⓒ Ⓓ	9. Ⓐ Ⓑ Ⓒ Ⓓ	17. Ⓐ Ⓑ Ⓒ Ⓓ	25. Ⓐ Ⓑ Ⓒ Ⓓ	33. Ⓐ Ⓑ Ⓒ Ⓓ
2. Ⓕ Ⓖ Ⓗ Ⓙ	10. Ⓕ Ⓖ Ⓗ Ⓙ	18. Ⓕ Ⓖ Ⓗ Ⓙ	26. Ⓕ Ⓖ Ⓗ Ⓙ	34. Ⓕ Ⓖ Ⓗ Ⓙ
3. Ⓐ Ⓑ Ⓒ Ⓓ	11. Ⓐ Ⓑ Ⓒ Ⓓ	19. Ⓐ Ⓑ Ⓒ Ⓓ	27. Ⓐ Ⓑ Ⓒ Ⓓ	35. Ⓐ Ⓑ Ⓒ Ⓓ
4. Ⓕ Ⓖ Ⓗ Ⓙ	12. Ⓕ Ⓖ Ⓗ Ⓙ	20. Ⓕ Ⓖ Ⓗ Ⓙ	28. Ⓕ Ⓖ Ⓗ Ⓙ	36. Ⓕ Ⓖ Ⓗ Ⓙ
5. Ⓐ Ⓑ Ⓒ Ⓓ	13. Ⓐ Ⓑ Ⓒ Ⓓ	21. Ⓐ Ⓑ Ⓒ Ⓓ	29. Ⓐ Ⓑ Ⓒ Ⓓ	37. Ⓐ Ⓑ Ⓒ Ⓓ
6. Ⓕ Ⓖ Ⓗ Ⓙ	14. Ⓕ Ⓖ Ⓗ Ⓙ	22. Ⓕ Ⓖ Ⓗ Ⓙ	30. Ⓕ Ⓖ Ⓗ Ⓙ	38. Ⓕ Ⓖ Ⓗ Ⓙ
7. Ⓐ Ⓑ Ⓒ Ⓓ	15. Ⓐ Ⓑ Ⓒ Ⓓ	23. Ⓐ Ⓑ Ⓒ Ⓓ	31. Ⓐ Ⓑ Ⓒ Ⓓ	39. Ⓐ Ⓑ Ⓒ Ⓓ
8. Ⓕ Ⓖ Ⓗ Ⓙ	16. Ⓕ Ⓖ Ⓗ Ⓙ	24. Ⓕ Ⓖ Ⓗ Ⓙ	32. Ⓕ Ⓖ Ⓗ Ⓙ	40. Ⓕ Ⓖ Ⓗ Ⓙ

ENGLISH TEST

Time: 45 Minutes—75 Questions

Directions: In the five passages that follow, certain words and phrases are underlined and numbered. In the right-hand column, you will find alternatives for the underlined part. In most cases, you are to choose the one that best expresses the idea, makes the statement appropriate for standard written English, or is worded most consistently with the style and tone of the passage as a whole. If you think the original version is best, choose "NO CHANGE." In some cases, you will find in the right-hand column a question about the underlined part. You are to choose the best answer to the question.

You will also find questions about a section of the passage, or about the passage as a whole. These questions do not refer to an underlined portion of the passage, but rather are identified by a number or numbers in a box.

For each question, choose the alternative you consider best and fill in the corresponding oval on your answer sheet. Read each passage through once before you begin to answer the questions that accompany it. For many of the questions, you must read several sentences beyond the question to determine the answer. Be sure that you have read far enough ahead each time you choose an alternative.

PASSAGE I

The Real Johnny B. Goode?

No one person invented rock and roll single-handedly, but for years both critics, and fans have agreed that (1) no individual is due more credit than Chuck Berry. The singer, songwriter, and guitarist behind such rock classics as "Maybelline" and "Johnny B. Goode" was a major influence (2) on everything from the songwriting of the Beatles to the guitar playing of Jimi Hendrix.

1. **A.** NO CHANGE
   B. critics and fans have agreed, that
   C. critics, and fans have agreed, that
   D. critics and fans have agreed that

2. **F.** NO CHANGE
   G. were a major influence
   H. were major influences
   J. have had a major influence

He sold millions of records and in 1986 among (3) the first class of inductees into the Rock and Roll Hall of Fame. But in 2000, the music world was

3. **A.** NO CHANGE
   B. was
   C. was among
   D. would have been among

shocked when Berry was sued by an old piano player of his, Johnnie Johnson claimed it was really he who had composed the music for nearly all of Berry's hits.
4

Could the great Chuck Berry is a fraud, and the virtually unknown Johnson the true force behind the songs that shaped rock and roll? It seemed distracting at first, but eventually even the biggest Berry fans had to admit that certain details seemed
5
6

to corroborate Johnson's story. The band that became the Chuck Berry Trio in 1955 was originally the Johnnie Johnson Trio, and Berry, a struggling local musician, had joined as a last-minute addition when a member fell ill before a St. Louis gig in 1953.
7
8

Although Berry claimed sole responsibility for the many hits that soon followed, his gift for composition mysteriously dried up after he
9

4. F. NO CHANGE
G. Johnson, claimed
H. Johnson, claiming
J. Johnson, who claimed

5. A. NO CHANGE
B. be
C. possibly was
D. DELETE the underlined portion.

6. Which word or phrase best emphasizes the shocking nature of the allegations?
F. NO CHANGE
G. silly
H. unthinkable
J. impossible to determine

7. Which of the following alternatives to the underlined portion would be LEAST acceptable?
A. to prove
B. to verify
C. to confirm
D. to dispute

8. If the writer were to delete the underlined portion, the paragraph would primarily lose:
F. an instance of foreshadowing.
G. an explanation of why the type of music Berry played was popular in the South.
H. a reminder of how cruel the music business can be.
J. evidence of how close Berry came to not being a rock star at all.

9. A. NO CHANGE
B. Since
C. On the other hand,
D. DELETE the underlined portion.

stopped working with Johnson. Berry was jailed in 1959 over shady goings-on at a nightclub he owned, and his only Top Ten hits after his 1963 release <u>was</u> [10] a silly novelty record called "My Ding-a-Ling" and a tune called "No Particular Place to Go," which was clearly just the Berry classic "School Days" with new lyrics. Even lifelong Berry fan Bruce Springsteen <u>from remarking</u> [11] years earlier that their songs were written in unusual keys for a guitar player—keys more commonly found in songs composed on piano. [12]

Why had Johnnie not spoken up at the time? Tragically, Johnson was plagued by alcoholism for most of his life, and took little notice of what went on outside the studio. He also knew far less about

10. **F.** NO CHANGE
G. had
H. were
J. being

11. **A.** NO CHANGE
B. had remarked
C. did remark
D. would remark

12. At this point, the writer is considering adding the following true statement:

> Berry had been in trouble with the law many times before, so allegations that he had cheated a former partner were hardly inconsistent with his character.

Should the writer make this addition?

F. Yes, as it provides relevant information.
G. Yes, because it proves Berry is a fraud.
H. No, because only Berry's talent is the issue, and not his character.
J. No, because it doesn't specify every crime of which Berry was accused.

things like rights and royalties than did the more educated and business-savvy Berry. [13]

A judge dismissed the suit because too much time had elapsed <u>until the songs in question were written,</u> (14) and Johnnie Johnson passed away in 2005, so the world will never know exactly who wrote what in all those immortal songs. Johnson never claimed he wrote them alone, however, and Chuck Berry still deserves his legendary status even if all he did was pen the lyrics and play the guitar—but maybe the name of Johnnie Johnson should be no less famous than his.

13. Given that all the following statements are true, which one, if added here, would most effectively conclude the paragraph and support information given in the preceding sentence?

A. As far as Johnson knew, what he was paid for his time at the end of a session was fair.
B. Many African-American musicians of that era never received the money they deserved.
C. Of course, how music publishing works has changed a great deal since the 1950s.
D. Later rock stars were even more educated, a notable example being Mick Jagger.

14. **F.** NO CHANGE
G. between the writing of most of the songs,
H. since the writing of the songs in question,
J. before any more songs could be written,

Question 15 asks about the preceding passage as a whole.

15. Suppose the author had intended to write an essay about how celebrities are almost never really the people we think they are. Would this essay fulfill that goal?

A. Yes, because it makes a strong case that one of the greatest rock stars of all time did not write his own songs.
B. Yes, because the essay just confirms what most people already suspected anyway.
C. No, because the essay deals only with Chuck Berry, and not celebrities in general.
D. No, because the concept of "celebrities" did not exist yet in the 1950s.

PASSAGE II

Stealing *Mona Lisa*

It is the world's most famous painting, and endlessly [16] admired, analyzed, parodied [17] for over 500 years. You'd think that any sane thief would set his sights on a less ambitious target. But in 1911, Leonardo da Vinci's masterpiece, the *Mona Lisa,* was stolen, and it remained missing [18] for two years.

Vincenzo Perrugia was an Italian immigrant who had worked at France's famous Louvre museum for barely a month, but this was [19] enough time for him to formulate a daring plan. Knowing that the museum would be closed for restorations on August 21, he hid inside at closing the night before. The following day, Peruggia tried his hardest to keep calm [20] until he found himself alone in the gallery where the *Mona Lisa* hung.

16. F. NO CHANGE
G. endlessly
H. it was endlessly
J. that has been endlessly

17. A. NO CHANGE
B. and parodied
C. and it was parodied
D. it was parodied

18. F. NO CHANGE
G. went missing and was stolen
H. had been stolen, remaining missing
J. was missing

19. Which of the following alternatives to the underlined portion would NOT be acceptable?
A. this was
B. which was
C. evidently
D. DELETE the underlined portion.

20. Given that all the choices are true, which one provides the most specific information about Perrugia's methods?
F. NO CHANGE
G. Perrugia somehow managed to evade detection
H. just as he would eventually tell his grandchildren, Perrugia remained in the museum
J. disguised in a smock, Perrugia walked around looking busy

He quickly snatched it off the wall and absconded into a stairwell, where he smashed the frame, then rolled up the painting and hid it in his smock. [21: off]

21. Which of the following alternatives to the underlined portion would be LEAST acceptable?
   A. from
   B. off of
   C. from of
   D. from off

He found the door at the bottom of the stairs locked, he smashed the knob and calmly reported the broken lock to a custodian on his way out of the building. [22: He found]

22. F. NO CHANGE
   G. Although he would find
   H. Just before he found
   J. Finding

Perrugia wasn't the only one in the Louvre that day who had a plan. [23] Many workers passed the empty space on the wall where they knew the *Mona Lisa* usually hung, but since restorations were taking place all day, just assumed that the museum's prized possession was being touched up or reframed as quickly as possible. [24] When it was discovered that the painting was gone, a massive manhunt began. Theorizing that a radical young artist might have stolen it as a publicity stunt, [25] police even arrested and questioned such figures as Pablo Picasso and surrealist poet Guillaume Apollinaire.

23. Given that all the choices are true, which one most effectively introduces the paragraph?
   A. NO CHANGE
   B. There's no record of how long it took for the lock to be repaired, if it ever was.
   C. The staff of the Louvre did not immediately realize that a theft had occurred.
   D. The Louvre had seen its share of troubles since it was first constructed as a fortress in the twelfth century.

24. F. NO CHANGE
   G. in private.
   H. by Italian artisans.
   J. automatically.

25. Which of the following alternatives to the underlined portion would be LEAST acceptable?
   A. out of ignorance
   B. as a form of protest
   C. to make a point
   D. as some pretentious prank

Perrugia hid the painting in his apartment and waited. As time passed, the search lost momentum and the <u>feared masterwork was gone forever.</u> 26

Fortunately, <u>Perrugia was motivated</u> 27 for the crime led to its recovery: he felt that the *Mona Lisa* belonged in da Vinci's native Italy, <u>from whence</u> 28 it had been stolen by Napoleon a century earlier. In 1913, he smuggled it there and offered it to the director of the Uffizi Gallery in Florence. Perrugia expected a hero's welcome and a reward for his patriotic crime, but gallery personnel stalled him while police were called, and he was arrested.

<u>Still, a lot of good came out of the business after all:</u> 29 the *Mona Lisa* was exhibited all over Italy for months before being returned to the Louvre, and as for Vincenzo Perrugia himself, the Italian courts took his patriotism (and the popularity of his crime in Italy) into consideration, and for the theft of the most priceless portable object on the face of the earth, he served only a few months in jail!

26. F. NO CHANGE
    G. gone masterwork was forever feared.
    H. masterwork was feared gone forever.
    J. masterwork was forever feared gone.

27. A. NO CHANGE
    B. the motivation had
    C. Perrugia being motivated
    D. Perrugia's motivation

28. F. NO CHANGE
    G. after which
    H. into there
    J. whereas

29. The writer would like to begin the final sentence with a phrase that indicates Perrugia might not have been as crazy as he seems. Given that all the choices are true, which one best accomplishes the writer's goal?
    A. NO CHANGE
    B. Still, his expectations were not entirely off-base:
    C. Curiously, it was the last time he ever felt the need to steal anything:
    D. Curiously, a war between France and Italy was only a few short years away:

Question 30 asks about the preceding passage as a whole.

30. Suppose the writer's goal had been to write a brief essay explaining the background, execution, and aftermath of a famous crime. Would this essay accomplish that goal?
   F. Yes, because it establishes that everyone knew about the theft at the time, even though some people don't nowadays.
   G. Yes, because it presents a sufficiently complete picture of Perrugia's theft of the *Mona Lisa.*
   H. No, because it tells us virtually nothing about why the *Mona Lisa* is so important.
   J. No, because it clearly states that Perrugia's punishment was not nearly harsh enough.

PASSAGE III

The following paragraphs may or may not be in the most logical order. Each paragraph is numbered in brackets, and question 45 will ask you to choose where Paragraph 1 should most logically be placed.

Whom Are You Calling a Barbarian?

[1]

His enemies <u>dubbed</u> (31) "The Scourge of God." His name is synonymous <u>to</u> (32) cruelty, mercilessness, and barbarism of all kinds. But has history really been fair to the fifth-century king and military

31. A. NO CHANGE
   B. dubbed him
   C. dubbed to him
   D. dubbed him for

32. F. NO CHANGE
   G. of
   H. as
   J. with

leader known to us as Attila the Hun? <u>It is modern historians who agree</u> [33] that it has not. Traditional views of this period in Europe have been based on Roman sources, which even at their best are still biased against Attila, and at worst contain outright lies. [34]

33. A. NO CHANGE
B. It is agreed by modern historians
C. Modern historians had finally agreed
D. Modern historians agree

34. If the writer were to delete the preceding sentence, the paragraph would primarily lose information that:
F. demonstrates that Roman historians were typically less honest than were historians from other cultures.
G. proves that modern Europe is more indebted to Rome for its culture than to any other ancient society.
H. explains the reasons behind the long-standing negative opinion of Attila.
J. explains which myths about Attila were invented by the Romans.

[2]

The Huns were not the nomadic tribe of brutes that popular culture has often portrayed them as being. At the time of Attila's birth in <u>406, the</u> [35] Huns were a vast and efficiently run nation stretching all the way from <u>Asias central seas</u> [36] to the west of what is now Germany, <u>and this was</u> [37] far larger and less fragmented than the Western Roman Empire then was. And unlike aristocratic Roman society, the Hun world was a meritocracy with little to no <u>separation because of class division</u> [38]. At least a few sources who

35. A. NO CHANGE
B. 406, and the
C. 406; the
D. 406. The

36. F. NO CHANGE
G. Asia's central seas
H. Asias central sea's
J. Asias' central sea's

37. A. NO CHANGE
B. this was
C. which was
D. DELETE the underlined portion.

38. F. NO CHANGE
G. class division
H. people being separated by class division
J. unfair class division keeping people apart

had lived in both societies said that they preferred the Hun civilization to the Roman.

Yes, the Huns had beards and wore furs, but this was only common sense: it was much colder where they lived than it was in Rome. [39]

[3]

Attila became king upon the death of his uncle in 434 and coexisting peacefully (40) with Western Rome for the first part of his reign. Roman armies in what is now France recruited soldiers from Hun lands with Attila's permission, and the two empires traded freely and even extradited criminals to each other. The trouble started in 450, when Honoria, the sister of the emperor, offered herself in marriage to Attila in an attempt to escape an arranged union with a much older senator. Valentinian, her brother, tried to deny that the offer was genuine, but Attila was

39. At this point, the writer is considering adding the following true statement:

> The Vikings wore even more furs and had even longer beards, and they sailed to America 500 years before Columbus!

Should the writer make this addition?

A. Yes, because it provides a much-needed additional example for the same point.
B. Yes, because this little-known fact should be provided to people whenever possible.
C. No, because it distracts the reader from the main focus of the essay.
D. No, because the essay does not explain whether the Huns and Vikings got along.

40. **F.** NO CHANGE
G. coexists in peace
H. coexisted peacefully
J. peaceful coexistence

understandably unwilling to pass up a chance to unite his royal line <u>with that of Rome</u> [41] and create the greatest empire in history. Rome was so frightened by this prospect that they aligned themselves with the Visigoths—formerly the common enemy of both the <u>Huns, and Rome further insulted Attila.</u> [42] Hun forces entered Italy in 452, and sacked several cities, but were forced to turn back before reaching the capital, as a famine prevented the army from obtaining sufficient food. Attila died in his native lands a year later, supposedly after partying too hard at a feast.

[4]

Contrary to popular belief, neither Attila nor any Hun commander ever sacked Rome (the Visigoths took the city in 410, and the Vandals in 454, but neither nation was aligned or even friendly with the Huns). Although his tactics were brutal by modern standards, <u>they were</u> [43] no more so than those of any military leader from that time, the "civilized" Romans included. Attila may be known as a monster in the West, but is revered as a national

41. **A.** NO CHANGE
B. with they're own
C. with Rome's one
D. plus the Roman one

42. **F.** NO CHANGE
G. Huns and Rome's, who had further insulted Attila.
H. Huns and Rome—further insulting Attila.
J. Huns everywhere. Rome thus insulted Attila further.

43. **A.** NO CHANGE
B. but they were
C. since they were
D. it was

hero in much of Eastern Europe to this day. <u>Should you visit that part of the world, you will be amazed at how often you see his name!</u> [44] [45]

44. Given that all of the following statements are true, which one provides the most relevant and specific information?
   - **F.** NO CHANGE
   - **G.** There is almost certainly at least one giant statue of him there!
   - **H.** In Budapest, there are more than ten "Attila Streets!"
   - **J.** Of course, the map of Eastern Europe is now very different from the one most Americans remember from school!

Question 45 asks about the preceding passage as a whole.

45. For the sake of logic and coherence, Paragraph 1 should be placed:
   - **A.** where it is now.
   - **B.** after Paragraph 2.
   - **C.** after Paragraph 3.
   - **D.** after Paragraph 4.

PASSAGE IV

The Christmas Truce

<u>When it started</u> [46] with the assassination of an Austrian nobleman in the summer of 1914, and by the end of that year all Europe was scarred by trenches full of soldiers and pits full of poison gas.

46.
   - **F.** NO CHANGE
   - **G.** Since it started
   - **H.** Although it started
   - **J.** It started

Tanks and warplanes <u>made their first appearances.</u> [47] Old-fashioned commanders accustomed to valiant charges on horseback sent countless waves of young men to instant death in the face of another new invention, the machine gun. The Great War, or World War I as it would come

47. Which of the following alternatives to the underlined portion would be LEAST acceptable?
   - **A.** were first put into use.
   - **B.** were first introduced.
   - **C.** were used in combat for the first time.
   - **D.** reared their ugly heads.

to be called, <u>was the deadliest conflict the Western World had ever seen.</u> [48] But out of its horror came one of the most reassuring accounts of the essential goodness of the human spirit.

On Christmas Eve of 1914, near the town of <u>Ypres, Belgium, German,</u> [49] and English forces had fought to a standstill from their opposed trenches. Both sides had sent miners to dig tunnels toward the enemy <u>line. Underground,</u> [50] each unit could hear the sounds of the <u>other's</u> [51] digging getting closer, and knew that the tunnels would soon meet and a firefight would erupt in the darkness at point-blank range.

At that moment, <u>every soldier must have thought that he was about to die.</u> [52] Recognizing the melodies, the men in the other tunnel responded, singing along in their own language. The singing picked up above ground, where the armies lit candles visible

48. The writer wishes to finish this sentence with a phrase that emphasizes the human cost of the war. Which of the following true statements best achieves that goal?
F. NO CHANGE
G. was the first modern war, involving horrors beyond description.
H. led directly to the deadly Spanish Flu epidemic.
J. is the only major war where the inhuman weapon of mustard gas was used.

49. A. NO CHANGE
B. Ypres, Belgium, German
C. Ypres, Belgium German
D. Ypres, Belgium, and German

50. Which of the following alternatives to the underlined portion would NOT be acceptable?
F. NO CHANGE
G. line, underground,
H. line; underground
J. line: underground

51. A. NO CHANGE
B. others
C. others'
D. other is

52. Given that all the choices are true, which one would be the best transition between the first and last parts of the paragraph?
F. NO CHANGE
G. you could have cut the tension with a knife.
H. soldiers from one side began singing Christmas carols.
J. no soldier in the tunnels had ever been more scared in his life.

to the enemy at the edges of their trenches. The fighting ceased, and slowly, some individuals even dared to cross No Man's Land and meet enemy soldiers in the <u>middle, where they exchanged</u> food [53] and drink from their respective homelands.

When word of the Christmas Truce got out, the high command on <u>both sides were furious</u> [54] and ordered the fighting to resume. When Christmas 1915 approached <u>again,</u> [55] they took steps to ensure that such things would not happen, ordering artillery bombardments on Christmas Eve and Christmas Day to make No Man's Land uncrossable. The commanders in the trenches had to follow orders, on pain of court martial. But <u>as the generals</u> [56] had never specified coordinates for the mandatory bombardments, entrenched officers in several locations came up with the idea of ordering wildly inaccurate shelling, allowing gift-giving between enemy combatants once again. <u>For example,</u> [57] in one location English and German soldiers even organized a soccer game in the middle of the battlefield.

53. Which of the following alternatives to the underlined portion would NOT be acceptable?
   A. middle. There, they exchanged
   B. middle to exchange
   C. middle they exchanged
   D. middle, exchanging

54. **F.** NO CHANGE
   G. both sides, they were furious
   H. both sides furiously
   J. both sides was furious

55. The best placement for the underlined portion would be:
   A. where it is now.
   B. after the word *they.*
   C. after the word *happen.*
   D. after the word *bombardments.*

56. **F.** NO CHANGE
   G. when the generals
   H. that the generals
   J. the generals

57. **A.** NO CHANGE
   B. In addition,
   C. Meanwhile,
   D. On the other hand,

By the time World War I ended in 1918, 16 million people had been killed in battle, three world powers had ceased to exist altogether, and nothing discernible had been accomplished. <u>The devastation ended up leading directly to the existence of both the Soviet Union and Nazi Germany.</u> [58] Just about the only good thing that came out of it was the story of a few young men who couldn't <u>understand or comprehend</u> [59] each other's languages but still decided that they would rather play soccer than fight.

58. If the writer were to delete the underlined sentence, the paragraph would primarily lose:

- **F.** an example of how World War I shaped the major conflicts of the twentieth century.
- **G.** the answer to a question posed at the beginning of the essay.
- **H.** an example of pure speculation on the part of the writer.
- **J.** some minor details unrelated to the main point.

59.
- **A.** NO CHANGE
- **B.** understand nor comprehend
- **C.** understandably comprehend
- **D.** understand

Question 60 asks about the preceding passage as a whole.

60. Suppose the writer had intended to write a brief essay focusing on acts of protest within the armed forces during wars. Would this essay fulfill that goal?

- **F.** Yes, because the Christmas Truce is the most famous battlefield protest of all time.
- **G.** Yes, because the Christmas Truce was spontaneous in origin, rather than being planned in advance.
- **H.** No, because it only discusses examples of soldiers acting in protest from one war.
- **J.** No, because American troops had not yet entered World War I at the time of the Christmas Truce.

PASSAGE V

Genius at the Last Minute

He was born in Oregon in 1954, the son of a schoolteacher mother <u>and his father had grown up</u> [61] in a Mennonite community. <u>He never liked or excelled in school,</u> [62] and chose to attend a "hippie college" in Washington State that had been founded only five years earlier and didn't even give grades.

He stayed in college for five years, <u>and</u> [63] writing articles and drawing cartoons for the campus paper.

<u>After graduation,</u> [64] he moved to Los Angeles to try to become a writer, but couldn't catch a break and wandered through a series of jobs: busing tables, washing dishes, and even working at a sewage

61. **A.** NO CHANGE
B. and father grew up
C. and whose father grew up
D. and a father who'd grown up

62. Which of the following alternatives to the underlined portion would NOT be acceptable?
F. never liked school or excelled in it,
G. neither liked nor excelled in school,
H. disliked school, which he didn't excel in it,
J. disliked and failed to excel in school,

63. **A.** NO CHANGE
B. where
C. in which
D. DELETE the underlined portion.

64. **F.** NO CHANGE
G. Although after graduation,
H. After graduation, when
J. After graduation, however,

treatment plant. Finally, he ended up working in a [65] record store, a job he was able to stand. [66]

To amuse himself and make a little extra money, he drew comic books about how miserable he was in Los Angeles and sold photocopies of them in the store.

The comics were sarcastic [67] black-and-white doodles featuring a family of odd-looking, dysfunctional rabbits, became popular with neighborhood artists and intellectuals, and soon he was getting paid to draw a daily strip featuring his odd rabbits for a local alternative newspaper. (The paper also gave him a music column, but he lost that after admitting that he [68] just made up the names of all the bands and albums he reviewed as a joke.)

65. Which of the following alternatives to the underlined portion would NOT be acceptable?

A. at
B. of
C. for
D. the register in

66. At this point, the writer is considering adding the following true statement:

The name of the store was Licorice Pizza.

Should the writer make this addition?

F. Yes, because it helps explain why he was able to stand the job.
G. Yes, because otherwise readers will wonder which store it was.
H. No, because it is a minor detail that disrupts the flow of the paragraph.
J. No, because many readers will not believe that this was really the store's name.

67. **A.** NO CHANGE
B. comics, sarcastic
C. sarcastically comic
D. sarcastic comic's

68. Which of the following alternatives to the underlined portion would NOT be acceptable?

F. he
G. he had
H. that he had
J. because he had

The rabbit strip, called *Life in Hell*, came to the attention of a successful producer, who contacted [69] the thirty-one-year-old cartoonist about the possibility to do [70] animated shorts for television. The artist was thrilled, but while waiting in the lobby of the producer's building before his big meeting, he had a series of terrifying thoughts. What if the television series bombed and ruined the reputation of his beloved comic?

Or what if he had to give up the rights to the characters, and no longer had any control over how they were used?

Crazy stuff happens to young artists all the time. [71] So just before being called into the meeting, he quickly drew another group of characters and named them after his own family: he used the real names of his parents and two little sisters, but invented another for the sarcastic, academically unmotivated male child, thinking that using his

69. **A.** NO CHANGE
B. producer then contacted
C. producer, and contacted
D. producer contacted

70. **F.** NO CHANGE
G. of doing
H. he could do
J. that this would do

71. Which of the following sentences makes for the best transition between the first and second parts of the paragraph?
A. NO CHANGE
B. At times like this, he wished he were still at college in Washington.
C. It was probably silly for him to be worrying so much.
D. He wanted the TV gig badly, but didn't want to risk losing *Life in Hell.*

own name would give away [72] how little work he had put into the idea. To the animator's great relief, the producer loved the hurriedly created new characters. Their first animated short debuted in 1987, and by the end of 1989 they had their own half-hour show.

By now, you may have guessed that the cartoonist's name, Matt Groening, [73] and that the family he invented off the top of his head in that lobby is now known to the whole world as *The Simpsons*. The cartoon in which they star [74] has become the longest-running sitcom in TV history, as well as one of the most beloved, by viewers and critics alike. Although it may not happen every day, don't [75] ever let anyone tell you that a work of genius was never done at the last minute.

72. Which of the following alternatives to the underlined portion would be LEAST acceptable?
- **F.** betray
- **G.** evince
- **H.** mask
- **J.** tip the producer off to

73.
- **A.** NO CHANGE
- **B.** name was Matt Groening
- **C.** name, was Matt Groening
- **D.** name, Matt Groening

74.
- **F.** NO CHANGE
- **G.** cartoon which they star in
- **H.** cartoon, which they star in,
- **J.** cartoon they star in which

75.
- **A.** NO CHANGE
- **B.** day, but don't
- **C.** day; don't
- **D.** day, don't people

STOP

If there is still time remaining, you may review your answers.

MATHEMATICS TEST

Time: 60 Minutes—60 Questions

Directions: Solve each problem, choose the correct answer, and then fill in the corresponding oval on your answer sheet.

Do not linger over problems that take too much time. Solve as many as you can; then return to the others in the time you have left for this test.

You are permitted to use a calculator on this test. You may use your calculator for any problems you choose, but some of the problems may best be done without using a calculator.

Note: Unless otherwise stated, all of the following should be assumed.

1. Illustrative figures are NOT necessarily drawn to scale.
2. Geometric figures lie in a plane.
3. The word *line* indicates a straight line.
4. The word *average* indicates arithmetic mean.

DO YOUR FIGURING HERE

1. If $3x - 5 = 7$, then $3x = ?$

A. $\frac{2}{3}$
B. $\frac{4}{3}$
C. 4
D. $\frac{22}{3}$
E. 12

2. What is the complement of 70°?

F. 10°
G. 20°
H. 30°
J. 80°
K. 110°

3. 70 is 10% of what number?

A. 7
B. 63
C. 77
D. 700
E. 7,000

DO YOUR FIGURING HERE

4. The sum of three consecutive integers is 99. What is the value of the greatest of the three integers?

F. 32
G. 33
H. 34
J. 35
K. 36

5. What is the area of the figure below?

A. 54 in.^{2}
B. 90 in.^{2}
C. 108 in.^{2}
D. 135 in.^{2}
E. 180 in.^{2}

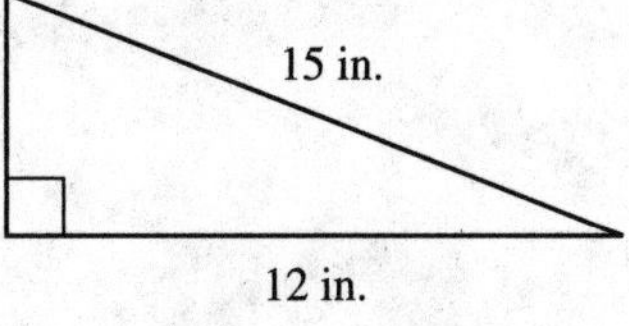

6. Miller earns $13.00 per hour for the first 40 hours he works each week. For each hour beyond 40 that he works in 1 week, Miller earns $19.50 per hour. Last week Miller earned $1,027.00. How many hours did Miller work last week?

F. 26
G. 30
H. 53
J. 66
K. 79

7. Which of the following inequalities is equivalent to $3 - 4(x + 7) < 19$?

A. $x > \frac{9}{2}$
B. $x < \frac{9}{2}$
C. $x < -11$
D. $x > -11$
E. $x < 11$

DO YOUR FIGURING HERE

8. Which of the following is equivalent to $3\sqrt{300} - 5\sqrt{75}$?
   F. $-2\sqrt{225}$
   G. $5\sqrt{3}$
   H. $15\sqrt{3}$
   J. $2\sqrt{225}$
   K. $15\sqrt{225}$

9. $|-2 + 3^2| - |-2 - 3^2| = ?$
   A. –24
   B. –4
   C. 0
   D. 18
   E. 26

10. For triangle *ABC*, $m\angle A = 75°$ and $m\angle B = 36°$. Which segment of triangle *ABC* is the longest?
   F. *AB*
   G. *BC*
   H. *AC*
   J. *AB* and *AC* are both the longest sides.
   K. Not enough information

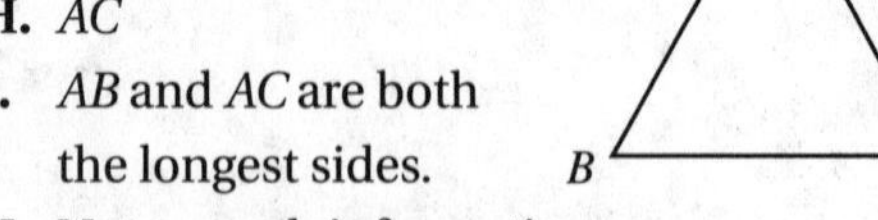

11. Which of the following is a factor of $3x^2 + x - 4$?
   A. $(x + 2)$
   B. $(x - 2)$
   C. $(3x - 4)$
   D. $(x + 1)$
   E. $(x - 1)$

DO YOUR FIGURING HERE

12. Which of the following lines passes through the point (–3, 5)?

F. $y = -2x - 3$
G. $y = -4x + 5$
H. $y = -x + 2$
J. $y = 4x + 5$
K. $y = 5x + 9$

13. If $f(x) = \dfrac{-x^2 + 4}{x}$, then $f(-2) = ?$

A. –4
B. –1
C. 0
D. 6
E. 10

14. Which of the following lines is parallel to $y = -\frac{3}{4}x + 2$ in the standard (x, y) coordinate plane?

F. $y = -\frac{3}{4}x$
G. $y = \frac{4}{3}x + 2$
H. $y = -\frac{4}{3}x + 2$
J. $y = \frac{3}{4}x + 2$
K. $y = \frac{3}{4}x - 2$

15. An aquarium has exactly two types of fish: goldfish and angelfish. If the ratio of goldfish to angelfish is 2:5 and there are 25 angelfish in the aquarium, how many total fish are in the aquarium?

A. 7
B. 32
C. 35
D. 50
E. 125

16. Three different lines in the same plane can intersect at how many points?
    - F. 1
    - G. 1 or 2
    - H. 1 or 3
    - J. 1, 2, or 3
    - K. 0, 1, 2, or 3

DO YOUR FIGURING HERE

17. If $-1 < a < 0$, $-4 < b < -3$, and $c = a - b$, then which of the following statements is true?
    - A. $c < a$
    - B. $c < b$
    - C. $c < a + b$
    - D. $c < 0$
    - E. $c > 0$

18. What is the slope of the line through the points (–2, 5) and (0, 8)?
    - F. $-\frac{3}{2}$
    - G. $-\frac{2}{3}$
    - H. $\frac{7}{8}$
    - J. $\frac{8}{7}$
    - K. $\frac{3}{2}$

DO YOUR FIGURING HERE

19. Rosemary and Caroline are baking cupcakes for a party. They are working from a recipe that will make 32 cupcakes. The recipe requires $2\frac{1}{2}$ cups of sugar to make 1 full batch. If they need to make 250 cupcakes for the party, which of the following amounts (to the nearest whole cup) is the LEAST amount of sugar they need to make all 250 cupcakes?

A. 5 cups
B. 10 cups
C. 15 cups
D. 20 cups
E. 25 cups

20. For the following triangle, $\angle B$ is a right angle, $BC = 8$, and $AC = 17$. What is the value of $\sin(C)$?

F. $\frac{8}{17}$

G. $\frac{15}{17}$

H. $\frac{\sqrt{353}}{17}$

J. $\frac{17}{15}$

K. $\frac{17}{8}$

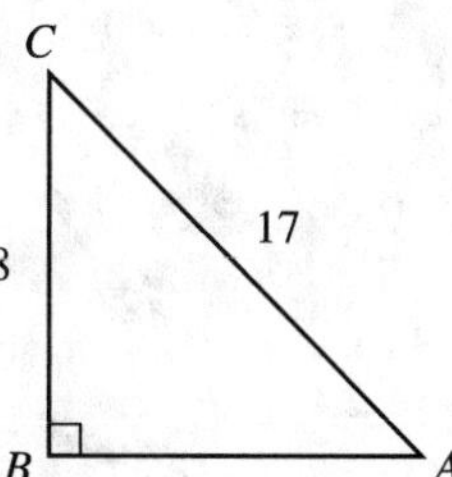

DO YOUR FIGURING HERE

Use the following information to answer questions 21–24.

The Knight family plans to remodel their kitchen. They have a total budget of $30,000 for the project. They have sorted the budget into 6 categories. Some of the budget amounts are shown in the table below.

Expense category	Budget amount
Appliances	$3,500
Cabinets	$7,000
Flooring	$4,000
Lighting	$2,500
Labor	?
Other	?
Total budget	$30,000

21. The amount budgeted for the Appliances category is the sum of the prices of 4 appliances. What is the average price per appliance?
    A. $ 583
    B. $ 625
    C. $ 700
    D. $ 875
    E. $1,000

22. What fraction represents the ratio of the budget for Lighting compared to the budget for Flooring?
    F. $\frac{5}{7}$
    G. $\frac{5}{8}$
    H. $\frac{1}{2}$
    J. $\frac{5}{14}$
    K. $\frac{1}{12}$

DO YOUR FIGURING HERE

23. In a circle graph illustrating the 6 budget amounts in the table, what should be the measure of the central angle of the Lighting sector?

A. 30°
B. 42°
C. 48°
D. 72°
E. 84°

24. Which of the following percentages is closest to the percent of the total budget for the Labor and Other categories combined?

F. 37%
G. 43%
H. 45%
J. 48%
K. 57%

---

25. If $5^3 \cdot 5^{-7} = \frac{1}{5^x}$, then $x = ?$

A. −21
B. −4
C. 4
D. 7
E. 21

26. In the figure below, m$\angle WYZ = 28°$ and $\overline{YM}$ bisects $\angle ZYX$. Which of the following is the measure of $\angle XYM$?

F. 76°
G. 78°
H. 84°
J. 90°
K. 152°

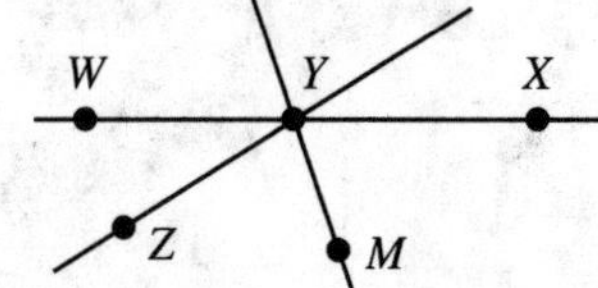

27. In the figure below, $\overline{AC}$ is a diameter of the circle and m$\angle BAC = 35°$. Find the measure of arc $\widehat{AB}$.

A. 35°
B. 60°
C. 70°
D. 90°
E. 110°

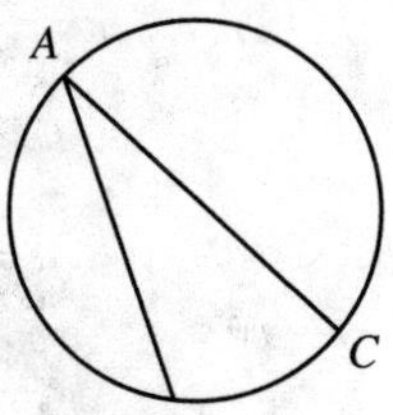

DO YOUR FIGURING HERE

28. Which of the following is the greatest common factor of $36m^4n^3p^5$ and $24m^2n$?

F. $6m^2n$
G. $6m^4n^3p^5$
H. $12m^2n$
J. $12m^2np^5$
K. $72m^2n$

29. The perimeter of a parallelogram is 56 and the length of one side is 12 inches. If it can be determined, what are the lengths, in inches, of the other three sides?

A. 12, 12, 20
B. 12, 10, 10
C. 12, 16, 16
D. 12, 32, 32
E. Cannot be determined from the given information

Use the following information to answer questions 30–32.

In the figure below, a gas station (at Y) and radar stations (at X and Z) lie on a horizontal east-west line, with X 5,000 feet due west of Y. An airplane (at W) is shown directly above the gas station, flying due east at a constant speed of 600 feet per second and at a constant altitude of 12,000 feet. The airplane is located at a straight-line distance of 13,000 feet from the radar station at X and 20,000 feet from the radar station at Z.

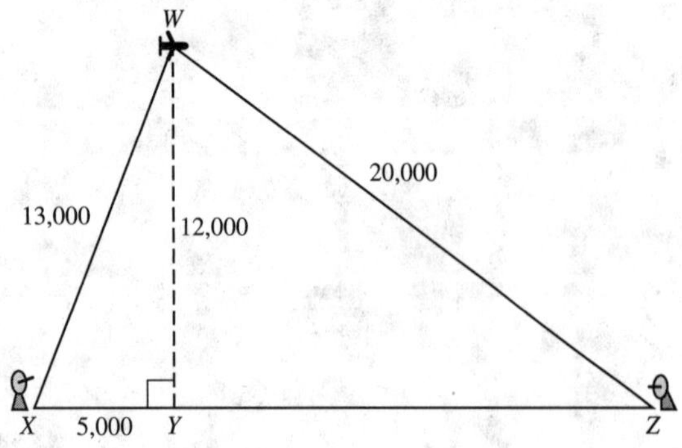

DO YOUR FIGURING HERE

30. Which of the following values is closest to the distance, in feet, between the two radar stations?

F. 12,000
G. 16,000
H. 18,000
J. 20,000
K. 21,000

31. Given that 1 mile is equal to 5,280 feet, which of the following is closest to the plane's rate of travel in miles per hour?

A. 88
B. 409
C. 528
D. 600
E. 681

32. Let *X*, *Y*, *Z*, and *W* lie in the standard (x, y) coordinate plane such that *X* is at (0, 0) and *Y* is at (5,000, 0). Which of the following equations represents the line between *Y* and *W*?

F. $x = 5{,}000$
G. $x = 12{,}000$
H. $x = 15{,}000$
J. $y = 5{,}000$
K. $y = 12{,}000$

---

33. What value of x will satisfy the following matrix equation?

$$\begin{bmatrix} 23y^2 & 13z \\ 2x-1 & -15w^3 \end{bmatrix} + \begin{bmatrix} -7 & 10 \\ -4x-2 & 13 \end{bmatrix} = \begin{bmatrix} 16 & 23 \\ 12 & -2 \end{bmatrix}$$

A. −7.5
B. −3.5
C. 1
D. 6.5
E. 13

DO YOUR FIGURING HERE

34. Which of the following is an expression for the area of the triangle below?

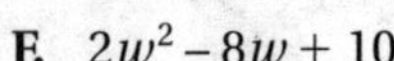

F. $2w^2 - 8w + 10$

G. $\dfrac{6w^2 - 24w + 21}{2}$

H. $6w^2 - 24w + 21$

J. $12w^2 - 48w + 42$

K. $(2w - 7)(w + 3)$

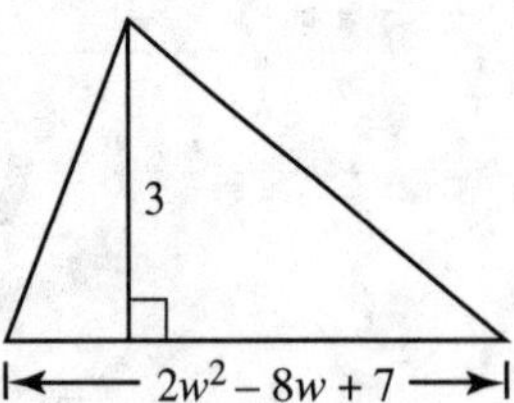

35. If ■ is defined for all real numbers x and y by $x■y = (x + y)(x - y)$, then $1■(2■2) = ?$

A. 0

B. 1

C. 3

D. 4

E. 5

36. Sophie has played 6 games of soccer scoring 0, 1, 3, 2, 4, and 1 goals respectively in those games. For game 7, which of the following values will NOT yield a median of 2 goals scored?

F. 1 goal

G. 2 goals

H. 3 goals

J. 4 goals

K. 5 goals

37. What is the center of the circle with equation $(x + 7)^2 + (y - 5)^2 = 121$?

A. (–7, –5)

B. (–7, 5)

C. (7, –5)

D. (7, 5)

E. (5, 11)

DO YOUR FIGURING HERE

38. Given the equation $3x - 7y = 21$, what is the equation in slope-intercept form?

F. $y = -\frac{3}{7}x + 3$

G. $y = -\frac{7}{3}x + 3$

H. $y = -\frac{3}{7}x - 3$

J. $y = \frac{3}{7}x + 3$

K. $y = \frac{3}{7}x - 3$

39. In the graph below, line *m* is parallel to line *n*. Find the value of *a*.

A. 17°

B. 22°
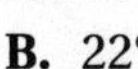
C. 27°
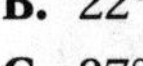
D. 32°
E. 37°

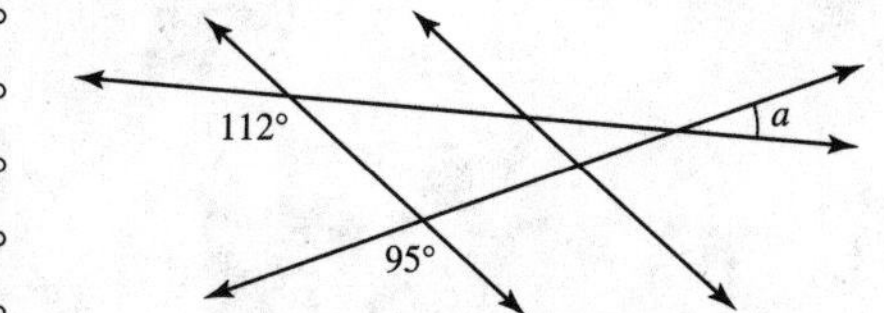

40. Dustin is in a 40-foot air traffic control tower at the local airport. He spots a plane that has just landed and using his protractor measures the angle of depression from the top of the tower to the landed plane to be 12°. How far from the base of the control tower is the plane?

F. $\frac{\tan(12°)}{40}$

G. $\frac{40}{\tan(12°)}$

H. $\frac{\sin(12°)}{40}$

J. $\frac{40}{\sin(12°)}$

K. $\frac{\cos(12°)}{40}$

41. For what values of x is the function $\sqrt{x-5}$ undefined in the real number system?

A. $x = 0$
B. $x = 5$
C. $x = -5$
D. $x < 5$
E. $x > 5$

DO YOUR FIGURING HERE

42. In the standard (x, y) coordinate plane, what are the coordinates of point A after the graph is reflected over the line $x = 7$?

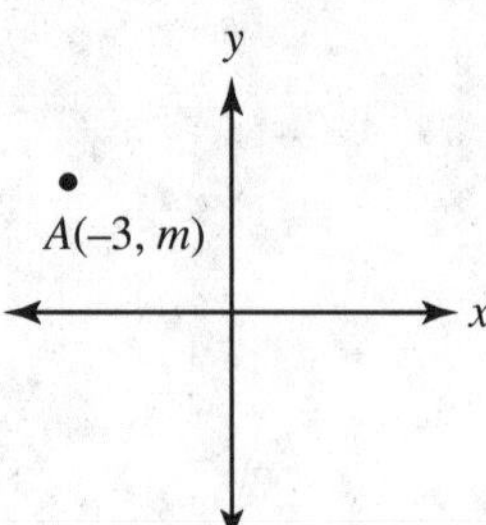

F. $(3, m)$
G. $(-3, -m)$
H. $(10, m)$
J. $(15, m)$
K. $(17, m)$

43. Given line segment AB with A $(-3, 2)$ and B $(5, 8)$, which of the following is the length of AB?

A. $\sqrt{34}$
B. $2\sqrt{10}$
C. 10
D. $9\sqrt{2}$
E. $\sqrt{170}$

44. Given similar rectangles *QUAD* and *RECT*, the ratio of sides *QU* to *RE* is 1:4. If the area of *QUAD* is 12, what is the area of *RECT*?

F. 0.75
G. 3
H. 12
J. 48
K. 192

DO YOUR FIGURING HERE

45. A parking lot downtown charges x dollars for the first hour and y dollars for each hour after the first. If Daniel parks in the lot for h hours where $h > 6$, which of the following equations represents P, the amount Daniel has to pay to park in the lot?

A. $P = h(x + y)$
B. $P = x + yh$
C. $P = y + x(h - 1)$
D. $P = xh + y(h - 1)$
E. $P = x + y(h - 1)$

46. Let $y = \frac{2x}{3z}$. What happens to the value of z as both x and y are doubled?

F. z remains the same
G. z doubles
H. z decreases by $\frac{1}{2}$
J. z quadruples
K. z decreases by a factor of $\frac{1}{4}$

47. If $\frac{w^6 t^5}{m^9} > 0$, then which of the following is true?

A. $w > 0$
B. $t > 0$
C. $m > 0$
D. $wt > 0$
E. $tm > 0$

48. Which of the following is equivalent to $2\log(x) + \frac{1}{2}\log(y) - 4\log(z)$?

F. $\log(2x + \frac{1}{2}y - 4z)$
G. $\log(x^2 z^4 \sqrt{y})$
H. $\log\left(\frac{x^2\sqrt{y}}{z^4}\right)$
J. $\log\left(\frac{xy}{4z}\right)$
K. $\log(2x^2 yz)$

DO YOUR FIGURING HERE

49. Given the following table, find $f(g(2))$:

x	$f(x)$	$g(x)$
1	-5	0
2	-10	3
3	-15	6
4	-20	9

A. –15
B. –10
C. 0
D. 3
E. 6

50. The number of fish, p, a small pond can sustain varies inversely with the square root of the amount of predators, q, in the pond. If a pond with 49 predators can sustain a population of 800 fish, how many fish could a pond with 100 predators sustain?

F. 560
G. 600
H. 650
J. 1,600
K. 2,000

51. Points $P(1, 1)$ and $Q(x, x^2)$ lie in the standard (x, y) coordinate plane. Which of the following is an expression for the slope between points P and Q when $x > 5$?

A. 0
B. $\frac{x^2+1}{x+1}$
C. $x + 1$
D. $\frac{x+1}{x^2+1}$
E. Undefined

52. Which of the following expressions is equivalent to $\frac{3 \cdot 3^{2x-5}}{3^{x+1}}$?

F. 3^{x-7}
G. 3^{x-5}
H. 3^{x-3}
J. 3^{x-1}
K. 1

DO YOUR FIGURING HERE

53. What fraction is located exactly halfway between $\frac{3}{8}$ and $\frac{4}{5}$ on the standard number line?

A. $\frac{15}{40}$

B. $\frac{17}{40}$

C. $\frac{1}{2}$

D. $\frac{7}{13}$

E. $\frac{47}{80}$

54. Mike has taken 4 tests in algebra so far. His average after 4 tests is 85%. If he has not received a grade lower than 80% on any tests, what is the highest possible score Mike could have achieved on one test?

F. 96%
G. 97%
H. 98%
J. 99%
K. 100%

55. Given $|x-3| > x-3$, what is the solution set for the inequality?

A. $x > 3$
B. $x < 3$
C. $x > 0$
D. $x < 0$
E. All real numbers

DO YOUR FIGURING HERE

56. For $i^2 = -1$, which of the following is equivalent to $\frac{i+7}{i-5} \cdot i$?

F. -1

G. $\frac{6}{13} - \frac{17}{13}i$

H. $\frac{6}{13} + \frac{17}{13}i$

J. $-\frac{1}{2} - \frac{3}{2}i$

K. $\frac{1}{2} + \frac{3}{2}i$

57. One square inch on the average pizza contains 50 calories. Alex bakes a 12" diameter pizza and cuts it into 8 equal slices. If his dad eats 3 slices and Alex only eats 2, approximately how many more calories did Alex's dad eat than he did?

A. 100

B. 700

C. 1,400

D. 2,100

E. 2,200

58. Given $\tan(\theta) = v$, where $0° \leq \theta \leq 90°$, which of the following could be an expression for $\cos(\theta)$?

F. $\frac{v}{\sqrt{1+v^2}}$

G. $\frac{\sqrt{1+v^2}}{v}$

H. $\frac{1}{\sqrt{1+v^2}}$

J. $\sqrt{1-v^2}$

K. $\frac{\sqrt{1-v^2}}{v}$

DO YOUR FIGURING HERE

59. Lisa, Carl, Max, Jenny, and Andy go to watch a movie and all sit next to each other in the same aisle. Andy must sit at either end of the group, but everyone else can sit anywhere within the group. How many possible seating arrangements are there?

A. 15

B. 48

C. 56

D. 92

E. 120

60. In the standard (x, y) coordinate plane, points (m, n) and $\left(m-2, n+\frac{2}{g}\right)$ lie on the graph of the equation $y=\frac{1}{3}x-t$, where $t>1$. What is the value of g?

F. −3

G. $-\frac{1}{4}$

H. 1

J. $\frac{7}{5}$

K. $\frac{123}{5}$

If there is still time remaining, you may review your answers.

READING TEST

Time: 35 Minutes—40 Questions

Directions: There are four passages in this test. Each passage is followed by several questions. After reading a passage, choose the best answer to each question and fill in the corresponding oval on your answer sheet. You may refer to the passages as often as necessary.

PASSAGE I—LITERARY NARRATIVE

This passage is adapted from the short story "A&P" by John Updike (© 1961 by John Updike).

In walks these three girls in nothing but bathing suits. I'm in the third check-out slot, with my back to the door, so I don't see them until they're over by the bread. The store's pretty empty, so there was nothing much to do except lean on the register and wait for the girls to show up again. After a while they come around out of the far aisle, around the light bulbs. Queenie puts down the jar and I take it into my fingers icy cold. Kingfish Fancy Herring Snacks in Pure Sour Cream: 49¢.

Then everybody's luck begins to run out. Lengel comes in from the lot and is about to scuttle into that door marked MANAGER behind which he hides all day when the girls touch his eye. Lengel's pretty dreary, teaches Sunday school and the rest, but he doesn't miss that much. He comes over and says, "Girls, this isn't the beach."

Queenie blushes, though maybe it's just a brush of sunburn I was noticing for the first time. "My mother asked me to pick up a jar of herring snacks." Her voice kind of startled me, the way voices do when you see the people first, coming out so flat yet kind of tony, too, the way it ticked over "pick up" and "snacks." All of a sudden I slid right down her voice into her living room. Her father and the other men were standing around in bow ties and the women were in sandals picking up herring snacks on toothpicks off a big plate and they were all holding drinks the color of water with olives and sprigs of mint in them.

"That's all right," Lengel said. "But this isn't the beach." His repeating this struck me as funny, as if it had just occurred to him. He didn't like my smiling—as I say he doesn't miss much—but he concentrates on giving the girls that sad Sunday-school-superintendent stare.

Queenie's blush is no sunburn now, and the plump one in plaid pipes up, "We just came in for the one thing."

"That makes no difference," Lengel tells her, and I could see from the way his eyes went that he hadn't noticed she was wearing a two-piece before. "We want you decently dressed when you come in here."

"We are decent," Queenie says suddenly, getting sore now that she remembers her place, a place from which the crowd that runs the A&P must look pretty crummy. Fancy Herring Snacks flashed in her very blue eyes.

"Girls, I don't want to argue with you. After this come in here with your shoulders covered. It's our policy." He turns his back. I could feel in the silence everybody getting nervous, most of all Lengel, who asks me, "Sammy, have you rung up this purchase?"

I thought and said "No." I go through the punches, 4, 9, GROC, TOT—it's more complicated than you think. I uncrease the bill and pass a half and a penny into her narrow pink palm, and nestle the herrings in a bag and hand it over, all the time thinking.

The girls, and who'd blame them, are in a hurry to get out, so I say "I quit" to Lengel quick enough for them to hear, hoping they'll stop and watch me, their unsuspected hero. They keep right on going; the door flies open and they flicker across the lot to their car, leaving me with Lengel and a kink in his eyebrow.

"Did you say something, Sammy?"

"I said I quit."

"I thought you did."

"You didn't have to embarrass them."

"It was they who were embarrassing us. I don't think you know what you're saying," Lengel said.

"I know you don't," I said. "But I do." I pull the bow at the back of my apron and start shrugging it off my shoulders. A couple customers that had been heading for my slot begin to knock against each other, like scared pigs in a chute.

Lengel sighs and begins to look very patient and old and gray. He's been a friend of my parents for years. "Sammy, you don't want to do this to your Mom and Dad," he tells me. It's true, I don't. But it seems to me that once you begin a gesture it's fatal not to go through with it. I fold the apron, "Sammy" stitched in red on the pocket, and put it on the counter, and drop the bow tie on top of it. "You'll feel this for the rest of your life," Lengel says, and I know that's true too, but remembering how he made that pretty girl blush makes me so scrunchy inside. One advantage to this scene taking place in summer, I can follow this up with a clean exit, there's no fumbling around getting your coat and galoshes, I just saunter into the electric eye in my white shirt that my mother ironed the night before, and the door heaves itself open, and outside the sunshine is skating around on the asphalt.

I look around for my girls, but they're gone. There wasn't anybody but some young married screaming with her children about some candy they didn't get. Looking back in the big windows, I could see Lengel in my place, checking the sheep through. His face was dark gray and his back stiff, as if he'd just had an injection of iron, and my stomach kind of fell as I felt how hard the world was going to be to me hereafter.

1. The point of view from which the passage is told is best described as that of a (an):

A. young man relating a significant event in his life.
B. young man explaining to his parents why he has quit his job.
C. adult describing exactly what he should have done differently at a turning point in his life.
D. adolescent boy imagining what his life might be like in the future.

2. The passage contains recurring references to all of the following EXCEPT:

F. the narrator's family.
G. the other customers.
H. supermarket chains.
J. the girls' attire.

3. The first three paragraphs (lines 1–32) establish all of the following about the narrator EXCEPT that he:

A. is fascinated by the girls.
B. is new at his job.
C. dislikes his manager.
D. feels socially inferior to Queenie.

4. It can reasonably be inferred from the passage that the narrator aspires to be seen as:

F. romantic and poetic.
G. intellectual but rebellious.
H. tough but cultured.
J. principled and heroic.

5. Based on the narrator's account, life in his hometown is characterized by all of the following EXCEPT:

A. a tendency toward conformity.
B. an awareness of class hierarchy.
C. a mistrust of organized religion.
D. people knowing one another's business.

6. According to the narrator, which of the following articles of his clothing is the property of the store?
   F. His shirt
   G. His coat
   H. His bow tie
   J. His galoshes

7. When the narrator refers to Queenie "getting sore now that she remembers her place" (lines 47–48), he is most likely referring to the fact that she is:
   A. much younger than Lengel and himself.
   B. backed up by her two friends.
   C. a stranger to this town.
   D. wealthier than Lengel and himself.

8. Details in the passage most strongly suggest that the narrator's decision to quit ended up seeming most admirable from the point of view of:
   F. himself.
   G. the manager.
   H. his parents.
   J. Queenie.

9. The narrator indicates that Lengel the manager is extremely:
   A. forgiving.
   B. observant.
   C. skeptical.
   D. philosophical.

10. According to the passage, the narrator's decision to quit is most strongly motivated by his desire to:
    F. impress the girls.
    G. rebel against his parents.
    H. get out of his hometown.
    J. finally stand up to Lengel.

PASSAGE II—SOCIAL SCIENCE

This passage is adapted from the essay "Into the Heart of India's Bone Trade" by Scott Carney, which appeared on NPR online in 2007.

Medical students across the world rely on anatomical models to become informed doctors. What many don't realize is that a large number of these models are stolen from graves in Calcutta, India.

For 200 years, the city has been the center of a shadowy network of bone traders who snatch up skeletons in order to sell them to universities and hospitals abroad. In colonial times, British doctors hired thieves to dig up bodies from Indian cemeteries. Despite changes in laws, a similar process is going strong today.

Throughout parts of Calcutta, many of the cemeteries have been empty for generations. "When I die, when I'm gone, my body will also be stolen," says Mohammad Jinnah Vishwas, a farmer who lives in the village of Amdanga. "Before we didn't understand where all the bones were going, now we know that they were taken by criminals."

A legal multimillion-dollar business throughout the 1970s, the export of human remains was banned by India in 1986 following rumors that traders were murdering people for their bones. The new law pushed most of the major companies out of business.

"It is kind of a sad situation because [my father] loved the business so much, and he saw it drift away from him," says Craig Kilgore, whose family founded Kilgore International, which at one point was the principal supplier of bones to the United States.

At least one organization, however, has managed to survive underground. Most prominently, a firm called Young Brothers—located conveniently between the city's biggest morgue and largest cemetery—has excelled in the black market. It has taken a bold approach—advertising its bone selection in catalogues and going to extreme measures to maintain its supply, according to a former clerk who requested anonymity for fear of retaliation.

"They took the bodies from the river, from the graveyard, and from the hospital. More than 5,000 dead bodies I have seen," she says.

In 2001, Javed Ahmed Khan, Calcutta's health department chief, started receiving complaints about Young Brothers. The main storefront, neighbors said, was emitting a stench so horrible that it could be detected several blocks away. Neighbors also reported that they had seen bones drying on the roof and skeletons boiling in massive tubs.

A raid against the business, led by Khan, confirmed suspicions. "I went inside and saw two rooms full of human skeletons. There were huge bowls where skeletons were dipped to remove the fats and all that," Khan says.

In addition to three truckloads of bones, Khan said, he found invoices for shipments headed to the United States, Europe, and Singapore. Despite the evidence, the owner of Young Brothers was released just a few days later.

"We won the case," says Vinesh Aron, the proprietor of Young Brothers. He denied a request to be interviewed, but when asked whether skeletons were recovered from his building, he said, "Those were all export materials." This answer hits on the hollowness of the rules governing the bones trade. Under the law, any bones being exported are technically "illegal"—but the question for police is often whether they are illegal enough to bother prosecuting.

That became evident again in May, when police intercepted a massive cache of human remains along a well-established smuggling route. The bleached white bones from over 100 people could have fetched around $70,000 had they made it to the United States. Whether the goods will ever be submitted as evidence in court is unclear.

"It depends on the seriousness that society places on it," says Rajeev Kuman, director inspector general of police in Calcutta. Kuman says he doesn't have enough resources to enforce the law. The fact that it's legal to import the bones into the United States and Europe, and that the "victims" are already dead, only serves to make the situation that much murkier.

Few retailers in the United States possess a steady supply of human bones. Those that do often purchase them through a chain of middlemen that spans the globe. The longer the chain, the easier it is to avoid considering the nature of that primary link.

11. Which of the following assumptions would be most critical for a reader to accept in order to agree fully with the author's claims in the passage?

- **A.** The root of the problem lies within the attitudes of Indian law enforcement.
- **B.** Local superstitions are keeping the illegal Indian bone market in business.
- **C.** The situation in India is no different than in any other Asian nation.
- **D.** Matters will not improve until American bone buyers insist upon greater accountability.

12. In the context of the passage, the statement "The longer the chain, the easier it is to avoid considering the nature of that primary link" (lines 93–95) most nearly suggests that:
    F. American bone buyers have become complacent because they do not have to deal directly with criminals.
    G. the general public does not believe that medical skeletons are made of real human bones.
    H. larger criminal enterprises are harder to stop than smaller ones.
    J. the bigger the bones, the more money criminals are able to get for them.

13. It can most reasonably be inferred from the passage that regarding the Indian bone trade, the author feels:
    A. anger that the American media refuse to report on the problem.
    B. fear that the criminals behind the enterprise will target him for exposing them.
    C. sympathy for the people living in the conditions that are perpetuating the problem.
    D. skepticism of whether the problem is really as widespread as people say.

14. The main purpose of the sixth paragraph (lines 33–42) is to:
    F. establish that location is the primary factor determining which criminal enterprises will be more successful than others.
    G. demonstrate the extreme boldness with which some bone-trafficking organizations operate.
    H. convince the reader that the word of the former clerk can be trusted.
    J. confirm the reader's suspicions that Young Brothers has been involved in illegal bone trafficking.

15. The main function of the eleventh paragraph (lines 64–73) is to:
    A. establish that even flagrant violators of the bone laws will not necessarily end up convicted.
    B. explain that Young Brothers had not been involved in illegal activity after all.
    C. shift the question of blame to local police.
    D. complain that American media have difficulty penetrating the veil of silence concerning Indian bone trafficking.

16. The passage notes all of the following as major contributors to the problem of illegal bone trafficking EXCEPT the:
    F. power and influence of the criminals.
    G. unfeasibility of prosecution.
    H. frequent unreliability of witnesses.
    J. willful ignorance of the American market.

17. The passage indicates that Calcutta law enforcement would do more about illegal bone trafficking if:
    A. they were permitted to use the sort of weaponry necessary to win a fight with the traffickers.
    B. they were better able to trust their own officers.
    C. the cemeteries from which the bones were stolen lay inside their jurisdiction.
    D. the public placed enough importance on the issue for the government to properly fund prosecution.

18. The passage implies that the skeletal remains of a single human might be worth approximately:
    F. $100
    G. $200
    H. $700
    J. $70,000

19. The passage implies that all of the following people oppose illegal bone trafficking EXCEPT:
    A. Craig Kilgore.
    B. Vinesh Aron.
    C. Javed Ahmed Khan.
    D. Mohammad Jinnah Vishwas.

20. The passage implies that the "catalogues" mentioned in line 39 would most likely be sent to:
    F. medical students.
    G. other criminals.
    H. American media outlets.
    J. superstitious locals.

PASSAGE III—HUMANITIES

Passage A is adapted from Mary Shelley's introduction to the 1831 second edition of her 1819 novel *Frankenstein.* Passage B is adapted from *Frankenstein* itself.

Passage A by Mary Shelley

The Publishers of the Standard Novels, in selecting "Frankenstein" for one of their series, expressed a wish that I should furnish them with some account of the origin of the story. I shall thus give a general answer to the question so frequently asked me—How I, then a young girl, came to think of and to dilate upon so very hideous an idea?

It is not singular that, as the daughter of two persons of literary celebrity, I should very early in life have thought of writing. As a child I scribbled, and my favourite pastime was to "write stories." Still I had a dearer pleasure than this, which was the formation of castles in the air—the indulging in waking dreams, which had for their subject the formation of a succession of imaginary incidents. My dreams were at once more fantastic and agreeable than my writings. In the latter I was a close imitator—rather doing as others had done than putting down the suggestions of my own mind. What I wrote was intended for other eyes, but my dreams were all my own.

I did not make myself the heroine of my tales. Life appeared to me too commonplace as regarded myself. I could not figure that romantic woes or wonderful events would ever be my lot, but I was not confined to my own identity, and I could people the hours with creations far more interesting to me than my own sensations.

After this my life became busier, and reality stood in place of fiction. My husband was very anxious that I should prove myself worthy of my parentage and enroll myself on the page of fame. He was forever inciting me to obtain literary reputation, which even on my own part I cared for then, though since I have become infinitely indifferent to it.

I thought and pondered—vainly. I felt that blank incapability of invention which is the greatest misery of authorship. *Have you thought of a story?* I was asked each morning, and each morning I was forced to reply with a mortifying negative.

When I placed my head on my pillow, I did not sleep, nor could I be said to think. My imagination, unbidden, possessed and guided me. I saw the pale student of unhallowed arts kneeling beside the thing he had put together. I saw the hideous phantasm of a man stretched out, and then, on the working of some powerful engine, show signs of life, and stir with an uneasy motion. His success would terrify the artist; he would rush away from his odious handiwork, horror-stricken. He would hope that, left to itself, the slight spark of life which he had communicated would fade. He sleeps; but he is awakened; the horrid thing stands at his bedside, opening his curtains, and looking on him with yellow, watery, but speculative eyes.

I opened mine in terror. Swift as light and as cheering was the idea that broke in upon me. "I have found it! What terrified me will terrify others; and I need only describe the spectre which had haunted my midnight pillow." On the morrow I announced that I had *thought of a story.*

And now, once again, I bid my hideous progeny go forth and prosper. I have an affection for it, for it was the offspring of happy days, when death and grief were but words, which found no true echo in my heart.

Passage B by Mary Shelley

It was on a dreary night of November that I beheld the accomplishment of my toils. With an anxiety that almost amounted to agony, I collected the instruments of life around me, that I might infuse a spark of being into the lifeless thing that lay at my feet. The rain pattered dismally against the panes, and my candle was nearly burnt out, when, by the glimmer of the half-extinguished light, I saw the dull yellow eye of the creature open; it breathed hard, and a convulsive motion agitated its limbs.

How can I describe my emotions at this catastrophe, or how delineate the wretch whom with such infinite pains and care I had endeavoured to form? His limbs were in proportion, and I had selected his features as beautiful. Beautiful! Great God! His yellow skin scarcely covered the work of muscles and arteries beneath; his hair was of a lustrous black, and flowing; his teeth of a pearly whiteness; but these luxuriances only formed a more horrid contrast with his watery eyes, that seemed almost of the same colour as the dun-white sockets in which they were set, his shrivelled complexion and straight black lips.

I had worked hard for nearly two years, for the sole purpose of infusing life into an inanimate body. I had desired it with an ardour that far exceeded moderation; but now that I had finished, the beauty of the dream vanished, and breathless horror and disgust filled my heart. Unable to endure the aspect of the being I had created, I rushed out of the room and continued a long time traversing my bed-chamber, unable to compose my mind. I slept, but I was disturbed by the wildest dreams. I thought I saw Elizabeth, in the bloom of health, walking in the streets of Ingolstadt. Delighted and surprised, I embraced her, but as I imprinted the first kiss on her lips, her features appeared to change, and I thought that I held the corpse of my dead mother in my arms. I started from my sleep with horror when, by the dim and yellow light of the moon, as it forced its way through the window shutters, I beheld the wretch—the miserable monster whom I had created.

Questions 21–25 ask about Passage A.

21. When Shelley writes "once again, I bid my hideous progeny go forth and prosper" (lines 65–66), she most nearly means that:

A. she is launching the new edition of her most famous novel into the world, as she did with the first.

B. she is prone to daydreaming about earlier times in her life when she was happier.

C. she feels confident that the new edition will make more money than the first did, regardless of what the critics say.

D. she is reluctant to publish the story but has no choice.

22. Passage A indicates that Shelley came to consider her earliest attempts at writing to be:

F. cynical attempts at widespread popularity.

G. unwilling to confront death and grief.

H. too unrealistic to be critically respected.

J. inorganic and insufficiently personal.

23. Shelley's claim that "since I have become infinitely indifferent to it" (lines 35–36) is meant to suggest that, over the course of the previous decade, she has:
   A. learned to write well without being emotionally affected by her subject matter.
   B. become more interested in writing nonfiction than unrealistic fiction.
   C. come to care far less about getting famous for her writing.
   D. developed a method of expertly disguising her own literary voice.

24. In the sixth and seventh paragraphs of Passage A (lines 43–64), Shelley explains the genesis of her realization that:
   F. her own psyche could in fact be the wellspring of effective literature.
   G. a tale of horror would be the last sort of book anyone expected from her.
   H. her novel would sell better if she wrote from the point of view of a male protagonist.
   J. she had already thought of the perfect story many years ago, when she was a child.

25. In Passage A, Shelley implies that, in the years since she wrote the first edition of *Frankenstein*:
   A. she has been surprised by how dramatically the public's taste in novels has changed.
   B. she has experienced profound personal tragedy in her own real life for the first time.
   C. she has been somewhat annoyed by how frequently the book's message is misinterpreted.
   D. her relationship with her parents has become less stressful and more one of mutual respect.

Questions 26–27 ask about Passage B.

26. In the second paragraph of Passage B (lines 81–94), the narrator describes his creation in a manner that:
   F. emphasizes the exhaustive degree of biological knowledge and long process of trial-and-error that went into creating him.
   G. apologizes for the creature's bizarre appearance by attempting to explain it logically and dispassionately.
   H. ironically juxtaposes the glory of the scientific knowledge involved in his creation with the grotesque form of the creature itself.
   J. emphasizes the personal jealousy he feels regarding the creature's prodigious physical strength.

27. Within Passage B, the narrator's dream in lines 105–115 functions symbolically to represent the idea that:
   A. true love gradually becomes impossible for anyone who knows too much about science.
   B. though the narrator has literally created life, he has metaphorically created death.
   C. death is a natural and inevitable part of life that should be embraced rather than feared.
   D. family is ultimately more important than either work or wisdom.

Questions 28–30 ask about both passages.

28. Both Passage A and Passage B highlight Shelley's taste for presenting:
   F. contrasting points of view via the device of frame narrative.
   G. necessary information in a roundabout fashion, in order to build suspense.
   H. the concepts of both death and genius as mere illusions.
   J. the depths of the human imagination as the source of true horror.

29. Based on Shelley's description in Passage A of her writing process, which of the following methods is likely to depict a way in which she might have gone about composing Passage B?
   A. Trying to analyze and then imitate other novels that have been widely regarded as terrifying
   B. Allowing herself to feel frightened and then writing in a way that puts the reader in her position
   C. Doing research into the biological mechanisms that cause fear and logically discerning how best to activate them
   D. Jotting down unstructured notes while half-asleep and then examining them in the morning

30. Elsewhere in the essay from which Passage A is adapted, Shelley writes:

> Invention, it must be humbly admitted, does not consist in creating out of void, but out of chaos; the materials must, in the first place, be afforded: it can give form to dark, shapeless substances, but cannot bring into being the substance itself. Invention consists in the capacity of seizing on the capabilities of the subject, and in the power of moulding and fashioning ideas suggested to it.

How do these statements apply to both Shelley's approach to storytelling as depicted in Passage A and the narration of her character Victor Frankenstein provided in Passage B?
   F. They suggest that Shelley considered the origins of both art and life itself to be mysterious, and the role of any "creator" to be that of a conduit for an external force.
   G. They amount to a cynical admission that every artistic idea is ultimately a copy of another, and that every supposedly "original" idea is actually "monstrous."
   H. They describe Shelley's conviction that the concept of "inspiration" is actually a lie, and that all true beauty is the result of a process that is messy and ugly.
   J. They suggest Shelley's viewpoint that all artistic creation is actually an act of destruction because we can only find words for what is already dead in our hearts.

PASSAGE IV—NATURAL SCIENCE

This passage is adapted from "Magnetic Attraction" by Robert L. Park, Prof. emeritus of Physics, U. of Maryland.

In the early 16th century, the power of lodestone (magnetite) to attract iron filings without touching them suggested great power. Paracelsus, the famous Swiss alchemist and physician, began using powdered lodestone in salves to promote healing. William Gilbert, however, physician to Queen Elizabeth I and father of the scientific study of magnetism, pointed out that the process of grinding the lodestone into powder destroyed the magnetism. Nevertheless, a century later, magnetic cures were introduced into England by Robert Fludd as a remedy for all disease. The patient was placed in the "boreal position" with the head north and the feet south during the treatment.

By far the most famous of the magnetizers was Franz Mesmer (1734–1815), who carried the technique from Vienna to Paris in 1778 and soon became the rage of Parisian society.

Dressed in colorful robes, he would seat patients in a circle around a vat of "magnetized water." While Mesmer waved magnetic wands over them, the patients held iron rods protruding from the vat. He would later discover that the cure was just as effective if he left the magnets out and merely waved his hand. He called this "animal magnetism."

Benjamin Franklin, in Paris on a diplomatic assignment, suspected that Mesmer's patients did indeed benefit from the strange ritual because it kept them away from the bloodletting and purges of other Paris physicians. Those physicians bitterly resented Mesmer, an outsider who was attracting their most affluent patients. At the urging of the medical establishment, King Louis XVI appointed a royal commission to investigate his claims. This remarkable group included Franklin, then the world's greatest authority on electricity; Antoine Lavoisier, the founder of modern chemistry; and Joseph Guillotine, the physician whose famous invention would one day be used to sever the head of his friend Lavoisier.

The commissioners designed a series of ingenious tests in which some subjects were deceived into thinking they were receiving Mesmer's treatment when they were not, and others received the treatment but were led to believe they had not. The results established beyond any doubt that the effects were due solely to the power of suggestion. Their report, never surpassed for clarity or reason, destroyed Mesmer's reputation in France, and he returned to Vienna.

Nevertheless, magnetic therapy eventually crossed the Atlantic. Its most famous practitioner in the United States was Daniel Palmer, who in 1890 opened Palmer's School of Magnetic Cure in Davenport, Iowa. Like Mesmer, Palmer soon discovered that his patients recovered just as quickly if he omitted the magnets and merely "laid on hands." Thus was founded "chiropractic therapy," and the school became Palmer's College of Chiropractic.

In recent years, an enormous amount of research has been done on the effect of magnetic fields on the human body, driven not by magnetic therapy, but by safety considerations associated with the phenomenal growth in the use of magnetic resonance imaging (MRI) for medical diagnoses and research. MRI subjects the whole body to a magnetic field about a hundred times stronger than the localized field of even the most powerful therapy magnet. Happily, no ill-effects have been found from exposure to MRI fields. Indeed, there are almost no effects at all—just a few reports of faint sensory responses, such as a slight metallic taste and visual sensations of flashing lights if patients move their eyes too rapidly. The fact is that the stuff we're made of just isn't very magnetic.

That's why scientists were surprised two years ago when Dr. Carlos Vallbona at the Baylor College of Medicine in Houston reported results of a double-blind trial of magnets in the treatment of 50 patients suffering post-polio pain. Some of the patients were treated with commercial therapy magnets; others were treated with sham magnets. Seventy-six percent of those treated with real magnets reported a decrease in pain, while only 19 percent receiving the placebo felt an improvement. The most frequent claim, which Vallbona supports, is that magnets promote the flow of blood to the treated area.

It's easy to check. An excess of blood shows up as a flushing or reddening of the skin. That's why the skin turns red when you apply heat; blood is being diverted to the heated area to serve as a coolant. But you will discover that placing a magnet of any strength against your skin produces no reddening at all. There is no indication that Vallbona tried this.

The argument is that blood, because it contains iron, should be attracted by the magnets. The iron in hemoglobin, however, is not ferromagnetic.

The hemoglobin molecule itself is very weakly paramagnetic, but the fluid that carries the red cells, consisting mostly of water, is diamagnetic—it is weakly repelled. Indeed, small animals have even been levitated in powerful magnetic fields.

As medical scams go, magnet therapy may not seem like a big deal. Magnets generally cost less than a visit to the doctor and they certainly do no harm. But magnet therapy can be dangerous if it leads people to forego needed medical treatment. Worse, it tends to reinforce a sort of upside-down view of how the world works, leaving people vulnerable to predatory quacks if they become seriously ill. It's like trying to find your way around San Francisco with a map of New York. That could be dangerous for someone who is really sick—or really lost.

31. One of the main ideas established by the passage is that:

A. Benjamin Franklin helped to start a feud between Franz Mesmer and other physicians.
B. English scientists did more than Swiss ones to develop the science of magnetic therapy.
C. if it hadn't been for Franz Mesmer, we wouldn't have MRI technology now.
D. the alleged benefits of magnetic therapy are dubious at best.

32. Which of the following did the most to turn public opinion against Mesmer's theories?

F. The execution of Lavoisier
G. Benjamin Franklin's writings on electricity
H. The findings of the royal commission
J. The urging of King Louis XVI

33. The main purpose of the fifth paragraph (lines 54–63) is to establish that:

A. poorly supported medical theories became popular in the United States despite the lack of evidence.
B. Mesmer's theories were in fact not sufficiently disproved after all.
C. The bodies of some people are more magnetic than those of others.
D. Daniel Palmer ended up being a more important scientist than Franz Mesmer.

34. The passage states that, on the whole, human blood is actually:

F. ferromagnetic.
G. repelled by magnetic fields.
H. predominantly composed of iron.
J. capable of levitating small animals.

35. The passage notes that the MRI:

A. was invented in 1890.
B. is used primarily to treat post-polio pain.
C. promotes the flow of blood.
D. is about 100 times stronger than a therapy magnet.

36. As it is used in line 90, the word *placebo* most nearly means:

F. phony treatment.
G. powerful magnet.
H. traditional cure.
J. psychological boost.

37. As it is used in line 117, the word *quacks* most nearly means:

A. theories.
B. treatments.
C. dishonest therapists.
D. animal-borne diseases.

38. The passage indicates that skin turns red when exposed to heat because:
    F. heat is absorbed and stored in the skin.
    G. one function of blood is cooling hot skin.
    H. hemoglobin is very weakly magnetic.
    J. humans are not very magnetic.

39. The passage most strongly emphasizes that the process of bloodletting was:
    A. an important step in the development of magnet therapy.
    B. still popular in France long after it had ceased to be popular in America.
    C. harmful enough to make magnet therapy appear beneficial.
    D. indirectly involved with the discovery of hemoglobin.

40. According to the passage, the only legitimate experiment that involved magnet therapy was conducted by:
    F. Benjamin Franklin.
    G. Daniel Palmer.
    H. William Gilbert.
    J. Carlos Vallbona.

If there is still time remaining, you may review your answers.

SCIENCE TEST

Time: 35 Minutes—40 Questions

Directions: There are six passages in this test. Each passage is followed by several questions. After reading a passage, choose the best answer to each question and fill in the corresponding oval on your answer sheet. You may refer to the passages as often as necessary.

You are NOT permitted to use a calculator on this test.

PASSAGE I

Tornado intensity is commonly estimated by analyzing damage to structures and then correlating it with the wind speed required to produce such destruction. This method is essential to assigning tornadoes specific values on the *Fujita Scale* (F scale) of tornado intensity (see Figure 1).

Damage f scale		Little Damage	Minor Damage	Roof Gone	Walls Collapse	Blown Down	Blown Away
		f 0	f 1	f 2	f 3	f 4	f 5
Windspeed F scale		F 0 (17 m/s–32; 40 mph–73)	F 1 (32–50; 73–113)	F 2 (50–70; 113–158)	F 3 (70–92; 158–207)	F 4 (92–116; 207–261)	F 5 (116–142; 261–319)
To convert f scale into F scale, add the appropriate number							
Weak Outbuilding	–3	f 3	f 4	f 5	f 5	f 5	f 5
Strong Outbuilding	–2	f 2	f 3	f 4	f 5	f 5	f 5
Weak Framehouse	–1	f 1	f 2	f 3	f 4	f 5	f 5
Strong Framehouse	0	F 0	F 1	F 2	F 3	F 4	F 5
Brick Structure	+1	–	f 0	f 1	f 2	f 3	f 4
Concrete Structure	+2	–	–	f 0	f 1	f 2	f 3

Figure 1

A tornado is formed when the following occurs: (1) warm, moist air rises into cool, dry air; (2) when the barrier is breached, a bulge of warm, moist air expands and condenses to form a cloud; (3) as air moves upward, the resulting instability creates a spiral of air called a *mesocyclone*; (4) cold air moves downward and rain falls as the cloud becomes a *supercell*; (5) cool, moist air from rain cycles back into a cloud, forming a spinning wall-cloud; and (6) horizontal spiraling wind "tubes" are pushed upward by warm, moist air, forming a tornado. (See Figure 2.)

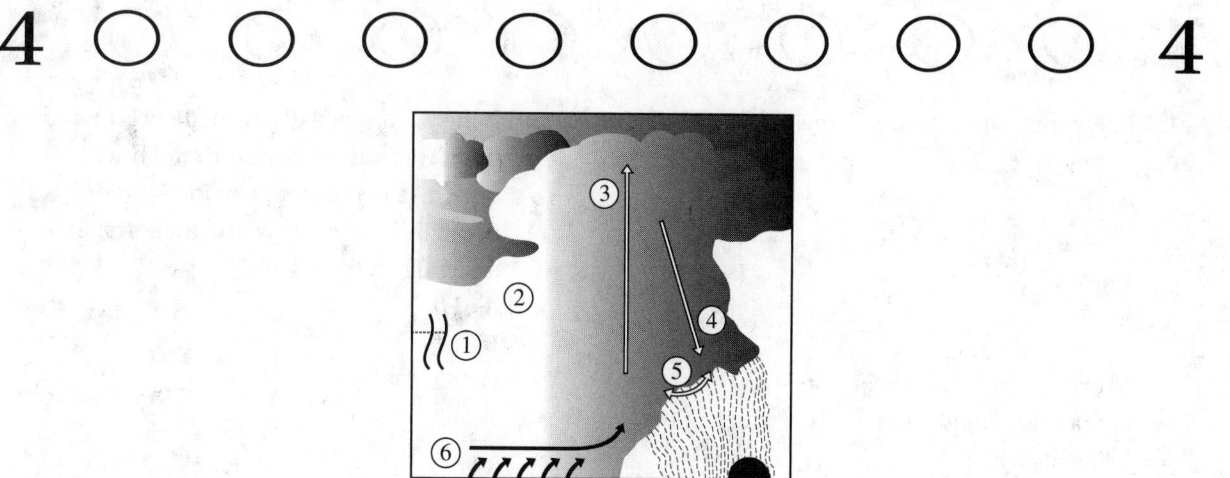

Figure 2

The United States has the most tornadoes of any country, and most of these tornadoes form in an area of the central United States known as "Tornado Alley." Figure 3 displays a geographical (state-by-state) breakdown of the occurrence of tornadoes in the United States in 2005.

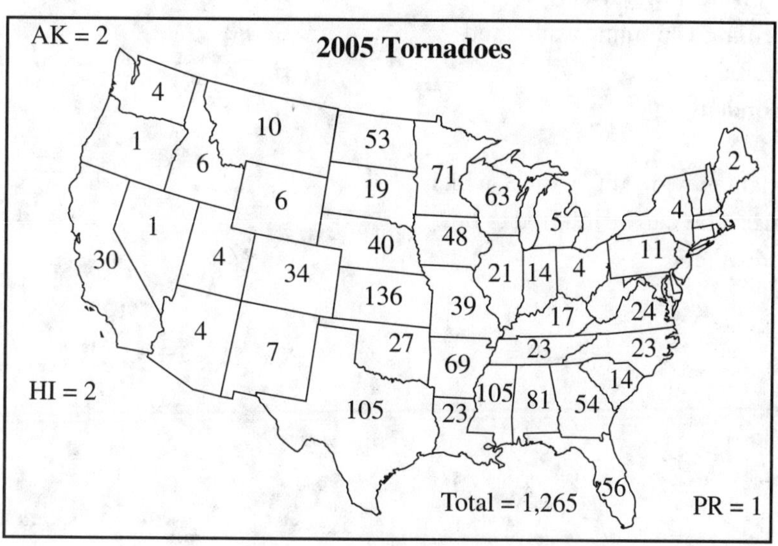

Figure 3

1. In Figure 2, the tornado is labeled with which number?

A. 1
B. 3
C. 5
D. 6

2. A tornado with an intensity of F4 on the Fujita Scale could have winds of which of the following speeds?

F. 70 mph
G. 155 mph
H. 190 mph
J. 210 mph

3. Which of the following does NOT precede the formation of a mesocyclone?

A. Warm air flowing upward
B. Cool air forming a spinning wall-cloud
C. Cloud formation
D. Moist air condensing

4. Based on the data provided in Figure 3, which of the following states can be inferred to be part of "Tornado Alley?"

F. Texas
G. Florida
H. Michigan
J. Washington

5. If the wind speed of a tornado was unknown, but it was observed that several brick buildings in the area sustained minor damage, what value would the tornado be assigned on the F scale?

A. F0
B. F1
C. F2
D. F3

6. In the aftermath of a small-town tornado, the most severe damage observed included collapsed walls on brick buildings, and missing roofs from strong frame houses. According to the intensity scale, what is the strongest possible tornado that could have hit the town?

F. F1
G. F2
H. F3
J. F0

PASSAGE II

Acid deposition delivers acids and acidifying compounds to the Earth's surface. Once on the surface, they move through soil, vegetation, and surface waters and, in turn, set off a cascade of adverse ecological effects. Acid deposition occurs in three forms: wet deposition, which falls as rain, snow, sleet, and hail; dry deposition, which includes particles, gases, and vapor; and cloud or fog deposition, which occurs at high altitudes and in coastal areas. Acid deposition is comprised of sulfuric acid, nitric acid, and ammonium derived from sulfur dioxide (SO_2), nitrogen oxides (NO_x), and ammonia (NH_3). Sulfuric and nitric acid lower the pH of rain, snow, soil, lakes, and streams.

Table 1

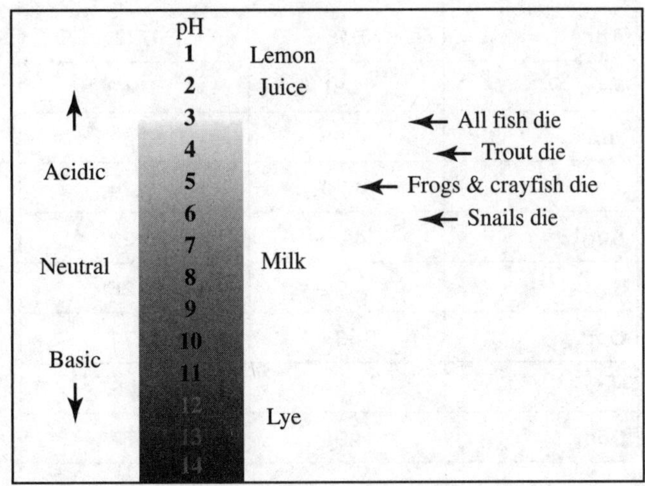

Study 1

A specially designed collection bucket was used to gather rain samples. The collector opened automatically during wet weather, allowing the precipitation to fall into the collection bucket, and then closed as soon as the precipitation stopped. The sample was then taken to a laboratory, where it was weighed and its acidity was measured. Finally, the concentrations of important inorganic chemicals found in the precipitation were analyzed. The results are shown in Table 2.

Table 2

Sample	pH	Cl (mg/L)	Mg (mg/L)	Na (mg/L)	NH_3 (mg/L)
1	5.41	0.02	0.002	0.010	0.01
2	5.28	0.09	0.009	0.029	0.05
3	5.43	0.15	0.008	0.084	0.03
4	5.16	0.08	0.006	0.038	0.01
5	5.45	0.00	0.002	0.003	0.00

Study 2

Another study was done to compare the average pH of precipitation across various months. The same procedure was used as in Study 1, and the results are shown in Table 3.

Table 3

Month	Average pH	Precipitation (cm)
Jan	4.58	8.45
Feb	4.77	8.20
Mar	4.90	7.01
Apr	5.16	17.12
May	4.81	11.48
Jun	4.68	51.67
Jul	4.79	9.24
Aug	4.18	23.52
Sep	4.92	42.26
Oct	4.34	9.74
Nov	4.89	11.76
Dec	4.91	4.67

7. It is known that precipitation with a higher concentration of chlorine (Cl) does more damage to bodies of water than precipitation with a lower concentration of Cl. Based on this information, which sample tested in Study 1 would cause the most harm to rivers?
   A. Sample 1
   B. Sample 2
   C. Sample 3
   D. Sample 4

8. Based on the results of Study 2, it can be concluded that the deposition is least acidic during which season?
   F. Spring
   G. Summer
   H. Fall
   J. Winter

9. Based on the results of Study 1, which of the following can be concluded about the relationship between sodium (Na) concentration and the acidity of deposition?
   A. The lower the concentration of Na, the more basic the precipitation.
   B. The higher the concentration of Na, the more basic the precipitation.
   C. The higher the concentration of Na, the more acidic the precipitation.
   D. There is no correlation between the concentration of Na and acidity of the precipitation.

10. During which of the following months should there be the *least* concern for the health of frogs?
   F. January
   G. April
   H. August
   J. September

11. The precipitation collected in Study 1 is an example of which type of acid deposition?
   A. Wet deposition
   B. Dry deposition
   C. Cloud deposition
   D. Fog deposition

12. If the collection bucket used in Study 1 had been rinsed with sulfuric acid before collecting sample number 2, the resulting pH measurement would have been:
   F. impossible to determine.
   G. exactly 5.28.
   H. lower than 5.28.
   J. higher than 5.28.

13. Scientists in a southern area of the country discovered a "dead zone" in a nearby river that caused fish to die and float to the top of the water. However, snails, frogs, and crawfish seemed unaffected. According to the information in the tables, what could be the best explanation for this "dead zone"?
   A. The pH fell below a reading of 4 and was too acidic for the fish to survive.
   B. The pH rose above 5 and was too basic for the fish to survive.
   C. The pH fell below a reading of 6 and was too acidic for the fish to survive.
   D. The pH rose above 8 and was too basic for the fish to survive.

PASSAGE III

Blood type is a hereditary trait. The type is established by the genes inherited from the mother and father. The ABO system is widely accepted as the best blood classification system. In the ABO system, there are four types of blood: A, B, AB, and O. The combination of inherited genes is known as the *genotype* and the actual blood type is known as the *phenotype.* The genes ensure that only the blood cells of the proper blood type remain in the body.

Table 1

		Father's Blood Type			
		A	B	AB	O
Mother's Blood Type	A	A or O	A, B, AB, or O	A, B, or AB	A or O
	B	A, B, AB, or O	B or O	A, B, or AB	B or O
	AB	A, B, or AB	A, B, or AB	A, B, or AB	A, B, or AB
	O	A or O	B or O	A or B	O

The Rh (+/–) factor is inherited separately from the blood type. It is possible to have the Rh+ phenotype yet still carry the recessive gene for Rh–. The Rh+ (R) is the dominant gene and Rh– (r) is recessive. Table 2 shows the Rh phenotypes resulting from the various genotypes inherited from parents.

Table 2

Genotype	Phenotype
R R	Rh+
R r	Rh+
r r	Rh–

The surface of every red blood cell is covered with proteins. Rh factor and blood type determine the proteins and the compatibility of donated blood as shown in Table 3.

Table 3

Type	Can Donate Blood To	Can Receive Blood From
A+	A+ AB+	A+ A– O+ O–
O+	O+ A+ B+ AB+	O+ O–
B+	B+ AB+	B+ B– O+ O–
AB+	AB+	Everyone
A–	A+ A– AB+ AB–	A– O–
O–	Everyone	O–
B–	B+ B– AB+ AB–	B– O–
AB–	AB+ AB–	AB– B– O–

14. According to Table 1, parents with blood types O and B can only produce offspring with which blood types?
F. B or O
G. A or B
H. A or O
J. A

15. Parents with which blood types could produce offspring with AB+ blood?
A. O+ and A–
B. A– and B+
C. AB– and AB–
D. B+ and B+

16. A person who can donate blood to anyone could have parents with which of the following blood types?
F. A+ and AB–
G. AB– and AB–
H. B– and B–
J. AB+ and AB+

17. List all of the blood types possible for the offspring of parents of blood types A+ and O+.
A. A+ or O+
B. A+, A–, O–, or O+
C. O– or O+
D. AB+, A–, or O–

18. The genes that determine blood type are also responsible for:
F. Rh factor.
G. controlling the types of cells in the blood.
H. controlling blood volume.
J. creating proteins on white blood cells.

19. If a child suffered an injury that required a blood transfusion and was blood type AB+, what blood type(s) could the doctors safely give the child when treating his injury?
A. Only AB+
B. Only O–
C. A+ or B+
D. Any blood type

PASSAGE IV

In a study of the effects of Ritalin and Adderall on children with ADHD, subjects were given one of four possible doses of medication. Their behavior in social and academic settings was then monitored and rated. The four possible doses were placebo (P), Ritalin given once in the morning (R1), Ritalin given twice daily (R2), or Adderall given once in the morning (A1).

The results for each group were averaged. Figure 1 shows the average behavioral rating (on a scale of 0–15, with 0 meaning no undesirable behavior) at various time periods throughout the day. Figure 2 shows the percentage of children who demonstrated side effects at a moderate or severe level on at least one day.

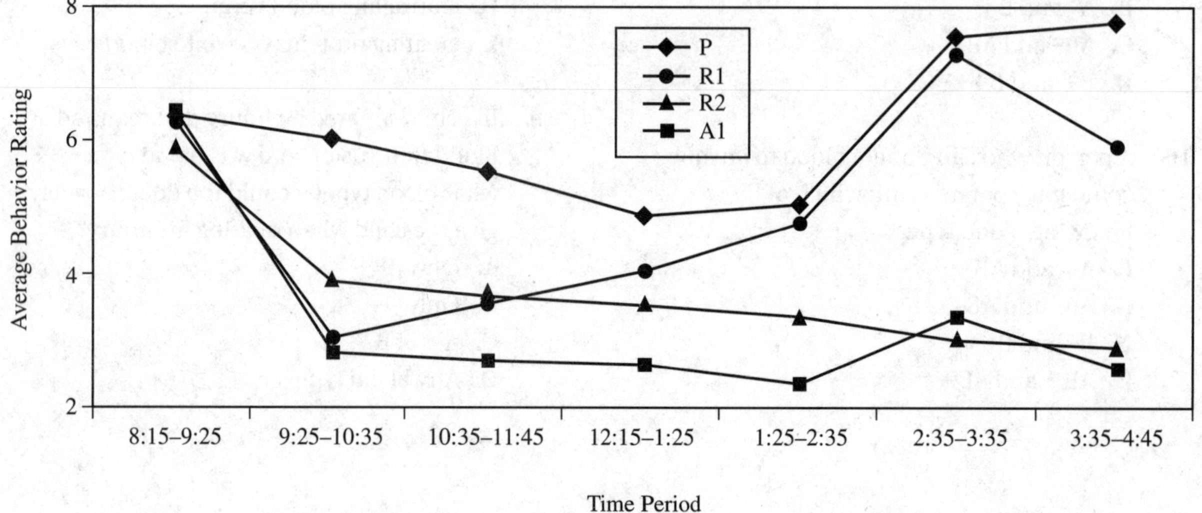

Figure 1

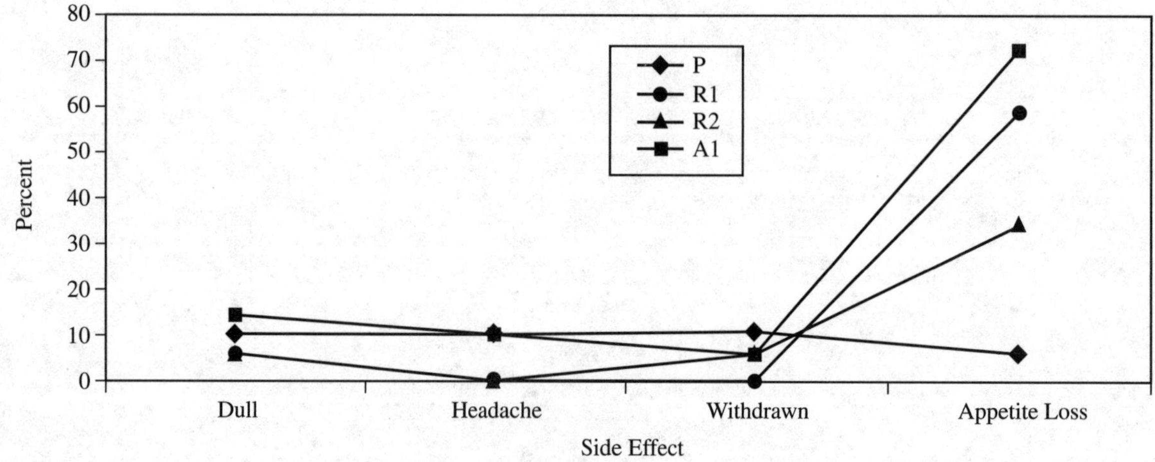

Figure 2

20. Based on Figure 1, during which of the following time periods was the average behavior rating most similar for the four groups of children?
    F. 8:15–9:25
    G. 9:25–10:35
    H. 10:35–11:45
    J. 3:35–4:45

21. A scientist claimed that children given one dose of Adderall daily would exhibit fewer behavior problems than children given either one or two doses of Ritalin daily. During which of the following time periods shown in Figure 1 are the results *inconsistent* with this claim?
    A. 9:25–10:35
    B. 10:35–11:45
    C. 2:35–3:35
    D. 3:35–4:45

22. According to Figure 2, for the group given Ritalin twice daily, the percentage of children who experienced an adverse side effect was greatest for which side effect?
    F. Dull
    G. Headache
    H. Withdrawn
    J. Appetite loss

23. According to Figure 1, which dose of medication was the least successful in controlling children's behavior problems from 3:35 to 4:45?
    A. P
    B. R1
    C. R2
    D. A1

24. Suppose four groups of children were given one of the four possible medication regimens. Between 12:15 and 1:25, one group had a behavior rating of 5. Which medication regimen was most likely given to them?
    F. P
    G. R1
    H. R2
    J. A1

25. Assume that an ideal medication is one that has the fewest side effects, yet is most effective. Based on the data provided, which dose of medication is the most ideal?
    A. P
    B. R1
    C. R2
    D. A1

26. If a parent was concerned about his son losing weight while taking ADHD medication, which of the following medications would have the least effect on appetite while still keeping a behavior rating below 4 after the first two hours of taking the recommended dosage?
    F. P
    G. R1
    H. R2
    J. A1

PASSAGE V

A solution consists of a solute dissolved in a solvent. For example, in a saltwater solution, the salt is the solute and the water is the solvent. Osmosis is the movement of solvent molecules across a barrier in order to equalize solution concentrations. When a saltwater solution is placed in a u-shaped tube with a selectively permeable barrier or semipermeable membrane, the phenomenon of osmotic pressure can be observed. Osmotic pressure is the pressure required to prevent the flow of a solvent across a barrier. In Figure 1, saltwater was poured in the right half of the tube and pure water was poured in the left half of the tube. As water passes from left to right in the figure below due to osmosis, the level of solution on the right rises. Eventually, the weight of the solution due to gravity becomes sufficient to prevent the further flow of water from right to left.

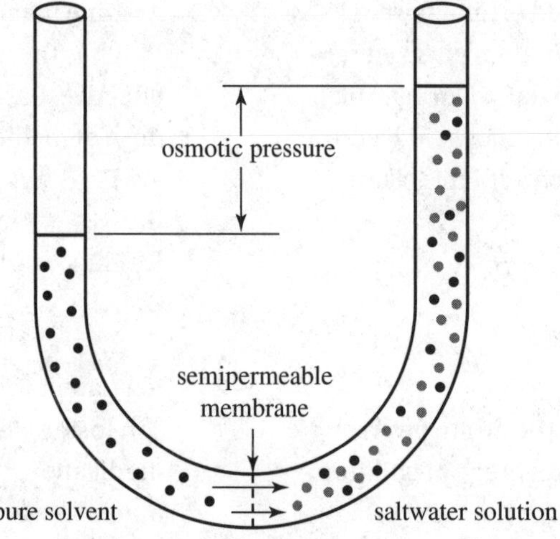

Figure 1

The following experiments were carried out to study how varying the molecular weight percentage of solvents and the temperature of solutions affects osmotic pressure. Table 1 shows the molecular weight percentages of the different solvents studied and Table 2 displays the temperatures of the various solutions used.

Table 1

Solution	Solution Concentration (% weight of solute)
1	5
2	10
3	15
4	20

Table 2

Trial	Temperature (°C)
1	20
2	30
3	40
4	50

Experiment 1

A 1000 ml u-shaped tube was fitted with a semipermeable membrane and 300 ml of solution was added on the right half and 300 ml of water was added on the left half. Table 1 shows the four solutions used in four separate trials of Experiment 1. The percent weight was measured by computing the ratio of the weight of the solute (salt) to the weight of the solution after dissolution. Every 5 seconds, the height of the solution on the right side of the tube was measured and recorded. Figure 2 shows the results of Experiment 1 recorded at 20°C.

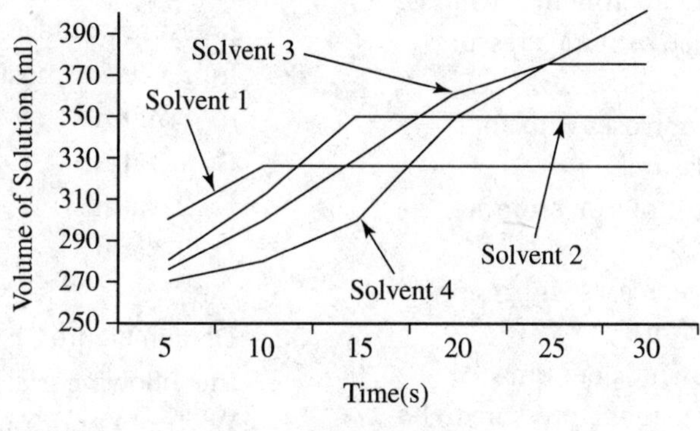

Figure 2

Experiment 2

Four more trials were performed but only the 10% solution was used. For each trial, the temperature was varied as shown in Table 2 and the results were graphed in Figure 3. In each trial, the height was measured 5 minutes after the water and solution were poured.

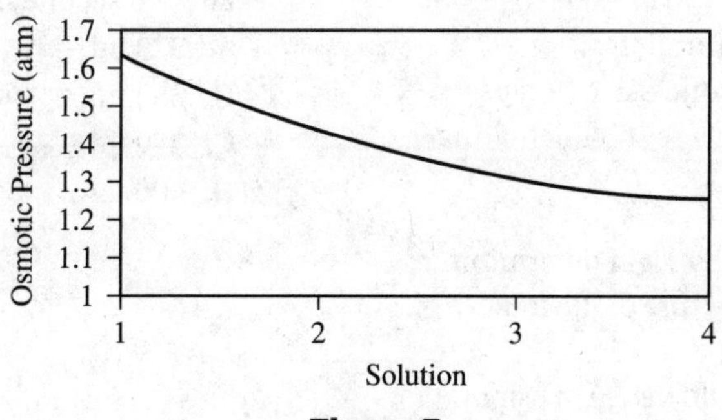

Figure 3

27. Based on Figure 2 and Table 2, which solution resulted in the greatest osmotic pressure after 30 seconds?

A. Solution 1
B. Solution 2
C. Solution 3
D. Solution 4

28. Based on the results of Experiment 2, what is the relationship between osmotic pressure and temperature?

F. Osmotic pressure increases with an increase in temperature.
G. Temperature and osmotic pressure are unrelated.
H. Osmotic pressure decreases with an increase in temperature.
J. Five minutes was insufficient time to allow the effects of osmotic pressure to be observed.

29. Based on Experiment 1, how does solution concentration affect osmotic pressure?

A. Osmotic pressure increases with concentration.
B. Osmotic pressure decreases with concentration.
C. There is no relationship between osmotic pressure and concentration.
D. The results were inconclusive because all solution heights were still fluctuating after 30 seconds.

30. Was Experiment 1 successful in determining the *relative* osmotic pressure of the four solutions tested?

F. Yes. There is a clear difference in osmotic pressure between the four solutions with Solution 1 having the greatest osmotic pressure.
G. Yes. There is a clear difference in osmotic pressure between the four solutions with Solution 4 having the greatest osmotic pressure.
H. No. All osmotic pressures were too similar to make any determination.
J. No. All solution heights were still fluctuating after 30 seconds.

31. *Reverse osmosis* occurs when the solvent flows from a solution of *higher* concentration to a solution of *lower* concentration. In Experiments 1 and 2, reverse osmosis can be observed by pouring more solution in the right side of the tube. Assuming the pressure required for reverse osmosis occurs at twice the osmotic pressure, approximately what pressure would a 30° solution have to reach for reverse osmosis to occur?

A. 0.7 atm
B. 1.2 atm
C. 2.8 atm
D. 3.2 atm

32. Data in Figure 2 is consistent with which of the following trials?

F. Trial 1 and Trial 3
G. Trial 1 only
H. Trial 2 only
J. Trial 2, Trial 3, and Trial 4

33. If scientists continued Experiment 1 under the same conditions, what would be the expected volume of the solution for Solvent 1 after 40 seconds?

A. 320 ml
B. 350 ml
C. 370 ml
D. 400 ml

PASSAGE VI

Students studying mirrors and reflection were given the following information:

There is a definite relationship between image characteristics and the distance an object is placed with regard to a concave mirror (see Figure 1). If an object is located beyond the center of curvature (C), its reflected image will be inverted (upside down) and smaller than the object itself. If an object is located precisely at C, the image will also be located at C; it will appear inverted and true to the object's actual size. When the object is placed between C and the focal length (F), the image will be inverted and larger than the object. When the object is located precisely at F, no image is formed whatsoever. Lastly, if an object is placed between F and the mirror, its image will appear upright and larger than the object.

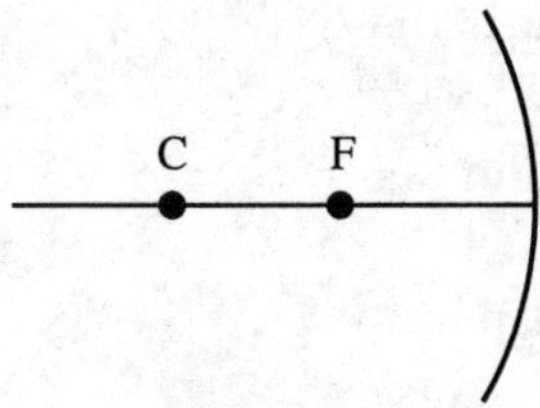

Figure 1

Given no further information, the students were asked to explain how the following magic trick is performed:

A famous Chinese magician conducts a classic magic trick utilizing a concave mirror with a focal length (F) of 1.6 m and a center of curvature (C) of 2.2 m. He is able to utilize the mirror in such a manner as to produce an image of a lightbulb at the same location and of the same size as the actual lightbulb itself.

Student 1

The lightbulb must have been placed exactly 1.6 m in front of the mirror, creating a perfect reflection. The image would thus be in the same location as the lightbulb, have the same dimensions as the lightbulb, and be an upright image.

Student 2

The lightbulb must have been placed exactly 2.2 m in front of the mirror. The image would then be in the same location and have the same dimensions as the actual lightbulb, although it would be inverted.

34. The students disagreed about which aspect of the lightbulb's image?
 F. Its size
 G. Its location
 H. Its orientation
 J. Its shape

35. The two explanations were similar to each other in that both explanations:
 A. assumed that the image was upright.
 B. assumed that the exact positioning of the lightbulb was important.
 C. correctly interpreted the information provided by the teacher.
 D. incorrectly interpreted the information provided by the teacher.

36. Placing the lightbulb in front of the mirror at which of the following distances would have resulted in an upright image?
 F. 1.0 m
 G. 1.6 m
 H. 2.2 m
 J. 2.6 m

37. Did Student 2 provide an adequate explanation of the magic trick?
 A. No. Student 2's explanation included an image that was upside down.
 B. No. If the lightbulb were placed at 2.2 m, it would not have produced an image.
 C. Yes. 2.2 m is the center of curvature. Placing an object at C results in an image of the same size in the same place.
 D. Yes. The magician specified that the image was inverted; Student 2 was the only student to account for this.

38. All of the following statements concerning concave mirror reflections are true EXCEPT:
 F. an object placed anywhere in front of C (closer to the mirror) will produce a reflected image that is larger than the actual object.
 G. an object placed anywhere in front of F (closer to the mirror) will produce an upright reflection.
 H. an object placed anywhere beyond F (farther from the mirror) will produce an inverted reflection.
 J. the only possible way to produce a reflected image equal in size to the actual object is to place the object precisely at C.

39. The teacher posed another question to the students. The students were told that the magician performed another trick in which he relocated the lightbulb so as to create the illusion that it had disappeared completely. How far in front of the mirror must the lightbulb have been placed in order to NOT produce a reflection?
 A. 1.3 m
 B. 1.6 m
 C. 2.0 m
 D. 2.2 m

40. Assume that Student 2's explanation is correct. If the magician wanted to create an image of the lightbulb that was smaller than the lightbulb itself, at which of the following distances in front of the mirror could he place the lightbulb?
 F. 1.6 m
 G. 2.0 m
 H. 2.2 m
 J. 2.5 m

If there is still time remaining, you may review your answers.

WRITING TEST

Time: 40 Minutes

Gender-Separate Education

More and more educators are supporting the notion that boys and girls should be taught separately through the end of high school. In addition to the "hormone-based" arguments that students in mixed-gender classrooms are distracted by "crushes" and/or worrying more about how they look than about learning, some psychologists believe that boys and girls have different learning styles. Additionally, many feminist scholars make the argument that girls learn better when they are not intimidated or drowned out by the typically louder and more aggressive boys. Still, many people find ideas based on the notion of "separate but equal" distasteful on general principle, since in practice it usually turns out to be the case that things that are separate sooner or later end up being unequal one way or another.

Read and carefully consider these perspectives. Each suggests a particular way of thinking about the debate on gender-separate education.

Perspective One	Perspective Two	Perspective Three
Schools should do whatever they can to ensure that students get the best educations possible. If reliable research indicates that both boys and girls learn better in single-gender classrooms, then that's all that matters.	When students grow up, the real world is never going to provide them with an ideal environment free of distractions. Teenagers will get distracted by anything, and if it isn't the opposite sex, then it will be something else. Boys and girls should get used to being around each other when they're young, rather than suddenly needing to learn to do so as adults.	The suggestion that all students will be distracted by the opposite sex marginalizes gay students, and the idea that boys learn one way and girls another ignores the reality of the students who are in the process of questioning their gender identity, adding more stress to an already stressful experience. For the students' own sake, and all of society's, we need to be making traditional notions about gender less rigid, rather than reinforcing them further.

ESSAY TASK

Write a unified, coherent essay concerning gender-separate education. In your essay, be sure to:

- clearly state your own perspective on the issue and analyze the relationship between your perspective and at least one other perspective
- develop and support your ideas with reasoning and examples
- organize your ideas clearly and logically
- communicate your ideas effectively in standard written English

Your perspective may be in full agreement with any of those given, in partial agreement, or completely different.

Planning Your Response

Your prewriting notes on this page will not be considered in your score.

Use the following space to brainstorm ideas and map out your response. You may want to think about the following as you analyze the given prompt:

Strengths and weaknesses of the three viewpoints

- What good points do they make, and what potential objections do they ignore?
- Why might they be convincing to readers, and why might their perspectives fall short?

Your previous experience, background knowledge, and personal values

- What is your viewpoint on this topic, and what are the pros and cons of this viewpoint?
- How will you craft an argument in support of your point of view?

If there is still time remaining, you may review your answers.

ANSWER KEY
Practice Test 3

English

1. **D**	16. **G**	31. **B**	46. **J**	61. **D**
2. **F**	17. **B**	32. **J**	47. **D**	62. **H**
3. **C**	18. **F**	33. **D**	48. **F**	63. **D**
4. **J**	19. **A**	34. **H**	49. **B**	64. **F**
5. **B**	20. **J**	35. **A**	50. **G**	65. **B**
6. **H**	21. **C**	36. **G**	51. **A**	66. **H**
7. **D**	22. **J**	37. **D**	52. **H**	67. **B**
8. **J**	23. **C**	38. **G**	53. **C**	68. **J**
9. **A**	24. **G**	39. **C**	54. **J**	69. **A**
10. **H**	25. **A**	40. **H**	55. **C**	70. **G**
11. **B**	26. **H**	41. **A**	56. **F**	71. **D**
12. **F**	27. **D**	42. **H**	57. **B**	72. **H**
13. **A**	28. **F**	43. **A**	58. **F**	73. **B**
14. **H**	29. **B**	44. **H**	59. **D**	74. **F**
15. **C**	30. **G**	45. **A**	60. **H**	75. **A**

Mathematics

1. **E**	13. **C**	25. **C**	37. **B**	49. **A**
2. **G**	14. **F**	26. **F**	38. **K**	50. **F**
3. **D**	15. **C**	27. **E**	39. **A**	51. **C**
4. **H**	16. **K**	28. **H**	40. **G**	52. **G**
5. **A**	17. **E**	29. **C**	41. **D**	53. **E**
6. **J**	18. **K**	30. **K**	42. **K**	54. **K**
7. **D**	19. **D**	31. **B**	43. **C**	55. **B**
8. **G**	20. **G**	32. **F**	44. **K**	56. **G**
9. **B**	21. **D**	33. **A**	45. **E**	57. **B**
10. **G**	22. **G**	34. **G**	46. **F**	58. **H**
11. **E**	23. **A**	35. **B**	47. **E**	59. **B**
12. **H**	24. **G**	36. **F**	48. **H**	60. **F**

ANSWER KEY
Practice Test 3

Reading

1. **A**	9. **B**	17. **D**	25. **B**	33. **A**
2. **H**	10. **F**	18. **H**	26. **H**	34. **G**
3. **B**	11. **D**	19. **B**	27. **B**	35. **D**
4. **J**	12. **F**	20. **F**	28. **J**	36. **F**
5. **C**	13. **C**	21. **A**	29. **B**	37. **C**
6. **H**	14. **G**	22. **J**	30. **F**	38. **G**
7. **D**	15. **A**	23. **C**	31. **D**	39. **C**
8. **F**	16. **H**	24. **F**	32. **H**	40. **J**

Science

1. **D**	9. **D**	17. **B**	25. **C**	33. **A**
2. **J**	10. **G**	18. **G**	26. **H**	34. **H**
3. **B**	11. **A**	19. **D**	27. **D**	35. **B**
4. **F**	12. **H**	20. **F**	28. **H**	36. **F**
5. **B**	13. **A**	21. **C**	29. **A**	37. **C**
6. **H**	14. **F**	22. **J**	30. **G**	38. **F**
7. **C**	15. **B**	23. **A**	31. **C**	39. **B**
8. **F**	16. **H**	24. **F**	32. **G**	40. **J**

HOW TO SCORE YOUR PRACTICE TEST

Step 1: Add up the number correct for each section and write that number in the blank under the Raw Score column on the Score Conversion Table. (Your goal is to get more questions correct on each subsequent practice test.)

Step 2: Using the Score Conversion Chart, find your scale score for each section and write it down. Then add up all four sections and divide by 4 to find your overall composite score. (Composite scores are rounded up at .5 or higher.)

SCORE CONVERSION TABLE

Section	Raw Score	Scaled Score
English	(out of 75)	____ / 36
Math	(out of 60)	____ / 36
Reading	(out of 40)	____ / 36
Science	(out of 40)	____ / 36
		Add and divide by 4
Overall Composite =		____ / 36

SCORE CONVERSION CHART

	Number Correct				
ACT Score*	English Section	Mathematics Section	Reading Section	Science Section	ACT Score*
36	75	60	40	40	36
35	74	59	39	39	35
34	73	58	38	38	34
33	72	57	37	—	33
32	71	56	36	37	32
31	70	54-55	35	36	31
30	69	53	34	35	30
29	67-68	51-52	33	34	29
28	65-66	49-50	32	33	28
27	64	46-48	31	31-32	27
26	62-63	44-45	30	30	26
25	60-61	41-43	29	28-29	25
24	58-59	39-40	27-28	25-27	24
23	55-57	37-38	25-26	24	23

(continued)

SCORE CONVERSION CHART (*Continued*)

	Number Correct				
ACT Score*	English Section	Mathematics Section	Reading Section	Science Section	ACT Score*
22	53-54	35-36	23-24	22-23	22
21	50-52	33-34	22	20-21	21
20	47-49	31-32	21	18-19	20
19	44-46	28-30	19-20	17	19
18	42-43	25-27	18	15-16	18
17	40-41	22-24	17	14	17
16	37-39	19-21	16	13	16
15	34-36	15-17	15	12	15
14	31-33	11-14	13-14	11	14
13	29-30	09-10	12	10	13
12	27-28	07-08	10-11	09	12
11	25-26	06	08-09	08	11
10	23-24	05	07	07	10
9	21-22	04	06	05-06	9
8	18-20	03	05	—	8
7	15-17	—	—	04	7
6	12-14	02	04	03	6
5	09-11	—	03	02	5
4	07-08	01	02	—	4
3	05-06	—	—	01	3
2	03-04	—	01	—	2
1	00-02	00	00	00	1

**These scores are based on student trials rather than national norms.*

SCORING YOUR ESSAY

As mentioned earlier in this text, two readers will evaluate your essay and each person will then assign it a score from 1 to 6. If, by chance, these two scorers disagree by more than 1 point, a third reader will step in and resolve the discrepancy. Performance on the essay will not affect your English, math, reading, science, or composite scores. You will receive two additional scores on your score sheet—a combined English/writing score (1–36) and a writing test subscore (1–12). Neither of these scores will affect your composite score!

The sample essay that follows reflects higher-level writing. It meets the criteria that ACT has put forth for essays that demonstrate effective writing skills.

- It takes a definite position.
- It addresses and expands on the counterargument.
- It has details that support the topic sentences and is well organized.
- It is not repetitive, and while there may be errors, they do not interfere with the competence of the essay.
- It is consistent and well balanced.
- The essay has a clear introduction and a conclusion that is not just a summary but ends with a significant thought.
- The vocabulary demonstrates good use of language and the sentence structure is varied.

ANSWER EXPLANATIONS

English

1. **(D)** In the phrase *both critics and fans have agreed,* two groups of people (*critics* and *fans*) are both doing the same thing—that is, both nouns are performing the same verb. Therefore, you don't need a comma before *and.* As for what they have agreed on, in the extended phrase *both critics and fans have agreed that no individual is due more credit than Chuck Berry,* there is also no need for a comma. The relative pronoun *that* introduces essential information (as opposed to *which,* which introduces nonessential or "extra" information). You do not need a comma in front of it (but you do in front of *which*).

2. **(F)** The phrase *singer, songwriter, and guitarist* refers to a single individual (Chuck Berry), and this is the noun phrase performing the verb in question. Choice F is the only one of the options with a singular verb (*was*). The other choices all have plural verbs. There is an added prepositional phrase trick: since *behind* is a preposition, *behind such rock classics as "Maybelline" and "Johnny B. Goode"* is a prepositional phrase that must be skipped over when determining agreement.

3. **(C)** The surrounding sentence informs us that there were multiple *inductees* into the Rock and Roll Hall of Fame in 1986, of whom Chuck Berry was one. Thus, we need the verb/preposition pairing *was among* (equivalent to "was one of" or "was part of").

4. **(J)** Since the sentence would be grammatically correct without the name *Johnnie Johnson,* the name is therefore set off with commas. The relative pronoun *who* is necessary after the comma because without it the subordinate clause would have no subject (just read the sentence without the name and you will see it sounds very wrong without *who*).

5. **(B)** The sentence is a question beginning with *Could.* You would not say *Could [blank] is?* but rather *Could [blank] be?* and so the choice with *be* is correct.

6. **(H)** *Unthinkable* means "nearly impossible to believe," and thus best emphasizes how shocking the allegations were. It is the most "extreme" of the four terms given as options.

7. **(D)** *Corroborate* means to support the validity of something. Therefore, the least acceptable choice is (D) dispute.

8. **(J)** The fact that Chuck Berry joined Johnson's band at the last minute when another member happened to get sick on the night Johnson's band was playing Berry's town was a very lucky coincidence from Berry's perspective, and emphasizes how easily his life could have gone a completely different way.

9. **(A)** The subordinating conjunction *although* is like a version of *but* that goes elsewhere in the sentence (you can see how the sentence would also work if you got rid of *although* but put a *but* after the comma). The ACT English often tries to trick you with *although* because it is a conjunction that can go at the beginning of the first of two independent clauses, instead of just at the beginning of the second. Here, it is the only one of the four choices that results in a complete correct sentence that means what you want it to mean.

10. **(H)** The noun performing the underlined verb is *hits,* and so the verb needs to be plural. *Were* is the only choice that is both plural and makes grammatical sense in context. This is a classic prepositional phrase trick. The prepositional phrase *after his 1963 release* needs to be skipped over when determining agreement.

11. **(B)** The sentence establishes that Springsteen's comment was made *years earlier*, and so *had remarked* is the only one of the choices that is grammatically correct and means what you want it to mean.

12. **(F)** Information establishing that Berry had been in trouble with the law several times and cheated other partners is absolutely relevant to a passage exploring the question of whether he also cheated Johnnie Johnson.

13. **(A)** The fact that Johnson was unaware that he was entitled to more money than he was paid for the recording sessions is information relevant to the question of why he didn't speak up at the time, which is exactly the question this paragraph is addressing.

14. **(H)** What the sentence means to say is that too much time had elapsed between the time that the songs were composed and the time of the lawsuit, and so the option beginning with *since* is the appropriate choice.

15. **(C)** The passage deals only with a specific set of allegations made against Chuck Berry, and not with any other celebrities, much less with celebrities in general. (The fact that the passage deals only with one example and not an entire category is a very common answer on ACT English final "Suppose the Author ..." questions!)

16. **(G)** The first thing to notice is that this sentence has more than one underlined portion; you must always be aware when this is the case, because the answers to both questions will affect each other (though there will never be more than one correct combination of answers). Since the part of the sentence before the comma is an independent clause, the part after it must either be a dependent clause or an independent clause with a conjunction. Choice G, *endlessly*, creates a grammatically correct "afterthought clause," a dependent descriptive clause preceded by a comma.

17. **(B)** The string of verbs constitutes a list, and so you need an *and* before the last of them: *endlessly admired, analyzed, and parodied* (either a comma or no comma before the *and* that precedes the last item in a list is acceptable; the ACT English will **never** test you on this directly).

18. **(F)** This option results in two independent clauses separated by a comma + *and*, forming a correct sentence that means what you want it to mean.

19. **(A)** Replacing the underlined portion with *this was* would result in a comma splice, and so this is the choice that is NOT acceptable.

20. **(J)** Choice J informs us that Perrugia disguised himself as one of the workers and walked around the museum pretending to work, and so it is the only one of the choices that provides specific information about how Perrugia avoided detection in the museum for so long.

21. **(C)** All of the other prepositions or combinations of prepositions are appropriate in context (although some are less formal than others), but *from of* is utter nonsense, and so it is the option that is LEAST acceptable.

22. **(J)** Because the subsequent clause is an independent one, the first clause of the sentence needs to be a dependent one. *Finding* is the only option that results in a sentence that is not a comma splice and means what you want to say.

23. **(C)** Since the subsequent sentence explains why people took so long to notice that the *Mona Lisa* had been stolen, the best opening sentence is the one that introduces this idea, even if some of the others relate to the end of the previous paragraph. (With questions about introductory sentences on the ACT English, it is always best to read a few sentences ahead and pick the sentence that best introduces the ones after it, rather than basing your answer on the previous paragraph!)

24. **(G)** Although all of the options result in complete correct sentences, only *in private* explains why no one was alarmed by the *Mona Lisa*'s absence (they assumed it was being worked on by museum staff in another room).

25. **(A)** Since it is inconceivable that another artist could be unaware of the *Mona Lisa*'s fame and importance, *out of ignorance* makes no sense as an explanation for an artist's motivation for stealing it, and so it is the choice that is the LEAST acceptable. The other three choices are so similar that they are essentially different ways of saying the same thing. (It is always a good idea to look for "which of these things is not like the other" on NOT and LEAST questions!)

26. **(H)** The *masterwork was feared gone forever* is the only one of the choices that makes sense and says what you mean to say. If it sounds strange, this may be because it is a situation where *to be* may be omitted, which you might not be used to hearing. The sentence means that the masterwork was feared to be gone forever.

27. **(D)** Since the verb of this independent clause is *led*, what goes in the underlined part needs to be a noun phrase performing that verb. *Perrugia's motivation* is the only noun phrase that forms a concise, correct sentence.

28. **(F)** Although you may not be used to seeing the formal phrase *from whence*, you should still understand from context that the painting was stolen *from* Italy, and that the other choices make no sense.

29. **(B)** The phrase *his expectations were not entirely off-base* is a way of saying that the things he believed were partially accurate, which is a paraphrase of the phrase *Perrugia might not have been as crazy as he seems* from the question.

30. **(G)** The passage does in fact explain the background, execution, and aftermath of a famous crime and this is all the question asks for. The explanation in choice G, the second of the *Yes* options, simply restates the demands of the question.

31. **(B)** *Dubbed* is a transitive verb that means *called* or *named*. So, just as you would have to say *his enemies called him* or *his enemies named him*, you have to say *his enemies dubbed him*.

32. **(J)** Preposition usage in English is largely idiomatic. The phrase is *synonymous with* because that is simply what we say. It is one of those things that you just have to know from reading a lot. (Preposition-choice questions are becoming more common on the ACT English, so make sure to make an effort to start noticing such things!)

33. **(D)** Although all four choices are correct complete sentences, the other three choices are awkward and/or unnecessarily complex. *Modern historians agree* is the simplest and most succinct way to put it. (On style questions, always pick the simplest way of putting

something as long as it makes a correct sentence, unless the question is specifically asking for something more complex, such as "the most detailed description.")

34. **(H)** The sentence says that most people's ideas about Attila come from Roman writers, and that these writers were unfair to him. Choice H is basically a paraphrase or summary of this.

35. **(A)** *At the time of Attila's birth in 406* is a dependent introductory clause, and so is followed by a comma. Although the rest of the sentence is long, and contains other underlined portions that should be double-checked alongside this answer, this introductory phrase could not constitute an independent clause no matter what. (Remember, when you see that two of the other choices are a semicolon and a period, this means they cancel each other out and the right answer must be a comma!)

36. **(G)** How many *Asias* are we talking about? One. And does it possess anything? Yes (the *central seas*). How many *seas* are we talking about? More than one. And do they possess anything? No. And so we need the singular possessive *Asia's* and the plural nonpossessive *seas.* It is as simple as that.

37. **(D)** Deleting the underlined portion makes the rest of the sentence into a succinct and grammatically correct "afterthought clause" describing the aforementioned *nation.*

38. **(G)** Simply saying *class division* concisely communicates the same information, whereas the other three choices are wordy and redundant.

39. **(C)** The Vikings, how they dressed, and when they sailed to America are all irrelevant to Attila, and distract the reader from the main idea.

40. **(H)** What we need here is the past tense verb *coexisted* and the modifying adverb *peacefully.*

41. **(A)** *That* is a pronoun standing in for the idea of Rome's royal line, and so the phrase *to unite his royal line with that of Rome* is correct.

42. **(H)** *Formerly the common enemy of both the Huns and Rome* is an appositive clause containing extra information, and is here set off with dashes (setting it off with commas would also be correct, but is not an option). The sentence then picks up with *further insulting Attila,* which grammatically matches up with the part of the sentence before the appositive. (On the ACT English, dashes usually come in pairs, so when you see a dash earlier in the sentence, expect the underlined part to contain the second one!)

43. **(A)** The presence of *Although* turns the first clause into a dependent one, and so the remainder of the sentence needs to be an independent clause. And since the noun being replaced here is *tactics,* the pronoun and verb need to be plural.

44. **(H)** The question asks for *relevant and specific information,* and only choice H provides a concrete example supporting the idea of Attila's high esteem in contemporary Eastern Europe.

45. **(A)** Paragraph 1 begins by building suspense about the identity of its subject, who is still a mystery until the third sentence (which also explains who Attila is). All this indicates that Paragraph 1 is definitely supposed to come first. (If a paragraph had been in the wrong place the whole time, then something probably would have sounded "off" while

you were reading the passage; if nothing did, then the paragraphs were probably in the right order!)

46. **(J)** The subsequent clause begins with a conjunction, which means that this first clause needs to be an independent one. *It started* is the only one of the choices that accomplishes this.

47. **(D)** *First reared their ugly heads* does not make sense in context, whereas the other three choices all indicate the first time. Hence, choice D is the least acceptable.

48. **(F)** The question asks for a phrase that *emphasizes the human cost of the war* (in other words, something about how many people died). Only choice F, which explains that more people died in World War I than in any war in Western history, does this.

49. **(B)** There must be a comma between *Ypres* and *Belgium*, separating the name of the city from the name of the country. There must also be a comma after *Belgium*, since this is where the appositive phrase beginning with the word *near* ends. Since both German and English forces are performing the verb *had fought*, there should not be a comma between *German* and *and*.

50. **(G)** Merely inserting a comma between *line* and *underground* would create a comma splice, and so this is the choice that is NOT acceptable.

51. **(A)** The phrase *each other* is tricky when it comes to possession. There are two armies, but relative to each army there is only one other, and so we need the singular possessive *other's: each army could hear the sound of the other's digging.* (Because *digging* is a gerund, it takes a possessive.)

52. **(H)** Although every choice seems fine if you don't read ahead, the subsequent sentence makes reference to melodies being recognized and someone's singing being responded to. Therefore, what we need here is a sentence establishing that someone was singing, and only choice H accomplishes this. (Always read ahead a little before answering "What sentence/phrase should go here?" questions!)

53. **(C)** This results in a run-on sentence (with the second of two independent clauses beginning at the word *they*), whereas the other three choices all result in grammatically correct sentences. Hence, it is the one that is NOT acceptable.

54. **(J)** Though it refers to a group of people, the phrase *high command* itself is singular, and so takes the singular verb *was*. This is a classic prepositional phrase trick: the prepositional phrase *on both sides* must be skipped over. (Though more than one high command is involved, the phrase itself is still singular.)

55. **(C)** Logically, the word *again* would have to modify something that already took place at least once. Since the truce was the thing that already took place, *again* should follow *happen* (since the noun phrase *such things* refers to the truce and is performing the verb *happen*).

56. **(F)** What we need preceding *the generals* is a word meaning "since" or "because." Of the choices, only *as* accomplishes this.

57. **(B)** Although every choice would result in a grammatically correct sentence, only the introductory phrase *in addition* accurately describes the information that follows, whereas the other three choices do not make sense in context.

58. **(F)** If neither Nazi Germany nor the Soviet Union would have existed if it hadn't been for World War I, then this phrase explains how World War I indirectly led to both World War II and the Cold War, the major conflicts of the twentieth century.

59. **(D)** The word *understand* by itself is all that is necessary. The other choices are all either redundant or grammatically incorrect. (When three choices are several words long and the fourth choice is one word, the fourth choice is almost always correct, as long as it results in a complete sentence!)

60. **(H)** The passage does not discuss protests within the armed forces in general, but only one individual famous instance of this. (The fact that the passage only discusses one specific example, rather than a larger phenomenon in general, is a very common answer to "Suppose the Author ..." questions on the ACT English!)

61. **(D)** The descriptive phrase *the son of* needs to extend in parallel ways to the phrases *a mother* and *a father*; both nouns need to function as objects of the preposition *of*. Only choice D accomplishes this.

62. **(H)** This incorrectly attempts to link two independent clauses with the relative pronoun *which* as though it were a conjunction. Hence, it is the choice that is NOT acceptable.

63. **(D)** Deleting the underlined portion makes the second half into a dependent descriptive clause that adds more information to the initial independent clause.

64. **(F)** The sentence (before the list that follows the colon) is two independent clauses separated by a comma and a conjunction. Only the introductory prepositional phrase *After graduation* preserves the first half of the sentence as an independent clause and refrains from adding any unnecessary elements.

65. **(B)** Preposition usage is largely idiomatic, and in certain situations more than one preposition (or phrase involving a preposition) could be correct. In this case, every choice would be acceptable besides *of*. Hence, choice B is the one that is NOT acceptable.

66. **(H)** The name of the store is not important, and so this is a minor detail that interrupts the flow of the paragraph.

67. **(B)** Reading the entire sentence reveals that the main verb is *became*, which is being performed by the noun *comics*, and that therefore everything between them should be a descriptive appositive phrase set off with commas.

68. **(J)** Either including or omitting the word *that* is acceptable, and either including or omitting the word *had* is acceptable (with varying degrees of formality). Inserting the word *because* in addition to *after admitting*, however, is grammatically incorrect, and so choice J is the option that is NOT acceptable.

69. **(A)** *Strip* is the subject of the sentence, and *came* is the main verb. The word *producer* should end the initial independent clause, followed by a comma and a dependent clause beginning with the relative pronoun *who*.

70. **(G)** Preposition usage in English is largely idiomatic. The phrase *the possibility of doing* is correct simply because it is what we say. There are some other phrases that could also be correct here, but none of the other three options are. It is one of those things that you

just have to know from reading a lot. (Preposition-choice questions are becoming more common on the ACT English, so make sure you start noticing such things!)

71. **(D)** Only this phrase both summarizes his concerns and explains his motivation for what he does next, thereby linking the two halves of the paragraph. Any of the other choices might well be true, but they are not sufficiently explanatory at this point in the passage.

72. **(H)** What we need here is a word or phrase meaning "give away" (in the sense of *reveal*, like with a secret). All the other choices mean "give away," but *mask* means "conceal," which is the opposite. Hence, it is the one that is LEAST acceptable.

73. **(B)** What is needed here is an independent clause subordinated to the relative pronoun *that*, and only *the cartoonist's name was Matt Groening* (uninterrupted by a comma) accomplishes this.

74. **(F)** The prepositional phrase *in which they star* adds important information to the noun *cartoon*, and does not need to be set off with any commas.

75. **(A)** The first clause is a dependent one beginning with *Although*, and so the part of the sentence after the comma needs to be an independent clause. (The conjunction *Although* is like a *but* that goes at the beginning of the first clause instead of the beginning of the second, and so the ACT English often tries to fool you using *although*!)

Mathematics

1. **(E)** If you add 5 to both sides, you get $3x = 12$.

2. **(G)** Complementary angles are two angles whose sum is 90°: 70°+ 20° = 90°; therefore, the complement of 70 is 20.

3. **(D)** You can set up an equation using the words of the problem to get $70 = 0.10(x)$. Solve for x by dividing both sides of the equation by 0.10 to get $x = 700$.

4. **(H)** You can find the three consecutive integers by either guessing and using your calculator, or you can set up an equation if that is what you prefer. Either way you will find the three consecutive integers whose sum is 99 are 32, 33, and 34. The greatest of these integers is 34.

5. **(A)** To find the area of a triangle, use the formula $A = \frac{1}{2}b \cdot h$. To find the height of this triangle, either use the Pythagorean Theorem, or realize this is a 9–12–15 right triangle, so the height must be 9. Now that we know the height, substitute into the area formula to get $A = \frac{1}{2}(12)(9) = 54$.

6. **(J)** $1{,}027 - (13 \times 40) = 507$ in overtime pay. $507 ÷ 19.50 = 26 overtime hours. The hours for the week would be $40 + 26 = 66$.

7. **(D)** First subtract 3 from both sides to get $-4(x + 7) < 16$, then distribute to get $-4x - 28 < 16$. Now add 28 to both sides: $-4x < 44$. Finally, divide both sides by -4, but don't forget to switch the inequality symbol to get $x > -11$.

8. **(G)** You could solve this problem using your calculator to get a decimal approximation, then plug the answers into your calculator to get a similar decimal approximation.

For those who prefer to do it using algebra: $3\sqrt{300} - 5\sqrt{75} \rightarrow 3\sqrt{100 \cdot 3} - 5\sqrt{25 \cdot 3} \rightarrow$ $3 \cdot 10\sqrt{3} - 5 \cdot 5\sqrt{3} \rightarrow 30\sqrt{3} - 25\sqrt{3}$. Subtract to get $5\sqrt{3}$.

9. **(B)** $|-2 + 3^2| - |-2 - 3^2| = |7| - |-11| = 7 - 11 = -4$.

10. **(G)** The longest side of a triangle is always opposite the largest angle in the triangle. To find the missing angle C, use the fact that the sum of the three angles of a triangle is 180° to get $180 - 75 - 36 = 69°$. Since angle A is 75°, it is the largest of the three angles and, therefore, the side opposite, BC, is the longest side.

11. **(E)** $3x^2 + x - 4$ can be factored to get $(x - 1)(3x + 4)$ making the factors $(x - 1)$ and $(3x + 4)$.

12. **(H)** Substituting $(-3, 5)$ into the equation $y = -x + 2$ gives $5 = -(-3) + 2 \rightarrow 5 = 5$. Since this is a true statement, the equation $y = -x + 2$ passes through the point.

13. **(C)** Substituting -2 for x into the equation gives $\frac{-(-2)^2 + 4}{-2}$. Simplifying using order of operations yields $\frac{-4+4}{-2} \rightarrow \frac{0}{-2} = 0$.

14. **(F)** Two lines are parallel if they have the same slope. The given equation is in slope-intercept form, $y = mx + b$, where m is the slope. In this equation, the slope is $-\frac{3}{4}$. The only answer that has the same slope is $y = -\frac{3}{4}x$.

15. **(C)** You can set up a proportion to find the number of goldfish: $\frac{2}{5} = \frac{x}{25}$. Cross multiply and solve for x to get $x = 10$, the number of goldfish. However, the question asks how many TOTAL fish, so add $10 + 25 = 35$ fish.

16. **(K)** The 3 lines could be parallel yielding no points of intersection, they could all intersect at the same point giving 1 point of intersection, or 2 lines could be parallel with the third crossing the other 2 giving 2 points of intersection, and finally the 3 lines could intersect to form a triangle making 3 points of intersection. See the diagram below.

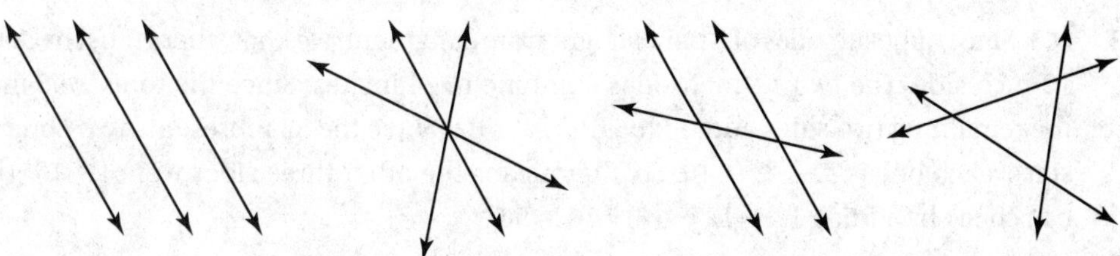

17. **(E)** Since $c = a - b$, and b is negative, its value actually gets added to a because subtracting a negative number is the same as adding a positive. When b is added to a the result will always be a positive number. Testing some numbers in the range of a and b will help lead you to the right answer.

18. **(K)** To find the slope between 2 points use the slope formula $\frac{y_2 - y_1}{x_2 - x_1}$ to get $\frac{8-5}{0-(-2)}$. Simplify to get $\frac{3}{2}$. Always be careful and check your signs when using the slope formula; it is easy to make an integer error or a sign error.

19. **(D)** Setting up a proportion to solve for how much sugar they need gives $\frac{2\frac{1}{2}}{32} = \frac{x}{250}$. Cross multiply and solve for x to get $x \approx 19.5$, which rounds to 20.

20. **(G)** Recall that the $\sin(C) = \frac{\text{opposite}}{\text{hypotenuse}}$. To find the side opposite angle C, either use the Pythagorean Theorem, or memorize the special 8–15–17 right triangle. Calculating AB gives $8^2 + x^2 = 17^2 \rightarrow x = 15$. Now, using the above fact, $\sin(C) = \frac{15}{17}$.

21. **(D)** The average is $3{,}500 \div 4 = 875$.

22. **(G)** $\frac{2{,}500}{4{,}000}$ reduces to $\frac{5}{8}$.

23. **(A)** $\left(\frac{2{,}500}{30{,}000}\right) \times 360 = 30$.

24. **(G)** $\left(\frac{3{,}500 + 7{,}000 + 4{,}000 + 2{,}500}{30{,}000}\right) = 57\%$. This represents the known amounts. To find the portion for the Labor and Other categories take $100\% - 57\% = 43\%$.

25. **(C)** Using the rules of exponents we get $5^3 \cdot 5^{-7} = 5^{3+(-7)} = 5^{-4}$. Recall that a negative exponent just means take the reciprocal of the base to get $5^{-4} = \frac{1}{5^4}$. Therefore, $x = 4$.

26. **(F)** WYX is a straight line making it 180°. Since $\angle WYZ = 28°$, the remaining angle ZYX must equal $180 - 28 = 152$. YM bisects angle ZYX, making each angle $\frac{152}{2} = 76°$.

27. **(E)** Recall that an angle that lies on a circle is exactly $\frac{1}{2}$ of its intercepted arc, making arc $BC = 2(35) = 70$. Since AC is a diameter of the circle, the total arc from A to C measures 180°. To find arc AB take $180 - 70 = 110°$.

28. **(H)** To find the greatest common factor of two numbers, first find the largest number that divides into both 24 and 36. Testing various numbers gives 12 as the GCF. To find the GCF of two like variables, always take the smallest power. The GCF of m^4 and m^2 is m^2 because it is the smaller power. Doing this for n and p as well gives the answer $12m^2n$.

29. **(C)** Since opposite sides of a parallelogram are congruent, we know there must be another 12-inch side. The two 12-inch sides combine to 24 inches. Since the total is 56 inches, the remaining two sides add up to $56 - 24 = 32$. Since the 32 represents two congruent sides, each one is $32 \div 2 = 16$. So, that means the other three sides were 12, 16, 16. We can check by adding $12 + 12 + 16 + 16 = 56$.

30. **(K)** Since $\triangle WYZ$ is a right triangle, we can use the Pythagorean Theorem to find the missing side $\overline{YZ}$. Solve $YZ^2 + 12{,}000^2 = 20{,}000^2$. $YZ = \sqrt{20{,}000^2 - 12{,}000^2} = 16{,}000$. Since the question asks for the distance between the two radar stations, add 5,000 and 16,000 for the answer 21,000.

31. **(B)** $\frac{600 \text{ feet}}{\text{seconds}} \times \frac{1 \text{ mile}}{5{,}280 \text{ feet}} \times \frac{60 \text{ seconds}}{1 \text{ minute}} \times \frac{60 \text{ minutes}}{1 \text{ hour}} = 409$ miles/hour.

32. **(F)** The desired line is a vertical line. Vertical lines have equations of the form $x = h$ and the x-coordinates of all of the points on this line are 5,000, so $x = 5{,}000$ is the equation of the line.

33. **(A)** In matrix addition, you add elements in the same position to get the sum. Therefore, $(2x - 1) + (-4x - 2) = 12$. Solve the equation to get $-2x - 3 = 12 \rightarrow x = -7.5$.

34. **(G)** Use the formula $A = \frac{1}{2}b \cdot h$ to find the area of the triangle to get $A = \frac{1}{2}(2w^2 - 8w + 7)(3) = \frac{6w^2 - 24w + 21}{2}$.

35. **(B)** To evaluate 1■(2■2) begin inside the parentheses. To evaluate 2■2, substitute 2 into the given equation for both x and y to get $(x + y)(x - y) = (2 + 2)(2 - 2) = 0$. Therefore, the original problem becomes 1■0. Evaluate this expression by plugging $x = 1$ and $y = 0$ to get $(1 + 0)(1 - 0) = 1$.

36. **(F)** If she scores just 1 goal in game 7, her overall goals scored would be 0, 1, 1, 1, 2, 3, 4. The median (middle number) in that set is 1, not 2.

37. **(B)** Recall the standard form of a circle $(x - h)^2 + (y - k)^2 = r^2$, where h and k represent the center of the circle. To find the center, take the opposite of each number after the x and y. For this problem, the opposite of positive 7 and negative 5 gives a center of (−7, 5).

38. **(K)** Solving for y gives $3x - 7y = 21 \rightarrow -7y = -3x + 21 \rightarrow y = \frac{3}{7}x - 3$.

39. **(A)** Using supplementary angles, parallel lines, triangles, and vertical angles you can arrive at the correct answer. See the diagram below for help.

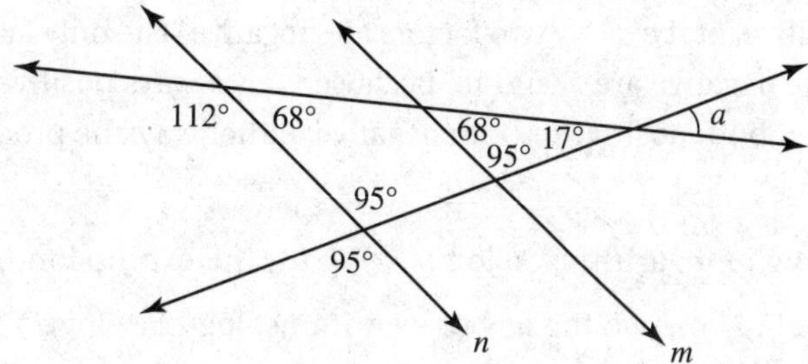

40. **(G)** To start this problem, draw and label a diagram. If the angle of depression from the control tower to the plane is 12°, then the angle of elevation from the plane to the tower is also 12°. Let x be the distance from the plane to the tower, then use $\tan(12) = \frac{40}{x}$. Solve for x to get $x \cdot \tan(12) = 40 \rightarrow x = \frac{40}{\tan(12)}$.

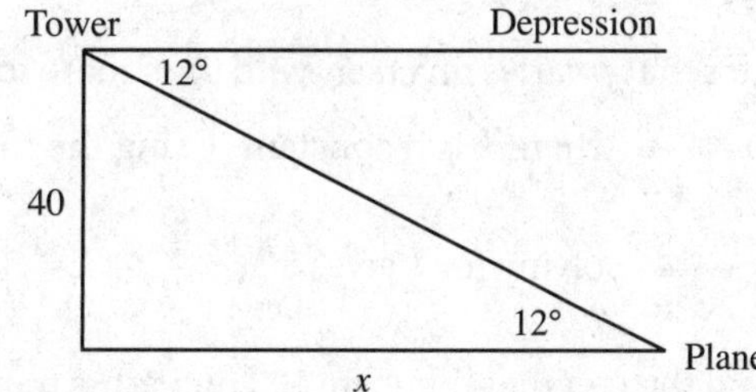

41. **(D)** A square root function is undefined in the real number system whenever the expression under the radical is less than zero. Set $x - 5 < 0$ and solve to get $x < 5$.

42. **(K)** The distance from $(-3, m)$ to the line $x = 7$ is $7 - (-3) = 10$ units. When reflected over the line, the point will move from its location 10 units left of $x = 7$ to its new location 10 units right of $x = 7$. The only point that is 10 units to the right of $x = 7$ is $(17, m)$.

43. **(C)** Using the distance formula $d = \sqrt{(x_2 - x_1)^2 + (y_2 - y_1)^2}$ we get

$$d = \sqrt{(5-(-3))^2 + (8-2)^2} = \sqrt{64+36} = \sqrt{100} = 10$$

44. **(K)** If the ratio of the sides of the two rectangles is 1:4, the ratio of the areas is $(1{:}4)^2 =$ 1:16. Set up a proportion to get $\frac{1}{16} = \frac{12}{x}$. Solve to get $x = 192$.

45. **(E)** For the first hour Daniel pays x dollars, so he pays $1(x)$ for the first hour. After the first hour, he pays y dollars for the remaining $h - 1$ hours, so he pays $y(h - 1)$. Add the expressions for the first hour and the remaining hours to get $P = x + y(h-1)$.

46. **(F)** First, solve for z to get $3z \cdot y = 2x \rightarrow z = \frac{2x}{3y}$. Now, to find out what happens as x and y are doubled, substitute $2x$ and $2y$ in place of them to get $\frac{2(2x)}{3(2y)}$. Simplify to get $\frac{2x}{3y}$, which is the same expression as what z originally started as. You could also substitute numbers like $x = 1$, $y = 1$ into the problem, then plug in $x = 2$, $y = 2$ to see what happens to z when x and y are doubled.

47. **(E)** The only way a product and quotient of three things can be greater than zero is if all factors are positive, or if exactly two factors are negative. The only factors in the expression that can be negative are t^5 and m^9 because w^6 is always positive. This means that t and m are either both positive or both negative. Either way, the product $t \cdot m$ would be positive.

48. **(H)** Using a law of logarithms, $a \log b = \log b^a$, the expression becomes $\log(x^2) + \log(\sqrt{y}) - \log(z^4)$. Now, use the law of logarithms, $\log(a) + \log(b) = \log(a \cdot b)$, to get $\log(x^2 \cdot \sqrt{y}) - \log(z^4)$. Finally, use the law of logarithms, $\log(a) - \log(b) = \log\left(\frac{a}{b}\right)$ to get $\log\left(\frac{x^2\sqrt{y}}{z^4}\right)$.

49. **(A)** To evaluate $f(g(2))$ start inside the parentheses by finding $g(2)$. To find $g(2)$ from the table, look where $x = 2$, and read $g(x) = 3$; therefore, $g(2) = 3$. Now, evaluate $f(3)$ using the table the same way to get $f(3) = -15$.

50. **(F)** The problem states that p varies inversely with the square root of q, meaning we can set up an equation $p = \frac{k}{\sqrt{q}}$ where k is a constant. Using the initial criteria $q = 49$ and $p = 800$, we get $800 = \frac{k}{\sqrt{49}}$. Solving for k gives $800 = \frac{k}{7} \rightarrow k = 5{,}600$. Now that we know the constant, use it and the fact that there are 100 predators to get $p = \frac{5{,}600}{\sqrt{100}} = 560$.

51. **(C)** To find the slope between two points, use the slope formula $m = \frac{y_2 - y_1}{x_2 - x_1}$ and substitute in the points to get $\frac{x^2 - 1}{x - 1}$. Now, simplify the answer by factoring to get $\frac{(x+1)(x-1)}{x-1}$. Cancel like factors to get $x + 1$, as long as $x \neq 1$. Since the problem states "for $x > 5$," we don't have to worry about this hole.

52. **(G)** Using the laws of exponents we first get $\frac{3^1 \cdot 3^{2x-5}}{3^{x+1}} = \frac{3^{2x-4}}{3^{x+1}}$. Then, use the laws of exponents to divide and get $3^{2x-4-(x+1)} = 3^{x-5}$.

53. **(E)** A good way to find a number that is halfway between two numbers is to find the average of those two numbers. To find the average of $\frac{3}{8}$ and $\frac{4}{5}$, add them up and divide by 2. A calculator can be handy for this step, or you can do it by hand. Either way, you should get $\frac{47}{80}$.

54. **(K)** For Mike to achieve the highest grade on one test, we want the other 3 tests to be as low as possible. The problem states that he never scored lower than 80%, so assume he scored an 80 on each of his first 3 tests and let x be the score on his fourth test. Set up an equation to find x using the fact that his average is an 85: $\frac{3(80) + x}{4} = 85$. Solve for x to get $x = 100$.

55. **(B)** To solve an absolute value inequality, split the problem into two inequalities without an absolute value. The first inequality stays exactly as the problem was written but without the absolute value bars: $x - 3 > x - 3$. Solving this inequality yields $-3 > -3$, which has no solution. The other inequality we get from splitting up the absolute value is $x - 3 < -(x - 3)$. Solve this inequality to get $x < 3$.

56. **(G)** Multiplying $\frac{i+7}{i-5} \cdot \frac{i}{1}$ gives $\frac{i^2 + 7i}{i-5}$. Recall that $i^2 = -1$; therefore, the expression becomes $\frac{-1+7i}{i-5}$. Now, multiply the top and bottom of the fraction by $i + 5$ ($i + 5$ is the *conjugate* of the denominator) to get $\frac{-1+7i}{i-5} \cdot \frac{i+5}{i+5} = \frac{-i-5+7i^2+35i}{i^2-25}$. Simplify to get $\frac{34i-12}{-26}$. Divide the top and bottom by 2 to get $\frac{-6+17i}{-13} \rightarrow \frac{6}{13} - \frac{17}{13}i$.

57. **(B)** First calculate the area of the pizza by using the formula $A = \pi r^2$ to get $A \approx 113.1$. If each square inch contains 50 calories, there is a total of $113.1 \cdot 50 = 5{,}655$ calories. Alex's dad eats 3 out of 8 slices, or in other words, $\frac{3}{8}$ of the pizza, which is $\frac{3}{8}(5{,}655) = 2{,}120$ calories. Alex eats two slices or $\frac{2}{8}(5{,}655) = 1{,}414$ calories. Subtract Alex's calories from his dad's to get $2{,}120 - 1{,}414 \approx 700$ calories.

58. **(H)** Start by drawing a right triangle with unknown angle θ as seen in the diagram below. Since $\tan(\theta) = v$, then we know the $\frac{\text{opposite}}{\text{adjacent}}$ from angle θ is $\frac{v}{1}$. Now, find the missing side using the Pythagorean Theorem to get it: $\sqrt{1^2 + v^2}$. Now, using SOH-CAH-TOA, $\cos(\theta) = \frac{\text{adjacent}}{\text{hypotenuse}} = \frac{1}{\sqrt{1+v^2}}$.

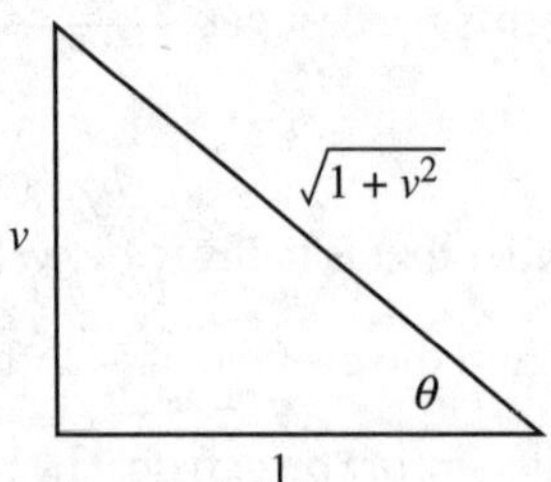

59. **(B)** Andy only has two possible places to sit, but the other four people can sit anywhere. Starting with just the arrangements for the other 4 people, we get $4 \cdot 3 \cdot 2 \cdot 1 = 24$ possible seating arrangements for them. Then, multiply the answer by 2 for the two possible choices for Andy to get $2 \cdot 24 = 48$ total arrangements.

60. **(F)** If the two points lie on the graph of the equation, then their slope must equal $\frac{1}{3}$, which is the slope of the equation. Using the slope formula and setting it equal to $\frac{1}{3}$, we get $\frac{n+\frac{2}{g}-n}{m-2-m} = \frac{1}{3}$. Simplify the numerator and denominator to get $\frac{\frac{2}{g}}{-2} = \frac{1}{3}$. Keep simplifying to get $\frac{-1}{g} = \frac{1}{3}$. Solve to get $g = -3$.

Reading

1. **(A)** As is often the case on the Literary Narrative section, the broadest answer is the correct one here. The passage sounds like a young man talking, and "relating a significant event" is so open-ended that there's really no way for it to be wrong. (If nothing is wrong, then it's right!)

2. **(H)** Although the story takes place in a supermarket, specific supermarket chains are never mentioned aside from line 49, and no other chain is mentioned besides the one in which the story is set.

3. **(B)** Although it's strongly implied that Sammy is young, there's no real indication that he is new at his job. He could easily have worked there for years.

4. **(J)** Sammy mentions thinking of himself as a hero in line 67, and his decision to quit is a stand on principle (if a minor and foolish one).

5. **(C)** Although Sammy makes jokes about Lengel being a Sunday-school teacher in lines 16 and 37–38, there is no indication that the locals in general are mistrustful of organized religion.

6. **(H)** The fact that Sammy turns in his bow tie after quitting (lines 89–90) establishes that it is the store's property.

7. **(D)** The reason that *the crowd that runs the A&P must look pretty crummy* to Queenie is that she is richer than they are, as implied in lines 19–32.

8. **(F)** There is never any indication that anyone besides Sammy finds his decision to quit admirable. Even Sammy himself barely feels this way by the end.

9. **(B)** We are told twice that Lengel "doesn't miss that much" (lines 17 and 36).

10. **(F)** Sammy explicitly states in lines 65–67 that he quit solely to try and impress the girls.

11. **(D)** The final paragraph, about how "a chain of middlemen" makes it easier for buyers to avoid considering where the bones come from, places blame on the fact that the bone buyers in other nations turn a blind eye to criminal practices.

12. **(F)** The "long chain" is the chain that separates Western buyers from the criminals who actually first obtain and prepare the bones. Western buyers are able to ignore the root problem or plead ignorance because they never have to deal directly with the criminals.

13. **(C)** All of the quotations that the author selected for use emphasize the horrifying environment and the fear and powerlessness of the people. The dominant emotion of the piece is sympathy for the people caught up in all of this.

14. **(G)** The paragraph emphasizes the fact that Young Brothers acquires bones openly from every conceivable location and even goes so far as to advertise despite the fact that their business is nominally illegal. The point here is the flagrancy of the enterprise.

15. **(A)** After the quote from Aron, the rest of the paragraph is concerned with explaining that, for various reasons, the laws concerning bone trafficking do not always get enforced.

16. **(H)** The passage never mentions anything about the reliability of witnesses (indeed, it implies that very few cases ever come to trial, and so witnesses would hardly be an issue).

17. **(D)** Lines 82–89 establish that, in the eyes of police themselves, they are powerless until society decides that it cares enough about the issue to give them the resources they need to enforce the law.

18. **(H)** Lines 77–78 state that the "bones from over 100 people could have fetched around $70,000," which works out to $700 per skeleton.

19. **(B)** Vinesh Aron is the owner of Young Brothers (lines 64–65), a bone-trafficking organization, and so would not oppose bone trafficking.

20. **(F)** It is established in lines 1–3 that the buyers of the bones are medical students. Therefore, they would be the audience for the catalogues.

21. **(A)** Passage A is adapted from Mary Shelley's introduction to a later edition of her famous novel, and so "once again" (i.e., for the second time) she is offering her "progeny" (a synonym for "offspring," as she is metaphorically the "parent" of the book) to the public.

22. **(J)** The second and third paragraphs of Passage A draw explicit contrast between Shelley's early attempts at writing and her personal fantasies. She states that only her fantasies were personal, whereas her early writing consisted of mechanical attempts to copy others.

23. **(C)** The antecedent of "it" in the sentence in question is "literary reputation"—i.e., getting famous for writing.

24. **(F)** The key phrase here is "what terrified me will terrify others." Shelley's epiphany was that the dreams and fantasies she had previously kept to herself had in fact been the key to success all along.

25. **(B)** Shelley closes her introduction by stating that her novel was originally written in "happy times, when death and grief were but words"—i.e., that although she was writing about horrible things, she had not yet experienced them, but now has. (Her husband, three of their children, and several of their close friends had all died in the interim.)

26. **(H)** In the paragraph in question, Victor Frankenstein begins by alluding to his meticulous scientific process, but then describes his emotional horror at seeing the result of that process come to life.

27. **(B)** Victor Frankenstein's quest was to create life, and he has done so, but the dream about his fiancée turning into his dead mother implies and foreshadows to the reader that the eventual results will be exactly the opposite.

28. **(J)** Shelley's autobiographical introduction describes her famous novel as being the product of a dream, and Victor Frankenstein's narration establishes that his aversion to his creation is an emotional reaction, rather than being the product of anything the Creature actually does (at least, not yet ...).

29. **(B)** As with Question #24, the key phrase here is "what terrified me will terrify others." Mary Shelley's grand realization was that her own personal imagination and psychology was the key to creating a work of genius.

30. **(F)** Mary Shelley (a great self-promoter, no matter how much she claimed not to care for fame) is clearly drawing an explicit comparison between her "creation" of the *Frankenstein* story and Victor Frankenstein's creation of the Monster. The "idea that broke in" in Passage A and the "spark of being" in Passage B are analogous to each other—in both cases, the creator merely harnesses a mysterious energy that originates elsewhere.

31. **(D)** The passage as a whole is concerned with the history of magnetic therapy and how there has never been any credible evidence to support it. (As is frequently the case with "main point" questions, the broadest answer is the correct one!)

32. **(H)** Lines 44–53 explain that the findings of Franklin's commission made Mesmer so unpopular that he had to flee France in disgrace.

33. **(A)** The paragraph begins with "Nevertheless" (i.e., "despite all this") and goes on to explain that the same discredited practices took hold in the United States, eventually developing into a new pseudomedical practice of dubious value.

34. **(G)** Lines 104–110 explain that human blood is actually diamagnetic, that is, repelled by magnets.

35. **(D)** Lines 70–74 state that an MRI field is about a hundred times stronger than a powerful therapy magnet. (The trick here is that 100 is written as a numeral in the answer choice, but written out as a word in the passage, so people who are scanning the passage quickly for a numeral will not see it.)

36. **(F)** A *placebo* is a fake treatment given to some patients in a medical experiment in order to rule out the psychological effect—in this case, the "sham magnets" of lines 87–88.

37. **(C)** The *predatory quacks* of line 118 are dishonest therapists. A *quack* is a doctor who believes (or pretends to believe) in false treatments.

38. **(G)** Lines 94–98 explain that skin gets red when it's heated because blood is being diverted to the area to act as a coolant.

39. **(C)** Lines 28–32 describe Benjamin Franklin correctly figuring out that magnet therapy only appeared to help because it was keeping patients away from the harmful treatments practiced by many other doctors at that time.

40. **(J)** Lines 81–93 describe an experiment conducted by Carlos Vallbona in which magnet therapy appeared to have beneficial effects, though no one knows why.

Science

1. **(D)** The tornado in Figure 2 is represented by the number 6. The paragraph above Figure 2 explains this (it is logical that the sixth and *final* step in the explanation would be the one that involves the tornado, since the paragraph is an explanation of how tornadoes are formed).

2. **(J)** The F4 box in Figure 1 (fifth box over, second one down) includes wind speeds from 207 to 261 mph.

3. **(B)** In the paragraph above Figure 2, a mesocyclone is formed in Step 3. Since a spinning wall-cloud is formed in Step 5, this would be the one that does NOT precede the formation of a mesocyclone.

4. **(F)** The paragraph above Figure 3 explains that "Tornado Alley" is in the central United States, and that the number over each state represents its number of tornadoes in 2005. Texas had 105 (higher than any of the other choices) and is in the central United States.

5. **(B)** The intersection box of the horizontal "Brick Structure" row and the vertical "Minor Damage" column says f0. The key within Figure 1 explains that the f scale (lower case) must then be *converted* into the F scale (upper case), and f0 + 1 = F1.

6. **(H)** According to the intensity scale, collapsed walls on a brick building are an F3 and missing roofs from strong frame houses occur during an F2 tornado. Therefore, the strongest tornado intensity possible is an F3.

7. **(C)** The sample with the highest concentration of chlorine in Table 2 (the table in Study 1) is Sample 3, with a concentration of 0.15 mg/L.

8. **(F)** In Table 3 (the table in Study 2), the highest grouping of numbers in the "Average pH" column occurs during the spring months: April, May, and March or June. (Remember that acidity is indicated by *low* pH, and so the *least* acidic deposition would be represented by the *highest* numbers.) Spring is still the right answer even though there are other individual high numbers in other months, and regardless of whether you count March or June as the third spring month.

9. **(D)** The order of the samples by acidity, from lowest pH to highest, is 4, 2, 1, 3, 5. The order of the samples by sodium concentration, from lowest to highest, is 5, 1, 2, 4, 3. The orders are neither the same as nor the reverse of each other, and therefore there is no correlation, neither a positive nor an inverse. (Remember that when the last choice is "no correlation" or "no relationship" or "date not included" or something weird like that, that is *probably* the answer, so test that one first!)

10. **(G)** The pH is highest in the month of April. Table 1 shows that frogs die at around a pH of 5. Clearly, the lower the pH, the greater the health risks for all animals. There is no definitive level but the question specifies *least* concerned. April is the best answer given the other three choices.

11. **(A)** The introductory paragraph above Table 1 explains that *wet deposition* refers to rain, snow, sleet, and hail. The paragraph in Study 1 explains that the samples in Study 2 were collected in the form of rain, and therefore they are examples of *wet deposition.*

12. **(H)** The introductory paragraph explains that sulfuric acid lowers the pH of rain. Since the samples in Table 2 were collected from rain, the pH of Sample 2 would necessarily be lower than its current pH of 5.28 had it been contaminated with sulfuric acid.

13. **(A)** According to Table 1, once the pH falls below 4 to a level 3 all fish will die, but frogs, crawfish, and snails can survive.

14. **(F)** As shown in Table 1, parents with blood types of O and B can only produce offspring with O or B blood as well. Whether the mother is O or B, whether the father is O or B, the results are the same.

15. **(B)** As Tables 1 and 2 make clear, to produce a child with blood type AB+, at least one parent must have a blood type with A in it (A or AB), at least one parent must have a blood type with B in it (B or AB), and at least one parent must be Rh+. The only one of the choices that has an A, a B, and a + in it is choice B.

16. **(H)** Table 3 shows that the "universal donor" is type O–. Table 1 shows that a child with type O blood could not possibly have a parent who has type AB blood (i.e., *neither* parent can be AB). When both parents have B– blood, B– or O– offspring will be produced.

17. **(B)** Parents with blood types A and O can produce either A or O offspring (Table 1). The Rh factor could be + OR – because both parents could carry the recessive gene for Rh–.

18. **(G)** In the opening paragraph, the passage clearly states, "The genes ensure that only the blood cells of the proper blood type remain in the body"—that is, they control the types of cells in the blood.

19. **(D)** According to Table 3, blood type AB+ is the universal recipient. Persons with this type can receive blood from anybody no matter what their blood type.

20. **(F)** All this question wants you to do is find the point at which the four lines in Figure 1 are the closest to one another. That would be the starting point, which represents 8:15–9:25.

21. **(C)** The text explains that lower numbers on the behavioral scale indicate better behavior, so all this question is asking you to do is find the point (out of the choices) where the line representing the Adderall kids (the one with the squares) is *not* the *lowest*. (Even if you didn't get that, choice C is still the only one of the choices where the line representing the Adderall kids is in a *different* place relative to the other four lines—when in doubt, pick the odd one out.)

22. **(J)** All this question wants you to do is find the point in Figure 2 where the line representing the double-dose Ritalin kids (the one with the triangles) is highest, which is over "appetite loss" (as it is for all the lines except the one representing the placebo kids).

23. **(A)** The text explains that lower numbers on the behavioral scale indicate better behavior, so all this question wants you to do is find the line in Figure 1 that is highest at the 3:35–4:45 mark, and it is the one representing the placebo kids (the one with the diamonds).

24. **(F)** According to the legend for Figure 1, the group with a 5 behavior rating corresponds to P—placebo.

25. **(C)** In Figure 1, the effectiveness order of the medications from most to least effective is A1, R2, R1. In Figure 2, the side-effects order of the medications from fewest to most is R1, R2, A1. The medication choice that "splits the difference" is R2.

26. **(H)** R2 medication consistently keeps the behavior rating at a 4 or lower for the duration of the day except within the first two hours, and while A1 medication does the same for the behavior rating, R2 manages the symptom of appetite loss better than A1. Therefore, the child would be less likely to lose weight while taking the prescribed medication.

27. **(D)** All this question wants you to do is find which line in Figure 2 is the highest at the 30-second mark. The lines stop before the 30-second mark, but it is still clear from extrapolation that the line representing Solvent 4 would be highest (it is continuing to rise when the other three have leveled off).

28. **(H)** Table 2 shows that Solutions 1–4 progressively increase in temperature. Figure 3 shows that osmotic pressure decreases as the number of the solution used rises. Therefore, as temperature increases, osmotic pressure decreases.

29. **(A)** Table 1 indicates that Solvents 1–4 progressively increase in terms of molecular weight percentage. Figure 2 shows that the solutions finish passing through the semipermeable membrane (i.e., the lines representing them level off) in the same order. Therefore, the lower the molecular weight percentage of a solvent, the more quickly the solution passes through a membrane.

30. **(G)** The line in Figure 2 that represents Solvent 4 has the greatest osmotic pressure.

31. **(C)** Table 2 indicates that the 30°C solution is Solution 2. In Figure 3, the height of the line above the Solution 2 hash mark is about 1.4 atm. Double this, and the answer choice that is closest is 2.8 atm.

32. **(G)** Experiment 1 indicates in the paragraph that the Figure 2 results are shown as recorded at the 20° trial, which according to Table 2 is Trial 1.

33. **(A)** The volume of Solvent 1 in the tube leveled out at 320 ml and remained there for the last 20 seconds of the experiment, so you would expect the volume to remain there through 40 seconds.

34. **(H)** Student 1 closes by specifying that the image would be upright, whereas Student 2 closes by specifying that the image would be inverted. Therefore, the students disagree about the image's orientation.

35. **(B)** The fact that both students open by specifying the distance between the object and the mirror, and then base their theories on it, shows that both know that the exact positioning of the lightbulb is important.

36. **(F)** The teacher's information specifies that an object must be between F and the mirror to appear upright, and the description of the magic trick specifies that F lies 1.6 m from the mirror. Therefore, an object 1.0 m away would produce an upright image.

37. **(C)** Student 2's explanation is perfectly accurate. The teacher's information specifies that an object at C will produce an exact but inverted image. (It is often the case on the ACT Science that remembering earlier questions in a passage can help you answer later ones!)

38. **(F)** This is not true because F is in front of C, and an object at F will produce no image at all (although an object at any point between C and the mirror *aside from F* will indeed produce a larger image).

39. **(B)** The teacher's information states that an object at F will produce no reflection, and the description of the magic trick states that F is 1.6 m away.

40. **(J)** The teacher's information states that objects placed beyond C will produce reflections smaller than the objects themselves. The description of the magic trick states that C is 2.2 m away. Therefore, an object at 2.5 m away will produce a reflection smaller than itself.

Writing Sample

Gender-Separate Education

(This essay would score in the 10–12 range)

A lot has been made recently of gender equality within education. In fact, the movement has taken on a whole new dimension over the last few years. Today, gender equality in the classroom is much more than boys and girls having equal rights; today, gender equality includes all people who identify as genders other than those listed on their birth certificates. From an early age, American children are now exposed to gender equality in all forms. This new openness places those in charge of educating children in a precarious position as they debate the age-old question of whether or not boys and girls learn better together or separated by gender. The three perspectives given on this topic each have some validity; however, none truly answer the question. Separating boys and girls during their school years is not the most effective method of creating an outstanding society through quality education. The instantaneous access to all forms of information through technology makes it clear that children should not be separated by gender in an attempt to promote better learning.

The view that students will eventually be distracted by something comes the closest to explaining how technology has made the question of gender-separate education a moot point. As perspective two points out, "the real world is never going to provide them with an ideal environment free of distractions." That "distraction" is technology and everything that goes with it. If parents want to keep their teenager away from the opposite sex in the classroom, they will need to cut off all social media, all news feeds, and all Internet access—essentially relegating their child to an education resembling what was once provided in antiquated one-room school houses. Because of technology, the world is a very small place—a place where we are all interconnected and dependent on each other for our daily interactions and information. Most teenagers learn via technology: their books are digital; their lessons are often delivered via group videos sessions; their teachers respond to them through messages and emails; and they converse with each other through emojis and text messages. A perfect example of technology making gender-separate education obsolete is the foreign language training program called Rosetta Stone. The key ingredient for success with Rosetta Stone is open dialogue with others who are native speakers of the language the learner is attempting to master. Even members of the United Nations and newly appointed foreign ambassadors use the one-to-one and group chat features of Rosetta Stone to quickly learn a new language. That's how the world works today: people learn rapidly and openly because of technology; there are no borders, no roadblocks, no discrimination or exclusion based on gender. Computers are impartial. Attempting to educate children equally through gender separation is like attempting to look at one's own face without using some type of mirror. It's simply impossible.

There are, of course, other opinions on gender-separate education. Perspective number one states that "if reliable research indicates that both boys and girls learn better in single-gender classrooms, then that's all that matters." This view has several weaknesses. Not only does it fail to provide any type of reliable research, it does not consider a host of other valid points. America is not a "separate but equal" society for a good reason. Separation based on the promise of equality always leads to one or more groups becoming marginalized. One only needs to look at the struggle of various socio-economic groups throughout America's history to see the truth: African Americans, wave after wave of immigrant groups, the entire LGBQT community, and of course women have all been marginalized because of the concept of separate but equal. Each of these groups is gaining true equality because they fight for the right to not be separate, and one fact is certain, only through inclusiveness will greatness as a society be achieved. This inclusiveness must begin in the classroom.

American society cannot afford to keep the genders separate during their most formative years, and in fact, it is impossible. Technology is the great equalizer; it provides all students access to previously unfathomable amounts of information. There is strength and power in knowledge, and to be truly knowledgeable, all students must interact with each other, regardless of gender. Technology allows all students to do this. There may be inherent differences in males and females, but those differences provide strength and knowledge for all. Educators and students know that the most effective learning happens in the spirit of cooperation between all participants regardless of gender.